Transact-SQL User-Defined Functions

Andrew Novick

Wordware Publishing, Inc.

Library of Congress Cataloging-in-Publication Data

Novick, Andrew N.
Transact-SQL user-defined functions / by Andrew Novick.
p. cm.
Includes bibliographical references and index.
ISBN 1-55622-079-0 (pbk.)
1. SQL server. 2. Database management. I. Title.
QA76.9.D3 N695 2003
005.75'85--dc22 2003020942
CIP

2320 Los Rios Boulevard
Plano, Texas 75074

Printed in the United States of America

ISBN 1-55622-079-0

10 9 8 7 6 5 4 3 2 1
0309

All inquiries for volume purchases of this book should be addressed to Wordware Publishing, Inc., at the above address. Telephone inquiries may be made by calling:

(972) 423-0090

To my parents, Toni and Larry Novick

Contents

Acknowledgments

This book is the product of a lot of work on my part, which was enabled by the direct and indirect support of many other people. I'd like to acknowledge their support and thank them for their help.

My family, especially my wife, Ulli, has been very supportive throughout the year that it's taken to create this book. There's no way it would have been completed without her help and encouragement.

Phil Denoncourt did a great job as technical editor. His quick turnaround of the chapters with both corrections and useful suggestions for improvements made completing the final version a satisfying experience. And it was on time!

The staff at Wordware has been very helpful, and I appreciate all their efforts. Wes Beckwith and Beth Kohler moved the book through the editing and production process effectively. Special thanks to Jim Hill for taking a chance on a SQL Server book and a fledgling author.

The technical background that made this book possible is the product of 32 years of computer programming and computer science education. Many people helped my education along, particularly Dan Ian at New Rochelle High School who got me started programming PDP-8s and Andy Van Dam at Brown.

Experience over the last 23 years has enabled me to build the knowledge of how to create practical computer software, which I hope is reflected throughout the book. For that I'm thankful to a handful of entrepreneurs who gave me the opportunities to build programs that are used by large numbers of people for important purposes: Larry Garrett, Alan Treffler, Lance Neumann, and Peter Lemay. Along with them I'd like to acknowledge the work of some of my technical colleagues without whom the work would never have been as successful or enjoyable: Bill Guiffree, Steve Pax, Dmitry Gurenich, Nick Vlahos, Allan Marshall, Carolyn Boettner, Victor Khatutsky, Marty Solomon, Kevin Caravella, Vlad Viner, Elaine Ray, Andy Martin, and many others.

Books don't just happen. They take a lot of work, and the people acknowledged here had a hand in making this book possible.

Introduction

User-defined functions (UDFs) are new in SQL Server 2000. This book examines the various types of UDFs and describes just about everything that you'll ever want to know in order to make the most of this new feature. In particular, we'll cover:

- The different types of UDFs
- Creating UDFs
- Using UDFs
- Debugging UDFs
- Documenting UDFs

Along the way, dozens of useful UDFs are created. They're available for you to use in future projects or to reference when you want to see an example of a particular technique.

I first encountered UDFs in SQL Server when I discovered that SQL Server didn't have them. That was a disappointment. It was also a problem because I had completed work on a database design that depended on the ability to create my own functions.

How I Came to Search for the Missing T-SQL UDF

The story of my search for the missing T-SQL UDF goes back to 1996. I was working at a small consulting company in Cambridge, Massachusetts, that specialized in government transportation projects. We'd just won a contract to create a pavement management system for the state of Mississippi in the southern United States. As part of the contract, the client had specified that we use Sybase 11 to develop the system.

Microsoft and Sybase had already split their partnership to develop SQL Server, but at the time they were both selling essentially the same product for Windows NT. Most importantly, both versions used the same dialect of SQL, Transact-SQL (aka T-SQL), which was created by Sybase as it developed SQL Server in the 1980s.

This was before the days of the quick 20 megabyte download and instant software trials, so we couldn't get our hands on the database product for a couple of months after the project start date. We didn't think it would be much of a problem, as there was plenty of design work to be done before development got under way.

Bill Guiffre, the lead programmer, and I, as project manager, began the design for the database and user interface. Using T-SQL wouldn't be much of a problem. After all, between the two of us, we'd developed similar applications with Oracle, Access, Watcom SQL (now Sybase SQL Anywhere), Informix, and a few other RDBMSs.

Then we made one unfortunate assumption. We assumed that T-SQL would have a way to create user-defined functions. After all, all the other RDBMSs that we'd used had such a facility. Oops!

For the pavement management system, we had planned to use UDFs for converting pavement measurements that were stored in the metric system into the imperial (aka U.S. standard) system of measurement for use in the application's user interface.

When the database arrived, Bill and I were plenty happy. I really liked the product and its integration into Windows. I started trying out a few of the tools and getting used to T-SQL. For a while, everything looked great.

The surprise came when I decided to code the unit conversion functions. `CREATE FUNCTION` worked in Oracle's PL/SQL, so I assumed that it would work in T-SQL as well. Of course it didn't work, and the documentation wasn't any help. We even put in a call to technical support to be sure we weren't missing something, but we weren't. T-SQL didn't include `CREATE FUNCTION` or any alternative.

In the grand scheme of things, our problem wasn't very difficult to overcome. We just did a little redesign. We added a couple dozen stored procedures and learned a few new techniques in PowerBuilder, the UI development tool, to make them work. All-in-all, the lack of UDFs set us back only two or three days. In a nine-month project, that was pretty easy to overcome. Chapter 12 has more about unit conversions and shows some of the alternative ways to code them now that SQL Server supports UDFs.

As SQL Server became my primary development database in the late 1990s, I waited a long time for the availability of UDFs. Finally, SQL Server 2000 made them available. I've used them on a couple of SQL Server 2000 projects since it was released. For the most part, I'm pretty happy with them. They do the job even if they have a few idiosyncrasies.

As I built a library of UDFs, I realized the need for more information than the Books Online provides. It just doesn't tell you very much except the basics of the syntax and some of the rules about what you can't do. Other T-SQL-oriented books weren't much help either. They pretty much stuck to the basics with not much more information than you'll find in the first half of Chapter 1 in this book.

Since there's so much more to UDFs than just the syntax of the `CREATE FUNCTION` statement, I decided the world needed a book on the subject. When my opportunity arose to write a book on UDFs, I decided to go for it; you're reading the product of that effort.

What's in the Book?

This book is divided into two parts. Part I is "Creating and Using User-Defined Functions." It discusses the SQL syntax required to create, alter, delete, manage, and use your own UDFs. Part II is "System User-Defined Functions." It describes the UDFs that Microsoft has added to SQL Server as tools for your use and for its own use to implement SQL Server functionality. My intention is that they be read in order, but if you're looking for information about a system UDF, you'll want to skip to the chapter that describes it.

Chapter 1 starts with a quick introduction to the three types of UDFs, which are:

- Scalar UDFs
- Inline table-valued UDFs
- Multistatement table-valued UDFs

It's an overview to give you the basics of creating and using UDFs—enough so that you can understand the rest of the chapter, which is devoted to the really big question "Why?" as in "Why would you use UDFs?"

I have a few answers to that question. The best reasons are:

- Code reuse
- Management of knowledge
- Simplification of programs

There are also reasons not to use UDFs. They revolve principally around performance, and they are covered in Chapter 1 with more detail in Chapters 3 and 11. The performance issue stems from the procedural nature of scalar and multistatement UDFs.

Once UDFs are introduced, Chapter 2 goes into depth about scalar UDFs. It covers how to create them, where you can use them, and how to control the permissions to use them. Most of what is written about scalar UDFs applies to the other types as well.

Before discussing the other types of UDFs, Chapters 3 through 6 go into depth about several topics that affect all UDFs. They're important enough to be discussed before getting into the details of the other types.

Chapter 3, "Working with UDFs in the SQL Server Tools," shows you how to use the principal SQL Server client tools: Query Analyzer, SQL Profiler, and Enterprise Manager. This isn't an introduction to the tools; I assume you're already familiar with them. The chapter sticks to the features that are particularly relevant to UDFs.

UDFs are different from stored procedures in several ways. Some of the most important differences are the restrictions placed on the T-SQL statements that can be used in a UDF. The restrictions are detailed in Chapter 4, "You Can't Do That in a UDF."

I sometimes find that almost half of my code is devoted to error handling. Chapter 5, "Handling Run-time Errors in UDFs," shows you what you can and cannot do in a UDF to handle an error. Sometimes it's less than you'd like, and the chapter discusses how to live within SQL Server's limitations.

There are many styles used to write T-SQL code—almost as many styles as there are programmers. Chapter 6, "Documentation, Formatting, and Naming Conventions," shows you aspects of my style and discusses why the conventions that I show are helpful when creating and maintaining UDFs.

Chapter 7, "Inline UDFs," and Chapter 8, "Multistatement UDFs," cover the two types of UDFs that haven't previously been given detailed treatment. Each of these chapters shows how these types of UDFs can be used to solve particular problems faced by the database designer and programmer.

The SQL Server GUI tools Query Analyzer and Enterprise Manager are great for handling individual UDFs. But anyone responsible for maintaining a database with a lot of UDFs ultimately needs to manage them with T-SQL scripts. Chapter 9, "Metadata about UDFs," describes SQL Server's system stored procedures, functions, and views that can be used to get information about UDFs.

Extended stored procedures are compiled code that can be invoked from T-SQL scripts. Fortunately, SQL Server allows the use of extended stored procedures in UDFs, as long as they don't return rowsets. Chapter 10, "Using Extended Stored Procedures in UDFs," shows which of these procedures can be used and how to use them. The most important of the extended stored procedures are those that allow the use of COM objects from a T-SQL script. The chapter creates an object with Visual Basic 6 and shows how it can be used and debugged.

Speaking of bugs, we can't escape testing. Chapter 11, "Testing UDFs for Correctness and Performance," gets into the details of writing tests and test scripts for UDFs. Most importantly, it discusses testing UDFs for performance, and demonstrates how much a UDF can slow a query.

With the discussion of how to create, manage, use, and test UDFs complete, Chapter 12, "Converting between Unit Systems," and Chapter 13, "Currency Conversion," tackle two common problems that can be solved with UDFs. The unit conversion problem is what first motivated me to want UDFs in SQL Server. It should be simple, right? In a sense, it is simple, but it provides an opportunity to examine the problems of numeric precision and a way to illustrate alternative methods for solving one problem. Currency conversion is similar in many ways to converting between unit systems with the exception that the variability of the conversion rate forces us to store the rate in a table and handle issues such as missing data and interpolation.

Microsoft used the availability of UDFs as part of its implementation of SQL Server 2000. It went beyond just extending the syntax of T-SQL to add a special class of system UDFs. Part II of the book is six chapters about the system UDFs and how to use them. It starts with Chapter 14, "Introduction to System UDFs," which gives you an overview of what system UDFs are available and the differences between system UDFs and the ordinary UDFs that you and I create. It covers four of the ten documented system UDFs, including the new `fn_get_sql` function that wasn't available before Service Pack 3.

Chapter 15, "Documenting DB Objects with fn_listextendedproperty," discusses how to create and retrieve SQL Server's extended properties. This is a new feature in the 2000 version that can be used to document a database or store other information related to database objects.

The amount of input/output (I/O) required of SQL Server is a key determinant of its performance. Chapter 16, "Using fn_virtualfilestats to Analyze I/O Performance," shows you that system UDF and how to slice and dice the statistics it generates to narrow down performance problems.

The SQL Profiler is a great tool for analyzing the performance of UDFs as well as other T-SQL code. Behind the scenes, it uses a set of system stored procedures for creating traces. Chapter 17, "fn_trace_* and How to Create and Monitor System Traces," shows you those system stored procedures and a group of four system UDFs that help you retrieve information about active traces in your SQL Server instance.

In addition to the ten system UDFs that are documented in the Books Online, there are a few dozen more undocumented UDFs declared in master. Some of these are true system UDFs and possess that special status. Others are just ordinary UDFs that are located in master and owned by **dbo**. Chapter 18, "Undocumented System UDFs," lists all of these UDFs. It also has a detailed treatment of several undocumented system UDFs that you might want to use.

The special status of system UDFs lets you create them in just one place, master, but use them in every database in the SQL Server instance. Chapter 19, "Creating a System UDF," shows you how to make your own. Most importantly, it shows how data access from a system UDF is different when the UDF has system status.

Three appendices wrap up the book. Appendix A is a complete list of the built-in functions in SQL Server 2000 along with an indication of whether the function is deterministic or nondeterministic. Appendix B has a chart with the keyboard shortcuts for the T-SQL debugger in SQL Query Analyzer. Finally, Appendix C describes some of the problems that I discovered in SQL Server 2000 during the course of writing this book.

What You Need to Know Before You Start

This is a text for intermediate and advanced SQL Server programmers and DBAs. You'll need basic familiarity with SQL Server 2000 (or at least version 7). By "basic familiarity," I mean that you know:

- Relational concepts and the SQL statements `SELECT`, `INSERT`, `UPDATE`, and `DELETE`.
- The rudiments of T-SQL, including the control of flow statements `IF ELSE`, `WHILE`, `BEGIN`, and `END`.
- Some of the built-in functions and built-in constants of SQL Server 2000, such as `SUBSTRING`, `DATEPART`, `COALESCE`, and `@@ERROR`.
- The use of the four principal SQL Server client utilities:
  - SQL Query Analyzer
  - Enterprise Manager
  - SQL Profiler
  - Books Online

It's not that you need to know everything about these topics, but I don't introduce them. What I do is concentrate on how each of them relate to UDFs.

Using the Download Files

The book is accompanied by a download zip file that you can retrieve from www.wordware.com/downloads/tsql or www.novicksoftware.com/transact-sql-user-defined-functions.htm. You should unzip the file into a directory tree where you can get at it from SQL Server's tools, such as Query Analyzer.

Most important in the download is the sample database named TSQLUDFS. It has the UDFs, stored procedures, tables, and views that are described in the book. This database makes it easy to try out the queries and other scripts that you'll find in every chapter. Instructions for attaching TSQLUDFS to your SQL Server are in the ReadMe.txt file that you'll find in the root of the download.

After you've attached the TSQLUDFS database to your SQL Server, please execute the script in the file Script to create LimitedDBA logins.sql and LimitedUser logins.sql. `LimitedDBA` and `LimitedUser` are SQL users that are used by some of the examples, particularly the ones about permissions. If your system only allows Windows logins or you don't have the permissions to create new users, you'll have to rely on the text of the book for the results of the queries that use them.

While many of the UDFs in TSQLUDFS are there just as examples, many more are very reusable. You may want to incorporate the UDF library into your projects. To make that easy, I've included a file, Reusable UDF Library.sql, that is a script to create over 100 of the functions that I think are most reusable along with two supporting views and a couple of stored procedures.

Various examples also use the pubs and Northwind Traders sample databases that come with SQL Server. At times you may want to create UDFs, views, or stored procedures in those databases. You might also change some of the data in the tables. For these reasons, I suggest that you make a backup of both of these databases. With a backup, you can always return the database to its original state. In addition to making a backup, I usually create a new database for each of the samples with "_Original" at the end of the name. I then restore the backup into the "_Original" version and make it read only. This gives me a place to look when I want to know the original contents of pubs or Northwind.

The download tree has a directory for every chapter of the book with one or more listing files. Most of the numbered listings in the book are not in files. The `CREATE FUNCTION` scripts for the UDFs are easily obtained from the TSQLUDFS database, and I don't duplicate them in the chapter download directories. You can retrieve them from the database using SQL Query Analyzer. One way to do this is to execute the system stored procedure `sp_helptext`. A description of `sp_helptext` is in Chapter 9. However, the easier way is by using the Object Browser window. Select the UDF that you want to work with, then use the context menu from the Object Browser and select the menu command Script Object to New Window As ➤ Create or Alter. You can then work with the UDF in a new Query Analyzer connection.

Most chapters have a file named Chapter X Listing 0 Short Queries.sql. This file has the short queries that illustrate how UDFs are used and various aspects of T-SQL. I started out creating these files so that I could be sure to verify each of the batches and so I could easily go back and retest each one. As I worked with the files, I said to myself, "If I was reading this book, I'd like to have this file so I could execute every query without opening a different file for each one." So I've included the Listing 0 file for each chapter in the chapter's directory.

Please don't run all the queries in the Listing 0 files all at once. Each query should be executed one at a time. To better show you how to do this, I've bracketed each query between a comment line that describes it and a `GO` command. You'll find the following query in the file Introduction Listing 0 Short Queries.sql in the directory Book_Introduction of the download tree. Once you've attached the TSQLUDFS database, open a Query Analyzer window and try it:

```
-- start in the TSQLUDFS database
USE TSQLUDFS
GO

-- short query to illustrate how Listing 0 files should be used.
SELECT 'Just a sample to show how the Listing 0 works'
GO

(Results)

---------------------------------------------
Just a sample to show how the Listing 0 works
```

To run just the second query, select from the start of the comment to the `GO` command and either press F5 or Ctrl+E, or use your mouse to select the green Execute arrow on Query Analyzer's toolbar. Figure I.1 shows the Query Analyzer screen just after I used the F5 key to run the query.

There are various other files in the chapter download tree. They are explained in the chapters.

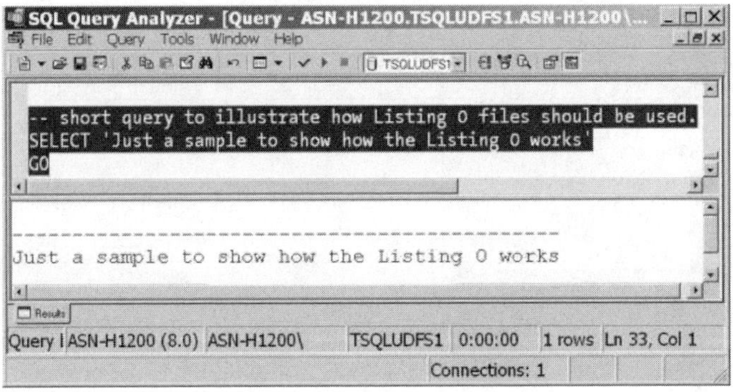

Figure I.1: Query Analyzer running a simple query

Finding the Links

There are a few hyperlinks scattered throughout the book. To make it easy to follow them, the links are reproduced at the bottom of the download page. They're listed by chapter and page. I'll try to correct any of the links if they move. The links are on the following page: www.novicksoftware.com/transact-sql-user-defined-functions.htm.

On to the Book

That's it for the preliminaries. However you choose to read this book, I hope it brings you the information that you're looking for. User-defined functions are a worthwhile tool for SQL Server programmers and DBAs to add to their arsenal.

If you have comments about the book, I'd like to hear from you. Please send your comments and questions directly to me at: anovick@NovickSoftware.com. Thanks.

Part I

Creating and Using User-Defined Functions

1

Overview of User-Defined Functions

SQL Server 2000 introduced three forms of user-defined functions (UDFs), each of which can be a great addition to your SQL repertoire. UDFs are SQL code subroutines that can be created in a database and invoked in many situations. The types are:

- Scalar UDFs
- Inline table-valued UDFs
- Multistatement table-valued UDFs

The initial sections of this chapter describe each type of UDF and show how to use them. An example or two accompanies each type of UDF. The intent is to give you a quick overview of the different types of functions and how to use them.

Once you get the overall idea of UDFs, the second part of this chapter discusses why you would use them. There isn't really anything that can be done in a UDF that couldn't be done in some other way. Their advantage is that they're a method for packaging T-SQL code in a way that's more reusable, understandable, and maintainable. The UDF is a technique for improving the development process.

As we consider why to use UDFs, we should also consider potential reasons not to use them. UDFs have disadvantages because of performance degradation and loss of portability, and we shouldn't ignore them. In particular, UDFs have the potential for introducing significant performance problems. The trick in using UDFs wisely is knowing when the potential problems are going to be real problems. Performance is a topic that comes up throughout this book.

Now let's get down to the meat. If you want to execute the queries in this chapter, they're all in the file Chapter 1 Listing 0 Short Queries.sql, which you'll find in the download directory for this chapter. I strongly suggest that you try it by starting SQL Query Analyzer and opening the file.

Introduction to UDFs

All three types of UDFs start with the `CREATE FUNCTION` keywords, a function name, and a parameter list. The rest of the definition depends on the type of UDF. The SQL Server Books Online does an adequate job of describing the `CREATE FUNCTION` statement, so I won't reproduce the documentation that you already have. The next sections each concentrate on one type of UDF and show how to create and use them through examples. Scalar UDFs are up first.

Scalar UDFs

Scalar UDFs are similar to functions in other procedural languages. They take zero or more parameters and return a single value. To accomplish their objective, they can execute multiple T-SQL statements that could involve anything from very simple calculations to very complex queries on tables in multiple databases.

That last capability, the ability to query databases as part of determining the result of the function, sets SQL Server UDFs apart from functions in mathematics and other programming languages.

Listing 1.1 has an example of a simple scalar UDF, `udf_Name_Full`. If you store names as separate first name, middle name, and last name, this function puts them together to form the full name as it might appear on a report or check.

Before we use `udf_Name_Full` in a query, permission to execute it must be granted to the users and groups that need it. The database owner (**dbo**) has permission to execute the function without any additional `GRANT` statements, so you may not run into this problem until someone else tries to use a UDF that you created. For any user or group other than **dbo**, you must grant `EXECUTE` permission before they may use the function. At the bottom of Listing 1.1, the `GRANT` statement gives `EXECUTE` permission to the `PUBLIC` group, which includes everyone. There is more on the topic of permissions for scalar UDFs in Chapter 2. That chapter also deals with the permissions required to create, alter, and delete UDFs. As **dbo**, you have all the permissions necessary to work with all your database objects. Other users require that you grant permission explicitly.

Listing 1.1: udf_Name_Full

```
-- These options should be set this way before creating any UDF
SET Quoted_Identifier ON
SET ANSI_Warnings ON
GO

CREATE FUNCTION dbo.udf_Name_Full (

    @FirstName  nvarchar(40) = NULL
  , @MiddleName nvarchar(20) = NULL
  , @LastName   nvarchar(40) = NULL
  , @SuffixName nvarchar(20) = NULL
)   RETURNS nvarchar(128) -- The person's full name
/*
* Concatenates the parts of a person's name with the proper
* amount of spaces.
*
* Related Functions: udf_Name_FullExample is a more procedural
*                       version of this function.
* Example:
select dbo.udf_Name_Full('John', 'Jacob'
                       , 'Jingleheimer-Schmitt', 'Esq.')
* Test:
PRINT 'Test 1 JJJ-S ' + CASE WHEN
'John Jacob Jingleheimer-Schmitt Esq.' =
dbo.udf_Name_Full('John', 'Jacob','Jingleheimer-Schmitt', 'Esq.')
                            THEN 'Worked' ELSE 'ERROR' END
****************************************************************/
AS BEGIN
   RETURN LTRIM(RTRIM( -- trim the whole thing
          -- Start with the first name
          ltrim(rtrim(@FirstName))

          -- Add in the middle name
          + CASE WHEN LEN(LTRIM(RTRIM(@MiddleName))) > 0
                 THEN ' ' + LTRIM(RTRIM(@MiddleName))
                 ELSE ''
                 END

          -- Add in the last name
          + CASE WHEN LEN(LTRIM(RTRIM(@LastName))) > 0
                 THEN ' ' + LTRIM(RTRIM(@LastName))
                 ELSE ''
                 END

          -- Finally the suffix name
          + CASE WHEN LEN(LTRIM(RTRIM(@SuffixName))) > 0
                 THEN ' ' + LTRIM(RTRIM(@SuffixName))
                 ELSE ''
                 END

         )) -- CLOSE OUT THE LTRIM(RTRIM( FUNCTIONS

END
GO

GRANT EXECUTE on dbo.udf_Name_Full to [PUBLIC]
GO
```

The Authors table in pubs stores separate first and last names in the columns au_fname and au_lname, respectively. Here's how you might use udf_Name_Full in a select list to combine them:

```
-- Get the first five authors and book titles.
SELECT TOP 5
       dbo.udf_Name_Full (au_fname, NULL, au_lname, NULL) as [Author]
     , Title
    FROM pubs..authors a
        INNER JOIN pubs..titleauthor ta
            ON a.au_id = ta.au_id
        INNER JOIN pubs..titles t
            ON ta.title_id = t.title_id
GO
```

(Results -- truncated on the right)

```
Author              Title
------------------- ---------------------------------------------------------
Cheryl Carson       But Is It User Friendly?
Stearns MacFeather  Computer Phobic AND Non-Phobic Individuals: Behavior Var
Livia Karsen        Computer Phobic AND Non-Phobic Individuals: Behavior Var
Michael O'Leary     Cooking with Computers: Surreptitious Balance Sheets
Stearns MacFeather  Cooking with Computers: Surreptitious Balance Sheets
```

dbo.udf_Name_Full is identified in the SELECT with a two-part name of owner.function_name. Two-part names using the owner prefix before the function name are required for scalar UDFs. They're optional for other types of UDFs. If the UDF is in a different database, it must be identified with the three-part name: database.owner.function_name.

In addition to columns, the parameters to the scalar function may also be constants or expressions. In the first invocation of udf_Name_Full in the next example, all parts of the name are constants. In the second invocation, the first and middle names are shortened in an expression to initials with periods. Here's the example:

```
-- calling a function with constants and expressions
SELECT dbo.udf_Name_Full('John', 'Jacob'
                        , 'Jingleheimer-Schmitt', 'Esq.') as [My Name Too]
     , dbo.udf_Name_Full(LEFT('Andrew', 1) + '.'
                        , LEFT('Stewart', 1) + '.'
                        , 'Novick'
                        , null) as [Author]
GO
```

(Results)

```
My Name Too                            Author
-------------------------------------- ------------------------
John Jacob Jingleheimer-Schmitt Esq.   A. S. Novick
```

In addition to T-SQL logic and calculations, a scalar UDF can read data using a SELECT statement.

The next UDF illustrates the ability to retrieve information using SELECT. It uses the data from EmployeeTerritories in the Northwind sample database that comes with SQL Server. The script moves into the Northwind database before creating the UDF:

```
USE Northwind
GO

-- These options should be set this way before creating any UDF
Set Quoted_Identifier ON
Set ANSI_Warnings ON
GO

CREATE FUNCTION dbo.udf_EmpTerritoryCOUNT (

    @EmployeeID int -- ID of the employee
)   RETURNS INT -- Number of territories assigned to the employee
AS BEGIN

    DECLARE @Territories int -- Working Count
    SELECT @Territories = count(*)
        FROM EmployeeTerritories
        WHERE EmployeeID = @EmployeeID

    RETURN @Territories
END
GO

-- EXEC permission is short for EXECUTE
GRANT EXEC ON dbo.udf_EmpTerritoryCOUNT to PUBLIC
GO
```

The logic of ufd_EmpTerritoryCOUNT is simple: Retrieve the number of territories for the EmployeeID given by the @EmployeeID parameter and return it as the result. This short query illustrates how it works. Employee 1 is the very famous Nancy Davolio.

```
-- Get the territory count for one employee
SELECT dbo.udf_EmpTerritoryCOUNT (1) as [Nancy's Territory Count]
GO

(Results)

Nancy's Territory Count
-----------------------
                      2
```

The select list isn't the only place where a UDF can be invoked. The next example uses udf_EmpTerritoryCOUNT in the WHERE clause and the ORDER BY clause in addition to the select list:

```
-- Get the 3 employees with the most territories
SELECT TOP 3 LastName, FirstName
, dbo.udf_EmpTerritoryCOUNT(EmployeeID) as Territories
    FROM Employees
    WHERE dbo.udf_EmpTerritoryCOUNT(EmployeeID) > 3
    ORDER BY dbo.udf_EmpTerritoryCOUNT(EmployeeID) desc
GO

(Results)

LastName         FirstName  Territories
---------------- ---------- -----------
King             Robert              10
Buchanan         Steven               7
Fuller           Andrew               7
```

Using `udf_EmpTerritoryCOUNT` three times in the same query is far from efficient because the SQL Server engine must execute the logic of the UDF each place the function is invoked for every row. That's nine times for the three rows in the results, plus additional times for rows that didn't make it to the result but had to be evaluated to see if the employee was one of the top three. However, the example is useful because it shows most of the places where a scalar UDF can be used. By the way, the `TOP 3` clause is used here to limit the output to the three employees with the most territories. The `TOP` clause is even more useful later in inline UDFs where it is required if you want the results of the UDF to be sorted.

UDFs may retrieve data, but they are prohibited from executing SQL statements that might change the database. Microsoft's SQL Server development team went to great lengths to enforce this restriction. There are additional limitations on UDFs. Most of them prevent functions from changing the database or causing any other side effects during execution. Chapter 4 is all about what you can't do in a UDF.

The two scalar UDFs presented in this section are not totally necessary. That may be strange to hear in a book devoted to UDFs. But it's possible to rewrite the `SELECT` statements that invoke the UDFs without using the functions. The scalar function gives the developer a way to simplify the coding process and create code that can be easily reused.

Scalar UDFs don't have to be as simple as the two shown so far. They can involve complex logic using all of the T-SQL control-of-flow language, cursors, and other T-SQL features. We'll see examples of these techniques in the chapters that follow.

The T-SQL scalar UDF is very similar to functions in other programming languages. Although they're called functions, inline table-valued UDFs are very different from scalar UDFs, and they serve a different purpose. The next section gives you a quick overview of them.

Inline User-Defined Functions

An inline user-defined function is created with a CREATE FUNCTION statement and takes parameters like a scalar UDF. The function header is where the similarities end. Instead of returning a single scalar value, inline UDFs return a table. The function body of an inline UDF consists of one, and only one, SELECT statement. Does this sound familiar?

Of course it does—an inline UDF is a view. The difference is that it has parameters, which can be used in the SELECT statement to modify the rowset that is returned by the function.

Understanding inline UDFs is easier with an example to work from. udf_EmpTerritoriesTAB works on data in the Northwind database and returns a list of the territories assigned to an employee. The EmployeeID is the first and only parameter. Here's the script to create it. It's in the Listing 0 file:

```
USE Northwind
GO

-- These options should be set this way before creating any UDF
SET Quoted_Identifier ON
SET ANSI_Warnings ON
GO

CREATE FUNCTION dbo.udf_EmpTerritoriesTAB (

    @EmployeeID int -- EmployeeID column

)   RETURNS TABLE
/*
* Returns a table of information about the territories assigned
* to an employee.
*
* Example:
select * FROM udf_EmpTerritoriesTAB(2, 2, 3)
****************************************************************/
AS RETURN

SELECT TOP 100 PERCENT WITH TIES -- TOP Makes ORDER BY OK
       et.TerritoryID
     , t.TerritoryDescription as [Territory]
     , t.RegionID
    FROM EmployeeTerritories et
         LEFT OUTER JOIN Territories t
             ON et.TerritoryID = t.TerritoryID
    WHERE et.EmployeeID = @EmployeeID
    ORDER BY t.TerritoryDescription

GO

GRANT SELECT ON dbo.udf_EmpTerritoriesTAB to [PUBLIC]
GO
```

The columns of the table returned by udf_EmpTerritoriesTAB are determined by the select list. They're drawn from the EmployeeTerritories (alias et) and Territory (alias t) tables. However, the TerritoryID column could just as well have been taken from Territories. One of the columns, TerritoryDescription, has a column alias so that the rowset uses the column name that I prefer. The function's parameter, @EmployeeID, is used in this WHERE clause:

```
            WHERE et.EmployeeID = @EmployeeID
```

to restrict the results to the territories of a single employee.

Check out the GRANT statement. There's no EXEC permission for an inline UDF. Like a view, the permissions for inline UDFs are SELECT, INSERT, UPDATE, DELETE, and REFERENCE. In this case, only the SELECT permission is granted. The restrictions on updates, inserts, and deletes that apply to views also apply to UDFs. In the case of udf_EmpTerritoriesTAB, the use of the TOP clause and the ORDER BY clause prevent the possibility of applying updates to the UDF.

You should also take note of the comment block under the RETURNS TABLE clause. In the interest of space, I've shortened or eliminated some of the comments that I usually insert into a UDF. As with all code, comments are essential to producing maintainable programs. Chapter 6 goes into detail about how I think UDFs should be documented.

Inline UDFs return rowsets and are invoked in the FROM clause of a statement, such as SELECT. They can also be used in the FROM clause of an UPDATE or DELETE statement.

udf_EmpTerritoriesTAB returns the territories for one employee. The employee must be specified as parameter one with the value of his or her EmployeeID column. The program that invokes udf_EmpTerritoriesTAB must know the EmployeeID based on other program logic. The UDF might be used to show an employee's territories on a master-detail form with the employee as the master and the territory list produced by udf_EmpTerritoriesTAB as the detail. The next script gets the EmployeeID using the name of the employee and then uses it to execute udf_EmpTerritoriesTAB:

```
DECLARE @EmpID int -- Working copy of the EmployeeID column
SELECT @EmpID = EmployeeID
    FROM Employees
    WHERE FirstName = 'Andrew' and LastName = 'Fuller'

-- Now use @EmpID to get the list of territories
SELECT * FROM udf_EmpTerritoriesTAB(@EmpID)
GO
```

```
(Results)

TerritoryID          Territory
-------------------- ------------------
01730                Bedford
02116                Boston
02184                Braintree
02139                Cambridge
01833                Georgetow
40222                Louisville
01581                Westboro
```

Like a table, view, or other rowset-returning function, the results of a UDF can be joined to other data. The next query uses that capability to join the results of `udf_EmpTerritoriesTAB` with the `Region` table. The combination is grouped to return just the RegionID and description of regions in which the employee has territories.

```
-- Get the EmployeeID of Andrew Fuller. Use it to get his regions
DECLARE @EmpID int -- Working copy of the EmployeeID column
SELECT @EmpID = EmployeeID
    FROM Employees
    WHERE FirstName = 'Andrew' and LastName = 'Fuller'

SELECT r.RegionID
     , r.RegionDescription as [Region]
    FROM udf_EmpTerritoriesTAB (@EmpID) t
        LEFT OUTER JOIN Region r
            ON t.RegionID = r.RegionID
    GROUP BY r.RegionID, r.RegionDescription
GO

(Results)

RegionID    Region
----------- --------------------------------------------------
          4 Southern
```

As it happens, Mr. Fuller has territories in only one region, Southern. In the example data contained in the Northwind database, all employees only have territories in a single region. In Chapter 2, we'll use a UDF to enforce the restriction of a salesman to a single region as a business rule.

I hope that gives you an idea of what can be done with inline UDFs. The next section is an overview of the third type of UDF, the multi-statement table-valued UDF. It combines some of the aspects of inline UDFs with other aspects of scalar UDFs.

Multistatement Table-Valued User-Defined Functions

Multistatement table-valued user-defined function is a mouthful of a name. I'll refer to them as multistatement UDFs. They're sort of a cross between the inline UDF, a stored procedure, and a scalar UDF. Like inline UDFs, they return rowsets and are used in the `FROM` clause of a SQL statement, such as `SELECT`. Like a stored procedure, they contain multiple lines of T-SQL, including control-of-flow statements, such as `IF` and `WHILE`, and cursors. Like the other types of UDFs, they can't change the state of the database.

Listing 1.2 shows `udf_DT_MonthsTAB`, which returns one row for each month that falls within a date range. You can find the `CREATE FUNCTION` script for it in the Listing 0 file so that you can easily create it in Northwind. It's also in the TSQLUDFS database. Let's first look at the function and then discuss how it is used.

Listing 1.2: udf_DT_MonthsTAB

```
SET quoted_identifier ON
SET ANSI_Warnings ON
GO

CREATE    FUNCTION dbo.udf_DT_MonthsTAB (

    @StartDT datetime -- Date in the first month
  , @EndDT   datetime -- Date in the last month
)   RETURNS @Months TABLE (
          [Year]        smallint   -- Year number
        , [Month]       smallint   -- Month number 1-12
        , [Name]        varchar(9) -- Month name January,...
        , Mon           char(3)    -- Jan, Feb..
        , StartDT       datetime   -- Date the month starts
        , EndDT         datetime   -- EOD of last day of month
        , End_SOD_DT    datetime   -- SOD of last day of month
        , StartJulian   int        -- Julian start date
        , EndJulian     int        -- Julian end date
        , NextMonStartDT datetime  -- Start date of next month
    )
/*
* Returns a table of months that are between two dates including
* both end points.  Each row has several ways to represent the
* month. The result table is intended to be used in reports that
* are reporting on activity in all months in a range.
*
* Example: -- to create a table of months in 2002
select * FROM dbo.udf_DT_MonBtwnTAB('2002-01-01', '2002-12-31')
**************************************************************/
AS BEGIN

DECLARE @MonStrt   datetime -- Start of month for looping
      , @NxMonStDT datetime -- Start of next month
      , @Julian0   datetime -- Origin of Julian calendar
```

```
-- Get the start of the first month
SET @MonStrt = CONVERT(datetime,
                      CONVERT(char(4), YEAR(@StartDT))
                      + '-'
                      + CONVERT(VARCHAR(2), MONTH(@StartDT))
                      + '-01')
SET @Julian0 = CONVERT(datetime, '1900-01-01')

WHILE @MonStrt <= @EndDT BEGIN
    SET @NxMonStDT = DATEADD(MONTH, 1, @MonStrt)

    INSERT INTO @Months ([Year], [Month] , [Name], Mon, StartDT
                    , EndDT, End_SOD_DT, StartJulian
                    , EndJulian, NextMonStartDT)
        VALUES (YEAR(@MonStrt)        -- Year
           , MONTH(@MonStrt)          -- Month
           , CASE MONTH(@MonStrt)     -- Name
                 WHEN 1 THEN 'January'   WHEN 2 THEN 'February'
                 WHEN 3 THEN 'March'     WHEN 4 THEN 'April'
                 WHEN 5 THEN 'May'       WHEN 6 THEN 'June'
                 WHEN 7 THEN 'July'      WHEN 8 THEN 'August'
                 WHEN 9 THEN 'September' WHEN 10 THEN 'October'
                 WHEN 11 THEN 'November' WHEN 12 THEN 'December'
                 END
           , CASE MONTH(@MonStrt)     -- Mon
                 WHEN 1 THEN 'Jan'    WHEN 2 THEN 'Feb'
                 WHEN 3 THEN 'Mar'    WHEN 4 THEN 'Apr'
                 WHEN 5 THEN 'May'    WHEN 6 THEN 'Jun'
                 WHEN 7 THEN 'Jul'    WHEN 8 THEN 'Aug'
                 WHEN 9 THEN 'Sep'    WHEN 10 THEN 'Oct'
                 WHEN 11 THEN 'Nov'   WHEN 12 THEN 'Dec'    END
           , @MonStrt                               -- StartDT
           , DATEADD (ms, -2, @NxMonStDT)           -- EndDT
           , DATEADD (dd, -1, @NxMonStDT)           -- End_SOD_DT
           , DATEDIFF(dd, @Julian0, @MonStrt)       -- StartJulian
           , DATEDIFF(dd, @Julian0, @NxMonStDT) - 1 -- EndJulian
           , @NxMonStDT               -- NextMonStartDT
           )
    SET @MonStrt = @NxMonStDT        -- On to next month
END -- WHILE

RETURN -- Function completed
END
GO

GRANT SELECT on dbo.udf_DT_MonthsTAB to PUBLIC
GO
```

If you're running the examples, please create udf_DT_MonthsTAB in the Northwind database now. It's used in the next few examples.

As with inline UDFs, permission to retrieve data is granted by granting SELECT permission on the function. There are no permissions for INSERT, UPDATE, or DELETE on a multistatement UDF.

udf_DT_MonthsTAB constructs a table of months between two dates. By itself a table of months isn't interesting. Typically, udf_DT_MonthsTAB is used in queries that report on some quantity by month. Having the months in a table ensures that no months are left out of the final results. In a query that follows, we'll use udf_DT_MonthsTAB to create a query that reports on sales shipped by month from the Northwind database. That's a little complicated, so first let's break it down into multiple parts. Here's a query that uses udf_DT_MonthsTAB to return a table of the first six months in 1998. Note that the results had to be broken into two sets so that they would fit into this book:

```
-- Exercise udf_DT_MonthsTAB to get the first 6 months in 1998
SELECT [Year], [Month] [M], Name, StartDT, EndDT
      , StartJulian [Start Jul], EndJulian [End Jul]
      , NextMonStartDT
    FROM udf_DT_MonthsTAB('1998-01-01', '1998-06-01') m
GO
```

(Results - first group of columns - reformatted to save space)

```
Year M Name     Mon StartDT                 EndDT
---- - -------- --- ----------------------- -----------------------
1998 1 January  Jan 1998-01-01 00:00:00.000 1998-01-31 23:59:59.997
1998 2 February Feb 1998-02-01 00:00:00.000 1998-02-28 23:59:59.997
1998 3 March    Mar 1998-03-01 00:00:00.000 1998-03-31 23:59:59.997
1998 4 April    Apr 1998-04-01 00:00:00.000 1998-04-30 23:59:59.997
1998 5 May      May 1998-05-01 00:00:00.000 1998-05-31 23:59:59.997
1998 6 June     Jun 1998-06-01 00:00:00.000 1998-06-30 23:59:59.997
```

(Results - second group of columns - reformatted to save space)

```
End_SOD_DT               Start Jul End Jul NextMonStartDT
------------------------ --------- ------- -----------------------
1998-01-31 00:00:00.000      35794   35824 1998-02-01 00:00:00.000
1998-02-28 00:00:00.000      35825   35852 1998-03-01 00:00:00.000
1998-03-31 00:00:00.000      35853   35883 1998-04-01 00:00:00.000
1998-04-30 00:00:00.000      35884   35913 1998-05-01 00:00:00.000
1998-05-31 00:00:00.000      35914   35944 1998-06-01 00:00:00.000
1998-06-30 00:00:00.000      35945   35974 1998-07-01 00:00:00.000
```

There are ten columns in the output. I only use a few of them in any one query. As a general-purpose function, udf_DT_MonthsTAB contains all the columns that might be used by different programmers in different situations. For instance, there are several different ways to represent the end of the month: EndDT, End_SOD_DT, EndJulian, and NextMonStartDT. Any one of these could be used to group datetime values into the month in which they belong. We'll see one possible method in the example that follows.

Now that we have a table of months, we need date-based data to combine it with in order to make our report. We can use the Northwind Orders and [Order Details] tables to produce rows of items shipped by date. The UnitPrice, Quantity, and Discount columns are combined to produce the Revenue for each item. Here's the query with its first five rows of output:

```
-- Months will be joined with this subquery in another example that follows
SELECT o.ShippedDate, od.ProductID
    , od.UnitPrice * od.Quantity
          * (1 - Discount) as Revenue
    FROM Orders o
        INNER JOIN [Order Details] od
           ON o.OrderID = od.OrderID
    WHERE (o.ShippedDate >= '1998-01-01'
           AND o.ShippedDate < '1999-07-01')

GO

(Results - first five rows)

ShippedDate                ProductID   Revenue
-------------------------- ----------- ------------------
1998-01-01 00:00:00.000             29           1646.407
1998-01-01 00:00:00.000             41          183.34999
1998-01-02 00:00:00.000             71              344.0
1998-01-02 00:00:00.000             14              279.0
1998-01-02 00:00:00.000             54          35.760002
```

Next, combine the two queries to produce a report of revenue per month for the first six months of 1998:

```
-- Report on Revenue per month for first six months of 1998
SELECT [Year], [Month], [Name]
     , CAST (SUM(Revenue) as numeric (18,2)) Revenue
    FROM udf_DT_MonthsTAB('1998-01-01', '1998-06-01') m
        LEFT OUTER JOIN -- Shipped Line items
               (SELECT o.Shippeddate, od.ProductID
                     , od.UnitPrice * od.Quantity
                          * (1 - Discount) as Revenue
                    FROM Orders o
                        INNER JOIN [Order Details] od
                           ON o.OrderID = od.OrderID
                    WHERE (o.ShippedDate >= '1998-01-01'
                         AND o.ShippedDate < '1999-07-01')
                ) ShippedItems
            ON ShippedDate Between m.StartDT and m.EndDT
    GROUP BY m.[Year], m.[Month], m.[Name]
    ORDER BY m.[Year], m.[Month]
GO

(Results)

Year   Month  Name      Revenue
------ ------ --------- --------------------
1998        1 January               83651.59
1998        2 February             115148.77
1998        3 March                 77529.58
1998        4 April                142901.96
1998        5 May                   18460.27
1998        6 June      NULL

Warning: Null value is eliminated by an aggregate or other SET operation.
```

To report on revenue per month, each row in the ShippedItems subquery is joined to the month that it falls within using the ON clause:

```
ON ShippedDate Between m.StartDT and m.EndDT
```

The GROUP BY clause and the SUM function aggregate the ShippedItems by month. The CAST function is used to produce two decimal places to the right of the decimal. The warning is issued because the SUM aggregate function is aggregating no rows in the month of June 1998. That's an important point because one of the reasons for using udf_DT_MonthsTAB and similar UDFs for reporting on months is that periods with no activity show up in the results instead of disappearing. The next chapter takes this point a little further when it discusses the pros and cons of using UDFs.

There are many other ways to use multistatement UDFs. Some, like udf_DT_MonthsTAB, are general-purpose functions that can be used with any database. There are also many uses that are tied to an individual database. Chapter 8 has much more information about multistatement UDFs and various ways to put them to work.

Now that you've been introduced to UDFs, why would you use them? Let me say something again that I said before: It's the economic benefits of creating UDFs, not the technical ones, that count the most. The next section discusses the economic arguments for and against using UDFs.

Why Use UDFs?

T-SQL programmers have lived without UDFs since Sybase created T-SQL in the mid-1980s. There has always been a way to achieve the desired results without them. So why do we need them? Obviously, we don't have to have them to use T-SQL effectively.

What do they add that's so useful? In my opinion, they add these factors to the software development equation for SQL Server code:

- Ability to build reusable code
- Better organization of code through modularization
- Ease of coding

These three factors are important enough to make it worthwhile to spend the time to learn how to use UDFs and learn how to use them well. I suppose that you agree, or you wouldn't be reading this book.

For almost all of us, programming is an economic activity. For me and, I suspect, most of you, it's been the focus of our professional life. Although many of us do some coding for fun, most of the uses of SQL Server are in business, government, and other organizations where there are economic costs and benefits associated with a database. UDFs have a part to play in the cost/benefit equation.

You're paying one of the costs of using UDFs—the learning curve—right now. The other costs of UDFs that I'm aware of are:

- Performance
- Loss of portability

The execution cost occurs when code that includes UDFs is used instead of faster alternatives. In this chapter and later ones, we'll discuss where the execution costs of UDFs come into play.

Using T-SQL UDFs diminishes the portability of the database. Of course, that could be said for stored procedures as well. T-SQL UDFs are not yet compliant with any technical standard. More importantly, they're not part of any de facto standard. When we choose to code in T-SQL, we're giving up most database portability. There is some prospect that that will change. There are efforts to extend SQL to include both object and procedural features. It's clear that we're not there yet, and won't get there for several years.

The prospect of reusing software between projects has been one of the best ways to sell a new technology to management. It requires an up-front investment in the original code but promises large returns down the road.

Reuse

Software reuse has been the Holy Grail of programming methodologies as long as I can remember. I recall Modular Programming, Structured Programming, Object-Oriented Programming, and, more recently, Component Design. All these methodologies have reuse as one of their primary objectives and as a major selling point.

Why not? If you can reuse code, you don't have to write it. With the high cost of developing systems, reuse looks like the way to go. While the history of software reuse is less spectacular than the hype that precedes each new technology, there have been some successes. The oldest model, and maybe the most successful, is the function library.

Function libraries have been a way to package tested code and reuse it since the days of FORTRAN. The function library paradigm of reuse comes from the age of Modular Programming. Programmers have been creating and reusing function libraries for many years, and UDFs fit most closely into this model.

The basic idea of the function library is that once written, a general-purpose subroutine can be used over and over again. As a consultant developing SQL, VB, ASP, and .NET applications, I carry around a library of a few hundred subroutines that I've developed over the years. Since SQL Server 2000 came on the scene, I've added a library of UDFs.

My UDF library has a lot of text- and date-handling functions. Listing 1.3 shows one of them, udf_Txt_CharIndexRev. The SQL Server built-in function CHARINDEX searches for a string from the front. udf_Txt_CharIndexRev searches from the back.

Listing 1.3: udf_Txt_CharIndexRev

```
CREATE FUNCTION  dbo.udf_Txt_CharIndexRev (

    @SearchFor varchar(255) -- Sequence to be found
  , @SearchIn varchar(8000) -- The string to be searched
)   RETURNS int -- Position from the back of the string where
                -- @SearchFor is found in @SearchIn
/*
* Searches for a string in another string working from the back.
* It reports the position (relative to the front) of the first
* such expression it finds. If the expression is not found, it
* returns zero.
*
* Example:
select dbo.udf_Txt_CharIndexRev('\', 'C:\temp\abcd.txt')
* Test:
PRINT 'Test 1    ' + CASE WHEN 8=
           dbo.udf_Txt_CharIndexRev ('\', 'C:\temp\abcd.txt')
                     THEN 'Worked' ELSE 'ERROR' END
PRINT 'Test 2    ' + CASE WHEN 0=
           dbo.udf_Txt_CharIndexRev ('*', 'C:\tmp\d.txt')
                     THEN 'Worked' ELSE 'ERROR' END
****************************************************************/
AS BEGIN

    DECLARE @WorkingVariable int
          , @StringLen int
          , @ReverseIn varchar(8000)
          , @ReverseFor varchar(255)

    SELECT @ReverseIn = REVERSE (@SearchIn)
         , @ReverseFor = REVERSE(@SearchFor)
         , @StringLen = LEN(@SearchIn)

    SELECT @WorkingVariable = CHARINDEX(@ReverseFor, @ReverseIn)

  -- return the position from the front of the string
  IF @WorkingVariable > 0
      SET @WorkingVariable = @StringLen - @WorkingVariable + 1
  -- ENDIF

    RETURN @WorkingVariable
END
GO

GRANT EXEC on dbo.udf_Txt_CharIndexRev to PUBLIC
GO
```

I find myself using udf_Txt_CharIndexRev every once in a while. Most often it's for parsing the extension off the end of a file name. Here's a sample query:

```
-- Return just the extension from a file name.
DECLARE @FileName varchar(128) -- The file name
SET @FileName = 'c:\temp\myfile.txt'

SELECT RIGHT (@FileName
            , LEN(@FileName)
            - dbo.udf_Txt_CharIndexRev('.', @Filename)
            ) as [Extension]
GO

(Results)

Extension
----------------
txt
```

Now that it's written, I don't have to write it again. Neither do you. You'll find many other reusable UDFs in this book and in the many SQL script libraries on the web.

Of course, I could have written the function in such a way that it wouldn't be very reusable. For example, I could have written the function to work with one specific column of one specific table. That would work just as well the first time I needed it.

The database that comes with this book contains over 100 functions. You'll find many that you can reuse. The rest are examples with reusable techniques.

Organizing Code through Modularization

Modularization means packaging something in a self-contained unit. The concept of modularization and the object-oriented concept of encapsulation are pretty similar. Someone builds a piece of code that contains some information or some algorithm, or both, and someone else can use it without knowing how it works.

So a project manager could assign the task of writing udf_DT_MonthsTAB to programmer Jack and the task of writing the report of revenue by month to programmer Jill. Of course, Jill has to wait for Jack to finish before she can start her work. As manager, I may be able to take advantage of unique skills by splitting up the work. And the function continues to be available as an aid for writing other reports.

Often, breaking down a problem and compartmentalizing it make it much easier to solve. UDFs are a tool that can compartmentalize one part of a problem and let you solve the rest. So sometimes UDFs make the job of writing SQL easier.

Ease of Coding

A good coder is a lazy coder. I don't mean knocking off work and heading to the beach or sitting at your desk playing Solitaire instead of working. I mean that a good coder looks for ways to do more with less: fewer lines of code and less effort. The point is to find easy ways to deliver what the customer needs so the programmer can move on to project completion.

We could live without the UDF `udf_EmpTerritoriesTAB` that was defined in the section on inline UDFs. Instead of:

```
SELECT * FROM udf_EmpTerritoriesTAB(@EmpID)
```

it's possible to write:

```
SELECT et.TerritoryID
     , t.TerritoryDescription as [Territory]
    FROM EmployeeTerritories et
         LEFT OUTER JOIN Territories t
             ON et.TerritoryID = t.TerritoryID
    WHERE et.EmployeeID = = @EmpID
    ORDER BY t.TerritoryDescription
```

If I use `udf_EmpTerritoriesTAB` only once, creating the UDF doesn't save any time. But the second time I use the function, I've probably made my life easier. I've also made the job of maintaining my code easier for the person who has to maintain it in the future. In some ways, you could call this "reuse within a project" as opposed to "reuse between projects," which was discussed in the previous section.

Another way that code becomes easier is in compartmentalizing problems. In many cases it's possible to replace a UDF with equivalent code. The result usually works faster, as we'll see in Chapter 11. However, that's a lot of work and these days project budgets don't expand very easily. Particularly when a task becomes complex, a UDF can come to your aid by biting off a chunk of the problem so that it's easier to attack the rest of the problem.

UDFs may make developing a solution easier, but they do have drawbacks. There are reasons not to use UDFs, and that's considered in the next section.

Why Not Use UDFs?

The two reasons that I'm aware of for not using UDFs were mentioned earlier. They are:

- Loss of portability
- Performance

I don't have much more to say about loss of portability. If you want your application to be portable between database management systems, don't use T-SQL; it's unique to SQL Server. That means you can't use stored procedures or UDFs.

Performance is another matter. There is a lot to say about the performance of UDFs. The next section scratches the surface, but you'll find more performance-related information in the rest of this book, particularly in Chapter 11.

Performance

When considering the execution cost, we should always ask ourselves, "Does it matter?"

Purists may say, "Performance always matters!"

I disagree. As far as I'm concerned, performance matters when it has an economic impact on the construction of a system. When your system has the available resources, use them. Other economic benefits of using UDFs and simplifying code usually outweigh performance concerns.

In the case of UDFs, the economic benefit to using them comes from more rapid software development. If used well, the three factors mentioned earlier—reuse, organization, and ease of coding—have a large impact on the development process.

The performance penalty comes in execution speed. The SQL Server database engine is optimized for relational operations, and it does a great job at performing them quickly. When SQL Server executes a UDF in a `SELECT` statement that uses a column name as a parameter, it has to run the function once for every row in the input. It sets up a loop, calls the UDF, and follows its logic to produce a result. The loop is essentially a cursor, and that's why there are many comparisons of UDFs to cursors. Cursors have a justified reputation for slowing SQL Server's execution speed. When overused, UDFs can have the same effect on performance as a cursor. But like a cursor, it's often the fastest way to write the code.

Over the last 17 years, I've managed many projects. I've got a pretty good record of completing them on time, and I've evolved the following philosophy about writing efficient code:

Writing code is an economic activity with trade-offs between the cost of writing code and the cost of running it. The best course of action is to write good, easy-to-maintain code and use a basic concern for performance to eliminate any obvious performance problem. But don't try to optimize everything. Then during testing, and as needed, refine any code that has become a performance issue. While this strategy permits some less than optimal code into a system, it helps your system get finished.

When it comes to using UDFs, I use them whenever they'll simplify, improve, or make development easier. When the execution speed of SQL code becomes an issue, I know to look at the use of UDFs as a potential cause. Most of the time, they're not the problem. When they are the problem, the reason usually jumps out at you fairly quickly and the code gets rewritten.

Summary

This chapter has served as an introduction to the three types of UDFs:

- Scalar UDFs
- Inline table-valued UDFs
- Multistatement table-valued UDFs

Chapters 2, 7, and 8 go into detail about each type.

By now you should have an understanding of what UDFs are and how they're used. They're a great tool. But as discussed in this chapter, there can be performance problems with UDFs. In fact, they can slow a query by a hundredfold. That can be quite a price to pay.

The choice to use a UDF is really a balancing act between the benefits and the costs associated with them. Most of the time, the benefits in reduced development time, improved organization, and ease of maintenance are worth both the effort involved and any performance penalty.

Now that you've seen an overview of UDFs and have heard my ideas about why to use them, it's time to drill down into the details of creating, debugging, using, and managing UDFs. The next chapter goes into depth on scalar UDFs. That is followed by several chapters that deal with the really practical issues of using the SQL Server tools, documentation, debugging, naming, and handling run-time errors. After those chapters, we get back to inline and multistatement UDFs in Chapters 7 and 8, respectively.

2

Scalar UDFs

> Scalar:
>
> 3. <programming> Any data type that stores a single value (e.g., a number or Boolean), as opposed to an aggregate data type that has many elements. A string is regarded as a scalar in some languages (e.g., Perl) and a vector of characters in others (e.g., C).
>
> *The Free On-line Dictionary of Computing*

I think that's a pretty good definition of the term scalar for programming. By the way, a string is a scalar in T-SQL.

Scalar UDFs return one and only one scalar value. Table 2.1 lists data types that can be returned by a scalar UDF. The types `text`, `ntext`, and `image` aren't on the list.

Table 2.1: Data types that can be returned by a UDF

binary	float	real	tinyint
bigint	int	smalldatetime	varbinary
bit	money	smallint	varchar
char	nchar	smallmoney	uniqueidentifier
datetime	nvarchar	sql_variant	
decimal	numeric	sysname	

The pattern followed by a scalar UDF is simple:

- Take in zero or more parameters.
- Do some computation on the parameters and on data in the database.
- Return a single scalar value.

That's all there is to it. The middle step can be as long a program as you care to write or just a single expression.

What a scalar UDF can't do is change the database or any operating system resource. This is referred to as a side effect. Microsoft has gone to great lengths to make it nearly impossible for UDFs to produce side effects. Some of these restrictions are discussed in the section "Using the

CREATE FUNCTION Statement." There's more on the subject in Chapter 4.

There is a principle behind the restrictions: Given the same parameters and the same state of the database, a scalar UDF should return the same value every time. In order to uphold that principle, SQL Server prohibits the use of built-in functions that return a different value each time they are invoked, such as `getdate()`. These functions are referred to as nondeterministic. The complete list is in the Books Online on the page for `CREATE FUNCTION`. There is a way around this restriction, which I'll show you in Chapter 4. But you really shouldn't be trying to get around it most of the time. The motivation behind the principle is the use of computed fields that reference UDFs in indexes and in indexed views. We'll pay particular attention to both of these uses of scalar UDFs.

In order to better understand which SQL statements a UDF can and cannot use, it's helpful to understand a common division of the SQL language into two parts:

- SQL Data Definition Language (SQL DDL)
- SQL Data Manipulation Language (SQL DML)

SQL DDL contains `CREATE TABLE` and similar statements that define database objects that contain data such as tables, views, indexes, rules, and defaults.

SQL DML[1] is for working with data. It consists of:

- Statements that manipulate data such as `SELECT`, `INSERT`, and `DELETE`
- Statements for SQL programming such as `IF ELSE` and `WHILE DO CONTINUE`
- The `DECLARE` statement that is used to create local variables in stored procedures, UDFs, triggers, and batches

The distinction between these two types of SQL is useful because it divides SQL into areas where particular features of UDFs are relevant.

The importance of determinism is only really apparent when using UDFs as part of the definition of tables and indexes. Therefore, most of the discussion of determinism is held off until the section "Using Scalar UDFs in SQL DDL."

While the scalar is only one of the three types of UDFs, many of the subjects in this chapter also apply to the other types. This is particularly true for the statements that control the permissions to create, drop, and

---

1 My reference, *A Guide to the SQL Standard* 4th Edition, by C.J. Date with Hugh Darwin, (Addison Wesley), doesn't make such a distinction. It puts statements like `IF` and `WHILE` in the "Persistent Stored Module" appendix because they're not yet part of the standard. I've placed `IF` and `WHILE` with the DML statements for clarity.

alter functions but also extends in part to control-of-flow statements, table variables, and determinism.

As with all chapters in this book, the short queries that illustrate the text have been collected into a file in the download named Chapter 2 Listing 0 Short Queries.sql. Run the SQL Query Analyzer and open this file if you want to execute the queries as you read.

Before you can use a UDF, it must be created. Let's start the process of creating scalar UDFs and the statements that let you manage them.

Creating, Dropping, and Altering Scalar UDFs

Scalar UDFs are created with the `CREATE FUNCTION` statement. As you'd expect, they're dropped with the `DROP FUNCTION` statement and changed with the `ALTER FUNCTION` statement. This section discusses the three statements but concentrates on `CREATE FUNCTION`.

The first issue to discuss is who has permission to execute `CREATE/DROP/ALTER FUNCTION` statements. Managing permissions on these statements is similar to managing permissions on other SQL DDL statements.

Permissions to Use CREATE/DROP/ALTER FUNCTION

To create a function, a user must have the statement permission called `CREATE FUNCTION`. There is a similar statement permission for `DROP FUNCTION` and one for `ALTER FUNCTION`. These permissions are granted by default to the fixed server role `sysadmin` and to the `db_owner` and `db_ddladmin` database roles. Any user who is in those roles has the permission to use these function management statements.

Like many other permissions, `CREATE FUNCTION` permission can be granted to other users who don't already have it based on their role membership. For example, junior DBAs might not automatically be a member of `db_ddladmin` and have these permissions. Here's a typical grant statement:

```
-- Allow LimitedDBA To create functions.
GRANT CREATE FUNCTION TO LimitedDBA
GO
```

`LimitedDBA` can now create any type of function, not just scalar UDFs.

If a user without `CREATE FUNCTION` permission tries to create a function, he will get the following message:

```
Server: Msg 262, Level 14, State 1, Procedure blah2, Line 1
CREATE FUNCTION permission denied in database 'TSQLUDFS'.
```

Permission to use the DROP FUNCTION and ALTER FUNCTION statements *cannot* be transferred to other users. It can only be obtained by role membership. Any attempt to do so results in an error message. Here's what happens if you try:

```
-- Try to grant DROP FUNCTION to LimitedDBA. It will fail unless
-- LimitedDBA is a member of sysadmin, db_owner or db_ddladmin.
GRANT DROP FUNCTION TO LimitedDBA
GO

(Results)

Server: Msg 165, Level 16, State 10, Line 1
Privilege DROP <object> may not be granted or revoked.
Server: Msg 156, Level 15, State 1, Line 1
Incorrect syntax near the keyword 'FUNCTION'.
```

Attempts to grant ALTER FUNCTION result in the same error message.

With CREATE FUNCTION permission but not DROP FUNCTION or ALTER FUNCTION, a user is able to run prepared scripts of functions. That's useful but limited functionality. A programmer or DBA developing a UDF needs to alter the UDF and in many cases delete it during the course of development. The typical programmer won't be able to get by using only CREATE FUNCTION permission.

The most logical solution for those developing UDFs is to add the appropriate DBAs and programmers to the db_ddladmin fixed database role. This can be done with Enterprise Manager or the sp_addrolemember procedure, as in this script:

```
-- Add LimitedDBA to the db_ddladmin fixed server role.
DECLARE @rc int
EXEC @rc = sp_addrolemember @rolename='db_ddladmin'
                          , @membername='LimitedDBA'
PRINT 'sp_addrolemember returned ' + Convert(varchar, @rc)
GO

(Results)

'LimitedDBA' added to role 'db_ddladmin'.
sp_addrolemember returned 0
```

Zero signifies that sp_addrolemember was successful.

If you have all your programmers in a group, the group can be added to the role. Be aware that being a member of db_ddladmin also confers the right to add all other types of database objects, such as tables, views, and stored procedures. If you want to limit which types of objects the group can manipulate, the DENY statement can be used to remove permissions for particular statements.

Only users with the fixed server role sysadmin or the db_owner and db_ddladmin database roles can grant permission on CREATE FUNCTION. However, the statement permissions can't be passed on using the WITH GRANT OPTION clause. So if **dbo** executed the following GRANT statement, it would fail:

```
-- Try to extend the right to GRANT CREATE FUNCTION
GRANT CREATE FUNCTION to LimitedDBA WITH GRANT OPTION
GO

(Result)

Server: Msg 1037, Level 15, State 2, Line 1
The CASCADE, WITH GRANT or AS options cannot be specified with
    statement permissions.
```

Likewise, when LimitedDBA attempts to grant CREATE FUNCTION permission to LimitedUSER, it fails, as illustrated by this script that was executed while logged in as LimitedDBA:

```
-- Try to pass on CREATE FUNCTION permission
SELECT current_user as [Logged in as]
GRANT CREATE FUNCTION to LimitedUSER
GO

(Results)

Logged in as
------------------------------------------------------------
LimitedDBA

Server: Msg 4613, Level 16, State 1, Line 2
Grantor does not have GRANT permission.
```

The other statements available to manage CREATE FUNCTION permission are REVOKE and DENY. These work with the CREATE FUNCTION statement permission the same way that they work with table permissions or permissions on other statements. Once granted, permissions are taken away with the REVOKE statement. Role membership is removed with the sp_droprolemembership stored procedure. The Listing 0 file has an example that revokes db_ddladmin from LimitedDBA.

If CREATE FUNCTION permission is granted to a group or role, it can be denied to a member of that group with the DENY statement. When resolving an overlapping permissions statement, DENY has higher precedence than GRANT. DENY can be removed with the REVOKE statement.

Once a user has permission for the CREATE FUNCTION statement, he or she can begin using it. There is no SQL Server functionality to limit the number or type of UDFs that the user can create.

Using the CREATE FUNCTION Statement

Scalar UDFs are created with the CREATE FUNCTION statement. Like other CREATE statements, it must be the first statement in a batch. Even the SET statements that are used in the CREATE FUNCTION scripts generated by SQL Query Analyzer are placed in a separate batch.

If you're unfamiliar with the term "batch," it refers to a group of SQL statements terminated by the batch separator. In Query Analyzer, the batch separator is always GO. In the command-line utilities isql and osql, the batch separator can be set for the duration of the session.

The typical script to create a function has a few SET commands, the CREATE FUNCTION statement, and one or more GRANT statements. Each of these groups is in a separate batch. The SET statements alter the way the T-SQL interprets all scripts that follow in the same session. The CREATE FUNCTION statement creates the function. Finally, the GRANT statement(s) give permission to use the function. The three different types of UDFs each have their own set of permissions that can be granted. The permissions for scalar UDFs are discussed in the section "Using Scalar UDFs." The inline and multistatement UDFs are discussed in Chapters 7 and 8, respectively.

The syntax of the CREATE FUNCTION script for a scalar UDF is:

```
CREATE  FUNCTION [ owner_name. ] function_name
    ( [ { @parameter_name [AS] scalar_parameter_data_type [ = default ] }
    [ ,...n ])
RETURNS scalar_return_data_type
[ WITH < function_option> [ [,] ...n] ]
[ AS ] BEGIN
    function_body
    RETURN scalar_expression
END
```

The Books Online gives definitions for each of the elements of the function declaration. The remarks that follow are my comments. Chapter 6 has additional information about how to format the CREATE FUNCTION script for maximum usefulness.

owner_name — While SQL Server allows each user to have his or her own version of a function, I find that having database objects owned by any user other than **dbo** leads to errors. I suggest that you always use **dbo** for the owner name. If you don't specify the owner name explicitly, the function is created with the current user as the owner. But you do not have to be the **dbo** to create a function owned by **dbo**.

function_name — You may have noticed that I use a naming convention for functions. They always begin with the characters "udf_". Most have a function group name, such as "Txt" for character string processing functions, and then a descriptive name. There's more on my naming convention in Chapter 6.

@parameter_name — Try to use as descriptive a name as possible. If the name doesn't tell the whole story, add a descriptive comment after the parameter declaration.

[= default] — Providing meaningful default values is a good practice. It tells the caller something about how the parameter can be used.

scalar_return_data_type — This is the return type of the function. You may use any of the return types listed in Table 2.1. You may also use any user-defined type (UDT) that's defined in the database as long as it resolves into one of the allowable types.

Note:

I usually encourage the use of UDTs. They add consistency to the definition of the database. However, in general purpose functions that are intended to be added to many databases, they complicate the process of distributing the function because the UDT must be distributed with any function that references it. Another complication is that UDTs can't be used when the `WITH SCHEMABINDING` option is used to create a UDF. For these reasons, you may decide to create the functions without referring to UDTs.

[WITH < function_option> [[,] ...n]] — The two options are `ENCRYPTION` and `SCHEMABINDING`. These are discussed in detail later in this chapter. Note that the `ENCRYPTION` method for functions and stored procedures has been broken and published on the Internet. Don't count on it to keep your code secure from anyone savvier than your kid sister!

[AS] BEGIN — I always start scalar function bodies with `AS BEGIN`, but you may omit the `AS` if you like.

function_body — The statements that are allowed or prohibited in the function body are covered following this summary.

RETURN scalar_expression — The `RETURN` statement specifies the result of the UDF. It's sometimes the only statement in the function. When possible, this is a good practice because limiting the number of statements that are executed while the function runs improves the performance of the function.

In many functions in this book you'll find one major part of the function that's not specified in the T-SQL syntax: the comment block. I'm a strong believer in using elements of the function header—the function name, parameter names, and return type—to convey as much information to the caller as possible. This keeps the amount of comments that are needed to a minimum. Chapter 6 is all about how to use naming conventions, comments, and function structure to make a function better, including an extensive discussion of the comment block.

Listing 2.1 is the `CREATE FUNCTION` script for the very simple string handling function `udf_Example_Palindrome`. It returns 1 when the parameter is the same from front to back as it is from back to front. To keep the function simple, it doesn't ignore punctuation or spaces as a human might.

Listing 2.1: `udf_Example_Palindrome`

```
SET Quoted_Identifier ON
SET ANSI_Warnings ON
GO

CREATE  FUNCTION dbo.udf_Example_Palindrome (

    @Input varchar(8000) -- Input to test for being a palindrome
)   RETURNS int -- 1 if @Input is a palindrome
/*
* A palindrome is the same from front to back as it is from back
* to front. This function doesn't ignore punctuation as a human
* might.
*
* Related Functions: udf_Txt_IsPalindrome is more robust.
*
* Example:
select dbo.udf_Example_Palindrome('Able was I ere I saw Elba')
* Test:
PRINT 'Test 1    ' + CASE WHEN 1 =
        dbo.udf_Example_Palindrome ('Able was I ere I saw Elba')
                    THEN 'Worked' ELSE 'ERROR' END
****************************************************************/
AS BEGIN

    RETURN CASE WHEN REVERSE(@Input) = @Input
                THEN 1
                ELSE 0
                END
END
GO

GRANT EXEC on dbo.udf_Example_Palindrome to [PUBLIC]
GO
```

You can see that the function uses most of the parts of the syntax but has no `WITH` clause or function body, just a `RETURN` statement. Most functions have a function body, and its contents are the subject of the next section.

The Function Body

The function body is a program written in a subset of SQL Server's script language T-SQL DML. As mentioned previously, DML stands for Data Manipulation Language. In essence, T-SQL DML consists of three parts:

- DECLARE statements, which create local variables, including TABLE variables.
- The T-SQL control-of-flow statements, such as WHILE, IF ELSE, and GOTO.
- SQL Data Manipulation Language (DML) statements, such as INSERT and SELECT.

Most of the three parts of DML can be used in the function body of a UDF. Unlike stored procedures, none of the SQL DDL, such as the CREATE TABLE statement, can be used in a UDF. UDFs may contain the full syntax of the DECLARE and the control-of-flow statements. Only a subset of SQL DML and no SQL DDL may be used in a UDF.

Although the function body is similar to the body of a stored procedure, there are many more restrictions on the statements that can be used in a function. DECLARE is one statement that's identical in a function to its use in stored procedures. The introduction of TABLE variables in SQL Server 2000 is an important innovation that affects many other statements, so we'll cover DECLARE first and then move on to the other statements.

Declaring Local Variables (Including TABLEs)

Local variables are created using the DECLARE statement. DECLARE works the same way in a function as it does in a stored procedure or batch. Variables may have any of the data types that a scalar function could return. You'll find the list in Table 2.1 at the beginning of the chapter. Like a scalar function, they can't have text, ntext, or image data types. A typical DECLARE statement might be:

```
DECLARE @I      int          -- Loop counter
      , @result varchar(128) -- working result of this function
      , @length smallint     -- length of the result so far
```

The statement declares several variables in a comma-separated list with comments at the end of each line. You may put each variable in its own DECLARE statement, if you prefer. The comments are recommended but, as always, not required.

SQL Server 2000 introduces the TABLE variable. It's a limited form of temporary table that is created with the DECLARE statement instead of

CREATE TABLE. TABLE variables are visible only within the function body of the function in which they are declared.

Unlike temporary tables, TABLE variables have very limited scope. They can't be passed to stored procedures or triggers. They also can't be accessed by functions other than the one in which the TABLE is declared. In addition to their use in scalar functions, we also saw in Chapter 1 that they're created in the RETURNS statement of a multistatement UDF.

TABLE variables have many of the same features, such as constraints and computed columns, as database tables. But most TABLE variables that I've ever created are pretty simple. This DECLARE statement for the @Emp TABLE variable demonstrates some of the available constraints.

```
DECLARE @Emp TABLE ( [ID] int Identity (1, 3) primary key
                   , EmpID int UNIQUE -- The original ID
                   , FirstName varchar(40) NOT NULL DEFAULT 'Pat'
                   , LastName varchar(40)  NOT NULL
                   , FullName as FirstName + ' ' + LastName
                   , BirthDATE smalldatetime
                   , HireDATE smalldatetime
                      CHECK (HireDATE > '1992-04-01')
                           -- Company Founded on 1992-04-01
                   , AgeAtHire int NULL
                   , guid uniqueidentifier
                   )
```

There are PRIMARY KEY, NOT NULL, NULL, UNIQUE, and CHECK constraints on the table and its columns. There's also an example computed column, FullName.

TABLE variables don't have storage related options such as ON filegroup or fillfactors. Also, they may not have foreign key constraints nor may indexes be created for them, other than indexes created implicitly for primary keys and unique constraints.

Once created, a TABLE variable is manipulated with the usual SQL DML statements: INSERT, UPDATE, DELETE, and SELECT. There is an example of using these statements in the section "Using SQL DML in Scalar UDFs."

Note:

Many programmers have the misconception that TABLE variables are stored only in memory. That's incorrect. While they may be cached in memory, TABLE variables are objects in tempdb and they are written to disk. However, unlike temporary tables, they are not entered into the system tables of tempdb. Therefore, using TABLE variables does not exhaust memory nor are they limited to available memory. They are limited only by the size of tempdb.

DECLARE statements are usually placed at the beginning of a function. They're followed by the function's logic, expressed in control-of-flow and other SQL DML statements.

Control-of-flow Statements and Cursors

If you've written T-SQL stored procedures, you're probably familiar with the control-of-flow statements of T-SQL such as WHILE BREAK CONTINUE, IF ELSE, WAITFOR, BEGIN END, and GOTO. You also may be familiar with cursors. All of these constructs work the same way in UDFs as they do in stored procedures, triggers, and SQL scripts. Since there are many books and tutorials on T-SQL control-of-flow language, I won't go over it again here. Many of the control-of-flow statements are used in the UDF udf_Num_IsPrime, which is shown in Listing 2.2.

Listing 2.2: udf_Num_IsPrime

```
CREATE FUNCTION dbo.udf_Num_IsPrime (

    @Num INT
)   RETURNS bit -- 1 if @Num is prime, otherwise 0
/* Returns 1 if @Num is prime. Uses a loop to check every odd
* number up to the square root of the number.
*
* Example:
SELECT dbo.udf_Num_IsPrime (31) [Is Prime]
     , dbo.udf_Num_IsPrime (49) [Not Prime]
****************************************************************/
AS BEGIN

    DECLARE @Divisor int
          , @N int
          , @resultBIT bit

    SET @resultBIT=1 -- Assume it's prime
    IF (@Num & 1) = 0 RETURN 0 -- Even numbers are not prime.

    SET @Divisor=3
    SET @N = SQRT(@Num)

    WHILE @Divisor<=@N BEGIN
        IF @Num % @Divisor=0 BEGIN
            SET @resultBIT=0 -- Not prime
      BREAK
     END
        SET @Divisor=@Divisor+2 -- Increment @divisor
   END

    RETURN  @resultBIT
END
GO

GRANT EXEC ON dbo.udf_Num_IsPrime TO [PUBLIC]
GO
```

However, control-of-flow statements and cursors are the statements that lead to the performance issues that can cause a UDF to slow your queries. Many purists advocate doing almost anything to avoid using a cursor or a `WHILE` loop. My opinion about using these statements is pretty plain from Chapter 1. When possible, relational constructs of SQL should be used instead of control-of-flow statements and cursors. But when using control-of-flow statements and cursors makes the process of creating your software faster, use them carefully.

Using SQL DML in Scalar UDFs

The following SQL DML statements may be used within a scalar function:

- `SELECT` statements that set the values of local variables either from expressions or by retrieving data from a database.
- `SET` statements that set the value of a single local variable from an expression.
- `SELECT`, `INSERT`, `UPDATE`, and `DELETE` on `TABLE` variables.
- `EXEC` statements that invoke extended stored procedures that do not return rowsets.

Notably absent from this list are the `INSERT`, `UPDATE`, and `DELETE` statements for tables in the database. They may not be used inside a UDF.

`SELECT` may be used to read data from the current database or any other database and to change the value of local variables within the function. In Chapter 1 we saw the `udf_EmpTerritoryCOUNT` function, which counts the number of territories assigned to an employee. That number was assigned to the local variable `@Territories` with the statement:

```
SELECT @Territories = count(*)
    FROM EmployeeTerritories
    WHERE EmployeeID = @EmployeeID
```

When a statement is assigning a value to a single local variable and when the right side of the equal sign is an expression, the `SET` statement may be used instead of `SELECT`. The `SET` that increments the divisor at the bottom of the `WHILE` loop in `udf_Num_IsPrime` (Listing 2.2) illustrates this:

```
    SET @Divisor=@Divisor+2 -- Increment @divisor
```

You'll find many other `SET` statements in the UDFs in this book. However, when several `SET` statements are used one after the other, it's a good idea to rewrite them into a single `SELECT` statement. This is because the overhead of a single `SELECT` is slightly less than the overhead for the individual `SET` statements and there are fewer statements to work with when debugging the function or tracing it with the SQL Profiler.

TABLE variables are very similar to database tables, and the INSERT, UPDATE, and DELETE statements are used to modify them. SELECT is often used to provide the values for an INSERT statement. This can be seen in Listing 2.3, which shows the udf_Example_TABLEmanipulation function. The function is contrived and could be done a zillion other ways, but it does show all four DML statements at work on a TABLE variable.

Listing 2.3: udf_Example_TABLEmanipulation

```
SET Quoted_Identifier ON
SET ANSI_Warnings ON
GO

CREATE FUNCTION dbo.udf_Example_TABLEmanipulation (

) RETURNS int -- Min age at hiring of employee with non-prime IDs.
/*
* An example UDF to demonstrate the use of INSERT, UPDATE, DELETE,
* and SELECT on TABLE variables.
* Uses data from the Northwind Employees table.
****************************************************************/
AS BEGIN

DECLARE @Emp TABLE ( [ID] int Identity (1, 3) primary key
                   , EmpID int UNIQUE -- The original ID
                   , FirstName varchar(40) NOT NULL DEFAULT 'Pat'
                   , LastName varchar(40)  NOT NULL
                   , FullName as FirstName + ' ' + LastName
                   , BirthDATE smalldatetime
                   , HireDATE smalldatetime
                     CHECK (HireDATE > '1992-04-01')
                          -- Company Founded on 1992-04-01
                   , AgeAtHire int NULL
                   , guid uniqueidentifier
                   )

DECLARE @MinAge int

INSERT INTO @Emp (EmpID, FirstName, LastName, BirthDATE, HireDATE)
    SELECT EmployeeID, FirstName, LastName, BirthDate, HireDATE
        FROM Northwind..Employees

-- Get rid of any Employee whose ID is a prime number.
DELETE FROM @Emp
    WHERE 1 = dbo.udf_Num_IsPrime ([id])

UPDATE @Emp
   SET AgeAtHire = DATEDIFF (y, Birthdate, HireDATE)

SELECT @MinAge = MIN(AgeAtHire) from @Emp

RETURN @MinAge
END
GO

GRANT EXEC on dbo.udf_Example_TABLEmanipulation to [PUBLIC]
GO
```

The last statement available for use in a scalar UDF is the EXEC statement. Most forms of the EXEC statement are prohibited in UDFs. The only allowed form is using EXEC on an extended stored procedure that doesn't return any rows. Using extended stored procedures in UDFs is the subject of Chapter 10.

The CREATE FUNCTION statement has two options that can be specified using the WITH clause. They each modify how SQL Server creates the UDF.

Adding the WITH Clause

The WITH clause is used throughout SQL to specify options to SQL statements. There are two options that can be specified on the CREATE FUNCTION or ALTER FUNCTION statements: ENCRYPTION and SCHEMABINDING. This subsection describes how the two options work. We'll discuss why you might or might not want to use them. It's possible to specify both options on the same function as they act independently. WITH ENCRYPTION is the easiest to describe, so let's start with it.

Specifying WITH ENCRYPTION

Normally the text of many SQL Server objects, such as stored procedures, views, triggers, and functions, is stored in the syscomments system table as plain readable text. The WITH ENCRYPTION option requests that the object's definition text be kept secret from all users, even the object's owner. WITH ENCRYPTION is available for all three types of UDFs, so the discussion here isn't specific to scalar UDFs.

WITH ENCRYPTION can be used to hide the definition of a UDF from the casual observer. However, by mid-2002, *the encryption method had been cracked and published on the Internet. DO NOT rely on* WITH ENCRYPTION *to protect the source code of a function from anyone with even the slightest amount of determination*.

The following script creates a short scalar UDF, udf_Example_WithEncryption, and requests that it be created WITH ENCRYPTION. The script is in the Chapter 2 Listing 0 Short Queries.sql file in the chapter download. It hasn't been added to the TSQLUDFS database.

```
-- CREATE FUNCTION script that uses WITH ENCRYPTION
SET QUOTED_IDENTIFIER ON
SET ANSI_WARNINGS ON
GO

CREATE FUNCTION dbo.udf_Example_WithEncryption (

    @Parm1 sql_variant -- take a parameter
```

```
)   RETURNS sql_variant -- Returns the value of @Parm1
    WITH ENCRYPTION
/*
* Example UDF to demonstrate the use of the WITH ENCRYPTION
* option on the CREATE FUNCTION statement.
*************************************************************/
AS BEGIN
    -- This is the body of the function.  All this one does is
    -- return the original parameter.
    RETURN @Parm1

END
GO
```

(Results)

```
The command(s) completed successfully.
```

The function works perfectly, as demonstrated by this query:

```
-- Use our example encrypted UDF
SELECT dbo.udf_Example_WithEncryption ('My string') as [A string]
     , dbo.udf_Example_WithEncryption (37.123)      as [A numeric]
     , dbo.udf_Example_WithEncryption (123e+34)     as [A float]
     , dbo.udf_Example_WithEncryption (
                  CAST('1956-07-10 22:44:00' as datetime)) as [A Date]
GO
```

(Results)

```
A string     A numeric    A float   A Date
------------ ------------ --------- -----------------------
My string    37.123       1.23E+36  1956-07-10 22:44:00.000
```

The difference between a function that is created using `WITH ENCRYPTION` and one that is created without it is that you can't retrieve the text of the `CREATE FUNCTION` script. We'll get to how to use the GUI tools in Chapter 3, so we're sort of skipping ahead a little, but when you request to see the definition of `udf_Example_WithEncryption` in Enterprise Manager, the text of the function is given as this line:

```
/*** Encrypted object is not transferable, and script cannot be generated. ***/
```

Of course, SQL Server still tries to help you use the UDF so you can still see the parameter list in Query Analyzer, as shown in Figure 2.1. But Query Analyzer and all the other SQL Server tools won't show the definition of the function.

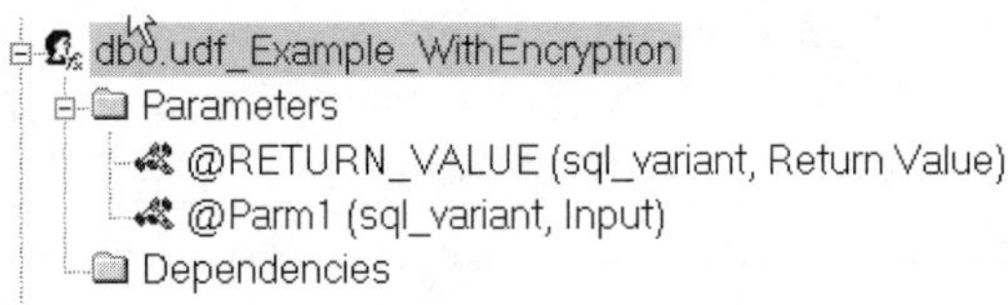

Figure 2.1: Query Analyzer showing the parameters to `udf_Example_WithEncryption`

The text tool for examining the definition of a UDF is `sp_helptext`. You'll learn more about it in Chapter 9. It won't reveal the text of the function, as shown by this attempt:

```
-- Try to retrieve the CREATE FUNCTION script with sp_helptext
DECLARE @rc int -- return code
EXEC @rc = sp_helptext udf_Example_WithEncryption
PRINT 'sp_helptext return code = ' + CONVERT(varchar(10), @rc)
GO

(Results)

The object comments have been encrypted.
sp_helptext return code = 0
```

All it tells us is that the comments have been encrypted.

Since `udf_Example_WithEncryption` doesn't do anything, you should probably clean it out of your database with the following batch:

```
-- Remove the udf_Example_WithEncryption function
DROP FUNCTION dbo.udf_Example_WithEncryption
GO
```

The refusal of SQL Server to generate the script of an object created using `WITH ENCRYPTION` makes source code control difficult. In fact, if you're planning on using it, be sure that you have some other mechanism for storing the source code of your UDFs. I suggest a tool like Visual SourceSafe.

So long as all you're looking for is protection from the casual observer, `WITH ENCRYPTION` can protect your source code. The best protection remains a scheme that restricts access to the database and only grants permission to use tools such as `sp_helptext` to trusted users.

`WITH ENCRYPTION` protects the source code of your functions. The other option on the `CREATE FUNCTION` statement is `WITH SCHEMABINDING`. It protects a UDF from modification in the results that it returns due to changes in the database objects that it references. It also provides that type of protection to any object that references your function.

Specifying WITH SCHEMABINDING

Once a UDF is created using the `WITH SCHEMABINDING` option, SQL Server prevents changes to any database object that is referenced by the UDF. Thus it protects the function definition from changes caused by changes in another object. This section discusses creating UDFs that have the `WITH SCHEMABINDING` option and also the effect of using the `WITH SCHEMABINDING` option on objects that reference the UDF.

The only two objects in SQL Server that can be created with the `WITH SCHEMABINDING` option are views and UDFs. However, as we'll see later, if you use a UDF in a computed column or in a table constraint, it cannot be altered, just as if it were schemabound.

There are two reasons for using the `WITH SCHEMABINDING` option:

- To prevent changes to one object from affecting other objects without retesting
- Because it's required for indexed views

The latter reason is usually the most important, and I believe it was the motivation for creating the `SCHEMABINDING` option in the first place. That's why this section discusses `WITH SCHEMABINDING` in the context of an indexed view.

Indexed views are a feature of SQL Server 2000. In order to create an index on a view, the view must be schemabound. And in order to be schemabound, all the views and UDFs that it references must be schemabound. In the process of creating the index, SQL Server must extract the fields that are in the index from the base tables and create index rows with data—even if the columns it extracts are computed.

In essence, the view is stored, or materialized, in the database. It's sort of like a table, but you don't manipulate data in the view; rather, you manipulate data in the base tables and SQL Server takes care of updating the index of the view. Oracle calls its analogous feature materialized views.

Think about that for a second. Every time you change a row in a base table that is referenced by an indexed view, SQL Server has to update the base table and the indexes in the base table that reference any modified columns. If there are any indexed views that reference modified columns, it also has to update any rows of the indexed view that might be affected. It's a big job, but hey, SQL Server's a great product, and it's up to the task.

The reason behind the creation of indexed views is that range scans of the indexed view are going to be lightning fast because SQL Server is storing a copy of the data in the order that it's needed. The only reason that you'd create an index on a view in the first place is that you need a particular query or group of queries to take advantage of the speed improvement provided by the index.

To demonstrate `WITH SCHEMABINDING` and indexed views at work, let's run a small experiment. The following script sets the session options so that they have the correct values for creating indexed views. It then creates two tables with some necessary constraints and populates the tables with sample data:

```
-- Set options for the correct creation of indexed views.
SET QUOTED_IDENTIFIER ON
SET ANSI_NULLS ON
SET ANSI_PADDING ON
SET ARITHABORT ON
SET CONCAT_NULL_YIELDS_NULL ON
SET NUMERIC_ROUNDABORT OFF
SET ANSI_NULLS ON
GO
```

(Results)

```
The command(s) completed successfully.

-- Create LocationCD Table
CREATE TABLE dbo.CalendarLocationCD (
    LocationCD char (2) NOT NULL
  , LocationName varchar (24) NOT NULL
    CONSTRAINT PK_CalendarLocationCD PRIMARY KEY  CLUSTERED (LocationCD)

)
GO
```

(Results)

```
The command(s) completed successfully.

-- Population script omitted from the text

-- Create the CalendarEvent Table
CREATE TABLE dbo.CalendarEvent (
    [ID] int IDENTITY (1, 1) NOT NULL
  , EventName varchar (32) NOT NULL
  , LocationCD char (2) NOT NULL
  , StartDT datetime NOT NULL
  , EndDT datetime NOT NULL
  , EventDate as dbo.udf_DT_SOD(StartDT)
  , CONSTRAINT CalendarEvent_PK PRIMARY KEY  CLUSTERED ([ID])
  , CONSTRAINT CalendarEvent_UNIQUE_LocationCD_StartDT UNIQUE
         (LocationCD, EventDate) -- Single Event Per Day
  , CONSTRAINT CalendarEvent_FK_CalendarLocationCD FOREIGN KEY
         (LocationCD) REFERENCES dbo.CalendarLocationCD (LocationCD)
)
GO
```

(Results)

```
The command(s) completed successfully.

-- Population script omitted from the text
```

Next we create a UDF to be used in a view but do it without schemabinding:

```
-- CREATE udf_DT_TimePart without SCHEMABINDING
CREATE FUNCTION dbo.udf_DT_TimePart (

   @DateTime datetime
)  RETURNS varchar(8)
/*
* Returns the time portion of a datetime as a character string
* in the form HH:MM:SS
* Example:
SELECT dbo.udf_DT_TimePart (Getdate())
***********************************************************/
AS BEGIN

RETURN LTRIM(SUBSTRING(CONVERT(varchar(30), @DateTime,120),12,8))

END
GO
GRANT EXEC, REFERENCES on dbo.udf_DT_TimePart to [PUBLIC]
GO
```

(Results)

```
The command(s) completed successfully.
```

Now try to create a view that uses the UDF. It must be created using the `WITH SCHEMABINDING` option in order to be indexed:

```
-- Try to create the view CalendarByLocation
CREATE VIEW CalendarByLocation
     WITH SCHEMABINDING
AS  SELECT CL.LocationCD
         , CL.LocationName
         , COUNT_BIG (*) AS [EventCount]
         , CE.EventDATE
         , LEFT(dbo.udf_DT_TimePart(StartDT), 5) StartsAt
        FROM dbo.CalendarEvent CE
           INNER JOIN dbo.CalendarLocationCD  CL
               ON CE.LocationCD = CL.LocationCD
        GROUP BY CL.LocationCD, CL.LocationName
              , CE.EventDATE
              , CE.StartDT
GO
```

(Results)

```
Server: Msg 4513, Level 16, State 1, Procedure CalendarByLocation, Line 4
Cannot schema bind view 'CalendarByLocation'. 'dbo.udf_DT_TimePart' is not schema
bound.
```

Ah ha! The rule that requires that all views and UDFs be referenced by a schemabound object hasn't been followed. Let's go back and modify `udf_DT_TimePart` so it qualifies:

```
-- Alter udf_DT_TimePart so it is schemabound
ALTER FUNCTION dbo.udf_DT_TimePart (

   @DateTime datetime
)  RETURNS varchar(8)
   WITH SCHEMABINDING
/*
* Returns the time portion of a datetime as a character string
* in the form HH:MM:SS
***************************************************************/
AS BEGIN

RETURN LTRIM(SUBSTRING(CONVERT(varchar(30), @DateTime, 120),12,8))

END
GO
```

(Results)

```
The command(s) completed successfully.
```

Now that `udf_DT_TimePart` is created using the `WITH SCHEMABINDING` option, let's try to create the view again:

```
-- Second try at creating the view CalendarByLocation
CREATE VIEW CalendarByLocation
     WITH SCHEMABINDING
AS  SELECT CL.LocationCD
         , CL.LocationName
         , COUNT_BIG (*) AS [EventCount]
         , CE.EventDATE
         , LEFT(dbo.udf_DT_TimePart(StartDT), 5) StartsAt
        FROM dbo.CalendarEvent CE
           INNER JOIN dbo.CalendarLocationCD  CL
               ON CE.LocationCD = CL.LocationCD
        GROUP BY CL.LocationCD, CL.LocationName
               , CE.EventDATE
               , CE.StartDT
GO
```

(Result)

```
The command(s) completed successfully.
```

Our view is created. Right now it's an ordinary view. Can it be indexed?

There are many restrictions on what views can be indexed, and I had to be pretty careful about constructing both `udf_DT_TimePart` and `CalendarByLocation` so that they qualify. Because almost all the queries on the view are for a single date for all locations, I've put `EventDate` first in the index. Here's the script to create the index on the view:

```
-- Create an index on CalendarByLocation
CREATE UNIQUE CLUSTERED INDEX [CalendarByLocation_IDX_CLUSTERED_byDate]
      ON CalendarByLocation (EventDate, LocationName, LocationCD, StartsAt)
GO
```

(Results)

```
The command(s) completed successfully.
```

That worked, and we now have an indexed view.

So let's say that we've inserted 1,000,000 rows into `CalendarEvent`. Our queries should still be running quickly due to the index on the view. That's fine, but what if we wanted to change `udf_DT_TimePart`? Let's say that instead of the colon between hours, minutes, and seconds we wanted a dash.

Can you imagine what SQL Server would have to do? Since the result of `udf_DT_TimePart` is in an index, it would have to get rid of the entire 1,000,000 row contents of the index and recreate it. Essentially, it would have to drop and recreate the index. That's exactly what schemabinding forces you to do. Changes to `udf_DT_TimePart` are prohibited until the `WITH SCHEMABINDING` option on the `CalendarByLocation` view is removed. You can't remove `WITH SCHEMABINDING` on `CalendarByLocation` until you drop the index on the view.

Creating UDFs using the `WITH SCHEMABINDING` option is a good practice, but it can be inconvenient, particularly during the early days of the development of a database. However, if you don't create UDFs `WITH SCHEMABINDING`, they can't be used in views or other UDFs that are schemabound. What I recommend is that:

- Scalar UDFs that perform computations but do not have data access are created using `WITH SCHEMABINDING`.
- Scalar UDFs that access data and all inline and multistatement UDFs are a judgment call.
- As new needs for `WITH SCHEMABINDING` occur, update your UDFs to include them.

The judgment call for UDFs that access data is mostly a matter of style and convenience. The advantage of using additional `WITH SCHEMABINDING` options is that UDFs are protected from changes that might modify or invalidate their definition. The disadvantage of `WITH SCHEMABINDING` is that it can become difficult to change your UDFs, even when the change won't affect the objects that are bound to it.

Now that you've seen how to create UDFs, let's turn our attention to using them. The next section goes over every way to invoke a scalar UDF. As with function creation, the discussion of using UDFs must start with the permissions that govern who can use them.

Using Scalar UDFs

Chapter 1 gave examples of several places where scalar UDFs can be used. This section goes into detail about using UDFs. For these purposes, as mentioned in the introduction, the world of SQL can be divided into two main groups:

- SQL Data Manipulation Language: DML
- SQL Data Definition Language: DDL

UDFs can be used in parts of both of them.

Recall that SQL DML consists of SELECT, INSERT, UPDATE, DELETE, EXEC, and the control-of-flow statements, such as IF and WHILE. There are many places in these statements where a UDF can be invoked. The rule of thumb is that you can use a UDF any place that you could use an expression. Use of scalar UDFs within DML is governed by the EXECUTE permission on the UDF.

Also recall that SQL DDL consists of the statements that create, drop, and alter database objects, such as tables and views. UDFs can be used in computed columns, CHECK constraints, views, and indexes. Use of scalar UDFs in DDL is governed by the REFERENCES permission on the UDF.

Permissions are required when using UDFs, and thus they're the first topic for this section. Once you see how to grant permissions to use UDFs, the rest of the chapter discusses all the places where they can be used in SQL DML and SQL DDL.

Granting Permission to Use Scalar UDFs

There are only two permissions that can be granted on scalar UDFs. The first one, EXECUTE, also known as EXEC, was mentioned in Chapter 1. It gives permission to use a scalar UDF in SQL DML statements. The second permission, REFERENCES, is required to use a scalar UDF in SQL DDL statements such as CREATE and ALTER. REFERENCES permission comes into play when creating table constraints, defaults, and computed columns. These uses are covered in the final section of this chapter, "Using Scalar UDFs in SQL DDL."

Permissions are given using the GRANT statement. Here's a typical GRANT statement for both EXECUTE and REFERENCES permissions on udf_DT_NthDayInMon:

```
-- Let the public use udf_DT_NthDayInMon
GRANT EXEC, REFERENCES on dbo.udf_DT_NthDayInMon to [PUBLIC]
GO
```

When permission to execute a UDF is granted to a user, the user can also be given the right to pass that permission on to others using the `WITH GRANT OPTION` clause. Here's an example that grants the right to use `udf_DT_NthDayInMon` to `LimitedDBA` and includes the right to pass on the permission:

```
-- Let LimitedDBA pass on permission to use udf_DT_NthDayInMon
GRANT EXEC, REFERENCES on dbo.udf_DT_NthDayInMon
                        TO LimitedDBA WITH GRANT OPTION
GO
```

Once `LimitedDBA` has the right to grant `EXEC` and `REFERENCES` to other users, the user can do so and can also pass on the right to pass it on. This is different from the statement permissions required to create and manage UDFs, which can't be passed on by those who hold them.

`REVOKE` and `DENY` are used for the `EXECUTE` and `REFERENCES` permissions in the same way that they are used for all other permissions. Check the Books Online if you need to know any details. The Listing 0 file also has an example of `REVOKE`.

Now that permission to use our UDFs has been granted, let's move on to show you how they can be invoked.

Using Scalar UDFs in SQL DML

There are many places in DML where a scalar UDF may be used. The basic rule of thumb applies: Scalar UDFs may be used where an expression may be used. The subsections that follow each take one or two of these places and show you how it works.

UDFs can be invoked with the same three-part object name that is used for other database objects: *`database_name.owner.function_name`*. For UDFs that don't use `SELECT` to get any data from the database, there is no problem invoking a UDF in a database other than the current one. However, because UDFs are executed in the database in which they are defined instead of the database from which they are invoked, UDFs that select data from tables may not return the results that you expect. There is more on what happens with cross-database references to UDFs in Chapter 19. For the remainder of this chapter, assume that each UDF is invoked from the database in which it was created.

Using Scalar UDFs in the Select List

You've seen scalar UDFs being used in a select list and a few other places in Chapter 1, but I'll try to push the envelope a little. Of course, the select list doesn't really offer much room for pushing, but let's try.

Our examples in this section use the `udf_DT_NthDayInMon` and `udf_DT_WeekdaysBtwn` functions from within the Northwind database. If you are executing the queries, your first step should be to create the two UDFs there. The file Chapter 2 Listing 0 Short Queries.sql has the `CREATE FUNCTION` scripts ready, if you want to run the queries as you read. The script also recreates a multistatement `udf_DT_MonthsTAB` function that was created in Chapter 1.

The first example is pretty trivial. It uses the UDF with hard-coded parameters:

```
-- Find this year's U.S. President's Day. 3rd Monday in February.
SELECT dbo.udf_DT_NthDayInMon (2003, 2, 3, 'MONDAY') as [2003's President's Day]
GO
```

(Results)

```
2003's President's Day
------------------------------------------------------
2003-02-17 00:00:00
```

Depending on our business rules, `udf_DT_NthDayInMon` might be useful for computing the billing date of a shipment. Let's say that our business rule is that a shipment should be billed on the second Tuesday of the month following the shipment. Here's a query that returns the billing date of the first four shipments for customer FRANK in 1998:

```
-- Get the bill date, grace period of FRANK's 1st 4 orders in 1998
SELECT TOP 4
       OrderID, ShippedDate
       , dbo.udf_DT_NthDayInMon (YEAR(DATEADD(Month, 1, ShippedDate))
                               , MONTH(DATEADD(Month, 1, ShippedDate))
                               , 2, 'TUESDAY') as [Billing Date]
       , dbo.udf_DT_WeekdaysBtwn (ShippedDate,
          dbo.udf_DT_NthDayInMon (YEAR(DATEADD(Month, 1, ShippedDate))
                               , MONTH(DATEADD(Month, 1, ShippedDate))
                               , 2, 'TUESDAY')
                          ) as [Grace Period]
    FROM Orders
    WHERE ShippedDate >= '1998-01-01' and ShippedDate < '1999-01-01'
       AND CustomerID = 'FRANK'
    ORDER BY ShippedDate
GO
```

(Results)

```
OrderID     ShippedDate             Billing Date        Grace Period
----------- ----------------------- ------------------- ------------
      10791 1998-01-01 00:00:00.000 1998-02-10 00:00:00           28
      10859 1998-02-02 00:00:00.000 1998-03-10 00:00:00           26
      10929 1998-03-12 00:00:00.000 1998-04-14 00:00:00           23
      11012 1998-04-17 00:00:00.000 1998-05-12 00:00:00           17
```

udf_DT_NthDayInMon is used twice in this query. The first time, it's used to compute the [Billing Date] column. The second time, the number of weekdays between ShippedDate and the billing date is calculated by udf_DT_WeekdaysBtwn. In business that's referred to as a grace period, thus the column name. In that expression the result of udf_DT_NthDayInMon is used as a parameter to a UDF.

There's no reason that a UDF can't be used in an aggregate function, as shown by the next example. It averages the grace period for all of FRANK's orders in 1998:

```
-- Get the # of orders and average grace period for FRANK in 1998
SELECT COUNT(*) as [Number of Orders]
     , AVG(dbo.udf_DT_WeekdaysBtwn (ShippedDate,
          dbo.udf_DT_NthDayInMon (YEAR(DATEADD(Month, 1, ShippedDate))
                                , MONTH(DATEADD(Month, 1, ShippedDate))
                                , 2, 'TUESDAY')
                             )
          ) as [Average Grace Period in Weekdays]
    FROM Orders
    WHERE ShippedDate >= '1998-01-01' and ShippedDATE < '1999-01-01'
        and CustomerID = 'FRANK'
GO

(Results)

Number of Orders Average Grace Period in Weekdays
---------------- --------------------------------
               4                               23
```

The rule of thumb holds. A UDF is an expression that can be used where an expression can be used. Next, let's extend that to other clauses: WHERE, ORDER BY, and SANTA. (Oh, I know. I can't fool you. There is no SANTA clause.)

Using Scalar UDFs in the WHERE and ORDER BY Clauses

Once again a UDF can be used anywhere in a WHERE clause and ORDER BY clause that an expression can be used. udf_EmpTerritoryCOUNT was used in the WHERE and ORDER BY clauses in Chapter 1. That query raised the issue of how often the UDF is invoked. The function must be invoked and its results calculated for every place that the UDF appears in the query. If the UDF is used in the select list, WHERE clause, and ORDER BY clause, it is invoked three times for each row. Fortunately, there is something that can be done about it.

To reduce the number of times the UDF is invoked in the WHERE clause, you should use the ability of the optimizer to short-circuit expressions. Within the same level of precedence, the optimizer evaluates expressions from left to right. When the expressions are combined with the AND operator and the first expression is false, there is no need to evaluate the second expression. Similarly, when expressions are combined with the OR operator and the first expression is true, there is no need to compute the second expression. All other things being equal, an expression involving a UDF should be the last expression in a series that's combined with the AND or the OR operators. An example helps.

Let's suppose that we're concerned that the grace period, the time before a bill is sent, may get too long. How about finding the cases where it's over 25 days for our customer FRANK? While we're at it, let's also order the shipments by the length of the grace period:

```
-- Grace periods over 25 days for FRANK in 1998
SELECT OrderID, ShippedDate
       , dbo.udf_DT_WeekdaysBtwn (ShippedDate,
           dbo.udf_DT_NthDayInMon (YEAR(DATEADD(Month, 1, ShippedDate))
                                 , MONTH(DATEADD(Month, 1, ShippedDate))
                                 , 2, 'TUESDAY')
                            ) as [Grace Period]
    FROM Orders
    WHERE ShippedDate >= '1998-01-01' AND ShippedDate < '1999-01-01'
          AND CustomerID = 'FRANK'
          AND 25 <= dbo.udf_DT_WeekdaysBtwn (ShippedDate,
                   dbo.udf_DT_NthDayInMon (YEAR(DATEADD(Month, 1, ShippedDate))
                                         , MONTH(DATEADD(Month, 1, ShippedDate))
                                         , 2, 'TUESDAY')
                                          )
    ORDER BY 3 DESC
```

(Results)

```
OrderID     ShippedDate             Grace Period
----------- ----------------------- ------------
      10791 1998-01-01 00:00:00.000           28
      10859 1998-02-02 00:00:00.000           26
```

The WHERE clause has four expressions combined with AND operators. By placing the three simple comparisons first, the expression that uses udf_DT_WeekdaysBtwn and udf_DT_NthDayInMon to calculate the grace period is only evaluated for rows that satisfy the first three conditions. This is the smallest number of rows possible.

The ORDER BY clause in the query also uses a method to limit the number of invocations of the two UDFs. Ordering can be done either by using the expressions to be ordered or by giving an integer that represents the column in the select list to be used for ordering. In this case, column 3 in the select list is our grace period calculation.

Normally I don't favor using column numbers in the ORDER BY clause. It's too easy to make a mistake by, for example, adding a column to the select list and forgetting to change the column number in the ORDER BY clause. However, because of the overhead of executing UDFs, I make an exception in this case. Using the column number eliminates the need for the query engine to execute the UDF again.

There are other places that scalar UDFs can be used. The next section shows how to use them in the ON clause of a JOIN.

Using Scalar UDFs in the ON Clause of a JOIN

The ON clause of JOIN operations tells SQL Server how to match records to produce the final result from the joined rowsets. As an expression, a UDF can be used in the ON clause of a JOIN.

In Chapter 1 in the section about multistatement UDFs, the final example query produced a report on revenue by month. Let's say that the accounting rules have changed and we want to book revenue when it's billed, rather than when the goods shipped. Here, the JOIN has been performed on the billing date instead of the shipping date:

```
-- Report on Billings per month for first 6 months of 1998
SELECT [Year], [Month], [Name]
     , CAST (SUM(Revenue) as numeric (18,2)) [Revenue-Billed]
    FROM udf_DT_MonthsTAB('1998-01-01', '1998-06-01') m
        LEFT OUTER JOIN -- Shipped Line items
               (SELECT o.ShippedDate, od.ProductID
                     , od.UnitPrice * od.Quantity
                           * (1 - Discount) as Revenue
                    FROM Orders o
                        INNER JOIN [Order Details] od
                           ON o.OrderID = od.OrderID
                        WHERE (o.ShippedDate >= '1997-12-01'
                               AND o.ShippedDate < '1998-06-01')
               ) ShippedItems
            ON dbo.udf_DT_NthDayInMon (
                                  YEAR(DATEADD(Month, 1, ShippedDate))
                                , MONTH(DATEADD(Month, 1, ShippedDate))
                                , 2, 'TUESDAY')
                  Between m.StartDT and m.EndDT
    GROUP BY m.[Year], m.[Month], m.[Name]
    ORDER BY m.[Year], m.[Month]
GO
```

(Results)

```
Year   Month  Name      Revenue-Billed
------ ------ --------- --------------------
  1998      1 January               60420.27
  1998      2 February              83651.59
  1998      3 March                115148.77
  1998      4 April                 77529.58
  1998      5 May                  142901.96
  1998      6 June                  18460.27
```

The query now has a non-NULL result for June 1998 because there are billings in that month even if there are no shipments. The ON clause that uses udf_DT_NthDayInMon is shown in the second shaded area. Listing 0 has both the original query from Chapter 1 and the refined query joined on the billing date.

The first shaded area is kind of interesting. It shows how the dates in the `WHERE` clause of the inline `SELECT` must to be modified. Since billing takes place one month after the shipment, the dates in the inline `SELECT` had to be moved up a month to the range '1997-12-01' through '1998-06-01'.

The `WHERE` clause in the inline `SELECT` isn't really necessary. We would get the same results without it because the `LEFT OUTER JOIN` statement limits the output rows to the months produced by the rowset returned by `udf_DT_MonthsTAB`, January through June 1998. However, there would be a performance penalty to pay.

What would have happened without that additional `WHERE` clause? Without it, the inner `SELECT` returns rows for all orders instead of just for orders in the time period of interest. That's 2155 rows instead of 763 rows, and `udf_DT_NthDayInMon` is evaluated for all of them. That's the potential performance penalty that was avoided by having the `WHERE` clause.

`SELECT` isn't the only DML statement in which you can use a UDF. The next section shows how to use them in `INSERT`, `UPDATE`, and `DELETE` statements.

Using Scalar UDFs in INSERT, UPDATE, and DELETE Statements

Using scalar UDFs in `INSERT`, `UPDATE`, and `DELETE` statements is similar to using them with `SELECT`. The rule of thumb applies: A UDF can be used where an expression can be used. Some of those places are:

- The `VALUES` clause on an `INSERT`
- On the right-hand side of the = in a `SET` clause of `UPDATE`
- In the `WHERE` clause of `DELETE` and `UPDATE`

All of these are straightforward uses of scalar UDF as an expression.

Expressions can also be part of some `SET` statements. There are actually two types of `SET` statements in SQL DML, only one of which may invoke a UDF. `SET` is the subject of the next subsection.

Using Scalar UDFs in SET Statements

There are two types of `SET` statements, but only one can invoke a UDF. The two types are:

- `SET` as an assignment statement
- `SET` to alter a database option for the connection

The assignment type of SET changes the value of a local variable. It has the form:

```
SET @local_variable  =  expression
```

This use of SET was discussed previously in this chapter in the section "Using the CREATE FUNCTION Statement." You won't be surprised to hear that the expression on the right-hand side of the equals sign can invoke a scalar UDF.

The second type of SET is used to change the value of a database option for the current connection. This type of SET doesn't take any expressions in any part of its syntax, and so there is no way to use a UDF in these SET statements. What is important and interesting is the way that the database options that are normally modified with a SET statement work when a UDF is executing. This topic is covered in Chapter 4, which discusses some of the subtleties of the execution environment of UDFs.

EXEC and PRINT are the last DML statements that can invoke a UDF. EXEC has a few flavors. All of them are tasted in the next section.

Using Scalar UDFs in EXECUTE and PRINT Statements

EXECUTE, or EXEC, is used for several purposes in T-SQL:

- To invoke stored procedures
- To invoke extended stored procedures
- To execute dynamic SQL

In SQL Server 2000 a rarely used variation on invoking a stored procedure allows you to invoke a UDF. Here's an example of a script that uses this form:

```
-- Invoking a UDF from an EXEC statement to find the first Mon in Oct.
DECLARE @1stMonInOct smalldatetime
EXEC @1stMonInOct = dbo.udf_DT_NthDayInMon 2003, 10, 1, 'MONDAY'
PRINT '2003''s U.S. Supreme Court session begins on '
      + CONVERT(varchar(11), @1stMonInOct, 100)
GO
```

(Results)

```
2003's U.S. Supreme Court session begins on Oct  6 2003
```

This use of a UDF is mentioned in the first paragraph of the Books Online page about CREATE FUNCTION and nowhere else in that document. It seems to be derived from a UDF's similarity to a stored procedure. Notice that there are no parentheses around the arguments to the function. This form of EXEC can be used in a stored procedure or a batch but not from within a UDF.

The last place to invoke a UDF with EXEC is from within a dynamic SQL statement. There's no restriction on using a UDF in a string executed dynamically. Here's an example of dynamic SQL that uses a UDF in a PRINT statement:

```
-- Invoking a UDF in dynamic SQL
DECLARE @SQL varchar(8000)
SET @SQL = 'PRINT dbo.udf_DT_NthDayInMon (YEAR(getdate()) '
                                + ', MONTH (getdate()) '
                                + ', 2, ''TUESDAY'')'
PRINT 'The statement is ->' + @SQL + '<-'
EXEC (@SQL)
PRINT 'End of Script'
GO
```

(Results - truncated on the right)

```
The statement is ->PRINT dbo.udf_DT_NthDayInMon (YEAR(getdate()) ...
Feb 11 2003 12:00AM
End of Script
```

I had forgotten about the PRINT statement. PRINT is just another example of a UDF being used where an expression can be used.

That wraps up the places that I'm aware of for using a UDF in SQL DML. DML covers the SQL used to manipulate data from batches, stored procedures, and triggers. All of these uses are governed by the EXEC permission on the UDF. The remaining uses of scalar UDFs are in SQL DDL statements that define tables, indexes, and views. They're the subject of the remainder of this chapter.

Using Scalar UDFs in SQL DDL

The REFERENCES permission governs the use of UDFs in table definitions. The places where a UDF is particularly interesting are:

- CHECK constraints
- Computed columns
- Indexes on computed columns

When a UDF is used in an index on a computed column, it's important that the UDF return the same answer every time it's invoked with the same parameters. That's the gist of determinism and the reason behind the many restrictions on the statements that can be executed in a UDF.

We'll start by discussing UDFs in CHECK constraints. They can be used to restrict the values that may be placed into a column. As CHECK constraints may use nondeterministic functions, determinism doesn't come into play.

To facilitate the discussion of computed columns, CHECK constraints, and indexes on computed columns, I've copied two tables from Northwind into the TSQLUDFS database. Northwind.dbo.Orders has been copied to TSQLUDFS.dbo.NWOrders, and Northwind.dbo.[Order Detail] has been copied to TSQLUDFS.dbo.NWOrderDetail. I did this because the scripts in this section make some important changes to the database, and I don't want you messing up your copy of Northwind. In addition to the tables, udf_Order_Amount is a UDF that calculates the amount of an order from the NWOrderDetail table. Listing 2.4 shows the CREATE FUNCTION script.

Listing 2.4: udf_Order_Amount

```
CREATE FUNCTION dbo.udf_Order_Amount (

    @OrderID int -- The order to determine the amount
)   RETURNS money -- Total amount of the order
/*
* Returns the amount of an order by summing the order detail.
****************************************************************/
AS BEGIN

    DECLARE @sum money -- working sum

    SELECT @sum = SUM(UnitPrice * Quantity)
        FROM NWOrderDetails
        WHERE OrderID = @OrderID

    RETURN @sum
END
```

There's no need for you to create this UDF. It already exists in TSQLUDFS.

After CHECK constraints, we discuss computed columns and then indexes on computed columns. That's where determinism becomes most important.

Using Scalar UDFs in CHECK Constraints

Constraints place limits on a table so that the table data satisfies the business requirements of the application. Some of the constraints that can be placed on a table include the primary key, foreign key, unique constraints, and CHECK constraints. The CHECK constraints limit the values that can be assigned to a column, or columns, of a table by applying a logical expression that must be true to allow the value in the column or columns. Ostensibly, there are two types of CHECK constraints:

- CHECK constraints on a column
- CHECK constraints on a table

Normally, a CHECK constraint on a column may only reference that column, and a CHECK constraint on a table may only reference columns in that table. Both types of CHECK constraints may use UDFs.

Because the UDF may reference data in another table, it may be used to circumvent the restriction on the data that a CHECK constraint can reference. Column CHECK constraints may only be added when the column is added to the table, which might also be at the time the table is created. SQL Server creates a constraint name for the CHECK constraint on a column, and it is, in effect, no different from a CHECK constraint on a table.

Let's start with simple constraints that use UDFs but don't access data. Continuing with our billing date example, let's suppose that grace periods have been growing too large for management's comfort and a new rule must be applied to the shipping department: Goods should not be shipped if the grace period would exceed 26 days. If you recall, the rule for the billing date is that it's on the second Tuesday of the month after the shipment, and the grace period is defined as the number of weekdays between ShippedDate and the billing date. The CHECK constraint to limit ShippedDate so that the grace period was no more than 26 days is:

```
-- Create a single column CHECK constraint to limit shipping when the
--     grace period is < 27 days.
ALTER TABLE NWOrders WITH NOCHECK
      ADD CONSTRAINT ShippedDate_GracePeriod_LessThan_27
      CHECK (27 > dbo.udf_DT_WeekdaysBtwn (
                ShippedDate,
                dbo.udf_DT_NthDayInMon
                          (YEAR(DATEADD(Month, 1, ShippedDate))
                         , MONTH(DATEADD(Month, 1, ShippedDate))
                         , 2, 'TUESDAY'
                          )
                                          )
             )
GO
```

The NOCHECK clause on the first line of the ALTER TABLE statement tells SQL Server not to apply this rule to rows that are already in the database. If the NOCHECK clause had been omitted, existing rows would have failed the test and the constraint would not have been created.

The CHECK constraint is removed with another ALTER TABLE statement. This batch removes the constraint that was just created:

```
-- Remove the constraint created above.
ALTER TABLE NWOrders
      DROP CONSTRAINT ShippedDate_GracePeriod_LessThan_27
GO
```

CHECK constraints may also use UDFs that select data from the database in order to decide if a column value is okay. This feature allows them to bypass the usual restriction that CHECK constraints only work on data in the same base table.

The next constraint uses udf_Order_Amount in the TSQLUDFS database to demonstrate this feature. Here's the script to create the constraint:

```
-- CHECK constraint to limit shipping when the order doesn't total 100
ALTER TABLE NWOrders WITH NOCHECK
      ADD CONSTRAINT Ship_Only_Orders_Over_100
      CHECK (ShippedDate is NULL
             OR dbo.udf_Order_Amount (OrderID) >= 100
             )
GO
```

To test that the constraint works, we'll need to find an order with a NULL ShippedDate that has an amount less than 100. We do it with this query:

```
-- Find Orders that can test the Ship_Only_Orders_Over_100 constraint
SELECT OrderID, ShippedDate
      , dbo.udf_Order_Amount(OrderID)
    FROM NWOrders
    WHERE ShippedDate IS NULL
       AND dbo.udf_Order_Amount(OrderID) <= 100
GO
```

(Result)

```
OrderID     ShippedDate    Amount
----------- -------------- ---------------------
      11019 NULL                         76.0000
      11051 NULL                         45.0000
```

The first order won't satisfy the constraint, so this next script uses it in an attempted update:

```
-- Try an update that violates the new constraint.
BEGIN TRAN
UPDATE NWOrders
    SET ShippedDate = GETDATE()
    WHERE OrderID = 11019
GO
ROLLBACK TRAN
GO
```

(Results)

```
Server: Msg 547, Level 16, State 1, Line 1
UPDATE statement conflicted with TABLE CHECK constraint
'Ship_Only_Orders_Over_100'. The conflict occurred in database 'TSQLUDFS',
table 'NWOrders'.
The statement has been terminated.
```

The constraint prevented the updating of order 11019 with the shipping date. In a real-world application, it's up to the application to recognize that the update failed and handle the failure. That's why it's rarely enough to only enforce business rules at the database level. The application must be aware of the rules and must communicate them to the user effectively. Had the restriction been enforced in a trigger, it would have been possible to raise a custom error, which can be more specific and easier for a user or program to handle.

When a UDF is used in a constraint, SQL Server doesn't allow any alterations to the function. It's almost as if it is schemabound to the computed column. This script attempts to alter `udf_Order_Amount`:

```
-- Attempt to alter udf_Order_Amount
ALTER FUNCTION dbo.udf_Order_Amount (

    @OrderID int -- The order to determine the amount
)   RETURNS money -- Total amount of the order
/*
* Test modification that always returns 17.
****************************************************************/
AS BEGIN
    RETURN 17
END
GO
```

(Results)

```
Server: Msg 3729, Level 16, State 3, Procedure udf_Order_Amount, Line 10
Cannot ALTER 'dbo.udf_Order_Amount' because it is being referenced by object
'Ship_Only_Orders_Over_100'.
```

The constraint has to be removed for the alteration to proceed.

With the capability to use UDFs in `CHECK` constraints, SQL Server 2000 allows you to enforce the type of business rules that formerly required triggers. Of course, triggers are still around. Many programmers and DBAs prefer to use declarative integrity validation through `CHECK` constraints rather than coding triggers.

Using Scalar UDFs in Computed Columns

The rules of data normalization into third normal form instruct us that the columns in a table should be dependent only on the columns in the key of the table, not on any other column. When one non-key column is dependent on another non-key column, it's called a "transitive dependency." For example, the `Northwind.[Order Details]` table has three non-key columns: `UnitPrice`, `Quantity`, and `Discount`. Together they can be used to compute an `[Extended Price]` column showing the amount to be paid for the line item. However, `[Extended Price]` would be dependent on those other three columns as well as on the key, creating a transitive dependency, and should be avoided. It should be avoided because keeping the `[Extended`

Price] column synchronized becomes quite a job for the user of the database and often leads to errors in the database.

Having the [Extended Price] column around would be a great convenience. Views are one solution to getting it without denormalizing the data. A view such as [Order Details Extended] could be defined on [Order Details], and it could be used instead of the base table.

There's another way. SQL Server allows the creation of computed columns. They're columns that are defined as a scalar expression. The expression may include other columns in the same row. Also, the expression can invoke a scalar UDF so long as the arguments to the UDF are constants, other columns in the table, or expressions involving other constants in the table. Having a column like [Extended Price] in the table would be very convenient, particularly for reporting purposes. Computed columns are added to a base table, but they are computed when they are referenced and not stored with the row.

A UDF that is used in a computed column is not restricted to using data in the table in which it is defined. It can do any computations that are allowed in a UDF, and it may select data from other tables in order to produce its result. This ability extends what could previously be done with a computed column.

To create an example of adding a computed column that is based on a UDF to a table and because you may not want to modify tables in your copy of Northwind, I've copied the Orders table from Northwind into the TSQLUDFS database with its data and called it NWOrders. The following example creates a computed column on TSQLUDFS.NWOrders using udf_DT_NthDayInMon:

```
-- Create the BillingDate computed column on NWOrders
ALTER TABLE NWOrders
     ADD BillingDate AS
        dbo.udf_DT_NthDayInMon (YEAR(DATEADD(month, 1, ShippedDate))
                               , MONTH(DATEADD(Month, 1, ShippedDate))
                               , 2, 'TUESDAY')
GO
-- Show a few rows of the new column
SELECT TOP 4 OrderID, ShippedDate, BillingDate
    FROM NWOrders
GO
```

(Results)

```
OrderID     ShippedDate             BillingDate
----------- ----------------------- -------------------
      10248 1996-07-16 00:00:00.000 1996-08-13 00:00:00
      10249 1996-07-10 00:00:00.000 1996-08-13 00:00:00
      10250 1996-07-12 00:00:00.000 1996-08-13 00:00:00
      10251 1996-07-15 00:00:00.000 1996-08-13 00:00:00
```

That's all there really is to using a UDF in a computed column. The UDF is an expression, and it can be used in a computed column on its own or as part of an expression that combines its result with other expressions.

As we saw with a constraint, using a UDF in a computed column binds the UDF to the column, and SQL Server prohibits any alteration to the function. An attempt to alter `udf_DT_NthDayInMon` receives this error message:

```
Server: Msg 3729, Level 16, State 3, Procedure udf_DT_NthDayInMon, Line 89
Cannot ALTER 'dbo.udf_DT_NthDayInMon' because it is being referenced by object
'NWOrders'.
```

The computed column would have to be dropped from the table before the UDF could be changed.

Computed columns extend a table by adding a new column. One interesting aspect of computed columns is that they can be indexed. That includes computed columns based on UDFs. This is where determinism really becomes important.

Creating Indexes on Computed Columns with UDFs

Creating an index on a computed column that uses a UDF is no different than creating the index on any other computed column. The most important consideration is that the UDF must be deterministic. That is, given the same parameters, the UDF must return the same result. To ensure that any UDF used in an indexed computed column is deterministic, SQL Server tests the UDF for this list of requirements before it allows the creation of the index:

- The UDF must be schemabound.
- All built-in and user-defined functions used by the function must also be deterministic.
- The body of the function may not reference any database tables or views. (It may reference `TABLE` variables that are created in the function.)
- The function may not call any extended stored procedures.

It isn't always obvious that a computed column meets all the requirements, so SQL Server provides the `IsIndexable` argument to the built-in `COLUMNPROPERTY` function to let you know if a column is indexable. The function `udf_Tbl_ColumnIndexableTAB`, which you'll find in the TSQLUDFS database, uses `COLUMNPROPERTY` to report on the indexability of any table column and on some related properties. Here's a call for the `NWOrders` table:

```
-- Which columns are indexable
SELECT COLUMN_NAME, DATA_TYPE, IsComputed as Comp
     , IsIndexable as Indexable, IsDeterministic as Deterministic
     , IsPrecise as Precise
   FROM udf_Tbl_ColumnIndexableTAB('NWOrders', default)
   ORDER BY ORDINAL_POSITION
GO
```

(Results – abridged)

```
COLUMN_NAME      DATA_TYPE     Comp Indexable Deterministic Precise
---------------- ------------- ---- --------- ------------- -------
OrderID          int           NO   YES       NO            NO
CustomerID       nchar(5)      NO   YES       NO            NO
EmployeeID       int           NO   YES       NO            NO
OrderDate        datetime      NO   YES       NO            NO
RequiredDate     datetime      NO   YES       NO            NO
ShippedDate      datetime      NO   YES       NO            NO
...
BillingDate      datetime      YES  YES       YES           YES
```

SQL Server tells us that it's possible to create an index on BillingDate. I actually had to go back and change the definition of the function udf_DT_NthDayInMon to make it deterministic. That was accomplished by removing the use of the DATEPART and DATENAME functions that were in the original version.

Only when SQL Server is satisfied that a computed column is deterministic can the index be created. This script creates an index on the BillingDate computed column created in the previous section:

```
-- Create an index on a computed column
CREATE INDEX NWOrders_BillingDate
    ON NWOrders (BillingDate)
GO
```

(Results)

```
The command(s) completed successfully.
```

Imagine what would happen if you could create an index on an expression that involved the GETDATE built-in function. You might do that if you wanted an index on the age, in months, of an order. Here's the imaginary syntax:

```
CREATE INDEX my_expression_index
    ON NWOrders (DATEDIFF(Month, OrderedDate, getdate()) DESC)
```

It wouldn't be that hard for the SQL engine to create the index. After all, it can calculate the result of the expression very easily. However, what would happen in the next instant? The value of the expression might change at any time as the month anniversary is passed. In this case the order of the rows wouldn't really change, but sometimes rows would have the same age in months and at other times they would not. Every time the SQL engine went to read the index, it would have to recalculate all the values. What you'd have wouldn't be any help as an index. It would be more like a view.

There is another set of requirements for the proper use of views on computed columns. A group of session options, listed in Table 2.2, must be set to consistent values. These options affect the results of evaluating some expressions. If they're not consistent, the results of any UDF might change.

Table 2.2: Session options that must be set to use an index on a computed column

Option	Setting in a UDF	Description
ANSI_NULLS	ON	Governs = and <> comparisons to NULL
ANSI_PADDING	ON	Governs right side padding of character strings
ANSI_WARNINGS	ON	Governs the use of SQL-92 behavior for conditions like arithmetic overflow and divide-by-zero
ARITHABORT	ON	Governs whether a query is terminated when a divide-by-zero or arithmetic overflow occurs
CONCAT_NULL_YIELDS_NULL	ON	Governs whether string concatenation with NULL yields a NULL
QUOTED_IDENTIFIER	ON	Governs the treatment of double quotation marks for identifiers
NUMERIC_ROUNDABORT	OFF	Governs whether an error is raised if a numeric expression loses precision

These options should be set when the index is created and in any session that hopes to use the index. If the session options are not set correctly when a query is made on the table, SQL Server ignores the index. Creating and maintaining it become a waste of effort.

For UDFs to be used in computed columns that are indexed, particular attention has to be paid to two of these options: QUOTED_IDENTIFIER and ANSI_NULLS. These options can only be set when the function is created or altered. Their run-time setting has no effect when the UDF is executed. Therefore, all UDFs should be created with these options ON. That's why you'll see this batch at the beginning of CREATE FUNCTION scripts:

```
SET ANSI_WARNINGS ON
SET QUOTED_IDENTIERS ON
GO
```

The other five session options must be set to the correct value at run time. Fortunately, ADO (OLE DB) and ODBC set every option except

ARITHABORT to the correct value. If you're going to create indexes on computed columns or on views, Books Online advises you to set the server-wide user option ARITHABORT to ON. I've included some batches that set all seven options as a precaution when executing the Listing 0 file.

Getting to the point where it's possible to index computed columns takes a bit of work. However, if a key query depends on the order of a computed column, creating the index can have sufficient performance advantages to be worth the trouble.

Before you go any further, you might want to remove the computed column, constraint, and the index that have been created in the TSQLUDFS database. Computed columns and constraints are removed from a table with the ALTER TABLE statement. Indexes are removed with a DROP INDEX statement. The Listing 0 file has the script to remove the objects that were created in this section.

Summary

Scalar UDFs are only one of the three types of functions, but they represent the most common type of UDF and the only one that doesn't return a rowset. This chapter has covered how to create and use them.

It is important to understand the permissions that govern the right to create, alter, and delete UDFs. The creation of all types of UDFs is governed by the statement permission CREATE FUNCTION. That permission is given to members of the db_ddladmin fixed database role, which includes the database owner. It can also be passed on to other users as needed. However, the ALTER FUNCTION and DROP FUNCTION permissions cannot be given to users who are not part of db_ddladmin.

Two permissions, EXECUTE and REFERENCES, govern the use of scalar UDFs in the two major parts of the SQL language: SQL DML and SQL DDL. EXECUTE permission governs the use of UDFs in SQL DML, the part of SQL that changes data. REFERENCES permission governs the use of UDFs in SQL DDL, the part of SQL that defines tables and other database objects.

Once permissions are granted, a simple rule of thumb applies: A scalar UDF can be used wherever an expression can be used. We saw how this works in the select list and in the WHERE and ORDER BY clauses. Other spots for using scalar UDFs include the ON clause of a JOIN and the right-hand side of a SET clause of the UPDATE statement.

If the table owner has REFERENCES permission on a scalar UDF, it can also be used in CHECK constraints and computed columns, including computed columns that are indexed. Using a UDF, a CHECK constraint or computed column allows calculations to be made on data that's not in the row being checked. This extends the power of these two features. Of course, the same functionality can also be achieved using triggers.

The creation of indexes on computed columns creates a new requirement for determinism of any functions used in the computed column definitions. This includes a prohibition on indexing a computed column that uses any scalar UDF that references data. Indexes can't be maintained without determinism, so it's a restriction that must be obeyed.

Scalar UDFs are the first of the three types of UDFs to get their own chapter. Inline UDFs and multistatement UDFs are covered in Chapters 7 and 8, respectively. Before we get to them, Chapters 3 through 6 cover topics that affect all functions. Let's move on to Chapter 3, which shows you how to use the SQL Server tools to work with UDFs.

3

Working with UDFs in the SQL Server Tools

Anyone working with the SQL Server 2000 tools should consider themselves fortunate. While they're not perfect and there's plenty of room for developing an even smoother, more productive environment for writing SQL and maintaining databases, they're darn good and a big improvement on their predecessors. Since UDFs are new in SQL Server 2000, this is the first set of SQL Server tools to work with UDFs.

Most of this chapter is devoted to the three principal GUI tools that programmers and DBAs use to manage SQL Server:

- Query Analyzer
- SQL Profiler
- Enterprise Manager

I assume you already know how to use all three of these tools. I'll be concentrating the discussion on features that are specific to UDFs. In particular:

- Debugging UDFs
- Understanding the performance implications of UDFs

The command-line tools OSQL and ISQL can still be used with UDFs. I find them much less useful than the GUI tools. ISQL is obsolete, and OSQL should really be the only DOS tool that you use with SQL Server 2000. About the only time that I use it is when I have a SQL script that I want to run from a Windows BAT or CMD file. The section "Enterprise Manager and Other Tools" covers them briefly.

In my consulting practice, I move around a lot and I find that Query Analyzer is the only tool that I choose to use for writing SQL. That way, no matter where I go I'm assured of having it available. It's also the tool I used to write and test the scripts in this book.

Query Analyzer

SQL Query Analyzer, or just Query Analyzer, is Microsoft's GUI tool for executing and analyzing SQL scripts. It's not the only tool available for the task. Microsoft provides two similar command-line tools—OSQL and the rather ancient ISQL. They're discussed in the final section of this chapter. In addition, there are third-party tools, some with excellent reputations. This section concentrates on Query Analyzer because that's the GUI tool available to everyone with SQL Server.

Those of you using MSDE may be more interested in alternative tools. Three ways to work with functions come from Microsoft: Access, Visual Studio, and Visual Studio .NET. All have some capability to work with UDFs. As of the summer of 2003, Access 2002 and Visual Studio .NET are the best of the Microsoft tools. Other companies have their own tools, but I rarely get to use them.

Let's start with the basics. Figure 3.1 shows the Query Analyzer window. The function list for the TSQLUDFS database is expanded and highlighted with the label (A). It shows the functions already defined in the database.

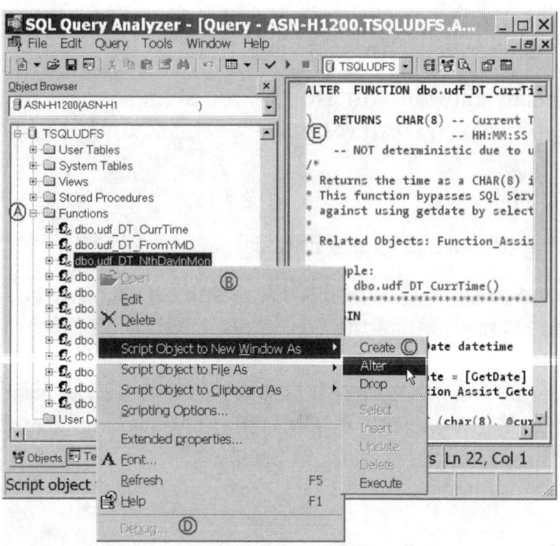

Figure 3.1: Query Analyzer showing the function list

By right-clicking on the function dbo.udf_DT_NthDayInMon, I brought up the context menu, labeled (B), and navigated down to the Script Object to New Window As ➢Alter menu item, labeled (C). That item creates a new connection and opens a new window with an ALTER script for the UDF that's selected. That's how I usually edit UDFs. Label (E) is in an already open window with an ALTER script for udf_DT_CurrTime.

At label (D) you'll notice that the Debug menu item is grayed out. Direct debugging of UDFs didn't make it into SQL Server 2000, which is a shame. However, with a little effort they can be debugged.

Debugging UDFs

Since it isn't possible to debug UDFs directly in SQL Server 2000, they have to be debugged by creating a stored procedure that invokes the UDF and then stepping into the UDF during the debugging session. This isn't very difficult.

All three types of UDFs can be debugged. The scalar and multistatement UDFs are the most interesting because they can have more than one statement, loops, conditional execution, and other debuggable features. Inline UDFs are only worth debugging for the sake of stepping into other UDFs that they might invoke. We'll start with scalar UDFs, and I'll also show an example of debugging a multistatement UDF.

The first step in the debugging process is to create the stored procedure for debugging. I always name the stored procedure by starting with the characters DEBUG_ followed by the name of the UDF. You'll find several DEBUG_ stored procedures in TSQLUDFS. For an example, let's use DEBUG_udf_DT_NthDayInMon, which is shown in Listing 3.1.

Listing 3.1: Debugging with DEBUG_udf_DT_NthDayInMon

```
CREATE PROCEDURE DEBUG_udf_DT_NthDayInMon  AS

DECLARE @dt datetime -- answer from udf_DT_NthDayInMon

-- First case taken from the function test
SELECT @dt = dbo.udf_DT_NthDayInMon(2003, 2, 3, 'Mon')
SELECT CAST('2003-02-17' as datetime) as [Correct Answer]
     , @dt as [udf_DT_NthDayInMon answer]
     , Case when '2003-02-17'=@dt THEN 'Worked' ELSE 'ERROR' END

-- Second case is harder one.  Should be 3/30/03
SELECT @dt = dbo.udf_DT_NthDayInMon (2003, 3, 5, 'SUNDAY')
SELECT CAST('2003-03-30' as datetime) as [Correct Answer]
     , @dt as [udf_DT_NthDayInMon answer]
     , Case when '2003-03-30'=@dt THEN 'Worked' ELSE 'ERROR' END
GO
```

The procedure has two test cases. The first one is the test taken from the function header. The second is a harder case that I made up for debugging.

Like the tests that I embed in function headers, `DEBUG_` procedures should be self-documenting. That's why each test case has two `SELECT` statements. The first is used to step into the function and get the answer. The second checks the answer and selects the result as part of a rowset for the user to see. It's important to return the results to the caller so he or she can see exactly what's returned. The SQL debugger doesn't highlight the return value as well as I would like. The second `SELECT` in each test shows the answer to the caller and checks the function's response for correctness.

The `DEBUG_` procedure should test the function's result for correctness and tell the caller if it is right or wrong. Reporting the correctness of the result, rather than the result itself, makes life easier both for the person who writes the test in the first place and for anyone maintaining the UDF after the first few days of creation. Don't forget Alzheimer's law, which is something about how easy it is to forget something, like the code you wrote a few weeks ago, but I don't remember.

There's no `GRANT` statement shown for the `DEBUG_` procedures. These procedures aren't for public consumption.

Select the stored procedure, right-click on the procedure name, and use the Debug menu item on the procedure's context menu to start debugging. Figure 3.2 shows the context menu as Debug is being selected.

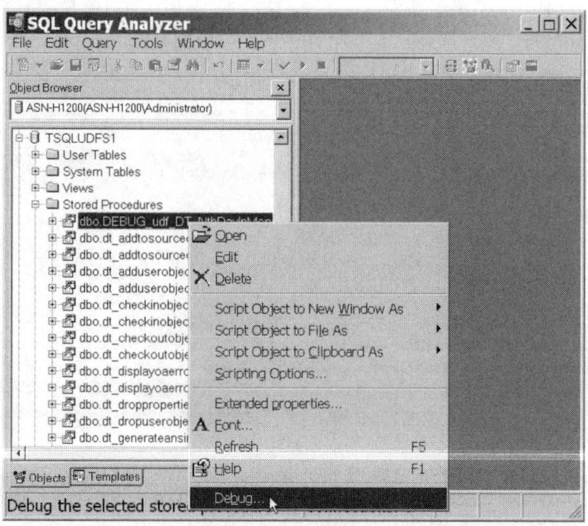

Figure 3.2: Beginning the debugging process

Selecting Debug brings up the Debug Procedure window shown in Figure 3.3. If you've given your `DEBUG_` proc any parameters, this is where you set the run-time value for them. I don't use any parameters for `DEBUG_` procs, so all I do is press the Execute button.

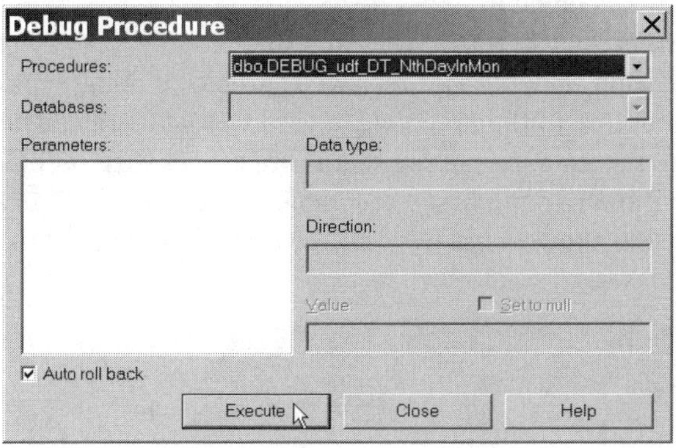

Figure 3.3: The Debug Procedure window

It's a good idea to leave the "Auto roll back" check box checked. Leaving it checked causes the debugger to surround the execution of your procedure with `BEGIN TRAN` and `ROLLBACK TRAN` statements. This prevents any undesired changes to the database from taking place. Of course, your UDF can't make any such changes, but your stored procedure might.

Once you press the Execute button, Query Analyzer brings up the debugging window, as shown in Figure 3.4. In the figure I've closed the Object Browser to give more room to view debugging information.

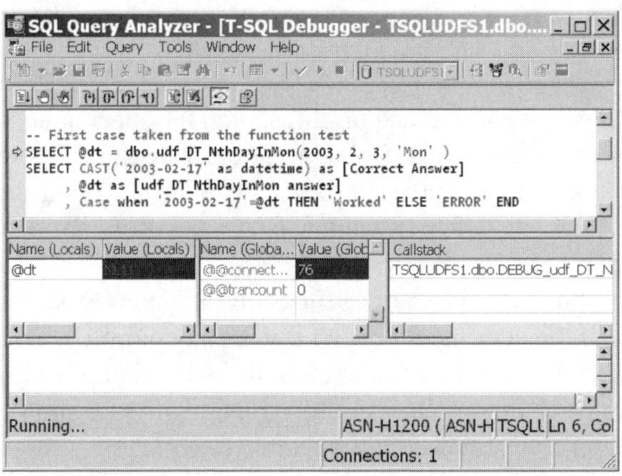

Figure 3.4: Debugging starting at the first statement of the proc

The debugger stops on the first executable statement of the `DEBUG_` proc. The yellow arrow in the left border points into the code window to show the next statement to be executed. Below the code window are the Locals window, the Globals window, and the Callstack.

The row of icons above the code window control execution of code during debugging. Each of the icons has a keyboard equivalent. A chart of keyboard shortcuts is given in Appendix B.

At this point, press F11 or use the Step Into icon  to start the function that we want to debug. If there were problems doing type conversion on the parameters to the function, an error would be raised before stepping into the function. Assuming that there are no such problems, the T-SQL Debugger steps to the first executable statement of `udf_DT_NthDayInMon`. Figure 3.5 shows what it looks like after I've adjusted the size of some of the windows.

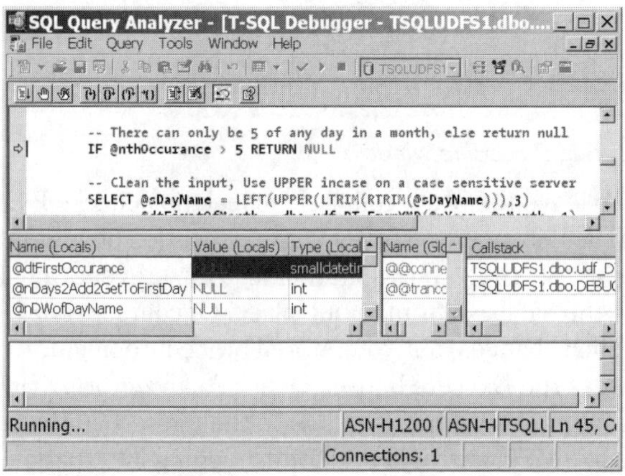

Figure 3.5: The first executable statement in udf_DT_NthDayInMon

There's almost never enough space on the screen for everything you'd like to see while using the T-SQL Debugger. Adjusting the windows helps to see the key facts. I like to make the Locals window pretty big and keep the Callstack in view. The Globals window isn't very useful for debugging UDFs, so I make it very narrow.

Step through the UDF with either the Step Into icon (F11) or Step Over icon (F10). If the statement doesn't invoke any more UDFs, there is no difference between the two ways to step. If the statement calls a UDF and you don't want to step into it, use Step Over. Figure 3.6 shows the debug window after I've stepped over several statements.

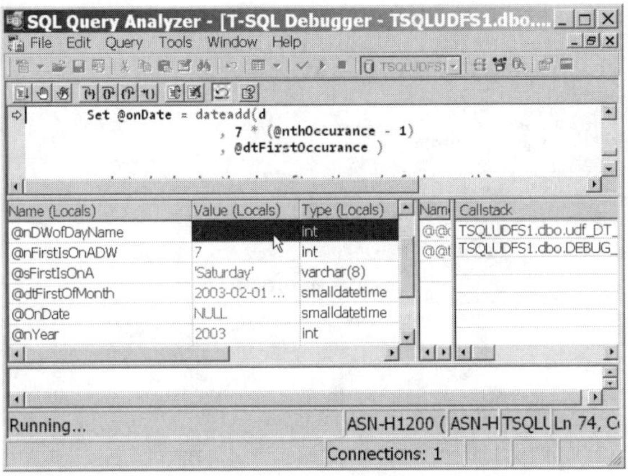

Figure 3.6: In the middle of debugging

I've enlarged the Locals window so I can see several of the local variables. You'll still have to scroll through the window to see them all. Either that or do what I did and purchase a very large monitor, or two, and a high-resolution, multi-monitor display card.

One of the most important aspects of the Locals window is that you can change the value of a local variable. This allows you to fix your intermediate results so you can limit the number of debugging trials needed to resolve an issue. This is the only way that you can change how the UDF executes as you debug it. Unlike some other debuggers, you cannot alter the order of execution of statements and you cannot change any of the statements themselves.

Once you've decided on a change, it's time to go back to the `ALTER` script for the function. Since the debugger places a lock on the function's definition, you must close the debugger window before you can alter the UDF. Once you've altered the function, you can debug the `DEBUG_` proc again. Unless you've changed the number or meaning of the parameters, there's no need to change the stored procedure.

After I was satisfied that I didn't need to make any changes to `udf_DT_NthDayInMon`, I pressed F5 and let the execution of the function and the stored procedure complete. Figure 3.7 shows the debugger in a completed state. The bottom panel has been enlarged to show the output of `DEBUG_udf_DT_NthDayInMon`.

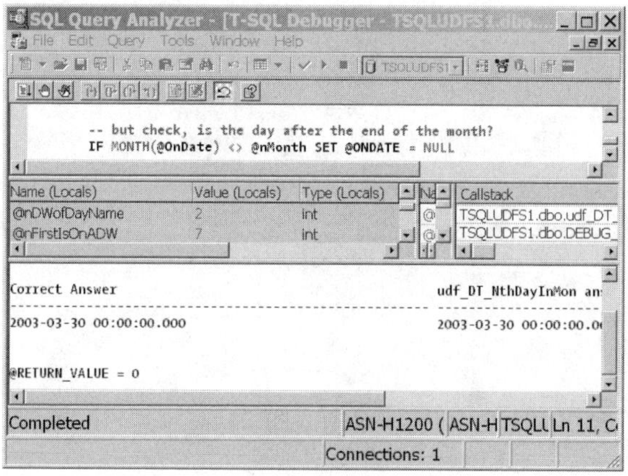

Figure 3.7: Debugging completed

The code window, Locals window, and Callstack remain as they were when I pressed F5 to complete execution. The gray shade of the Locals window indicates that you may no longer change the values it displays.

Note:

There is another available user interface for debugging UDFs: Visual Studio .NET. It has a direct interface to debugging and doesn't require setting up a stored procedure. I find the stored procedure method preferable because it always supplies parameters and tells me if the results were correct.

The T-SQL Debugger is a great tool that I use often. I'm looking forward to improvements in future releases of SQL Server.

Another great feature of Query Analyzer is the ability to create UDFs from templates. This is useful because you can create your own templates. The next section shows you how.

Creating UDFs with Templates

Templates are a general-purpose feature of Query Analyzer for creating SQL scripts by reusing text and substituting tokens in the text. The templates are text files with an extension of `TQL`. Nothing about templates is specific to functions. It's the templates themselves that can be written to create functions more easily.

Using a template is a two-step process. The two steps are:

1. Insert the template text into a Query Analyzer script window.
2. Bring up the substitution window.

The two steps correspond to the two advantages to using templates:

- They let you start each function with standard parts of the function, such as the function header, the comment block, the function body, and the `GRANT` statement.
- The substitution feature places the same text into every place where it is used in the function.

There's nothing magical about starting out with standard text for creating UDFs. You could do that with a plain text file. The advantage comes when you use the substitution feature to replace text strings, such as the function name, everywhere that they should appear in the text. This makes creation of a UDF faster, more consistent, and less error prone.

Take a look at Listing 3.2 on the following page for an example of how substitution works. It's the template I use for creating scalar UDFs. Strings in angle brackets (< >) are replaced during the substitution process. The substitution <scalar_function_name> is used in four places in the script, and when the substitution is performed the function name is entered identically in each place.

SQL Server ships with templates for creating each of the three types of functions. The download directory Templates has my version of all of the templates including inline and multistatement UDFs. If you like them, copy them to the directory where SQL Server keeps templates for creating UDFs: %Install Directory%\80\tools\Templates\SQL Query\Analyzer\Create Function, so they'll show up when you select a template.

The details of the comment block are discussed at length in Chapter 6 so I won't repeat them here. Let's step through a quick example of creating a function with a template.

The first step is to load the template into a query window. There are three ways to do this:

- Open a query window by connecting to the database and then using the Edit ➤ Insert Template menu item to load the template into the window.
- Use the Templates tab on the Object Browser, select a template, and use its context menu's Open item.
- Use Query Analyzer's File ➤ New menu item or Ctrl+N.

Listing 3.2: TSQL UDFS Create Scalar Function.tql

```
SET QUOTED_IDENTIFIER ON
SET ANSI_NULLS ON
GO

CREATE FUNCTION dbo.<scalar_function_name, sysname, udf_> (

    <parm1, sysname, @p1> <parm1_data_type, , int> -- <parm1_description, ,>
  , <parm2, sysname, @p2> <parm2_data_type, , int> -- <parm2_description, ,>
  , <parm3, sysname, @p3> <parm3_data_type, , int> -- <parm3_description, ,>
)   RETURNS <returns_data_type, ,int> -- <returns_description, ,>
    WITH SCHEMABINDING -- Or Comment about why not
/*
* description goes here
*
* Equivalent Template:
* Related Functions:
* Attribution: Based on xxx by yyy found in zzzzzzzzzzzz
* Maintenance Notes:
* Example:
select dbo.<scalar_function_name, sysname, udf_>(<parm1_test_value,,1>,
                         <parm2_test_value,,2>, <parm3_test_value,,3>)
* Test:
PRINT 'Test 1    ' + CASE WHEN x=dbo.<scalar_function_name, sysname, udf_>
           (<parm1_test_value,,1>, <parm2_test_value,,2>, <parm3_test_value,,3>)
                 THEN 'Worked' ELSE 'ERROR' END
* Test Script: TEST_<scalar_function_name, sysname, udf_>
* History:
* When          Who     Description
* ------------- ------- -----------------------------------------
* <date created,smalldatetime,YYYY-MM-DD> <your initials,char(8),XXX>
                        Initial Coding
****************************************************************/
AS BEGIN

    DECLARE @Result <function_data_type, ,int>

    SELECT @Result = fill_in_here

    RETURN @Result
END
GO

GRANT EXEC, REFERENCES ON [dbo].[<scalar_function_name, sysname, udf_>]
        TO [PUBLIC]
GO
```

Figure 3.8 shows the Query Analyzer as the TSQL UDFS Create Scalar Function.tql template is about to be loaded.

Once the Open menu item is selected, the window opens and the template is inserted, without modification, into the window. There's no need to show that because it's the same as Listing 3.2.

The next step is to select the Edit ➤ Replace Template Parameters menu item. This brings up the Replace Template Parameters dialog box that lets you enter your substitution text for each of the parameters in the template. Figure 3.9 shows the Replace Template Parameters dialog with the parameters that I'm interested in filled in just before I press the Replace All button.

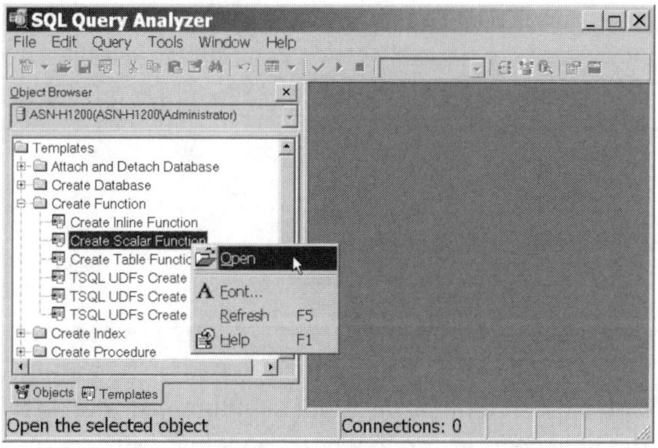

Figure 3.8: About to create a scalar UDF from a template

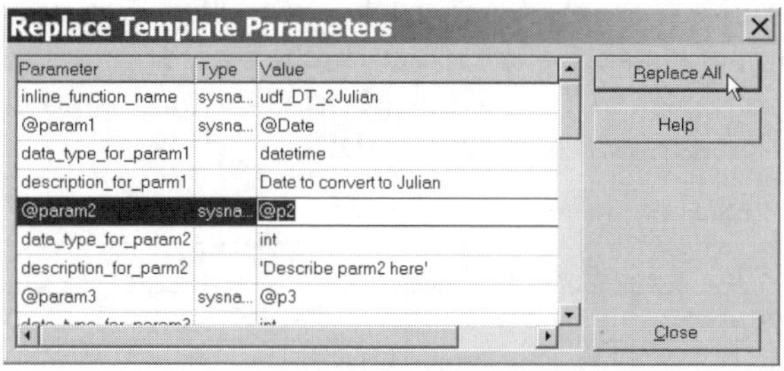

Figure 3.9: The Replace Template Parameters dialog box

The template parameters are replaced and your query window is left open, as shown in Figure 3.10, after I closed the Object Browser window.

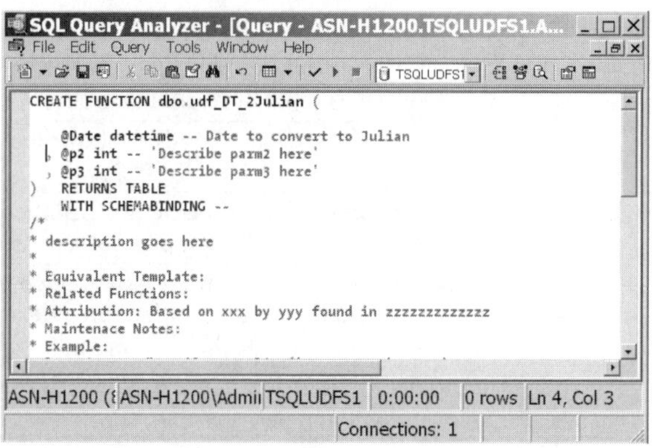

Figure 3.10: Query window after parameter replacment

Of course, there's still work to do to complete the UDF. For starters, since there's only one parameter to `udf_DT_2Julian`, `@p2` and `@p3` must be removed from the UDF. Also, there's the comment block to write. Templates are just a way to get a start on writing the UDF.

When it comes time to debug a UDF, Query Analyzer debugging is usually the most direct way to go. But you can't always replicate a real situation, and I often turn to SQL Profiler to help figure out what's happening in near real time.

SQL Profiler

SQL Profiler is a great tool that's been improved in SQL Server 2000. I'm not going to show you everything about how to use SQL Profiler. For that, I suggest you take a quick look at the Books Online and then start using it on a test system. This section concentrates on a few features of the SQL Profiler that are relevant to UDFs.

For the purpose of event tracing, UDFs are treated as stored procedures. Most but not all of the trace events in the stored procedure category are applicable to UDFs. Table 3.1 lists the stored procedure events and describes how they apply to UDFs.

Table 3.1: SQL Profiler events for stored procedures

Event	Description
RPC:Output Parameter	Not available for UDFs
RPC:Complete	Not available for UDFs
RPC:Starting	Not available for UDFs
SP:CacheHit	One event each time the UDF is found in the procedure cache
SP:CacheInsert	One event each time the UDF is compiled and inserted into the procedure cache
SP:CacheMiss	When a UDF is not found in the procedure cache
SP:CacheRemove	When a UDF is removed from the procedure cache
SP:Completed	When a UDF completes. TextData shows the statement that invoked the UDF.
SP:ExecContextHit	The execution version of a UDF has been found in the procedure cache. (Recompile not necessary)
SP:Recompile	A UDF was recompiled. This doesn't happen often but can be made to happen when an index on a table referenced by the UDF is dropped or created.
SP:Starting	Each time the UDF is started. TextData shows the statement that invoked the UDF.
SP:StmtCompleted	At the end of each executable statement within the UDF. `DECLARE` and comments are not executable.
SP:StmtStarting	At the start of each executable statement within the UDF. `DECLARE` and comments are not executable.

If you turn on all these events, you'll see either a CacheHit or a CacheMiss and then a CacheHit every time a UDF is invoked. The next event is an ExecContextHit followed by a StmtStarting event. Rather than my talking about what happens, the best way to become familiar with profiling UDFs is to try them out using the following series of steps.

Start by running this short script to get the object ID of two UDFs in the TSQLUDFS database:

```
-- Get the object ID of two UDFs for tracing
SELECT OBJECT_ID ('dbo.udf_SESSION_OptionsTAB')
          as [udf_SESSION_OptionsTAB]
     , OBJECT_ID ('dbo.udf_DT_age') as [udf_DT_age]
GO

(Results)

udf_SESSION_OptionsTAB udf_DT_age
---------------------- -----------
             837578022  1141579105
```

We'll put these object IDs into the trace filter. For a variety of reasons, there's a good chance that your object IDs will be different from the two above. Be sure to use the ones from the query that you run when we need them.

Start SQL Profiler and start a trace. Figure 3.11 shows the Events tab with the stored procedures events that I suggest you try. I usually use either SP:StmtStarting or SP:StmtCompleted but not both.

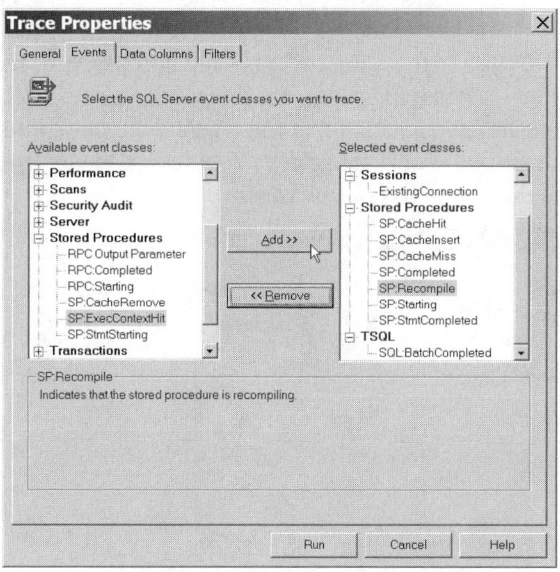

Figure 3.11: Adding stored procedure trace events

You can add all of the SP events if you like. The RPC events are not fired for UDFs.

Next, move over to the Data Columns tab. Figure 3.12 depicts this window after I added the ObjectID column to the Selected data list.

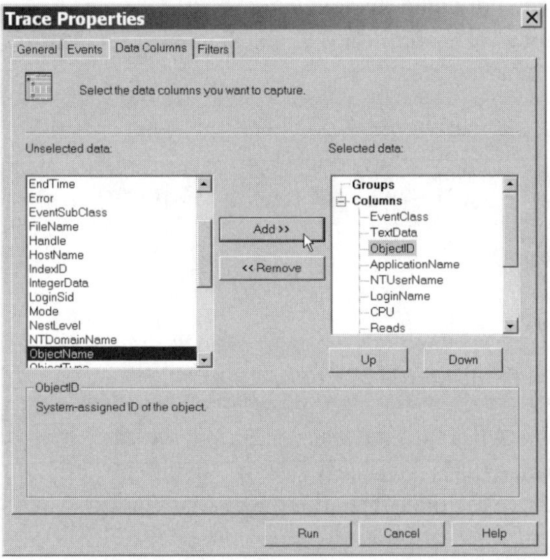

Figure 3.12: Data column selection

Finally, navigate to the Filters tab and down to the ObjectID tree node of the Trace event criteria tree and open it up. I suggest that you add the object IDs of `udf_DT_Age` to the filter. It isn't really necessary for tracing during this chapter's scripts; it's just a way to exercise a useful technique. Filtering the trace on the object ID(s) of the UDFs that you're interested in eliminates extraneous events that can be distracting. Figure 3.13 shows the Filters tab as the object ID is being added.

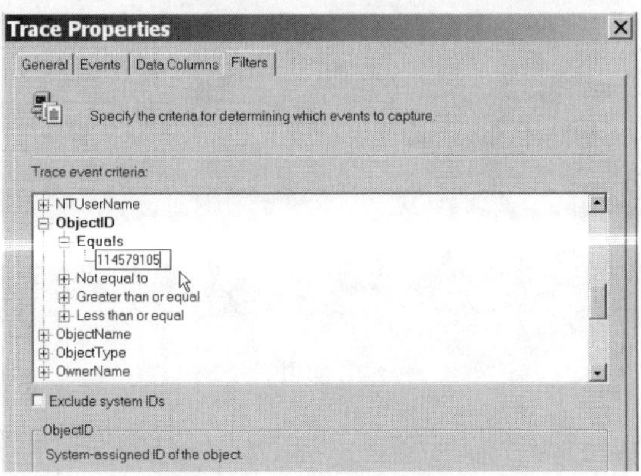

Figure 3.13: Filtering on the ObjectID column

To filter on a UDF, you should use ObjectID and not ObjectName. The tracing mechanism doesn't capture the name of a UDF, and so ObjectName isn't useful for filtering.

Now, flip back to Query Analyzer and run a few queries. Start with:

```
-- How old is the author
SELECT dbo.udf_DT_age('1956-07-10', null) as [Andy's Age]
GO
```

(Results)

```
Andy's Age
-----------
         47
```

Figure 3.14 shows the events that were traced during this script. Every statement in the UDF that was executed caused the SP:StmtCompleted event.

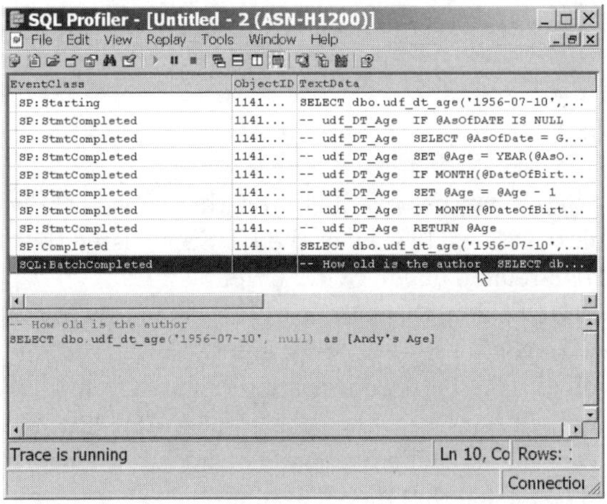

Figure 3.14: Events from tracing a single UDF

Next try a UDF that's filtered out:

```
-- Try a UDF that's not traced
SELECT dbo.udf_DT_FromYMD (2001, 2, 14)
GO
```

(Results)

```
------------------------------------------------------
2001-02-14 00:00:00
```

The only event you should see is the SQL:BatchCompleted event for the `SELECT` statement. That is assuming that you didn't remove SQL:BatchCompleted from the Events tab of the Trace Properties dialog box. Filters on the column don't filter out events that don't have a value for a data column, such as ObjectID. That's why SQL:BatchComplete shows up in the trace.

Now let's try to force a SP:Recompile event. Before you run the script, stop the trace. Open the properties window and remove the filter on ObjectID. Then restart the trace and run this script:

```
-- Try to force a recomple event.
SELECT dbo.udf_Order_Amount(10929) as [Amount of order 10929]
exec sp_recompile udf_Order_Amount
exec sp_recompile 'NWOrderDetails'
SELECT dbo.udf_Order_Amount(10929) as [Amount of order 10929]
GO
```

(Results)

```
Amount of order 10929
---------------------
            1174.7500
Object 'udf_Order_Amount' was successfully marked for recompilation.
Object 'NWOrderDetails' was successfully marked for recompilation.
Amount of order 10929
---------------------
            1174.7500
```

Although an extra SP:CacheMiss event is fired, there is no SP:Recompile event, even though `sp_recompile` was for the UDF. I've listed this in Appendix C as a UDF-related bug in SQL Server.

Recompiles on UDFs don't happen nearly as frequently as they do for stored procedures. As you'll see in Chapter 4, most of the statements that cause recompilation of stored procedures are prohibited from UDFs. Those are statements like `SET <session option>`, `CREATE TABLE`, `DBCC`, and `CREATE INDEX`. It is possible to get a recompile on a UDF when an index is created or dropped on a table that the UDF references. For the most part, you don't have to worry about recompiles of UDFs.

For more information about stored procedure recompiles, including a couple of videos about using the Windows Performance Analyzer and SQL Profiler, see the articles that I've published on my web site: http://www.NovickSoftware.com/Articles.htm.

The duration attributed to a UDF in the trace events can be a good indication of the resources it consumes. However, unless the statement is selecting data from the database, you'll often see a zero for duration. That's because the time to execute a single statement is usually less than SQL Profiler's measurement accuracy of three milliseconds. Take those zeros with a grain of salt. They add up in the end.

Another limitation on measuring the execution time of UDFs is the effect of the SQL Profiler on measurements. Running the profiler affects the time it takes to execute SQL statements; the measurement tool affects the results. (Didn't Heisenberg have something to say about that?)

I've tried to show some of the features of SQL Profiler that are very specific to UDFs. It's a great tool within its limitations. Chapter 17 is about a related group of system-defined functions that give you information about traces. It has a lot more information about tracing and measuring performance.

Before we conclude the topic of SQL Profiler, I just wanted to touch on one rather disappointing feature of SQL tracing. It's possible to generate a group of trace events, known as UserEvents, from code. Unfortunately, you can't generate them from a UDF.

Trying to Generate Your Own Trace Events from a UDF

SQL Server has an extended stored procedure, sp_trace_generateevent, that generates a user event. A user event only occurs when it's called. They're a great way for you to decide what gets traced. Unfortunately, even though sp_trace_generateevent is an extended stored procedure, it's impossible to invoke it from a UDF.

I was surprised by this limitation. UDFs are usually able to call extended stored procedures, even those whose name begins with sp_. So that you can test this limitation yourself, I've included a UDF to demonstrate that calls to sp_trace_generateevent compile but only generate an error when run. Listing 3.3 shows udf_Example_User_Event_Attempt, which has what looks like a valid call to sp_trace_generateevent.

Listing 3.3: udf_Example_User_Event_Attempt

```
CREATE FUNCTION dbo.udf_Example_User_Event_Attempt (

) RETURNS int -- just any integer
/*
* Example UDF that attempts to call the extended stored
* procedure sp_trace_generateevent. This demonstrates that the
* call fails with server message 557 in spite of
* sp_trace_generateevent being an extended and not a regular
* stored procedure.
*****************************************************************/
AS BEGIN

DECLARE @RC INT  -- the return code

EXEC @rc = master.dbo.sp_trace_generateevent 82
                      , 'From udf_example_user_event_attempt'
                      , 'this is the user data'

RETURN @RC
END
```

Try udf_Example_User_Event_Attempt with this script:

```
-- Try to generate a user event from inside a UDF
SELECT dbo.udf_Example_User_Event_Attempt()
GO

(Result)

Server: Msg 557, Level 16, State 2, Procedure udf_Example_User_Event_Attempt,
Line 15
Only functions and extended stored procedures can be executed from within
 function.
```

It's unfortunate that it doesn't work. We can always hope that Microsoft fixes it in the next service pack.

SQL Profiler can help solve all sorts of problems. Enterprise Manager and the other SQL tools are for more routine maintenance.

Enterprise Manager and Other Tools

There's not much to say about using UDFs in Enterprise Manager and the other tools, so I'll keep it short. The only other tools worth mentioning are OSQL and ISQL, the two text-based SQL execution tools. You can execute scripts with OSQL, which comes in handy when you want to automate script execution. ISQL is obsolete; use OSQL instead.

UDFs have their own node in Enterprise Manager's tree pane under the database's node. Enterprise Manager lets you create, alter, drop, and manage permissions for UDFs. The treatment of UDFs is no different than for other database objects. I find it easier to write CREATE FUNCTION scripts with Query Analyzer so I don't use Enterprise Manager's script-writing feature. The reasons are Query Analyzer's ability to execute examples, tests, and short scripts during the development process as well as its interface into the T-SQL Debugger. Enterprise Manager's functionality for dropping UDFs is occasionally useful because it lets you delete many UDFs at the same time.

The most useful feature of Enterprise Manager related to UDFs is its ability to script all UDFs and their dependent objects into a library. That's how the SQL scripts in the download directory were created. You'll find this capability as part of the All Tasks ➢Generate SQL Scripts item on each database's context menu.

Summary

For writing and debugging UDFs, stored procedures, and scripts, Query Analyzer and SQL Profiler are big improvements over their predecessors and pretty good tools. Their debugging capabilities don't rise to the level of Visual Studio .NET or some Java debuggers, but they get the job done.

Enterprise Manager is there for overall management of servers, databases, and database objects, including UDFs. It treats UDFs the same as other database objects, so all of Enterprise Manager's usual tools can be used on them.

The topic of what can and what cannot go into a UDF has come up several times. The next chapter is about what you can't do in a UDF. In some cases I'll show you a way around the limitation.

4

You Can't Do That in a UDF

As we learned in Chapter 2, there are many restrictions on the code that can be part of a UDF. While I speculate that the prime motivation for the restrictions is the need for determinism when indexing a computed field that references a UDF, it doesn't matter very much why you can't use a particular feature of T-SQL. This chapter discusses the features of T-SQL that may not be used in a UDF. I'll also show you a trick or two to get around some of these limitations.

T-SQL functions return scalar values or, in the case of inline and multistatement UDFs, rowsets to their callers. Many programming languages that have functions allow them to have side effects. That is, they modify the global state of the environment in which they run. This is in addition to returning information to their caller. Microsoft's SQL Server development team has tried to limit the ability of a UDF to have any side effects. It's also gone a long way to ensuring that UDFs return the same result every time that they are called. That is, they are deterministic.

Thus, the restrictions on UDFs fall into these broad principles. UDFs:

- May not invoke nondeterministic built-in functions
- May not change the state of the database
- Do not return messages to the caller

The restrictions apply to all three types of UDF. As a practical matter, many of them aren't applicable to inline UDFs due to the structure of an inline UDF as a single `SELECT` statement. They're in full force for scalar and multistatement UDFs.

We're going to start with the most obvious of the restrictions, the one on calling nondeterministic built-in functions. Then we'll work our way through the other restrictions from there.

Restriction on Invoking Nondeterministic Functions

UDFs may not call a nondeterministic built-in function! Well, that's part of the story because while there are certain functions that are clearly deterministic and others that are clearly nondeterministic, there is a group in between that can be called by a UDF. However, doing so makes the UDF nondeterministic.

Appendix A has a list of nondeterministic functions. I've tried to make that list as complete as possible by breaking out groups that are all nondeterministic based on the list from the Books Online.

Attempts to call any of the nondeterministic functions, such as GETDATE, in a UDF are rejected by the T-SQL parser, and the UDF is never created. Here's an example:

```
-- Try to create a UDF that returns seconds since a time
CREATE FUNCTION dbo.udf_DT_SecSince (
    @FromDate datetime
)   RETURNS INT -- Seconds since a time
AS BEGIN

    RETURN DATEDIFF (s, @FromDate, getdate())
END
GO

(Results)

Server: Msg 443, Level 16, State 1, Procedure udf_DT_SecSince, Line 7
Invalid use of 'getdate' within a function.
```

You'll find the same message if you try to use any of the other built-in functions in the list of always nondeterministic functions.

The Books Online lists two other groups in the article "Deterministic and Nondeterministic Functions." These are functions that are always deterministic and functions that are sometimes deterministic. The lists in Books Online are complete, so I won't show anything similar here.

What Books Online omits is a discussion of a group of functions that return the same result most of the time and may be used in UDFs. But use of these functions mark the calling function as nondeterministic. These functions include:

- DATEPART
- DATENAME

Why do they make a UDF nondeterministic? It's because a change in @@DATEFIRST changes the answer that they return. Any caller could change @@DATEFIRST before using a UDF that used one of the sensitive functions and then might get different results when the UDF is invoked with the default value of @@DATEFIRST. The potential for changing the results makes them unsuitable for use in a computed column that is indexed. You can still use them in UDFs that are never referred by an index.

There are two ways around the restriction on using nondeterministic functions:

- Take the value of the nondeterministic function as a parameter
- Select the nondeterministic function from a view

The next two sections cover these two techniques.

Take the Nondeterministic Value as a Parameter

This technique doesn't really get around the restriction; it's more of a way to live within the restriction. But it works, so it's worth mentioning. You remove to the nondeterministic function from the body of the function and add a parameter with the same data type that the nondeterministic function returns. You then rely on the caller to use the nondeterministic function, such as GETDATE, as the formal argument to the UDF. The next script illustrates this technique by adding a second parameter to the udf_DT_SecSince function that couldn't be created in the previous section:

```
-- Create a UDF that returns seconds since a time.
SET QUOTED_IDENTIFIER ON
SET ANSI_NULLS ON
GO
CREATE FUNCTION dbo.udf_DT_SecSince (
    @FromDate datetime
  , @ToDate   datetime
)   RETURNS INT -- Seconds since a time
AS BEGIN

    RETURN DATEDIFF (s, @FromDate, @ToDate)
END
GO

GRANT EXEC ON dbo.udf_DT_SecSince to [PUBLIC]
GO
```

To use it, supply GETDATE() as the second argument. Here's a sample:

```
-- Use udf_DT_SecSince
SELECT dbo.udf_DT_SecSince ('1964-02-09 20:05:00', getdate())
        as [Seconds since the Beatles appeared on Ed Sullivan]
GO
```

Supplying the second argument isn't convenient, and it makes the caller do the work. UDFs should make the caller's job easier, not harder. The next technique uses a view to get around the restriction on calling nondeterministic built-in functions.

Use the View Trick

While a nondeterministic built-in function can't be called directly from a UDF, it can be called indirectly. Creating a view that returns one column, the result of invoking the function, does this. This only works when the function doesn't take any arguments or when the arguments are fixed.

To continue with the time example, Listing 4.1 creates the view `Function_Assist_GETDATE`. The view has already been created in the TSQLUDFS database so you don't have to create it.

4.1: View to call GETDATE from a UDF

```
CREATE VIEW Function_Assist_GETDATE
/*
* A view to return one row, with one column, the current
* date/time from the built-in function GETDATE().  This
* view allows a UDF to bypass the restriction on access to
* the nondeterministic getdate() function.
*
* Attribution: Based on a newsgroup posting by Mikhail
*   Berlyant in microsoft.public.sqlserver.programming
*
* Example:
DECLARE @dtVar datetime
select @dtVAr = [GetDate] from Function_Assist_GETDATE
*********************************************************/

AS
    SELECT getdate() as [GetDate]
GO

GRANT  SELECT  ON [dbo].[Function_Assist_GETDATE]  TO [public]
GO
```

Now that `Function_Assist_GETDATE` is available, Listing 4.2 creates `udf_DT_CurrTime`, which uses it to return a character string with the current time.

Listing 4.2: udf_DT_CurrTime

```
CREATE FUNCTION dbo.udf_DT_CurrTime (

)   RETURNS  CHAR(8) -- Current Time string in the form
                     -- HH:MM:SS using 24-hour clock
    -- Nondeterministic due to use of getdate()
/*
* Returns the time as a CHAR(8) in the form HH:MM:SS
* This function bypasses SQL Server's usual restriction
* against using getdate by selecting it from a view.
*
* Related Objects: Function_Assist_Getdate
*
* Example:
select dbo.udf_DT_CurrTime()
**************************************************************/
AS BEGIN

    DECLARE @CurrDate datetime

    SELECT @CurrDate = [GetDate]
        FROM Function_Assist_Getdate

    RETURN CONVERT (char(8), @currDate, 108)
        -- 108 is HH:MM:SS 24-hour clock
END
GO

GRANT  EXECUTE  ON [dbo].[udf_DT_CurrTime]  TO [public]
GO
```

Using udf_DT_CurrTime doesn't require supplying any arguments. Just invoke it as in:

```
-- Use udf_DT_CurrTime
SELECT dbo.udf_DT_CurrTime() as [The time is now:]
GO

(Results)

The time is now:
----------------
12:33:58
```

Obviously, it's time for lunch. I'll go eat before discussing restrictions on access to data.

Restrictions on Data Access

As mentioned before, a UDF can select any data from any database that it can reach. The data access restriction is a prohibition on using INSERT, UPDATE, and DELETE. These statements can only be performed on TABLE variables declared within the UDF. Any attempt to insert, update, or delete a table in the database is rejected.

Along with the prohibition on using INSERT, UPDATE, and DELETE on database tables comes a restriction on any statement that would modify the state of transactions such as BEGIN TRAN, COMMIT TRAN, and ROLLBACK TRAN. @@Trancount isn't allowed either because it's nondeterministic.

One other restriction applies to UDFs. If a UDF selects any data other than from TABLE variables, the UDF becomes nondeterministic. This eliminates the possibility of it being used in a computed column that is indexed or in an indexed view.

Another highly restricted statement is EXEC, which is discussed in the next section. There is only one form of EXEC that can be used in a UDF.

Restrictions on the EXECUTE Statement

Most forms of EXEC are not allowed in a UDF. UDFs *may not*:

- Execute stored procedures
- Execute UDFs using an EXEC statement
- Execute dynamic SQL
- Execute extended stored procedures that return rowsets

UDFs are limited to executing extended stored procedures that do not return rowsets. Executing extended stored procedures is a topic itself, and I've made it the subject of Chapter 10. Here's an example code snippet that executes the xp_logevent extended stored procedure:

```
-- write a simple message to the log and the NT Event Log.
Declare @RC int -- return code
exec @rc = master..xp_logevent 60000, 'Illegitimi Non Carborundum'
```

If you executed it, you'll find a message in the Windows application event log and in the SQL Server log. xp_logevent can be used inside UDFs for reporting errors. That use is covered more fully in Chapters 5 and 10.

Of course, the restriction on executing dynamic SQL doesn't apply to referencing UDFs in a string that is dynamically executed. We saw that earlier in Chapter 2.

Another restriction on UDFs is not being able to refer to temporary tables. That's the subject of the next section.

Restriction on Access to Temporary Tables

One of the techniques often used by stored procedures and triggers is passing data between routines in temporary tables. This is also not available to UDFs, as temp tables may not be accessed by a UDF. UDFs *can't*:

- Create, alter, or drop temporary tables
- Select data from temporary tables
- Insert, update, or delete data from temporary tables

That pretty much covers what can be done with temporary tables. There's just no access to them from a UDF. Even if a stored procedure creates one and then creates the UDF dynamically, the temporary table is inaccessible. If I forgot to mention something that could be done with a temporary table, don't worry—you can't do it in a UDF.

In place of temporary tables, SQL Server 2000 provides the `TABLE` variable, which can be used in UDFs as well as in stored procedures, triggers, and SQL scripts. `TABLE` variables fill the need for short-term multi-row storage that sometimes comes up in the various types of procedures. They're very much like temporary tables.

`TABLE` variables were discussed at length in Chapter 2, so I won't repeat everything that was said there. One item that bears repeating is that `TABLE` variables are not just a memory object. They are created in tempdb in a special way. Although they use storage in tempdb, there are no entries for `TABLE` variables in the tempdb system tables. Small `TABLE` variables may be stored in memory, but larger ones eventually are written to and read back from disk.

Many stored procedures use temporary tables to communicate either among stored procedures or between triggers and stored procedures. That kind of communication isn't available to UDFs. Another mode of communication that isn't available from a UDF is messages.

Restriction on Returning Messages

Messages are returned by code by using either a PRINT statement or the RAISERROR statement. DBCC also uses messages to communicate most of its results rather than returning rowsets. UDFs don't return messages, so the three types of statements just mentioned are not allowed in a UDF.

The prohibition on using RAISERROR has implications for the handling of errors. What's a UDF to do when it recognizes an error? Chapter 5 discusses error handling in UDFs and the alternatives to RAISERROR, such as returning special values or NULL.

PRINT is often used to send messages to the console in a batch run by Query Analyzer or OSQL. I often use PRINT statements for debugging stored procedures. This option just isn't available when writing UDFs. Techniques for debugging UDFs were discussed in Chapter 3.

DBCC is used primarily for system maintenance tasks. Many of its options are used to analyze or fix the database. These uses are not available inside a UDF. If you want to use DBCC from SQL code, you'll have to use a stored procedure.

SELECT, TABLE, UPDATE, and DELETE statements can also generate a message saying how many rows the statement affects. I'm referring to the message:

```
(24 row(s) affected)
```

which is generated as the statement is executed. In stored procedures this message is often suppressed with the SET NOCOUNT ON statement. Even though these statements can be executed against TABLE variables, or against database tables in the case of SELECT, UDFs never return the message about the number of rows affected. It's as if SET NOCOUNT ON is executed as the UDF begins execution. No messages are returned.

Using SET for session options isn't allowed inside a UDF. The restrictions on SET and the required values for session options are the subject of the next section.

Restrictions on Setting Connection Options

Chapter 2 mentioned that there are two types of SET commands. The first type is an assignment statement for a single local variable. This is permitted in UDFs. The second type of SET statement changes a connection option. I'm sure that you're familiar with some of them, such as SET NOCOUNT and SET QUOTED_IDENTIFIER. The options are listed in the Books Online in the document for SET (described). This type of SET is not allowed in a UDF.

SET commands run on a session before execution of the UDF can affect the behavior of the SQL inside a UDF with two exceptions. ANSI_NULLS and QUOTED_IDENTIFIER are both "parse"-time options. The setting used inside the UDF during execution is not affected by any SET commands run on the session—only by the SET commands in effect when the UDF is created. This aspect of UDF execution confused me until I stumbled upon the Microsoft Knowledge Base Article: 306230 (formerly Q306230), which documents this feature. It is further explained in a subsection that follows.

No SET Commands Allowed

A quick example demonstrates the restriction on using SET. I tried to create this UDF to modify the DATEFIRST setting. Of course, it doesn't compile:

```
-- UDF that SETs DATEFIRST.  It won't compile.
CREATE FUNCTION udf_Test_SET_DATEFIRST (

    @NewDATEFIRST int -- new value of date first
)  RETURNS int -- The setting of Date first

AS BEGIN

    SET DATEFIRST @NewDATEFIRST

    RETURN @@DATEFIRST

END
GO
```

(Results)

```
Server: Msg 443, Level 16, State 2, Procedure udf_Test_SET_DATEFIRST, Line 9
Invalid use of 'SET COMMAND' within a function.
```

Changing the value of DATEFIRST doesn't make any code more nondeterministic than it already is, since using functions that are sensitive to DATEFIRST, such as DATEPART, already make a UDF nondeterministic. In any case, you can't SET DATEFIRST or use any SET command to change an option from within a UDF.

SET commands that have been executed before the UDF runs can change how the UDF executes, so it's important that they be set consistently. The next subsection demonstrates this feature, which turns out to be important for maintaining determinism along with the exceptions to the rule.

The Execution Environment of a UDF

One of the requirements that must be met for a UDF to be deterministic (that is, return the same result every time that it's called) is that it must react to execution errors, such as arithmetic overflow, in the same way every time it's run. The UDF must also handle expressions that compare a value to NULL the same way every time. The ANSI_NULLS setting governs how comparisons to NULL are evaluated. To ensure that UDFs return the same result every time they are run with the same inputs, UDFs should always be executed with the same settings for a group of options. The group is the same group that should be set when there are indexes on computed columns in the system.

The options that are always set the same way are shown in Table 4.1. These are the options that must always be set to a specific value when indexes on computed columns or indexes on views are created. This table is the same as Table 2.2 in the section on using UDFs in computed columns that are indexed.

Table 4.1: Session options and the required setting

Setting	Required Value	Description
ANSI_NULLS	ON	Governs = and <> comparisons to NULL
ANSI_PADDING	ON	Governs right side padding of character strings
ANSI_WARNINGS	ON	Governs the use of SQL-92 behavior for conditions like arithmetic overflow and divide-by-zero
ARITHABORT	ON	Governs whether a query is terminated when a divide-by-zero or arithmetic overflow occurs
CONCAT_NULL_YIELDS_NULL	ON	Governs whether string concatenation with NULL yields a NULL
QUOTED_IDENTIFIER	ON	Governs the treatment of double quotation marks for identifiers
NUMERIC_ROUNDABORT	OFF	Governs the generation of errors when numeric precision is lost during arithmetic operations

Listing 4.3 has the creation script of two UDFs that can be used to demonstrate how this works for the setting QUOTED_IDENTIFIER. The UDFs have already been created in the TSQLUDFS database under the correct setting of QUOTED_IDENTIFIER.

Listing 4.3: udf_Test_Quoted_Identifier_Off and _On

```
SET QUOTED_IDENTIFIER OFF
GO
SET ANSI_NULLS ON
GO

CREATE   FUNCTION dbo.udf_Test_Quoted_Identifier_Off (

) RETURNS BIT -- 1 if the Quoted IDENTIFIER property is ON
              -- inside the UDF.
/* Test UDF to show that it's the state of the quoted_identifier
* setting when the UDF is created that matters.  Not the
* state at run time.  This UDF was created when
* quoted_identifier was OFF.
***************************************************************/
AS BEGIN

 RETURN CAST (SESSIONPROPERTY ('QUOTED_IDENTIFIER') as BIT)

END
GO

GRANT EXEC on dbo.udf_Test_Quoted_Identifier_Off to [PUBLIC]
GO

SET QUOTED_IDENTIFIER ON
GO
SET ANSI_NULLS ON
GO

CREATE FUNCTION dbo.udf_Test_Quoted_Identifier_On (

) RETURNS BIT -- 1 if the Quoted IDENTIFIER property is ON
              -- inside the function.
/* Test UDF to show that it's the state of the quoted_identifier
* setting when the UDF is created that matters.  Not the
* state at run time.  This UDF was created when
* quoted_identifier was On.
***************************************************************/
AS BEGIN

 RETURN CAST (SESSIONPROPERTY ('QUOTED_IDENTIFIER') as BIT)

END
GO
GRANT EXEC on dbo.udf_Test_Quoted_Identifier_On to [PUBLIC]
GO
```

The most important thing to notice about Listing 4.3 is that the setting for QUOTED_IDENTIFIER is different for the two UDFs. It's off when creating udf_Test_Quoted_Identifier_Off and on when creating udf_Test_Quoted_Identifier_On. That's the only difference between the two functions.

Now that the function has been created, the following script shows how the setting that is in effect when a UDF is run has nothing to do with the current setting of QUOTED_IDENTIFIER. The setting depends only on the QUOTED_IDENTIFIER setting in effect when the UDF was created. Here's the script, which you'll find in this chapter's Listing 0 Short Queries.sql file.

```
-- To verify that QUOTED_IDENTIFIER is a parse time option
-- Begin the test here and ....
SET QUOTED_IDENTIFIER ON
GO
--
PRINT 'With QUOTED_IDENTIFIER ON'
SELECT dbo.udf_test_quoted_identifier_off() as [Off]
     , dbo.udf_test_quoted_identifier_on()  as [On]
GO

SET QUOTED_IDENTIFIER OFF
GO
PRINT 'With QUOTED_IDENTIFIER OFF'
SELECT dbo.udf_test_quoted_identifier_off() as [Off]
     , dbo.udf_test_quoted_identifier_on()  as [On]
GO
PRINT 'From OBJECTPROPERTY With QUOTED_IDENTIFIER OFF'

SELECT OBJECTPROPERTY
            (OBJECT_ID('dbo.udf_test_quoted_identifier_off')
           , 'ExecIsQuotedIdentOn') as [Off]
     , OBJECTPROPERTY
            (OBJECT_ID('dbo.udf_test_quoted_identifier_on')
           , 'ExecIsQuotedIdentOn') as [On]
GO
-- End execution of the script here.
```

(Results)

```
With QUOTED_IDENTIFIER ON
Off  On
---- ----
0    1

With QUOTED_IDENTIFIER OFF
Off  On
---- ----
0    1

From OBJECTPROPERTY With QUOTED_IDENTIFIER OFF
Off         On
----------- -----------
0           1
```

The first SELECT shows that setting QUOTED_IDENTIFIER ON doesn't change the behavior inside a UDF that was created with QUOTED_IDENTIFIER OFF. The second SELECT shows that setting QUOTED_IDENTIFIER OFF doesn't change the behavior inside a UDF that was created with QUOTED_IDENTIFIER ON. Finally, the last SELECT shows the state of the ExecIsQuotedIdentOn property for each UDF using the OBJECTPROPERTY function.

It's the object property ExecIsQuotedIdentOn that Query Analyzer uses when it creates the SET QUOTED_IDENTIFIER statement that it inserts at the top of scripts that it generates. In fact, it's because the QUOTED_IDENTIFIER and ANSI_NULLS settings are only in effect when the UDF is created that Query Analyzer puts them at the top of the CREATE FUNCTION or ALTER FUNCTION script each time they're generated.

If you recall the discussion of indexes on computed columns from Chapter 2, the successful indexing of computed columns, including those that invoke UDFs, requires that seven database settings always be set to specific states. The function udf_SQL_IsOK4Index, not listed, checks the session properties at run time to verify that the properties meet the indexing requirements. Listing 4.4 shows part of udf_Session_OptionsTAB, which reports on those options and several others.

These options can be queried using the SESSIONPROPERTY built-in function or by picking bits out of the @@Options built-in function. The latter approach is used by udf_Session_OptionsTAB. An abridged version of the function is shown in Listing 4.4. You'll find the full version in the database.

Listing 4.4: udf_Session_OptionsTAB **— abridged**

```
SET QUOTED_IDENTIFIER OFF -- Deliberately set off for this function
SET ANSI_NULLS OFF        -- Deliberately set off for this function
GO
CREATE   FUNCTION dbo.udf_Session_OptionsTAB (

) RETURNS @Options TABLE
              ([Set Option] varchar (32)
             , [Value]      varchar (17) -- @@LANGUAGE
                                         -- could be 17 chars.
              )
/*
* Returns a table that describe the current execution environment
* inside this UDF. This UDF is based on the @@OPTIONS system
* function and a few other @@ functions. Use DBCC USEROPTIONS
* to see some current options from outside of the UDF
* environment. See BOL section titled 'user options Option' in
* the section Setting Configuration Options for a description
* of each option.
*
* Note that QUOTED_IDENTIFER and ANSI_NULLS are parse time
* options and the code to report them has been commented out.
* See MS KB article 306230
*
* Example:
select * from udf_Session_OptionsTAB ()
```

```
*************************************************************/
AS BEGIN

    DECLARE @CurrOptn as int -- holds @@Options

    SET @CurrOptn = @@OPTIONS -- get it once

    INSERT INTO @Options ([Set Option], [Value])
        VALUES ('DISABLE_DEF_CNST_CHK'
               , CASE WHEN @CurrOptn & 1 = 1
                      THEN 'ON' ELSE 'OFF' END
               )

. . .

    INSERT INTO @Options ([Set Option], [Value])
        VALUES ('ANSI_NULL_DFLT_ON'
               , CASE WHEN @CurrOptn & 1024 = 1024
                      THEN 'ON' ELSE 'OFF' END
               )
    INSERT INTO @Options ([Set Option], [Value])
        VALUES ('ANSI_NULL_DFLT_OFF'
               , CASE WHEN @CurrOptn & 2048 = 2048
                      THEN 'ON' ELSE 'OFF' END
               )
    INSERT INTO @Options ([Set Option], [Value])
        VALUES ('CONCAT_NULL_YIELDS_NULL'
               , CASE WHEN @CurrOptn & 4096 = 4096
                      THEN 'ON' ELSE 'OFF' END
               )
    INSERT INTO @Options ([Set Option], [Value])
        VALUES ('NUMERIC_ROUNDABORT'
               , CASE WHEN @CurrOptn & 8192 = 8192
                      THEN 'ON' ELSE 'OFF' END
               )
    INSERT INTO @Options ([Set Option], [Value])
        VALUES ('XACT_ABORT'
               , CASE WHEN @CurrOptn & 16384 = 16384
                      THEN 'ON' ELSE 'OFF' END
               )
    INSERT INTO @Options ([Set Option], [Value])
        VALUES ('@@DATEFIRST', CONVERT(varchar(17), @@DATEFIRST)
               )
    INSERT INTO @Options ([Set Option], [Value])
        VALUES ('@@LOCK_TIMEOUT'
               , CONVERT(varchar(17), @@LOCK_TIMEOUT)
               )
    INSERT INTO @Options ([Set Option], [Value])
        VALUES ('@@TEXTSIZE'
               , CONVERT(varchar(17), @@LOCK_TIMEOUT)
               )
    INSERT INTO @Options ([Set Option], [Value])
        VALUES ('@@LANGUAGE'
               , CONVERT(varchar(17), @@LANGUAGE)
               )
    RETURN
END
```

The following script demonstrates that the options are changed. It changes a few options and then runs both DBCC USEROPTIONS and udf_Session_OptionsTAB to show their run-time values:

```
-- SET some options and then see the output of DBCC USEROPTIONS and
--         SELECT * FROM udf_Session_OptionsTAB()
SET DATEFIRST 4
SET TEXTSIZE 200000000
SET ARITHABORT OFF
SET ARITHIGNORE ON
SET NOCOUNT OFF
SET QUOTED_IDENTIFIER OFF
SET CURSOR_CLOSE_ON_COMMIT ON
SET ANSI_WARNINGS OFF
SET ANSI_PADDING OFF
SET ANSI_NULL_DFLT_ON OFF
SET NUMERIC_ROUNDABORT ON
SET XACT_ABORT ON

PRINT 'FROM DBCC'
DBCC USEROPTIONS

PRINT 'FROM udf_Session_OptionsTAB'
SELECT * FROM udf_Session_OptionsTAB()
GO
```

(Results - reformatted and abridged)

```
FROM DBCC
Set Option               Value
------------------------ --------------------
textsize                 200000000
language                 us_english
dateformat               mdy
datefirst                4
arithignore              SET
numeric_roundabort       SET
xact_abort               SET
disable_def_cnst_chk     SET
cursor_close_on_commit   SET
ansi_nulls               SET
concat_null_yields_null  SET

(11 row(s) affected)

DBCC execution completed. If DBCC printed error messages, contact your system
administrator.
FROM udf_Session_OptionsTAB
Set Option                       Value
-------------------------------- -----------------
DISABLE_DEF_CNST_CHK             ON
IMPLICIT_TRANSACTIONS            OFF
CURSOR_CLOSE_ON_COMMIT           ON
ANSI_WARNINGS                    OFF
ANSI_PADDING                     OFF
ARITHABORT                       OFF
ARITHABORT SESSIONPROPERTY       OFF
ARITHIGNORE                      ON
NOCOUNT                          OFF
```

```
ANSI_NULL_DFLT_ON             OFF
ANSI_NULL_DFLT_OFF            OFF
CONCAT_NULL_YIELDS_NULL       ON
NUMERIC_ROUNDABORT            ON
XACT_ABORT                    ON
@@DATEFIRST                   4
@@LOCK_TIMEOUT                -1
@@TEXTSIZE                    -1
@@LANGUAGE                    us_english

(18 row(s) affected)
```

It's a good idea to close the Query Analyzer session right now. The database options have been mixed up, and you wouldn't want to use it any more.

The restriction on SET is the last of the restrictions that I'm aware of. Don't be surprised if you encounter one or two others in obscure situations. I've tried to be thorough, but there may be more restrictions that I just haven't run across.

Summary

Microsoft has gone to great lengths to restrict user-designed functions so that they observe strict design principles that prevent side effects and ensure determinism to the maximum extent possible. UDFs were created with two principles in mind:

- Functions shouldn't have side effects.
- Functions should be deterministic whenever possible.

These principles have lead to the many restrictions placed on UDFs. If you keep them in mind as you code your UDFs, you won't be quite so surprised when a CREATE FUNCTION script is rejected by the T-SQL parser. By observing the principles, UDFs can be used in computed columns that are indexed and in indexed views.

The restrictions on UDFs that were discussed in this chapter raise another issue: How should a UDF report error conditions? The UDF can't use RAISEERROR or the PRINT statement, and other strategies are off-limits. What should it do? That's the subject of Chapter 5.

5

Handling Run-time Errors in UDFs

Due to all the restrictions discussed in the previous chapter, there are very limited choices for how to handle errors inside a UDF. Beyond the prohibitions on executing stored procedures, PRINT statements, RAISERROR, etc., SQL Server behaves differently when executing UDFs than when executing other types of T-SQL code. In particular, there's no opportunity to handle run-time errors.

Without the usual error handling mechanism, the potential solutions to handling run-time errors that occur in UDFs are:

- Detect errors before they happen and handle them on your own.
- Let them happen and rely on the code that called the UDF to handle the errors.

You'll never detect every possible error condition, although it's possible to detect the most obvious errors and do something that is more meaningful than allowing the error to be raised. What's more meaningful than the error? When you're working with scalar UDFs, about the only meaningful action you can take is to set the return value of the function. One of the options to discuss is using either NULL or a special numeric value as the return value for the function.

This chapter starts by showing how the handling of errors inside UDFs is different from the handling of errors in other types of T-SQL such as stored procedures. That is done by first setting up a demonstration of how error handling works in most T-SQL and then creating examples of how it works in the three types of UDF.

In the search for better ways to handle errors inside UDFs, I've tried various solutions. Unfortunately, only a few of the normal solutions are available to the coder of UDFs. As shown in Chapter 4, SQL Server won't let you use the RAISERROR statement inside a function. It is possible to cause an unrelated error, such as divide-by-zero, to stop execution of the program. But that's a messy solution and would confuse anyone who came along and used the function without knowledge of this unusual behavior. I don't recommend it, but I have experimented with it as a possible solution. I'll go into more details in the section "Causing Unrelated Errors in UDFs."

Let's start by showing how SQL Server treats errors that occur in a UDF differently than it treats other errors. Understanding this is very important when writing non-trivial UDFs.

Error Handling Inside UDFs

In order to illustrate how error handling inside UDFs differs from other error handling, I've created a stored procedure, usp_Example_Runtime_Error, that creates a run-time error and shows how SQL Server handles it when it's in a stored procedure. The procedure is shown in Listing 5.1, and you'll find it in the TSQLUDFS database.

The procedure is constructed so that it can be similar to a UDF, udf_Example_Runtime_Error, that follows. The proc uses a TABLE variable with a CHECK constraint on the EvenNumber column. This constraint raises an error when an attempt is made to put an odd value into the EvenNumber column.

The first thing that the procedure does is insert a row into @SampleTable that satisfies the CHECK constraint. It next updates the row so that it has the valid rowcount and the error code after the insert is performed.

The second insert has an odd value for EvenNumber, which raises an error. Execution of the stored procedure continues with the next statement, which selects @@ERROR, @@ROWCOUNT, and SCOPE_IDENTITY for updating the row. Since @@ERROR turns out to be non-zero, the UPDATE is skipped by the procedure's logic and a message is printed instead.

Listing 5.1: `usp_Example_Runtime_Error` stored procedure

```
CREATE PROCEDURE usp_Example_Runtime_Error AS

DECLARE @SampleTable TABLE (
           ID int IDENTITY (1,1)
         , EvenNumber int CHECK (EvenNumber % 2 = 0)
         , [Error] int
         , [RowCount] int
         )

DECLARE @myError int -- local @@Error
      , @myRowcount int -- local @@RowCount
      , @myID int

SET NOCOUNT ON
SET XACT_ABORT OFF

INSERT INTO @SampleTable (EvenNumber) Values (2)
SELECT @myError = @@Error, @myRowCount = @@RowCount
     , @myID = Scope_Identity ()

IF @myError = 0
    UPDATE @SampleTable
        SET [Error] = @myError, [RowCount] = @myRowCount
        WHERE [ID] = @myID
ELSE
    PRINT 'No Update after first insert due to error '
        + CONVERT(varchar(10), @myError)
-- ENIDF

INSERT INTO @SampleTable (EvenNumber) Values (3)
SELECT @myError = @@Error, @myRowCount = @@RowCount
     , @myID = Scope_Identity ()
IF @myError = 0
    UPDATE @SampleTable
        SET [Error] = @myError, [RowCount] = @myRowCount
        WHERE [ID] = @myID
ELSE
    PRINT 'No Update after second insert due to error '
        + CONVERT(varchar(10), @myError)
-- ENDIF

SELECT * from @SampleTable -- Return the rows to the caller
```

Before running this query in Query Analyzer, press Ctrl+T to turn on the Query ➤ Results in Text menu item. Because of the mixing of messages and result sets, text is the best way to view the output of this batch. Now, run the procedure and see what happens:

```
-- use usp_Example_Runtime_Error to demonstrate normal error handling
DECLARE @RC int, @ErrorAfterProc int
EXEC @RC = usp_Example_Runtime_Error
SELECT @ErrorAfterProc = @@ERROR
PRINT '@@Error After Proc = ' + CONVERT(varchar(10), @ErrorAfterProc)
PRINT 'Return Code=' + CONVERT(varchar(10), @RC)
GO
```

```
(Results)

Server: Msg 547, Level 16, State 1, Procedure usp_Example_Runtime_Error, Line 29
INSERT statement conflicted with COLUMN CHECK constraint
'CK__@SampleTa__EvenN__1B89C169'. The conflict occurred in database 'tempdb', table
'#1A959D30', column 'EvenNumber'.
The statement has been terminated.
No Update after second insert due to error 547
ID          EvenNumber  Error       RowCount
----------- ----------- ----------- -----------
          1           2           0           1

@@Error After Proc = 0
Return Code=0
```

A message about the second insert failing is returned to the caller, in this case Query Analyzer. That's followed by the message that comes from the PRINT statement about the error. The fact that this message gets returned at all is proof that execution of the stored procedure continued after the error was raised. Next, the resultset that comes from the SELECT * FROM @SampleTable statement is returned with one row. Finally, the PRINT statement in the batch shows us that the return code from the procedure is 0.

You might have noticed the SET XACT_ABORT OFF statement in the stored procedure usp_Example_Runtime_Error. The behavior of the procedure depends on this setting. If XACT_ABORT is ON, a stored procedure terminates as soon as any error is encountered, and the current transaction is rolled back. SQL Server's behavior inside a UDF is similar to but not exactly the same as if XACT_ABORT was set ON while it was executed.

The best way to see exactly what's happening in the procedure is to debug it. That's hard to show you in a book, so I'll leave it for you to try on your own.

Listing 5.2 shows udf_Example_Runtime_Error, which is as similar to usp_Example_Runtime_Error as I could make it. UDFs can't have PRINT statements so I had to remove them. Also UDFs can only return rowsets or scalar results, not both. I chose returning the scalar result.

Listing 5.2: udf_Example_Runtime_Error, to demonstrate error handling

```
CREATE   FUNCTION dbo.udf_Example_Runtime_Error (

) Returns int -- Error code from the last statement
/*
* Example UDF to demonstrate what happens when an error is
* raised by a SQL statement.
*
* Example:
SELECT * from dbo.udf_Example_Runtime_Error()
****************************************************************/
AS BEGIN

DECLARE @SampleTable TABLE (
          ID int IDENTITY (1,1)
```

```
        , EvenNumber int CHECK (EvenNumber % 2 = 0)
        , [Error] int
        , [RowCount] int
        )

DECLARE @myError int -- local @@Error
      , @myRowcount int -- local @@RowCount

-- First insert works and doesn't raise an error.
INSERT INTO @SampleTable (EvenNumber) Values (2)
SELECT @myError = @@Error, @myRowCount = @@RowCount
IF @myError = 0
    UPDATE @SampleTable
        SET [Error] = @myError, [RowCount] = @myRowCount
-- ENDIF

-- The next insert raises an error
INSERT INTO @SampleTable (EvenNumber) Values (3)
SELECT @myError = @@Error, @myRowCount = @@RowCount
IF @myError = 0
    UPDATE @SampleTable
        SET [Error] = @myError, [RowCount] = @myRowCount
-- ENDIF

RETURN @myError
END
```

The following query demonstrates the crux of the difference between error handling in UDFs and error handling in other T-SQL:

```
-- use udf_Example_Runtime_Error to show how UDFs are different.
DECLARE @RC INT, @Var2 int, @ErrorAfterUDF int
SELECT @RC = dbo.udf_Example_Runtime_Error ()
     , @Var2 = 2
SELECT @ErrorAfterUDF = @@Error
PRINT '@@ERROR after UDF = ' + CONVERT(varchar(10), @ErrorAFterUDF)
PRINT '   RC= ' + COALESCE(CONVERT(varchar(10), @RC), ' IS NULL')
PRINT 'Var2 = ' + COALESCE(CONVERT(varchar(10), @Var2),' IS NULL' )
GO
```

(Results)

```
Server: Msg 547, Level 16, State 1, Procedure udf_Example_Runtime_Error, Line 34
INSERT statement conflicted with COLUMN CHECK constraint
'CK__@SampleTa__EvenN__3D0AB0C5'. The conflict occurred in database 'tempdb', table
'#3C168C8C', column 'EvenNumber'.
The statement has been terminated.
@@ERROR after UDF = 0
   RC=  IS NULL
Var2 =  IS NULL
```

The UDF is terminated as soon as the error is encountered. The `SELECT` statement that calls the UDF is also terminated. Execution resumes with the next statement after that `SELECT`. In this case it's the `SELECT @ErrorAfterUDF = @@ERROR` statement. Notice that `@@ERROR` is set to 0, not 547!

The fact that the @@ERROR value is available inside the UDF and not available to the statement returned after the UDF is executed means that it's almost impossible to handle errors generated by UDFs in any intelligent way. I've listed this in Appendix C as a bug along with a small number of other issues that I've found with the implementation of UDFs. This is not an insurmountable problem. The error message is sent back to the calling application and will eventually be discovered. But it's inconsistent and makes it impossible to write good error handling code in T-SQL.

There are a couple of other things to notice. @RC is NULL. It never gets set. Also, take a look at @Var2. It's in the SELECT statement to illustrate that when the UDF is terminated, other parts of the SELECT are not executed.

Error handling in multistatement UDFs is similar to error handling in scalars. The TSQLUDFS database has udf_Example_Runtime_Error_Multistatement that you can use to demonstrate how it works. The procedure DEBUG_udf_Example_Runtime_Error_Multistatement has a reasonable demonstration and can be used to debug the UDF.

Error handling in inline UDFs is different from the other two types of UDFs. When an error occurs during the execution of an inline UDF, the statement stops running. However, the rows that have already been created are returned to the caller and @@ERROR is set to the error code that caused the problem.

udf_Example_Runtime_Error_Inline, shown in Listing 5.3, illustrates what happens by causing a divide-by-zero error when the column expression 100/Num is evaluated for the third row.

Listing 5.3: udf_Example_Runtime_Error_Inline

```
CREATE   FUNCTION dbo.udf_Example_Runtime_Error_Inline (

) RETURNS TABLE
/*
* Example UDF to demonstrate what happens when an error is
* raised by a SQL statement.  This is an inline UDF.
*
* Example:
SELECT * from dbo.udf_Example_Runtime_Error_Inline()
****************************************************************/
AS RETURN

SELECT Num
     , 100 / Num as [100 divided by Num]
    FROM (          SELECT 1 as Num
          UNION ALL SELECT 2
          UNION ALL SELECT 0 -- Will cause divide by 0
          UNION ALL SELECT 4
         ) as NumberList
```

Here's what happens when executing the UDF:

```
-- execute the inline UDF that generates an error
DECLARE @myError int, @myRowCount int -- local @@ variables
SET NOCOUNT OFF
SELECT * FROM udf_Example_Runtime_Error_Inline()
SELECT @myError = @@Error, @myRowCount = @@Rowcount
PRINT '@@Error = ' + CONVERT(VARCHAR(10), @myError)
PRINT 'Rowcount= ' + CONVERT(VARCHAR(10), @myRowCount)
GO

(Results)

Num         100 divided by Num
----------- ------------------
          1                100
          2                 50

(3 row(s) affected)

Server: Msg 8134, Level 16, State 1, Line 3
Divide by zero error encountered.
@@Error = 8134
Rowcount= 3
```

Only two rows really get returned, although Query Analyzer seems to think that there are three rows in the result. `@@ERROR` is set after the statement terminates to the correct error code.

I suggest that you experiment with UDF error handling further. To make that easy, I've included DEBUG stored procedures for all three `Example_Runtime_Error` UDFs. You also have the scripts in this section.

Errors inside UDFs are handled in a way that's much different from the way they're handled in other T-SQL scripts. There is no opportunity for examining `@@ERROR` so that the UDF can decide how to proceed after an error occurs. SQL Server has decided that the UDF terminates and the code that calls the UDF is responsible for handling the error. That leads us to the ways that we might avoid these problems in the first place.

Testing Parameters and Returning NULL

The function udf_Num_LOGN is a good candidate for the strategy of testing inputs before use and returning NULL. The function, which is shown in Listing 5.4, returns the logarithm of a number, *N*, to any desired base. The built-in LOG function returns the natural logarithm of *N*, using the base *e*.

Listing 5.4: udf_Num_LOGN

```
CREATE  FUNCTION dbo.udf_Num_LOGN(

    @n    float -- Number to take the log of
  , @Base float -- Base of the logorithm, 10, 2, 3.74
)   RETURNS float -- Logorithm (base @base) of @n
    WITH SCHEMABINDING
/*
* The logorithm to the base @Base of @n. Returns NULL for any
* invalid input instead of raising an error.
*
* Example:
SELECT dbo.udf_Num_LOGN(1000, 10), dbo.udf_Num_LOGN(64, 4)
     , dbo.udf_Num_LOGN(0, 3), dbo.udf_Num_LOGN(3, 0)
****************************************************************/
AS BEGIN

    IF @n IS NULL OR @n <= 0 OR
       @Base IS NULL OR @Base <= 0 OR @Base = 1
           RETURN NULL

    RETURN LOG(@n) / LOG(@Base)
END
```

Logarithm functions present many opportunities for errors because the mathematical definition of logarithm is undefined for values less than or equal to 0. Also, it's 0 for @Base=1. In the case of udf_Num_LOGN, a base of 1 could cause a divide-by-zero error if it wasn't prevented. Thus, any inputs that are less than or equal to 0 or a base of 1 will result in some type of error.

SQL Server's LOG() function always raises "Domain error" when it gets invalid input, and the message text "A domain error occurred" is printed when this occurs in Query Analyzer. But a domain error is not like most other SQL Server errors. It doesn't seem to have a message number or severity level associated with it. Although the message can be suppressed with SET ARITHIGNORE ON, it doesn't return NULL; it seems to just not return any result at all. This makes it a good candidate for creating a meaningful alternate treatment.

udf_Num_LOGN has a check for invalid inputs, and when it finds one, it returns NULL. The check could be omitted and the caller could be left to handle the result. However, in the case of logarithms, the meaning of NULL is pretty close to the meaning of mathematically undefined. So returning NULL produces a pretty meaningful result, one that could not be mistaken for a valid answer. That's why I've added the check to the function.

Returning Special Values

An alternative to returning NULL is to return a special value that represents the error situation. I understand that SAS, a statistical analysis package, has always made extensive use of this technique. It works in statistics because many statistical variables are positive by their definition. The negative values can be used for special meanings. As you'll see in Chapter 13, currency conversion is another candidate for using special values because there is a range of values stored by the data type (numeric) that are not legitimate exchange rates.

Table 5.1 shows the special values used for physical quantities in an analytic program that I worked on several years ago. Since the physical quantities could never be negative, these values worked very well. The quantities became input into a Markov model. Because of the way it was constructed, the negative sign propagated through the Markov model and showed where its results were unusable.

Table 5.1: Special values used by an analytic program

Value	Meaning
–1	Unknown error
–2	Not applicable
–3	Input too high
–4	Input too low
–5	Input bad format
–6	Input illegal
–7	Input bad length
–8	Division by zero
–9	Other math error
–10	Aggregation error
–11	Calculation result is too high
–12	Calculation result is too low
–13	Calculation based on missing value

I don't expect anyone to be doing Markov models in SQL. It's the wrong place for that type of code. However, a database is a great place to store model results and generate reports, and using the special negative values may afford a way to communicate problems in a way that's more detailed than just returning NULL.

Causing Unrelated Errors in UDFs

Even though I recommend against it, it's worth taking a look at how the technique of causing unrelated errors in UDFs might work. The only reason that I could ever imagine that I'd resort to this technique is out of total desperation to have a UDF stop executing when some sort of impossible situation had arisen. It hasn't happened to me yet.

Listing 5.5 creates a function, udf_Test_ConditionalDivideBy0, that can cause a divide-by-zero error. The error is optional based on the input parameter. You'll find the function in the TSQLUDFS database.

Listing 5.5: udf_Test_ConditionalDivideBy0

```
CREATE FUNCTION dbo.udf_Test_ConditionalDivideBy0 (

    @bCauseError BIT -- 1 if divide-by-zero error is requested.
)   RETURNS INT -- Always returns zero, if it returns at all.
/*
*  Creates a divide-by-zero error conditionally based on the
* @bCauseError parameter.
*
* Example:
select au_fname, au_lname, dbo.udf_Test_ConditionalDivideBy0(0)
    FROM pubs..authors -- does not produce an error
select au_fname, au_lname, dbo.udf_Test_ConditionalDivideBy0(1)
    FROM pubs..authors -- produces an error
***************************************************************/
AS BEGIN

    DECLARE @TestVar int -- working variable

    IF @bCauseError = 1
        SET @TestVar = 1 / 0

RETURN 0
END
```

The following queries illustrate what happens when you execute a SELECT that calls this function using three variations:

```
-- Query with UDF that doesn't divide by zero
SELECT top 2 au_id, au_fname, au_lname
    , dbo.udf_Test_ConditionalDivideBy0(0) [Don't Divide by Zero]
    FROM pubs..authors
GO

(Results)

au_id       au_fname au_lname       Don't Divide by Zero
----------- -------- -------------- --------------------
409-56-7008 Abraham  Bennet                            0
648-92-1872 Reginald Blotchet-Halls                    0
```

```
-- Now we do request a divide-by-zero
SELECT TOP 2 au_id, au_fname, au_lname
     , dbo.udf_Test_ConditionalDivideBy0(1) [Request Divide by Zero]
    FROM pubs..authors
GO
```

(Results)

```
Server: Msg 8134, Level 16, State 1, Procedure udf_Test_ConditionalDivideBy0, Line 24
Divide by zero error encountered.


-- But if the right session options are set there is no error raised
SET ANSI_WARNINGS OFF
SET ARITHABORT OFF
SET ARITHIGNORE ON
SELECT TOP 2 au_id, au_fname, au_lname
     , dbo.udf_Test_ConditionalDivideBy0(1) [Request Divide by Zero]
    FROM pubs..authors
GO
```

(Results)

```
au_id       au_fname  au_lname       Request Divide by Zero
----------- --------- -------------- ----------------------
409-56-7008 Abraham   Bennet                              0
648-92-1872 Reginald  Blotchet-Halls                      0
```

The first query doesn't have any code that raises an error. The second query calls udf_Test_ConditionalDivideBy0 with a parameter 1 that causes the divide-by-zero result to be raised and the error message to be returned to the caller with no results. The final query has three calls to SET that change SQL Server's handling of divide-by-zero errors, and no error is raised.

To reiterate, I don't advocate causing divide-by-zero errors in the middle of queries. This section is here to illustrate that it could be done and how errors are handled. But as the last query shows, if certain SET options are left in unexpected settings, no error gets raised.

Reporting Errors in UDFs Out the Back Door

Every once in a while, an error appears so grievous that it's essential that it be reported. As we've seen, the usual techniques of using a RAISEERROR statement or PRINT statement to get a message back to the caller aren't available in UDFs. One way to get the message out is with the xp_logevent extended stored procedure. It's able to write a message that goes into the SQL Server management log and at the same time to the Windows NT application event log.

This is technique should be used with a great deal of caution but can be a lifesaver. The best use that I've found for it is for writing messages about conditions that you thought were impossible or nearly impossible but that seem to be occurring. You can test for these conditions in your UDF code, write a message, and keep going if you want.

Listing 5.6 shows `udf_SQL_LogMsgBIT`, which is a UDF that calls `xp_logevent`. I prefer to use this intermediate UDF instead of putting calls to `xp_logevent` in my other code, but there may not be any real advantage to doing so. If you read the function's comments, you'll notice that it mentions a little trick: When defining a view, you can add a column that invokes this UDF. It would cause a message to be written to the SQL log every time the view was used.

Listing 5.6: `udf_SQL_LogMsgBIT`

```
CREATE FUNCTION dbo.udf_SQL_LogMsgBIT (

    @nMessageNumber int = 50001 -- User-defined message >= 50000
  , @sMessage varchar(8000) -- The message to be logged
  , @sSeverity varchar(16) = NULL -- The severity of the message
      -- may be 'INFORMATIONAL', 'WARNING', OR 'ERROR'
)   RETURNS BIT -- 1 for success or 0 for failure
/*
* Adds a message to the SQL Server log and the NT application
* event log. Uses xp_logevent. xp_logevent can used whenever
* in place of this function.
* One potential use of this UDF is to cause the logging of a
* message in a place where xp_logevent cannot be executed
* such as in the definition of a view.
*
* Example:
select dbo.udf_SQL_LogMsgBIT(default,
                   'Now that''s what I call a message!', NULL)
****************************************************************/
AS BEGIN

DECLARE @WorkingVariable BIT

IF @sSeverity is NULL
    EXEC @WorkingVariable = master..xp_logevent @nMessageNumber
                                              , @sMessage
ELSE
    EXEC @WorkingVariable = master..xp_logevent @nMessageNumber
                                              , @sMessage
                                              , @sSeverity
END
-- xp_logevent has it backwards
RETURN CASE WHEN @WorkingVariable=1 THEN 0 ELSE 1 END
END
```

This script gives you a quick picture of how it might work:

```
-- Detect an unusual situation and report it.
DECLARE @rc int, @SentMsg BIT
SET @rc = 37 -- 37 is our example unusual situation
IF @rc = 37 -- AND yada yada yada
   SET @SentMsg = dbo.udf_SQL_LogMsgBIT (default,
         'Special situation 37 occured in Chapter 5.', NULL)
GO
```

You can view the SQL Server message log with Enterprise Manager. Figure 5.1 shows what the bottom of the log looks like just after I ran the script.

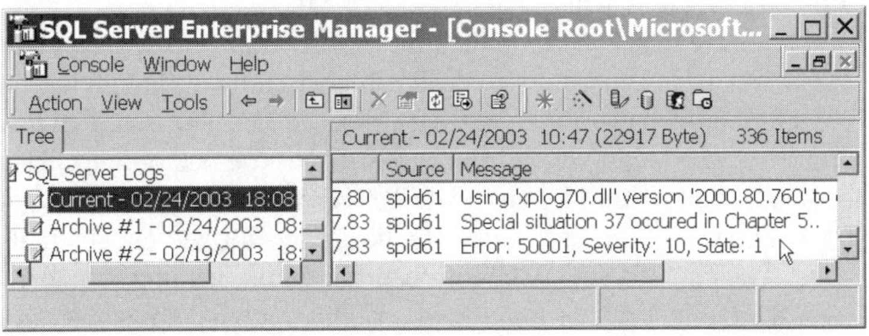

Figure 5.1: Enterprise Manager showing the SQL Server message log

Chapter 10 has an entire section on using `xp_logevent`, so I won't elaborate any more here. It's a technique that comes in handy in a pinch. Be careful not to overuse it, or you'll fill your event log in a hurry.

Summary

This chapter has shown how SQL Server handles errors that occur in UDFs differently than it handles errors that occur in other T-SQL. This can be a real problem and one that must be dealt with.

I've shown you a variety of techniques for dealing with the error handling issue in your UDF code. These techniques boil down to:

- Let the error happen and make the caller responsible for handling it.
- Find errors by careful checking of parameters and intermediate values, and return `NULL` for invalid values.
- Return a special value for the function that tells the caller what type of error occurred.

I've also shown two techniques that should be reserved for desperate times:

- Generating an unrelated error, such as divide-by-zero, from within a UDF
- Sending a message to the SQL message log and NT event log

Neither should be used casually. Rather, they should be reserved for when you really need them.

Whatever your choice when writing each UDF, error handling remains your responsibility, and it shouldn't be ignored. To be successful at it, it's important to remain aware of what SQL Server is doing with each potential error and how your code expects to handle it.

I'm sure that you've noticed the comment blocks that I put at the top of every UDF. I think they're pretty important even though they're time consuming to write. You might have noticed that I format T-SQL with separators at the beginning of lines instead of at the end of lines. Also, what about the names that I give to UDFs? They follow a pretty specific pattern. The next chapter is about the best ways for writing and maintaining code. The choices you make for documentation, naming, and formatting have a big effect on the long-term usability and maintainability of UDFs.

6

Documentation, Formatting, and Naming Conventions

What does this next function do?

```
Create function getcommaname (@f varchar(20),@m varchar(20),@l
       varchar(40),@s Varchar(20))returns Varchar(128) as begin
declare @t varchar(64) set @t = ltrim(rtrim(@l))
if len(@t) > 0  set @t = @t + ',' if len(ltrim(rtrim(@f))) > 0
set @t = @t + ' ' + ltrim(rtrim(@f))
if len(ltrim(rtrim(@m))) > 0 set @t = @t + ' ' + ltrim(rtrim(@m))
if len(ltrim(rtrim(@s))) > 0
set @t = @t + ' ' + ltrim(rtrim(@s)) return @t end
```

Take a minute and try to figure it out. Better yet, try to use it. You'll find the script in the Chapter 6 Listing 0 Short Queries.sql file in the chapter's download directory. The procedure has already been added to the TSQL-UDFS database. If you want to run the script, you'll have to do it in another database or drop the function first.

If you're like me, you copied the text into Query Analyzer and reformatted it so it was easier to read or copied just the function declaration into Query Analyzer and added a SELECT statement that executed it.

It's been a long time since I've seen a professional programmer try to use a function that is as badly formatted as the one above, but it makes a point: The presentation of a function has a lot to do with its usability. This chapter is about how to make functions more useful through the way they are formatted, named, and documented.

When I say "useful," you've got to ask, "Useful to whom?" In most cases, it's other programmers and DBAs:

- Application programmers — The users of the functions. They want to know what it does and how to use it to create the application.
- Maintenance programmers — The programmers who must make a change to a function or fix a bug in the function. They want to know how the function works, how to test the function, and any important gotchas, such as a related function, that must be changed whenever the function in question is modified. They also want the function's code laid out in an easy-to-read way.
- Database administrators — The people who protect the integrity of the database and keep the applications going. They want to know what the function does and if it's the code that's making their system slow.

Any of these people might be the original author of the function. A couple of weeks after writing any code, I'm hard pressed to recite what it does, much less the exact calling sequence of a function.

One problem with writing a chapter on programming conventions such as variable naming, comment formats, and SQL statement formats is that there's no right answer. I've been working with SQL for decades and with SQL Server UDFs for a few years, and I think I have something to say about how to write them. I can explain why I think a convention is the best choice, but there are always going to be good arguments for some other way. Please take this chapter the way it's intended: the well-intentioned conventions from an experienced programmer who's spent some time thinking about how to produce good code.

With that said, for purposes of illustration, Listing 6.1 shows the function udf_Name_FullWithComma, which concatenates the parts of a name to form a last name first, first name last string. It's used as an example throughout this chapter. Let's start with an explanation of how I format SQL statements.

Listing 6.1: udf_Name_FullWithComma

```
SET QUOTED_IDENTIFIER ON
SET ANSI_NULLS ON
GO

CREATE FUNCTION dbo.udf_Name_FullWithComma (

    @sFirstName nvarchar(20) = N'' -- First Name
  , @sMiddleName nvarchar(20) = N'' -- Middle or Initial
  , @sLastName nvarchar(40) = N'' -- Last Name
  , @sSuffixName nvarchar(20) = N'' -- Suffix name, like Jr or MD
)   RETURNS nvarchar(128)
    WITH SCHEMABINDING -- Or comment why not
```

```
/*
*  Creates a concatented name in the form
*  @sLastname, @sFirstName @sMiddleName @SuffixName
*  in the process it is careful not to add double spaces.
*  Prefix names such as Mr. are not common in this type of
*  name and are not supported in this function.
*
* Example:
select dbo.udf_NameFullWithComma (au_Fname, null, au_lname, null)
        from pubs..authors
* Test:
print 'Test 1 JJJS Jr ' + case when N'Jingleheimer-Schmitt, John J. Jr.'
                     = dbo.udf_NameFullWithComma ('John', 'Jacob',
                                   'Jingleheimer-Schmitt', 'Jr.')
                      THEN 'Worked' ELSE 'ERROR' END
*********************************************************************/
AS BEGIN

    DECLARE @sTemp nvarchar(128) -- Working copy of the name

    SET @sTemp = ltrim(rtrim(@sLastName))
    IF LEN(@sTemp) > 0
        SET @sTemp = @sTemp + N','
    IF LEN(ltrim(rtrim(@sFirstName))) > 0
        SET @sTemp = @sTemp + N' ' + ltrim(rtrim(@sFirstName))

    IF LEN(ltrim(rtrim(@sMiddleName))) > 0
        SET @sTemp = @sTemp
                     + N' '
                     + UPPER(left(ltrim(@sMiddleName), 1))
                     + N'.'

    IF LEN(ltrim(rtrim(@sSuffixName))) > 0
        SET @sTemp = @sTemp + N' ' + ltrim(rtrim(@sSuffixName))

    RETURN @sTemp
END
GO
```

Separator First Formatting

You may have already noticed that the formatting of the SQL statements used in this book is slightly unusual. Over the last two years, I've come to use a system that I call "Separator First Formatting," or SFF. I've seen a few other programmers use it, so I'm not the only one.

The principal practice in SFF is to put separators, such as commas and "and" and "or" operators, at the start of a new line. We'll go into the details in a second.

There are several reasons for using the SFF system:

- **Documentation** — SFF doesn't add documentation; it's intended to promote it by making it easier to include documentation on each line to explain the code.

- **Typeability** — Ease of adding and removing lines in a series.
- **Visibility** — Some of the separators, such as join operators and “and” logical operators, are extremely important and get visual prominence by starting the line.
- **Flexibility** — By putting separators at the beginning of the line, it becomes easy to comment it out by adding a double dash at the beginning of the line. (Query Analyzer has a hot key, Ctrl+Shift+C, that inserts the double dash.)

When formatting with separators first, almost all separators start their own line. That leads to a lot of lines, but most importantly, when combined with T-SQL’s double-dash comment, it makes it easier to put an explanatory comment on each, and sometimes every, line. Here’s an example:

```
-- SELECT with Separator First Formatting
SELECT a.au_id
    , [dbo].[udf_Name_FullWithComma](au_fname, null
                              , au_lname, null) as Name -- so it's sortable
    , au_fname, au_lname -- sent so client grid can sort
    , t.title
    , ta.royaltyper
    FROM pubs..authors a with (nolock)
        RIGHT OUTER JOIN pubs..titleauthor ta WITH (NOLOCK)
            on a.au_id = ta.au_id
        INNER JOIN pubs..titles t WITH (NOLOCK)
            on ta.title_id = t.title_id
    WHERE t.type = 'trad_cook'
      and ta.royaltyper > 50 -- 50 cents. authors aren't paid well.
    ORDER BY Name
            , t.title -- multiple titles per author.
GO
```

For starters, each subclause (FROM, WHERE, ORDER BY) of the SELECT statement starts a new line indented one tab stop from the start of the SELECT. The first entry in the list goes on the line with the subclause. That’s a compromise to keep the code slightly more compact.

In most circumstances, every entry in a list after the first goes on its own line. There will be exceptions. For one, the arguments to a function call rarely belong on their own line. Therefore, the lines:

```
    , dbo.udf_NameFullWithComma(au_fname, null
                              , au_lname, null) as Name -- so it's sortable.
```

are broken only when it was necessary to do so for line wrapping in this book. Sometimes space considerations are more important and several lines are combined. For example, this line has two fields on it because they’re covered by the same comment:

```
    , au_fname, au_lname -- sent so client grid can sort on these columns.
```

My overriding decision criteria for layout is to make the code more readable. It's just too bad that I don't get paid by the line of code.

I try to put each table in the FROM clause on its own line with any WITH clause. WITH clauses are hints instructing SQL Server how to perform the query. This line pulls in information from the pubs.titleauthor table:

```
        RIGHT OUTER JOIN pubs..titleauthor ta WITH (NOLOCK)
```

Notice that I almost always use a table alias. I also use column aliases for every expression but avoid them when the column is not an expression.

Throughout this book I've tried to put SQL keywords in uppercase. I've done that so that they are visually distinct. When writing SQL for any purpose except publication, I type in all lowercase (except variable names that have uppercase letters embedded). The coloring that Query Analyzer uses is sufficient to differentiate the parts of SQL. Besides, typing all those uppercase characters is harder on the fingers.

You may discover almost as many formatting conventions as there are programmers. SFF works for me because it makes the SQL more readable and easier to change. For example, to add another column to the end of the select list, all that is necessary is to put in the new line. There's no need to change the line before the new one to add a comma after the expression. The same works in reverse. By putting the separators at the start of a line, it's only necessary to put a double dash at the start of a line to eliminate it. There's no need to go to the previous line and adjust the commas. For example, to eliminate the second conditional expression from the WHERE clause, just add a double dash, as in:

```
    WHERE t.type = 'trad_cook'
      -- and ta.royaltyper > 50 -- 50 cents. authors aren't paid well.
```

The second set of double dashes that delimited the original comment is ignored.

In a function creation script, SFF comes into play in the parameter list, as you can see from this function declaration:

```
CREATE FUNCTION dbo.udf_Name_FullWithComma (

    @sFirstName nvarchar(20) = N'' -- First Name
  , @sMiddleName nvarchar(20) = N'' -- Middle or Initial
  , @sLastName nvarchar(40) = N'' -- Last Name
  , @sSuffixName nvarchar(20) = N'' -- Suffix name, like Jr or MD
)   RETURNS nvarchar(128)
    WITH SCHEMABINDING -- Or comment why not
/*
* The function comment block goes here
***************************************************************/
AS BEGIN
```

To make the CREATE FUNCTION script easy to maintain:

- Put the opening parenthesis on the line with the function name.
- Skip a line.
- Put each parameter on its own line.
- Use default values when possible.
- Comment each parameter.
- Put the right parenthesis that closes the parameter list on a line with the RETURNS clause.
- Add the WITH SCHEMABINDING line. It has the WITH SCHEMABINDING line or a comment that says why the function is not schemabound. If you add WITH ENCRYPTION, it also goes here.
- Finally, the AS BEGIN goes on its own line.

Not only do these practices make formatting a little easier, they document the parameters. One of the reasons to get every parameter on its own line is to leave room for the comment describing how the parameter is used. Unless the name "says it all," each parameter deserves a comment describing how to use it.

Header Comments

The first place to find information about the function is in the header. It's often the only place that any information is available. While it would be useful to have complete program documentation for all functions, I find that that's rarely in the project plan. The benefits to good documentation are just too far in the future for many project managers (myself included) to decide that they're worthwhile. That's why I devote some attention to the header.

The place to start a function is with a template. A template is a text file that can be used as the starting point for a SQL script. It has the extension .TQL. SQL Server ships with templates for Query Analyzer that can be used to get your function creation process started. I've enhanced these templates by adding the comment header and more formatting to create my own templates that I use in place of the ones from SQL Server. Listing 6.2 shows the function template for starting a function that returns a scalar value. You'll find it in the companion materials in the Templates directory (\Templates\Create Function\Create Scalar Function.tql) along with two other templates for creating UDFs that return tables. Using templates was discussed in Chapter 3 in the "Query Analyzer" section.

Listing 6.2: Header template file (Create Scalar Function.tql)

```
SET QUOTED_IDENTIFIER ON
GO
SET ANSI_NULLS ON
GO

CREATE FUNCTION dbo.<scalar_function_name, sysname, udf_> (

    <parm1, sysname, @p1> <parm1_data_type, , int> -- <parm1_description, ,>
  , <parm2, sysname, @p2> <parm2_data_type, , int> -- <parm2_description, ,>
  , <parm3, sysname, @p3> <parm3_data_type, , int> -- <parm3_description, ,>
)   RETURNS <returns_data_type, ,int> -- <returns_description, ,>
    WITH SCHEMABINDING -- Or comment about why not
/*
* description goes here
*
* Equivalent Template:
* Related Functions:
* Attribution: Based on xxx by yyy found in zzzzzzzzzzzz
* Maintenance Notes:
* Example:
select dbo.<scalar_function_name, sysname, udf_>(<parm1_test_value,,1>,
                        <parm2_test_value,,2>, <parm3_test_value,,3>)
* Test:
PRINT 'Test 1    ' + CASE WHEN x=dbo.<scalar_function_name, sysname, udf_>
(<parm1_test_value,,1>, <parm2_test_value,,2>, <parm3_test_value,,3>)
                     THEN 'Worked' ELSE 'ERROR' END
* Test Script: TEST_<scalar_function_name, sysname, udf_>
* History:
* When          Who     Description
* ------------- ------- -----------------------------------------
* <date created,smalldatetime,YYYY-MM-DD>          <your initials,char(8),XXX>
                              Initial Coding
* © Copyright 2003 Andrew Novick http://www.NovickSoftware.com
*****************************************************************/
AS BEGIN

    DECLARE @Result <function_data_type, ,int>

    SELECT @Result = fill_in_here

    RETURN @Result
END
GO

GRANT EXEC, REFERENCES ON [dbo].[<scalar_function_name, sysname, udf_>]
       TO [PUBLIC]
GO
```

The following describes each section of the header:

* description

The function is described here. A simple description of what the function does will suffice. If the function has any unusual behavior, it should be mentioned. For example, the types of errors in the input that cause the function to return `NULL` might be important.

Some UDFs are simple enough that they can be replaced by an expression. Doing so usually makes the SQL code more complex, but it will always execute faster. This section gives the template that can be used to replace an invocation of the function. For an example, see `udf_DT_2Julian` in the TSQLUDFS database. The function user might use the replacement in a performance-sensitive situation.

* Related Functions

Here we discuss any functions that are frequently used together with this function and, most importantly, why the other function is related. It's a heads-up to the user of the function and the maintenance programmer.

* Attribution

This section tells something about how the function was created. If it was copied from the net or if it was based on someone else's idea, that would be stated here. I generally only consider this section when I'm writing for publication. Of course, I do that a lot these days. Between this book and the UDF of the Week Newsletter, I've written several hundred UDFs in the past year.

* Maintenance Notes

These are notes to any programmer who is going to maintain the function. It might be something about where to look to get the algorithm for the function or which other functions use the same algorithm and should be changed in synch with this one.

* Example

This gives a simple example of how the function might be used. The line with "Example" starts with an asterisk, but the lines of the example that follows do not. That's so the example can be selected and executed within Query Analyzer without changing any of the text or having to remove the asterisk. Here's a sample section:

```
* Example:
SELECT dbo.udf_Name_FullWithComma ('John', 'Jacob'
                              , 'Jingleheimer-Schmitt', default)
```

To execute the sample, select the line or lines with the SELECT statement and use the F5 key or green execution arrow to run the query. In the interest of space, the example section is typically left on a single line. SFF formatting used elsewhere is skipped. Given the simple nature of the example, this rarely presents a problem. Of course, no harm would come if you chose to reformat the examples.

It may be more difficult to provide a meaningful example for inline and multistatement UDFs than it is for scalar UDFs. The two types that return tables usually depend on the state of the database, while scalars don't.

* Test

A few simple tests go here. They are not intended to be a comprehensive test that proves that the function works—just some simple tests that can verify that the function isn't screwed up after a simple change has been made.

```
PRINT 'Test 1 JJJS Jr ' + case when 'Jingleheimer-Schmitt, John J. MD'
                       = dbo.udf_NameFullWithComma ('John', 'Jacob',
                                  'Jingleheimer-Schmitt', 'Jr.')
                        THEN 'Worked' ELSE 'ERROR' END
```

The test should check its own result. It shouldn't just print the result and leave it to the programmer to do the checking. That would put an additional burden on the programmer executing the test, wasting his or her time. After all, whoever wrote the test knows the answer that the function should produce. The results of executing the test are:

```
Test 1 JJJS    Worked
```

When there is a series of tests, there will be a series of results. Hopefully they'll all say "Worked," so it's easy for the maintenance programmer to know that at least at a simple level, any change he or she made hasn't damaged the function.

Although I'd like to have tests that are easy to run and verify for all UDFs, it's much easier to code them for scalar UDFs than for inline or multistatement UDFs. Of course, that's because it's pretty easy to check the single scalar return value and much more complex to validate a recordset that the other function types return.

* Test Script

This gives the location of a comprehensive test of the function. The test might be embedded in a stored procedure or a script file. Since the comprehensive tests are not published along with this book, this section is not included in any of the functions published here. Chapter 11 is all about testing and what to put into the test.

* History

As the function is modified, each programmer should leave a short description of who made the change, when the change was made, and what was changed. In the interest of saving space in the function headers, the history sections are left out of the functions in this book.

* Copyright

If a copyright notice is needed, this is where it goes. Since you bought this book, you have the right to use any of the functions published in it. You can put them in a database and include them in software. The only right that is reserved is the right of publication. You may not publish the functions in an article without permission, which can be obtained by writing to me.

Notice the copyright symbol (©) on the copyright line. Although it's not an ASCII symbol, it shows up in the fonts that are most likely to be used for viewing script text.

That's what I put in a header. There are two additional types of information that I've seen in function headers that I omit.

What's Not in the Header

Everyone has his or her own convention. Mine is driven by what I think will provide cost-effective communication between the function author and subsequent reader. The less there is to write and maintain, the better. That's why I don't put the following two sections into the function header comment.

* Parameters

It's a common practice in many programming languages for programmers to maintain a parameters section in the comment header of each function. In the case of a T-SQL function, the parameters are in the declaration of the function at the top of the file with their data type. It isn't necessary to repeat them in the comment header. Doing so would require that the comment header and the function header be maintained synchronously. Any time a programmer has to keep an item of documentation synchronized with a line of code, you're asking for trouble. The temptation to code first and document later is great, and the documentation is often forgotten. I find that it's better to use a double-dash comment right after the data type of the function and leave the parameters out of the comment header.

* Algorithm and Formulas

The algorithm or the formula that is used to create the function could be in the function header. Instead, I prefer to put it in the body of the function. The algorithm description is usually not needed by the function user. In cases where it is helpful to the user, include the algorithm in the description.

Naming Conventions

There are many naming conventions. Throughout this book, you'll see a pretty consistent convention for naming functions, parameters, local variables, tables, and views that make up the database. My convention is a little bit different, but there's a method behind the madness, and I'll explain why here. First up are names for UDFs.

Naming User-Defined Functions

When you pick a name for a user-defined function, what are you trying to do? When I name a function, I want three things to happen. I want the programmer who sees the function to know:

- That it is a user-defined function
- Something about what the function does
- How to use the return value

Very importantly, I also want any programmer working on a project with me to be able to find the function after it's written. Having two programmers write the same function or doing without the benefits of an already written function is a productivity loss. If a way can be found to eliminate that loss, everyone is happier: management, the programmer who found the function, and me.

However, I don't want to write programming manuals. Not only don't I want to spend my time writing program documentation manuals, but my clients don't want to pay me to do it. Everything needed for finding the function and deciding if it's applicable to the situation needs to be in the function. That's why there is so much documentation in the function headers in this book. There isn't going to be any external documentation unless I can figure out how to write a program that creates it.

The name is the part of the function that lets it be found. Some of my ideas are influenced by long-term exposure to Intellisense in Visual Studio. If you're not familiar with it, it's the technology that Microsoft has built into its Visual Studio integrated development environment (IDE) that helps complete the names of variables by displaying a list of the known variables that are in scope and that start with the characters you just typed. Sadly, Intellisense isn't part of SQL Server 2000. I strongly suspect that when SQL Server is integrated with .NET, we'll see it.

Figure 6.1 illustrates how Intellisense shows the list of functions available while editing a small Visual Basic 6 program. While editing, I typed three characters, "Tex," and then pressed Ctrl+Space. That brings up a list of all the names in scope that begin with "Tex." These include all of my library functions in the Text group and the TextBox group. I can then scroll up or down to find the function that I'm interested in.

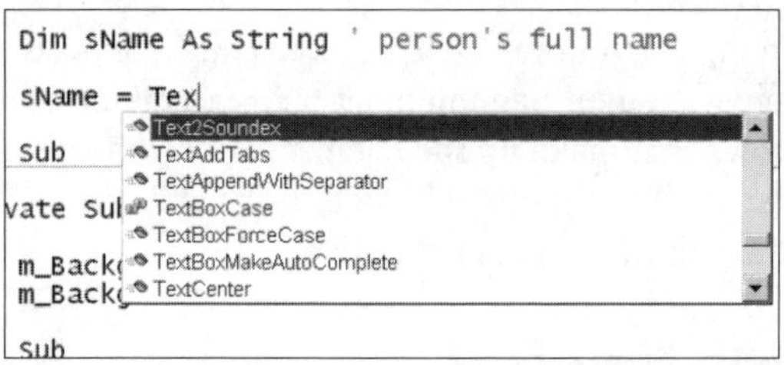

Figure 6.1: Intellisense at work in a Visual Basic program

In the English language, naming functions with the group name followed by the action sounds somewhat unnatural. It's more natural to put the verb first and a name function `GetSoundex` than `Text2Soundex`, as shown in Figure 6.1. I have to ask, "How is starting 500 function names with Get ever going to help anyone find the function or even understand what it does no matter how natural it sounds?" I've never heard a satisfactory answer to that question, and so I've reversed the order of most names to maximize the ease of finding the function that the programmer is looking for.

Here is how I break down function names:

udf_<group><object><action><domain>

Obviously, the `udf_` prefix tells anyone who sees such a reference that they're looking at a user-defined function. That's only one of the possible prefixes that could be used for UDFs. For system UDFs, Microsoft uses `fn_`. Chapter 19 shows you how to create your own system UDFs. Unless that's what you're doing, don't use the `fn_` prefix.

I'm not totally convinced that the expenditure of four characters in every name is worth the extra typing involved, but for now, that's my convention. You might want to use something shorter or possibly no prefix. Is any prefix needed to make it obvious that a UDF is in use? On a related note, see the sidebar "Owner Name Saves a Bit of CPU" about using the owner name in object references for a small performance gain.

<group> is used to organize functions as well as other SQL objects. Table 6.1 is a list of the groups used in this book. Most of these are pretty generic. As I develop an application, I add groups specific to that application.

Table 6.1: Groups used to organize SQL objects

Group	Description
Currency	Monetary currency conversion
DT	Date and time calculation and manipulation
Example	Examples of techniques. The functions are written for this book and are useful only as illustrations.
BitS	For working with strings that represent the bits of a longer data type
Func	UDF-related functions
Instance	Related to the SQL Server instance
Lst	Functions for working with lists
Name	Works with people's names
Num	Numeric functions
Object	Functions for working with SQL objects
Proc	Stored procedure-related functions
Session	Functions related to the current SQL Server session
SQL	Functions for working with SQL Server information
SYS	Operating system-related functions
Tbl	SQL table-related functions
Test	Functions used to test a particular technique
Trc	For working with SQL Server traces
Trig	Trigonometric functions
Txt	Text manipulation
TxtN	Text manipulation for Unicode strings
Unit	Units of measure conversion

<object> and **<action>** suggest that, when possible, functions should specify the object that is going to be operated on and the action that is performed on the object. This is usually a noun-verb combination.

<domain> is used to tell the user about the returned value. Later in this chapter, the methodology of naming columns with a "domain" is described.

Each domain is usually associated with a user-defined type. They can be used with functions when they add value.

For example, there is a function named `udf_Name_SuffixCheckBIT` that is shown in Listing 6.4. It's used when cleaning data consisting of names to verify that a suffix name is among the list of known suffixes. The name `udf_Name_SuffixCheckBIT` is broken down in Table 6.2.

Table 6.2: Breakdown of a sample function name

Characters	Part of the Name
udf_	Standard prefix
Name	Group of functions. In this case, it is functions for manipulating names.
Suffix	Object that's being worked on. In this case, it is a suffix name like Jr. or Sr. or III.
Check	Action that's being taken on the object
BIT	The domain BIT says that it returns the SQL Server data type BIT, which is used for a true/false meaning. BOOL is an alternative name that's less SQL Server specific.

Listing 6.4: `udf_Name_SuffixCheckBIT`

```
CREATE  FUNCTION dbo.udf_Name_SuffixCheckBIT (

    @sSuffixName nvarchar(255) -- possible suffix name
)   RETURNS BIT -- 1 when @sSuffixName is a common suffix name
/*
* Returns 1 when the name is one of the common suffix names. Such
* as Jr., Sr., II, III, IV, MD, etc. Trailing periods are ignored.
*
* Example:
-- Look for Suffix Names not on the standard list.
select FirstName, Lastname, SuffixName from ExampleNames
        WHERE 0=dbo.udf_Name_SuffixCheckBIT (SuffixName)
* Test:
PRINT 'Test 1 BAD ' + case when 0 =
                    dbo.udf_Name_SuffixCheckBIT ('BAD')
                                 THEN 'Worked' ELSE 'ERROR' END
print 'Test 2 Jr.    ' + case when 1 =
                    dbo.udf_Name_SuffixCheckBIT ('jr.')
                                 THEN 'Worked' ELSE 'ERROR' END
****************************************************************/
AS BEGIN

DECLARE @sTemp nvarchar(255) -- Working copy of the suffix name
                             -- stripped of punctuation
      , @bRC BIT             -- our working return code

    -- Null is OK
    IF @sSuffixName is NULL RETURN 1

    -- Clean up the string by
        -- trimming
        -- uppercasing, in case of a case-sensitive SQL Server
```

```
    SET @Stemp = UPPER(LTRIM(RTRIM(@sSuffixName)))
    IF RIGHT (@sTemp, 1) = '.'
        SET @sTemp = LEFT(@sTemp, LEN(@sTemp) - 1)

    SET @bRC = CASE WHEN @sTemp in ('JR', 'SR', 'II', 'III', 'IV'
                                  , '2ND', '3RD', '4TH', 'MD'
                                  , 'ESQ', 'ESQRS'
                                  , 'PHD', 'PH.D'
                                  , 'DDS' -- dentist
                                  , 'DVM' -- Veterinarian
                                    )
                    THEN 1
                    ELSE 0
                    END

    RETURN @bRC

END
GO
```

Owner Name Saves a Bit of CPU

Every time SQL Server resolves an object name, it must search its cache. When the user who is logged in is not the **dbo**, some extra cache misses, and therefore extra searches are needed to find the object. Furthermore, specifying the owner name in all object references appears to result in less reads, which can be even more important than cache misses. To illustrate this point, log in as the **dbo** and create two stored procedures with the script in Listing 6.3. The first stored procedure does not use an owner reference, while the second one does. The procedures have already been added to the TSQLUDFS database so you don't have to add them.

Listing 6.3: Creating stored procedures to illustrate owner references

```
create procedure usp_ExampleSelectWithoutOwner
as
    select * from cust
go

grant exec on usp_ExampleSelectWithoutOwner to public
go

create procedure dbo.usp_ExampleSelectWithOwner
as
    select * from dbo.cust
go

grant exec on usp_ExampleSelectWithOwner to public
go
```

To see what's really happening, start the SQL Profiler and add these events: SP:CacheHit, SP:CacheMiss, SP:StmtStarting, SP:StmtCompleted, and SP:ExecContextHit. Also include the ObjectID and Reads in the data columns.

Now log in as a user who is not **dbo** but is a member of the PUBLIC group. If you've created the two "Limited" user IDs, LimitedUser would fit the bill. Execute the following batch:

```
-- You should log in as a user that is not dbo before running these queries
-- These generate different cache misses.  Use SQL Profiler to watch them.
exec usp_ExampleSelectWithoutOwner

exec dbo.usp_ExampleSelectWithOwner
go
```

The difference between the two stored procedures shows up in two places. The second line of trace shows the CacheMiss. This is the miss when the stored procedure is looked up because the first EXEC statement doesn't specify **dbo** at the start of the stored procedure reference. SQL Server tries to find the procedure under the name of the logged-in user. When the second EXEC statement starts, it performs a lookup on dbo.usp_ExampleWithOwner, and there's no miss.

EventClass	TextData	Reads
SQL:StmtStarting	exec usp_ExampleSelectWithoutOwner	
SP:CacheMiss		
SP:ExecContextHit		
Audit Object Permission ...	-- usp_ExampleSelectWithoutOwner e...	
SP:Starting	exec usp_ExampleSelectWithoutOwner	
SP:StmtCompleted	-- usp_ExampleSelectWithoutOwner s...	0
SP:Completed	exec usp_ExampleSelectWithoutOwner	
SQL:StmtCompleted	exec usp_ExampleSelectWithoutOwner	21
SQL:StmtStarting	exec dbo.usp_ExampleSelectWithOwner	
SP:ExecContextHit		
Audit Object Permission ...	-- usp_ExampleSelectWithOwner exec...	
SP:Starting	exec dbo.usp_ExampleSelectWithOwner	
SP:StmtCompleted	-- usp_ExampleSelectWithOwner sele...	0
SP:Completed	exec dbo.usp_ExampleSelectWithOwner	
SQL:StmtCompleted	exec dbo.usp_ExampleSelectWithOwner	14

Figure 6.2: Profiler results when owner is not specified

The second place the difference shows up is in the total number of reads for each EXEC statement. When the owner name is not placed on the EXEC, seven extra reads are required. This appears to all come from the cache miss since the SP:StmtCompleted events for SELECT * from CUST lines don't show any reads.

Naming Columns

Column names should tell the programmers as much as possible about what is stored in the column. In many programming environments, naming convention dictates that the data type of a variable become part of the name. For example, the Hungarian notation commonly used in C++ and often in Visual Basic starts each variable with a one- to three-character prefix that denotes the type of the variable. For example, `s` or `str` indicate string and `f` indicates float.

However, the data type isn't something that should go into a column name. Microsoft recommends against using Hungarian notation when naming columns, and I agree (see http://www.microsoft.com/technet/treeview/default.asp?url=/technet/prodtechnol/sql/plan/inside6.asp). When the data type of a column changes, the name of the column might also have to change. That has a ripple effect on stored procedures, functions, and views. The pain involved in changing all the code in stored procedures and views when a data type changes is not worth the benefits in adding the additional description in the column name. What's more, client programs such as Windows applications and reports might also have to change.

Domain Names

However, when a column describes an entity from an application domain, I sometimes use a domain name and associated data type. For example, when working with stockbrokers, one domain is `ExchangeCD`, which stores the codes for stock exchanges. When working with roads, there are two domains that store measurements of kilometers: lengths of road segments and markers that designate a position relative to the start of the road. There is more on these domains in Chapter 12, "Converting between Unit Systems."

For `ExchangeCD`, I might create the user-defined type (UDT) `DomainExchangeCD` with this script:

```
EXEC sp_addtype N'DomainExchangeCD', N'CHAR(3)', N'not null'
```

Then I can use it wherever an `ExchangeCD` is stored, as in:

```
CREATE table ExchangeMembership
    ( BrokerID Int
    , ExchangeCD DomainExchangeCD
    )
GO
```

I'd also use it to define parameters to UDFs. But that's where we're going to run into a problem. Here's a script that attempts to create a UDF that uses the DomainExchangeCD UDT to define the data type of its parameter:

```
-- Try to create a UDF with a UDT and SCHEMABINDING
CREATE  Function dbo.udf_Exchange_TestCodeBIT (

    @ExchangeCD DomainExchangeCD -- Which exchange, NYSE, NASD, etc.
)   RETURNS BIT
    WITH SCHEMABINDING
AS BEGIN
   RETURN CASE WHEN @ExchangeCD in ('NYSE', 'DAX', 'AMEX')
               THEN 1 ELSE 0 END
END
GO
```

(Results)

```
Server: Msg 2012, Level 16, State 1, Procedure udf_Exchange_TestCodeBIT, Line 0
User-defined variables cannot be declared within a schema-bound object.
```

UDTs can't be used in a UDF that is created with SCHEMABINDING. Your choices are to either give up the UDT and put the data type in the parameter declaration or drop SCHEMABINDING. Since SCHEMABINDING might be needed by views or UDFs that call the UDF, I'm in favor of not using the UDT and keeping SCHEMABINDING.

Listing 6.5 shows udf_Exchange_MembersList, a UDF that returns a list of members of a stock exchange. I had originally written it with the parameters as a DomainExchangeCD, but when I added WITH SCHEMABINDING, I had to replace the UDT with CHAR(3). You'll find the function in the TSQLUDFS database along with the tables that it selects from.

Listing 6.5: udf_Exchange_MembersList

```
CREATE Function dbo.udf_Exchange_MembersList (

    @ExchangeCD CHAR(3) -- Which exchange, NYSE, NASD, etc.
)   RETURNS TABLE
    WITH SCHEMABINDING
/*
* Returns a TABLE with a list of all brokers who are members of
* the exchange @ExchangeCD.
*
* Example:
SELECT * from dbo.udf_Exchange_MembersList('NYSE')
****************************************************************/
AS RETURN

   SELECT B.BrokerID
        , B.FirstName
        , B.LastName
        FROM dbo.Broker b
            INNER JOIN dbo.ExchangeMembership EM
                ON B.BrokerID = EM.BrokerID
        WHERE EM.ExchangeCD = @ExchangeCD
```

Using the domain name tells the programmer something about what the column stores. It doesn't tell about the type. `DomainExchangeCD` could have been stored as a `tinyint` without changing any of the scripts above, except the one that created the type in the first place.

The reason given earlier to avoid Hungarian notation when naming columns is no longer a problem when a domain name is used. It would make no difference to the code in any stored procedure or view when the definition of a domain name was changed from, let's say, `integer` to `Numeric (18,2)`. That's not to say that changing a UDT is easy; it's not.

Naming Function Parameters and Local Variables

When naming function parameters and local variables, I basically use Hungarian notation by adding a prefix that gives the data type. It's handy when reading code that may be half a page or more from the original `DECLARE` statement. I find it an aid to understanding the code. The problems associated with adding the data type as part of a column name don't apply to function parameters and local variables. That's because they're never referenced outside of the database object that creates them.

As you've seen above, when there is a domain name available, use it. If not, I put the type in front of the variable name, as in:

```
DECLARE @mPrice Money -- our charge for the item
      , @nMyRowCount int -- local copy of @@RowCount
      , @sMessage varchar(256) -- Error msg created locally
```

Yes, that's a little inconsistent. If you want to put the type at the end, I wouldn't object. The goal is to put maximum explanatory power in the variable or parameter name.

Summary

Almost any naming convention is better than no convention. Through the conventions for naming, documenting, and formatting in this chapter, I've tried to show:

- A way to format SQL with separators at the start of a line for readability and easier manipulation of the text.
- A header format for functions that provides the documentation needed by the users of the function and those charged with maintaining it in the future.

- A convention for naming functions and other objects that attempts to maximize the ease in finding the correct function sometime after it's written.

Locating the function is simplified by starting it with a combination of the `udf_` prefix and a group name that splits all the functions into more memorable categories. A noun-verb pair that tells the prospective caller what object is manipulated and what type of manipulation occurs follows the group.

The objective is always to communicate fully to the users of the function and to the person responsible for maintaining the function in the future. What else is a name for?

Now that you've read about various topics regarding creating UDFs, it's time to take a more detailed look at inline and multistatement types. They are subject to most of the same rules as scalars, but each type has its own peculiarities. Chapter 7 covers inline UDFs, and Chapter 8 covers multistatement UDFs.

7

Inline UDFs

Inline UDFs are a form of SQL view that accepts parameters. The parameters are usually used in the WHERE clause to restrict the rows returned, but they can also be used in other parts of the UDF's SELECT statement. Inline UDFs can be convenient, but they don't have all the features available to views.

Like views, inline UDFs can be updatable and can have INSERT, UPDATE, and DELETE permissions granted to them. Unlike views, there is no WITH CHECK OPTION clause to prevent insertion of rows that, given the parameters, would not be returned by the UDF. This limits the usefulness of updatable views in many situations.

Although it's not part of standard SQL, views and inline UDFs can be sorted with an ORDER BY clause if there is a TOP clause in the SELECT statement. This technique can add value to inline UDFs at the cost of a potential for duplicate sort operations.

One use of inline UDFs that I've found particularly productive is to create a pair of inline UDFs for paging web applications that display a screen's worth of data from a larger set of rows. A section of this chapter shows how to use this technique and the trade-offs that seem to work best.

Permissions are required both for creating and for using inline UDFs. We can't do anything without them, so they're the first subjects for this chapter.

Managing Permissions on Inline UDFs

Since the basics of permissions were covered in Chapters 1 and 2, this section explores only the few differences that exist between permissions for scalar UDFs and those for inline UDFs. The most important differences arise because inline UDFs return a table instead of a scalar value.

Permissions to Create, Alter, and Drop Inline UDFs

The statement permissions CREATE FUNCTION, ALTER FUNCTION, and DROP FUNCTION are the same permissions used for creating both scalar and multistatement UDFs. You can't split permissions between types of UDFs (not that I've ever found a reason to try to split them). Usually, the programmers who write UDFs are members of the database role db_ddladmin. That role has the necessary permissions to manage UDFs.

Permission to Use Inline UDFs

There are five permissions available for using inline UDFs: SELECT, INSERT, UPDATE, DELETE, and REFERENCES. You've seen the SELECT permission already. It's required to retrieve data from the UDF. INSERT, UPDATE, and DELETE permissions let you make an inline UDF updatable. This is similar to making a view updatable and places similar requirements on the SELECT statement. Those requirements for updatable inline UDFs are examined thoroughly in a later section of this chapter.

I haven't found a use for the REFERENCES permission on an inline UDF. If you know of one, please drop me an e-mail at anovick@NovickSoftware.com. TIA.

As with stored procedures, views, and the other types of UDFs, the owner of an inline UDF must have permission on the underlying tables, views, and functions referenced by the UDF. All users of the UDF only need permission on the UDF itself. Views and stored procedures are often used this way to convey permission to restricted objects. The inline UDF is now an alternate choice for conveying permissions.

Creating Inline UDFs

The essential fact of inline UDFs is that they are a type of view, one that allows for parameters that can be used in the single SELECT statement that makes up the body of the inline UDF. Chapter 1 covered the essentials of how to create an inline UDF, but there are a few things to add to that discussion.

Chapter 6 discussed naming conventions for UDFs, and the policies discussed there apply to inline UDFs as well as scalars. One convention that I've been following for naming both inline and multistatement UDFs is to end the name with the characters "TAB." It's supposed to indicate that the function returns a table and thus suggest where in a SQL statement the UDF can be used. I do make exceptions to this convention when adding the extra characters either makes a name too long or when the name already tells the programmer that this UDF returns a table.

We've already seen several inline UDFs in previous chapters. Most of them use their parameters in the WHERE clause to restrict the rows returned by the function. The parameters can also be used in:

- The select list as part of an expression that's returned by the UDF
- The ON clause of a JOIN to affect the join criteria
- The ORDER BY clause

Inline UDFs can have inline SELECT statements, GROUP BY, HAVING, and any other clause that could go into a SELECT with the exception of COMPUTE, COMPUTE BY, FOR XML, FOR BROWSE, OPTION, and INTO. The SELECT statement is also subject to the restrictions discussed in Chapter 4. For example, a UDF's SELECT can't reference temporary tables or TABLE variables.

As with all UDFs, there are two options that may be used in a WITH clause when the UDF is created: SCHEMABINDING and ENCRYPTION. SCHEMABINDING ties the UDF to the objects that it references, preventing changes to those objects unless the binding is removed. ENCRYPTION secures the CREATE FUNCTION script from being viewed by casual users. However, it's not very secure. As mentioned elsewhere in this book, the formula to decrypt SQL objects, including UDFs, has been published on the web.

In the FROM clause of the SELECT, all references to tables, views, or other UDFs should use a two-part name that includes the name of the object owner. It's usually **dbo**. There are two reasons for the owner qualification:

- It's slightly more efficient because SQL Server doesn't have to check to see if there's an object of that name owned by the current user.
- It's required if you're going to use the WITH SCHEMABINDING clause.

Qualifying the name is always a good idea because it ensures that you avoid any errors caused by having multiple versions of a UDF in the database. That might result in invoking the wrong UDF at run time.

A few SQL Server features that are available for views are not available for UDFs:

- The WITH CHECK OPTION is not available. This affects updatability.
- Indexes can't be created on UDFs. They're available for views.
- INSTEAD OF triggers. UDFs don't have any triggers.
- The WITH VIEW_METADATA clause is not available.

This mixture of feature availability makes the inline UDF a possible substitute for views but not a sure thing. There are enough features that are not available when using a UDF that you might decide that a view is preferable, even if it doesn't have parameters. The code that uses the view can qualify its SELECT statement to limit the rows returned and achieve the same result achieved using the UDF. You'll have to examine the specific circumstances to choose between these two alternatives.

The ability to create inline UDFs quickly is aided by the use of a template file. The next section shows you a template that has several modifications from the one provided with SQL Server.

Template for Inline UDFs

Chapters 3 and 6 showed you the template that I use for creating scalar UDFs. Listing 7.1 has a template that can be used to create inline UDFs. You'll find this template file in the Templates directory of the download for this book. The following are some of the features that Listing 7.1's template has. The one included with SQL Server don't have these features.

- SET QUOTED_IDENTIFIER ON and SET ANSI_NULLS ON start the file to ensure that they're set in every UDF.
- **dbo** always owns the UDF. I recommend that only **dbo** own database objects.
- No DROP statement for the UDF. If the UDF already exists, change CREATE to ALTER.
- Inclusion of a comment block with a place for a description, an example, test cases, and the modification history.
- The WITH SCHEMABINDING clause is in the template. I suggest that you either use WITH SCHEMABINDING or have a comment that says why not.
- A GRANT statement for easily giving SELECT to PUBLIC.

There are two GRANT statements at the bottom of the file. The first is the one that's almost always used to give SELECT permission to PUBLIC. The second GRANT statement is in the file for use with an updatable UDF. It's commented out because it's only used on rare occasions.

The procedure for turning the template into an inline UDF is the same procedure that was shown in Chapter 3 for turning the template for a scalar UDF into a working function. There's no need to repeat it here, so we can move on to creating inline UDFs.

Listing 7.1: Template for creating inline UDFs

```
SET QUOTED_IDENTIFIER ON
SET ANSI_NULLS ON
GO

CREATE FUNCTION dbo.<inline_function_name, sysname, udf_> (

    <@parm1, sysname, @p1> <parm1_data_type, , int> -- <parm1_description, ,>
  , <@parm2, sysname, @p2> <parm2_data_type, , int> -- <parm2_description, ,>
  , <@parm3, sysname, @p3> <parm3_data_type, , int> -- <parm3_description, ,>
)   RETURNS TABLE
    WITH SCHEMABINDING -- Or relevant comment.

/*
* description goes here
*
* Related Functions:
* Attribution: Based on xxx by yyy found in zzzzzzzzzzzz
* Maintenance Notes:
* Example:
select * FROM dbo.<inline_function_name, sysname, udf_>
   (<parm1_test_value, , 1>, <parm2_test_value, , 2>, <parm3_test_value, , 3>)
* Test:
* Test Script: TEST_<inline_function_name, sysname, udf_>
* History:
* When          Who     Description
* ------------- ------- -----------------------------------------
* <date created,smalldatetime, YYYY-MM-DD>            <your initials,char(8), XXX>
Initial Coding
***************************************************************/
AS RETURN

SELECT
    FROM
    WHERE
    GROUP BY
    HAVING
    ORDER BY

GO

GRANT SELECT ON [dbo].[<inline_function_name, sysname, udf_>]
        TO [PUBLIC]
-- GRANT INSERT, UPDATE, DELETE ON
--          [dbo].[<inline_function_name, sysname, udf_>]  TO [PUBLIC]
GO
```

Creating a Sample Inline UDF

Listing 7.2 shows a sample inline UDF, `udf_Category_ProductCountTAB`. To make our lives easier, it's already been created in the TSQLUDFS database. However, because it accesses data in a database different from the one in which it was created, it can't be created using `WITH SCHEMABINDING`.

Listing 7.2: udf_Category_ProductCountTAB

```
CREATE FUNCTION udf_Category_ProductCountTAB (

    @MinProducts int = NULL -- Min products in the count
                            -- Null for all
) RETURNS TABLE
  -- SCHEMABINDING not allowed across databases.
/*
* Categories and their count of products.
* Example:
SELECT * from dbo.udf_Category_ProductCountTAB(NULL) -- All prod
SELECT * from dbo.udf_Category_ProductCountTAB(9)-- >=9 products
***********************************************************/
AS RETURN

SELECT c.CategoryID, c.CategoryName, COUNT(ProductID) as NumProducts
    FROM Northwind.dbo.Categories c
        LEFT OUTER JOIN Northwind.dbo.Products p
           on c.CategoryID = P.CategoryID
    GROUP BY c.CategoryID, c.CategoryName
    HAVING (@MinProducts IS NULL
            or COUNT(ProductID) >= @MinProducts)
GO
GRANT SELECT ON dbo.udf_Category_ProductCountTAB to PUBLIC
GO
```

There isn't much new to say about creating inline UDFs. It's a single SELECT statement that uses its parameters to drive the query. You'll see more examples throughout the chapter.

Once the inline UDF has been created, it's time to use it. Using inline UDFs is very much like using a regular view except with parameters. The syntax is what you'd expect: function-like.

Retrieving Data with Inline UDFs

Inline UDFs are used in the FROM clause like all other database objects that return rowsets. Syntactically, they go in the same place as tables, views, OPENROWSET, OPENXML, and multistatement UDFs. You've seen this already in Chapter 1.

Like other database objects that return rowsets, inline UDFs can have an alias. In fact, if you want to refer to the columns returned by the UDF, it must have an alias! There's no other way to distinguish the UDF's columns from other similarly named columns coming out of the FROM clause. Repeating the UDF's name is not an option.

Unlike scalar UDFs, inline and multistatement UDFs don't have to be qualified with the name of the owner when they are used. However, it is a good practice to qualify the owner name for two reasons previously mentioned: a small performance gain, and it's required when using WITH SCHEMABINDING.

As with all other objects, I suggest that **dbo** be the only user to own inline UDFs.

The previous section created the function `udf_Category_ProductCountTAB` in Listing 7.2. We can use it to retrieve categories that have nine or more products, as shown in this query:

```
-- Get products by category
SELECT *
    FROM dbo.udf_Category_ProductCountTAB(9)
    ORDER BY NumProducts asc
GO
```

(Results)

```
CategoryID  CategoryName    NumProducts
----------- --------------- -----------
          4 Dairy Products           10
          8 Seafood                  12
          1 Beverages                12
          2 Condiments               12
          3 Confections              13
```

In a report of categories, we might reuse this UDF to choose the product categories of interest. We'd join its resultset with the `Categories` table in order to pick up the description and any other columns of interest. Take a look at this example query:

```
-- Combine rowsets.
SELECT cp.CategoryName, c.[Description], NumProducts
    FROM dbo.udf_Category_ProductCountTAB (default) cp
       inner join  Northwind.dbo.Categories c
           ON c.CategoryID = cp.CategoryID
    ORDER BY cp.CategoryName
GO
```

(Results - Description truncated)

```
CategoryName    Description                                 NumProducts
--------------- ------------------------------------------- -----------
Beverages       Soft drinks, coffees, teas, beers, and ...           12
Condiments      Sweet and savory sauces, relishes, spre...           12
Confections     Desserts, candies, and sweet breads                  13
Dairy Products  Cheeses                                              10
Grains/Cereals  Breads, crackers, pasta, and cereal                   7
Meat/Poultry    Prepared meats                                        6
Produce         Dried fruit and bean curd                             5
Seafood         Seaweed and fish                                     12
```

Notice that without the alias, `cp`, the reference to the `CategoryName` column in the select list would be ambiguous. That points out the need to use aliases for all inline and multistatement UDF invocations.

Before anyone gets up in arms, I'm aware that joining `udf_Category_ProductCountTAB` with the `Categories` table is not the optimal way of getting the result that we desire. This query forces SQL Server to read the `Categories` table twice: a table scan to produce the resultset for `udf_Category_ProductCountTAB` and a seek using the clustered index on each of the categories in the resultset to find the matching `CategoryID` so that the `Description` column can be returned. A single query that included the description field would be better, either as the body of the UDF or to replace the query. When we realize this, we're faced with a choice: Either accept the suboptimal query or rewrite it.

To get the desired ordering, the previous two queries had `ORDER BY` clauses. The `SELECT` in the inline UDF can also have an `ORDER BY` clause but only if it has a `TOP` clause. By using both clauses, the results of the UDF are sorted. This has advantages and disadvantages, which are the subject of the next section.

Sorting Data in Inline UDFs

Most of the example inline UDFs that appear in this book begin with the clause `TOP 100 PERCENT WITH TIES` right after the `SELECT`. When the `TOP` clause is used in either an inline UDF or a view, SQL Server also requires/allows the use of an `ORDER BY` clause to sort the result.

`ORDER BY` clauses don't normally go into views. Traditionally, sorting the results of a view is done by using an `ORDER BY` clause in the `SELECT` statement that uses the view, not in the `CREATE VIEW` statement. That's the way it should be. Deferring the ordering process allows the SQL Server database engine to optimize its plan in light of the other parts of the query.

What I've found as I've created inline UDFs is that adding the `ORDER BY` clause to the UDF provides additional value to the developer that uses the UDF. Let's face it: The point in time when you, the UDF author, know most about the UDF is when you're creating it. This is the time when you're in the best position to determine the most useful order for the results. So why not?

Performance is the reason not to sort in the UDF definition. Only one order may be chosen for sorting when defining the inline UDF, but various uses of the function may require other orderings. There's no limitation on reordering the results of an inline UDF in the `SELECT` that calls it, even if the UDF's `SELECT` has an `ORDER BY` clause. But if the UDF and the calling `SELECT` both have `ORDER BY` clauses, the rows are sorted twice. That's a waste of effort. For small resultsets, the additional overhead won't be significant because the sorting happens in memory. If the amount of data is large enough so that the sort has to use disk resources, the double sorting can be a large percentage of the query execution time.

Once again, we're faced with a three-way trade-off between performance, functionality, and ease of coding. Like the other times that this trade-off was mentioned, you're going to have to decide. Do you want a UDF that makes the programming job easier, or are you more concerned with performance?

There are no hard and fast rules about when to choose performance, but the factors that I take into account are the number of rows that are likely to be returned by the UDF and the frequency of use. If the number of likely rows goes over one thousand or the frequency of invocation goes over once per minute, I think about it seriously and may remove the ORDER BY clause from the UDF. When in doubt, leave it out. The caller can always sort the function's resultset, and the SQL Server optimizer can do a better job of creating an optimal plan.

Updatable Inline UDFs

Inline UDFs can be updatable. When they are, you may perform inserts, updates, and deletes from them. This feature of UDFs works similarly to the updatability of views. There are a few rules to observe when writing an inline UDF that is updatable:

- Database objects must be referenced with two-part names.
- No TOP clause is allowed in the SELECT statement. This implies no ORDER BY clause.
- Other restrictions on the SELECT statement that would apply to an updatable view apply to an updatable UDF. For example, no DISTINCT clause, aggregate functions, GROUP BY, HAVING, or derived columns are allowed.

Unlike updatable views, there is no WITH CHECK OPTION clause. In a view, this clause restricts activity on the view to rows in the base table that are returned by the view. In other words, when WITH CHECK OPTION is used on a view, if a SELECT on a view wouldn't return the row, then the row can't be inserted into the view. As you'll see in the examples that follow, the WHERE clause on the SELECT statement in the UDF doesn't limit INSERT statements at all!

The story is different for UPDATE and DELETE statements. UPDATE and DELETE statements modify the base table only if the rows modified are in the resultset of the UDF. This is best shown with a short series of batches that attempt to insert, update, and delete an inline UDF and a similar view.

For the demonstration let's use the BBTeams table as the basis for our UDF. Our baseball teams are divided into two leagues: the National

League (NL) and American League (AL). Figure 7.1 shows the schema of the BBTeams table in a SQL Server diagram.

BBTeams

Column Name	Data Type	Length	Allow Nulls
ID	int	4	
Name	varchar	12	
League	char	2	
Manager	varchar	12	✓
Players	varchar	255	✓

Figure 7.1: Diagram of the BBTeams table

Listing 7.3 has udf_BBTeams_LeagueTAB that lists the teams in a league. Note the GRANT statement that gives SELECT, INSERT, UPDATE, and DELETE permissions to PUBLIC.

Listing 7.3: udf_BBTeams_LeagueTAB, an updatable inline UDF

```
CREATE FUNCTION dbo.udf_BBTeams_LeagueTAB (

    @LeagueCD char(2) -- Code for the league AL or NL
)   RETURNS TABLE
    WITH SCHEMABINDING
/*
* Returns the ID, Name, and Manager of all teams in a league
*
* Example:
select * FROM dbo.udf_BBTeams_LeagueTAB('NL')
*****************************************************************/
AS RETURN

SELECT [ID], [Name], League, Manager
    FROM dbo.BBTeams
    WHERE League = @LeagueCD
GO

GRANT SELECT, INSERT, UPDATE, DELETE
        ON dbo.udf_BBTeams_LeagueTAB    TO [PUBLIC]
GO
```

Listing 7.4 shows a view on the teams in the American League, BBTeams_AL. It's very similar to udf_BBTeams_LeagueTAB, but the WHERE clause forces it to return only teams in the American League. In addition, BBTeams_AL has the WITH CHECK OPTION clause so that teams in the National League can't be inserted.

Listing 7.4: BBTeams_AL, an updatable view on the American League

```
CREATE VIEW BBTeams_AL AS

SELECT ID, Name, League, Manager
    FROM BBTeams
    WHERE League = 'AL'
    WITH CHECK OPTION
GO

GRANT SELECT, INSERT, UPDATE, DELETE ON BBTeams_AL TO PUBLIC
GO
```

The following series of batches demonstrate that unlike the limits placed on `INSERT` statements into views that use `WITH CHECK OPTION`, the parameters to the inline function have no bearing on what can be inserted into the UDF. Start by listing the teams in the American League:

```
-- Get the list of teams in the American League
SET NOCOUNT OFF
SELECT * FROM dbo.udf_BBTeams_LeagueTAB ('AL')
GO

(Results)

ID          Name         League Manager
----------- ------------ ------ ------------
          2 Yankees      AL     Yogi
          7 Red Sox      AL     Zimmer

(2 row(s) affected)
```

An attempt to add a National League team to the view on the American League fails:

```
-- Try to add a NL team to the American League View
INSERT INTO BBTeams_AL
            (Name, League, Manager)
      VALUES ('Mets', 'NL', 'Casey')
GO

(Results)

Server: Msg 550, Level 16, State 1, Line 1
The attempted insert or update failed because the target view either specifies
WITH CHECK OPTION or spans a view that specifies WITH CHECK OPTION and one or
more rows resulting from the operation did not qualify under the CHECK OPTION
constraint.
The statement has been terminated.
```

Contrast that statement with a similar attempt to insert into udf_BBTeams_LeagueTAB. When we try to insert a National League team into the UDF with 'AL' as the argument, the INSERT succeeds:

```
-- Add a team to the National League through the AL
INSERT INTO dbo.udf_BBTeams_LeagueTAB ('AL')
            (Name, League, Manager)
      VALUES ('Mets', 'NL', 'Casey')
GO

(Results)

(1 row(s) affected)
```

The message indicates that one row is affected, confirming the success of the statement. The next queries verify the contents of the BBTeams table:

```
-- Verify that the insert worked
PRINT 'American League'
SELECT * FROM dbo.udf_BBTeams_LeagueTAB ('AL')
PRINT 'National League'
SELECT * FROM dbo.udf_BBTeams_LeagueTAB ('NL')
GO

(Results)

American League
ID          Name         League Manager
----------- ------------ ------ ------------
          2 Yankees      AL     Yogi
          7 Red Sox      AL     Zimmer

(2 row(s) affected)

National League
ID          Name         League Manager
----------- ------------ ------ ------------
          1 Dodgers      NL     Walt
          3 Cubs         NL     Joe
         11 Mets         NL     Casey

(3 row(s) affected)
```

Updates and deletes are different. They work only on rows that are returned by the UDF. It is as if the WHERE clause of the UDF was combined with the WHERE clause of the UPDATE or DELETE statement that's being executed. For example, these two statements don't modify the database as intended:

```
-- Updates and Deletes are affected by the parameters
UPDATE dbo.udf_BBTeams_LeagueTAB ('AL')
   SET Manager = 'Hodges'
   WHERE name = 'Mets'
DELETE FROM dbo.udf_BBTeams_LeagueTAB ('AL')
    WHERE [Name] = 'Mets'
GO

(Results)

(0 row(s) affected)


(0 row(s) affected)
```

Both of the statements modify zero rows because `udf_BBTeams_League-TAB('AL')` doesn't return any rows that satisfy the statement's `WHERE` clause. The UDF is updatable when supplied with arguments that return the rows we're trying to update. Here we go:

```
-- Updates only occur if the row is in the result of the UDF
UPDATE dbo.udf_BBTeams_LeagueTAB ('NL')
   SET Manager = 'Hodges'
   WHERE name = 'Mets'
GO

(Results)

(1 row(s) affected)
```

This last batch gets rid of the Mets so that you can run the experiment again some other time:

```
-- Clean up the data for the next experiment
DELETE FROM BBTeams WHERE [Name] = 'Mets'
GO
```

In my opinion, the lack of a `WITH CHECK OPTION` clause and the fact that the UDF parameters don't limit `INSERT` statements make updatable views preferable to updatable UDFs. At least with views, the limitations are explicit and consistent.

Using Inline UDFs for Paging Web Pages

In a typical data-driven web site, many pages include tables of data that are retrieved from a database. One of the design decisions that must be made is how much data the web server scripts should retrieve from the database when showing tables that might be hundreds of rows or more. After all, the resulting table might span several pages.

My answer is: Retrieve as little as possible. To support that strategy, I've found that inline UDFs are a great tool for managing web site paging. By combining use of the UDF's parameters with the `TOP` clause, the minimal number of rows can be retrieved for each page.

Retrieving Minimal Data for Each Web Page

Whether you're using ASP or ASP.NET, JSP, PHP, CGI, or some other programming tool to generate data-driven web pages, the issue of how much data to show on each page and how to show additional pages faces us all. Once you've decided on the amount of data to show, you then have to decide how much data to retrieve each time you go to the database.

A typical query might result in just a few or many thousands of rows of results. This depends on how you set up your searches and the search arguments supplied by the user. Once the number of rows retrieved gets beyond the number of rows that can be shown on the page, I find that retrieving them becomes counterproductive. It slows the time to complete the page. So how do you go about retrieving just the right amount of data?

Some of the things that I've learned about making data-driven web sites are:

- Database access is the most expensive component of the web application to scale up, and it should be optimized.
- The number of round-trips between the page generation engine and the database is the biggest determinant of database load. It should be kept to a low number, usually once per page.

The hope of reducing the number of round-trips has occasionally led me to try to cache data on the web server. I've usually found this disappointing. The frequency that users go beyond the first page of a long table is pretty low. This observation has led to the guideline to retrieve only the minimum amount of data. What's the minimum?

Showing more than 15 or so rows on a page makes the user have to scroll the page to see all the results. A little bit of scrolling isn't so bad. Hitting the Page Down key once or twice doesn't usually bother most users. However, users only occasionally look at the data past the first screen. I've come to the conclusion that it's best to keep pages short, at about the amount that can be shown on a single screen.

If the aim is to retrieve rows in screen size groups and not cache extra rows at the web server, an inline UDF works very well. The next section shows how to create UDFs to support the page forward and page back operations.

Creating the Inline UDF

Before creating the paging UDF, let's decide what should be on the page. For illustration purposes, we'll use the Northwind database and base the query on this scenario:

> The page must show all products ordered by the number of units in stock. In addition, it must show the number of units sold since inception of the database.

So the query to retrieve this data in the desired order is:

```
SELECT P.ProductID, P.ProductName, P.UnitsInStock
       , S.[Total Sold], C.CategoryName
    FROM Northwind.dbo.Categories C
      INNER JOIN Northwind.dbo.Products p
            ON C.CategoryID = P.CategoryID
      INNER JOIN (SELECT ProductID, SUM (Quantity) as [Total Sold]
                     FROM Northwind.dbo.[Order Details]
                     GROUP BY ProductID
                  ) as S
       ON P.ProductID = S.ProductID
    WHERE P.Discontinued <> 1
    ORDER BY UnitsInStock desc
```

How many rows should you retrieve? Since the numeric argument to the `TOP` clause must be a constant, use the largest number that could fit on a screen. The data transmission between the SQL Server and the web creation engine (ASP.NET, ASP, or some other) is usually over a fast connection, and there is little benefit to trying to save a few bytes at the potential cost of another database round-trip. If our typical screen fits 15 rows, `TOP 15` should be added as the first clause in the `SELECT` statement.

The ability to retrieve rows after the first page is displayed is essential. To accomplish this, it's necessary to save one or more columns that identify where the user is in the paging process. The selection of the columns to save depends on the ordering used in the query.

The columns used to identify position must uniquely identify the last row shown. It may be necessary to add additional columns to the `ORDER BY` clause to provide uniqueness. In fact, for our sample query, the `UnitsInStock` column doesn't provide uniqueness, and we must add an additional column or columns. While there might be some benefit to using `[Total`

Sales] as the second sort column, it's a field that could actually change between pages. We're better off using a combination of ProductName and ProductID. Why two columns? Because ProductName isn't guaranteed to be unique in the Products table of the Northwind database. Most of the time, ProductName provides a very understandable and useful ordering. But in the rare occasions where a page with two products with the same quantity for UnitsInStock have the same name and fall on the exact end of a page, we might produce an error if we don't also use the ProductID. The ORDER BY clause in our query becomes:

```
ORDER BY UnitsInStock desc
    , P.ProductName asc
    , P.ProductID asc
```

In the web page generation code, we'll have to save three scalar values, one for each of the sort variables: UnitsInStock, ProductName, and ProductID. In ASP or ASP.NET, these values can safely be saved in the SESSION object. Other web programming environments have their own way to save session-related values. The values are used when the second and subsequent pages are retrieved. The page generation code must then hand the values from the end of the last page back to the paging UDF as arguments, which can then be used in the WHERE clause. The declaration of the parameters is:

```
-- Parameters identify the last row shown. Default for first page.
   @LastUnitsInStock int = 20000000 -- Product.UnitsInStock
 , @LastProductName nvarchar(40) = '' -- Product.ProductName
 , @LastProductID int = 0 -- Product.ProductID
```

Each of them has a default value that is used to retrieve the first page. Providing the defaults simplifies retrieval of the first page and relieves the programmer of having to figure them out. Just use DEFAULT for each of the function arguments.

It's possible to use a page number or starting line number to store the user's position. I find that it's better to use values from the application to define where pages start and end. The problem with page and line numbers is that the insertion of rows in the database while the user is paging through the table can make the paging operation miss a row or a few rows. That ends up being classified as a bug. Although it may take a little more time, choosing a set of columns from the application is worth the effort.

The WHERE clause gets a little tricky. Of course, the P.ProductID = S.ProductID condition must remain in the query, and the three parameters must be compared to the corresponding columns in each of the rows so that we start where we left off. My first instinct is to code these comparisons as:

```
AND P.UnitsInStock <= @LastUnitsInStock
AND P.ProductName >= @LastProductName
AND P.ProductID >= @LastProductID
```

But that's wrong! The problem is that it only returns rows with ProductName columns that are greater than or equal to the last ProductName, even if they have lower UnitsInStock values. The same problem holds for ProductIDs. The correct coding of the WHERE conditions for positioning the results is:

```
AND (P.UnitsInStock <= @LastUnitsInStock
    OR (P.UnitsInStock = @LastUnitsInStock
        AND P.ProductName >= @LastProductName)
    OR (P.UnitsInStock = @LastUnitsInStock
        AND P.ProductName = @LastProductName
        AND P.ProductID >= @LastProductID)
    )
```

This retrieves rows that are after the last row shown. Using the less than or equal (<=) and greater than or equal (>=) comparison operators gives us one row of overlap between pages. Use just the less than (<) or greater than (>) comparison operators to eliminate the overlap.

Listing 7.5 pulls these changes together to create udf_Paging_ProductByUnits_Forward, our forward paging UDF. The name is long, but there's a method to creating it. After the usual udf_ designation, the second part of the name is the group, which identifies the UDF as one used for paging. The name ProductByUnits identifies the page that the function serves. Finally, Forward tells the direction that we're going.

Listing 7.5: udf_Paging_ProductByUnits_Forward

```
CREATE FUNCTION dbo.udf_Paging_ProductByUnits_Forward (

   -- Parameters identify the last row shown. Null for first page.
    @LastUnitsInStock int = 20000000 -- Product.UnitsInStock
  , @LastProductName nvarchar(40) = '' -- Product.ProductName
  , @LastProductID int = 0 -- Product.ProductID
)   RETURNS TABLE
/*
* Forward paging UDF for ASP page ProductByUnits
*
* Example:
SELECT *
    FROM udf_Paging_ProductByUnits_Forward
            (default, default, default) -- defaults for 1st Page
****************************************************************/
AS RETURN

SELECT TOP 15
       P.ProductID
     , P.ProductName
```

```
    , P.UnitsInStock
    , S.[Total Sold]
    , C.CategoryName
   FROM Northwind.dbo.Categories C
       INNER JOIN Northwind.dbo.Products p
          ON C.CategoryID = P.CategoryID
       INNER JOIN (SELECT ProductID
                       , SUM (Quantity) as [Total Sold]
                      FROM Northwind.dbo.[Order Details]
                      GROUP BY ProductID
                    ) AS S
          ON P.ProductID = S.ProductID
   WHERE P.Discontinued <> 1
          AND (P.UnitsInStock <= @LastUnitsInStock
              OR (P.UnitsInStock = @LastUnitsInStock
                  AND P.ProductName >= @LastProductName)
              OR (P.UnitsInStock = @LastUnitsInStock
                  AND P.ProductName = @LastProductName
                  AND P.ProductID >= @LastProductID)
              )
   ORDER BY P.UnitsInStock desc
          , P.ProductName asc
          , P.ProductID asc
GO
```

To retrieve rows for the first page, the SELECT statement is:

```
-- Get the first page of data
SELECT ProductID, ProductName, UnitsInStock as Units
          , [Total Sold], CategoryName as Cat
    FROM udf_Paging_ProductByUnits_Forward (default, default, default)
GO
```

(Results - abridged with some fields truncated)

```
ID    ProductName                    Units  Total Sold  Category
----- ------------------------------ ------ ----------- --------------
   75 Rhönbräu Klosterbier            125        1155 Beverages
   40 Boston Crab Meat                123        1103 Seafood
    6 Grandma's Boysenberry Spread    120         301 Condiments
...
   59 Raclette Courdavault             79        1496 Dairy Products
   65 Louisiana Fiery Hot Pepper Sau   76         745 Condiments
```

Parameter values are not supplied to retrieve the first page because defaults can be used. To retrieve the rows for the second page, use this SELECT statement:

```
-- Get the second page
SELECT ProductID as [ID], ProductName, UnitsInStock as Units
          , [Total Sold], CategoryName as Category
    FROM udf_Paging_ProductByUnits_Forward
             (76, 'Louisiana Fiery Hot Pepper Sauce', 65)
GO
```

```
(Results - only first three rows and the last row)

ID    ProductName                   Units  Total Sold  Category
----- ----------------------------- ------ ----------- --------------
   65 Louisiana Fiery Hot Pepper Sau   76         745 Condiments
   25 NuNuCa Nuß-Nougat-Creme          76         318 Confections
   39 Chartreuse verte                 69         793 Beverages
   ...
   52 Filo Mix                         38         500 Grains/Cereals
```

The previous SELECT statement has constants as arguments. Of course, your web page logic will construct the SQL statement using the variables that hold the key values from the last page shown.

You might ask, "Do I really need an inline UDF to accomplish this?" My answer is that it isn't essential; you could put the query inline in the web page creation script. But using the inline UDF has important advantages:

- The query plan is cached, which saves the time it takes to create the execution plan after the first time it's used.
- The effort to write the query is encapsulated in a database object for easy reuse.

As you've already heard, it's the latter reason that I think is most important. Separating the SQL logic from other page creation logic is a simplifying step that pays many times over in a reduction in complexity and thus in maintenance effort. For this reason, I almost always move all my SQL into stored procedures or UDFs and out of the web creation script.

How about paging backward? I know of two approaches to paging back based on the inline UDF technique:

- Save a stack with the key values for the start of each page as the user navigates forward.
- Write a corresponding UDF for reverse paging.

The first method requires that you save the key values for the top of each page and use them as the arguments to the forward paging UDF. Once you're saving one set of values, you might as well save an array, used as a stack. This approach involves more coding on the web page creation side and has the additional disadvantage that it could miss one or more rows if insertion of rows was going on at the same time as paging.

Writing the inline UDF to page in reverse is very similar to writing the forward paging UDF, with the addition of an extra sort operation. Listing 7.6 shows the CREATE FUNCTION script for udf_Paging_ProductBy-Units_Reverse.

Listing 7.6: udf_Paging_ProductByUnits_Reverse

```
CREATE FUNCTION udf_Paging_ProductByUnits_Reverse (

-- Parameters identify the last row shown. default for last page.
    @LastUnitsInStock int = -1 -- Product.UnitsInStock
  , @LastProductName nvarchar(40) = 'zzzzzzzzzzzzzzz'
                                    -- Product.ProductName
  , @LastProductID int = 2000000000 -- Product.ProductID
)   RETURNS TABLE
/*
* Forward paging UDF for ASP page ProductsByUnit
*
* Example:
SELECT *
    FROM udf_Paging_ProductByUnits_Reverse
            (default, default, default) -- defaults for last page
*************************************************************/
AS RETURN

SELECT TOP 100 PERCENT WITH TIES *
    FROM (
        SELECT TOP 15
               P.ProductID
             , P.ProductName
             , P.UnitsInStock
             , S.[Total Sold]
             , C.CategoryName
            FROM Northwind.dbo.Categories C
                INNER JOIN Northwind.dbo.Products p
                  ON C.CategoryID = P.CategoryID
                INNER JOIN (SELECT ProductID
                                 , SUM (Quantity) as [Total Sold]
                              FROM Northwind.dbo.[Order Details]
                              GROUP BY ProductID
                          ) AS S
                ON P.ProductID = S.ProductID
            WHERE P.Discontinued <> 1
                  AND (P.UnitsInStock > @LastUnitsInStock
                       OR (P.UnitsInStock = @LastUnitsInStock
                           AND P.ProductName < @LastProductName)
                       OR (P.UnitsInStock = @LastUnitsInStock
                           AND P.ProductName = @LastProductName
                           AND P.ProductID <= @LastProductID)
                      )
           ORDER BY P.UnitsInStock asc
                  , P.ProductName desc
                  , P.ProductID desc
     ) as RowsOnPreviousPage
    ORDER BY UnitsInStock desc
           , ProductName asc
           , ProductID asc
```

The inline SELECT statement RowsOnPreviousPage selects the 15 previous rows. This uses logic similar to the logic used when paging forward with the exception that the WHERE clause selects rows that are less than or equal to the first row on the last page. The outer SELECT is used to resort the rows into the presentation order.

By the way, to use the reverse paging function, the web page creation code must save the three key values from the first row on the page. These can be saved in the SESSION object in the same way that the key values from the last row on the page are saved for paging forward.

Inline UDF parameters combined with the TOP clause can be put to use retrieving just the right number of rows to show on each web page. This has proven to be an effective strategy in data-driven web sites.

Summary

This chapter has shown how inline UDFs are similar to views. The addition of parameters makes them more powerful. By using the parameters in the SELECT statement, choices that the user of a similar view would normally have to make are coded into the function. This makes the UDF simpler to use in the right situation.

While inline UDFs can be updatable, the differences between them and updatable views may not be sufficient to make the switch worthwhile. In particular, the absence of a WITH CHECK option and the inconsistent behavior of not checking inserts but checking updates and deletes makes me want to stick with updatable views rather than switching to updatable UDFs.

Web site paging is one application of inline UDFs that has proved to work well in practice. The capability to supply parameters and the use of the TOP clause facilitates moving the SQL required for paging logic out of the page generation script and into a compiled SQL object. By retrieving the right number of rows, database and network resources are consumed in proportion to the number of pages displayed.

Inline UDFs return a single rowset but can only contain one SELECT statement. If you require more program logic to achieve the desired results, a multistatement UDF may be what you need. The next chapter takes a detailed look at them.

8

Multistatement UDFs

Among the confusing aspects of multistatement UDFs is that they go by many different names. Some of the names you'll see for multistatement UDFs are:

- Multiline
- Multistatement
- Table-valued
- TABLE
- Table function
- Multistatement table-valued function
- TF (the type code used in `sysobjects`)

I've used "multistatement" in the text of this book because it's the name that Books Online uses. SQL Server's code, such as the `sp_help` system stored procedure, refers to them as table functions. Inline UDFs also return tables, so I think the term is somewhat confusing.

No matter what the name, they're a useful hybrid of a scalar and inline UDF. They return a table that is constructed by the T-SQL script in the body of the function. The table can be used in the `FROM` clause of any SQL statement, and they join the ranks of the rowset returning functions like `OPENROWSET` and `OPENXML`.

The logic in the body of the UDF can be extensive but must obey the same limitations on side effects that were documented in Chapter 5. Most importantly, multistatement UDFs can't execute stored procedures nor can they create or reference temporary tables or generate any messages. Their communication options are limited by design.

In this chapter, we examine them and concentrate on these topics:

- Permissions for multistatement UDFs
- Using cursors in UDFs
- Managing lists with UDFs

Permissions for managing and using multistatement UDFs are very similar to permissions on the other types of UDFs. The mix is slightly different due to the limits on what can be done with them.

Managing Permissions on Multistatement UDFs

Multistatement UDFs are similar enough to other UDFs that you already know how this is going to work. Permissions to create, change, and remove UDFs are the same as those used on scalar and inline UDFs. `SELECT` is the key permission used to retrieve data from one. There's no `EXEC` permission on multistatement UDFs.

Permissions to Create, Alter, and Drop Multistatement UDFs

The statement permissions `CREATE FUNCTION`, `ALTER FUNCTION`, and `DROP FUNCTION` are the same used for creating both scalar and inline UDFs. As mentioned before, you can't split permissions between types of UDFs. Usually, the programmers who write UDFs are members of the database role `db_ddladmin`.

Permission to Select on Multistatement UDFs

There are two permissions on multistatement UDFs: `SELECT` and `REFERENCES`. `SELECT` permission allows the caller to use the UDF in the `FROM` clause of a SQL statement. Just like the `REFERENCES` permission on inline UDFs, I've never found a use for the `REFERENCES` permission on a multistatement UDF.

As with the other types of UDFs, users of a multistatement UDF don't need permissions on the tables, views, and functions referenced by the UDF. Only the UDF owner, usually **dbo,** needs the permissions on the referenced objects.

Unlike inline UDFs, multistatement UDFs can never be updatable, and there are no permissions for `UPDATE`, `INSERT`, and `DELETE`. In some imaginary perfect world, updatable multistatement UDFs might be a good idea, but in practice there's no way for SQL Server to figure out where to put the data.

Creating and Using Multistatement UDFs

The multistatement UDF is sort of a cross between the other types:

- Its body is a T-SQL script.
- It returns a table.

The table returned by the UDF is a `TABLE` variable with a scope of the entire UDF. It's declared in the `RETURNS` clause in the function header.

Some of the useful features of the returned table are that it can have:

- An identity column
- A `ROWGUID` column
- A primary key
- `CHECK` clauses
- `NULL` and `NOT NULL` columns
- `UNIQUE` constraints
- Defaults

The table can't have:

- Indexes other than those created implicitly to implement the primary key and unique constraints
- Foreign key constraints
- Triggers
- A storage clause

The table returned by a UDF is treated like a `TABLE` variable. As such, it's an object in tempdb that is not stored in tempdb's system tables. Like `TABLE` variables, the pages of the table are written to disk in tempdb. Depending on the amount of data in the table and the available RAM, data pages from the table may or may not ever be removed from SQL Server's data cache and stored on disk. You only have to worry about this if the amount of data in the `TABLE` grows large relative to the available RAM or if there's a possibility of running out of space in tempdb.

Once the function header with the table definition is declared, you may write the function body. All the limitations on which T-SQL statements are allowed in a UDF that are discussed in Chapter 5 apply to multistatement UDFs. While this limits what you can do, it ensures that the UDF has no side effects.

The lack of side effects is one of the features of multistatement UDFs that distinguish them from stored procedures. In many ways, they're similar to a stored procedure that returns a single resultset. If you can live with the restrictions, including the restriction on calling stored procedures, a multistatement UDF is a good substitute for a procedure. The lack of side effects improves the maintainability of the code.

Chapter 1 had udf_DT_MonthsTAB as an example UDF. Listing 8.1 shows udf_Num_FactorialTAB, a simple multistatement UDF that returns a table of numbers and factorials.

Listing 8.1: udf_Num_FactorialTAB

```
CREATE FUNCTION dbo.udf_Num_FactorialTAB (

    @N bigint -- The number of factorials to return
)   RETURNS @Factorials TABLE (Number int, Factorial bigint)
/* Returns a table with the series of numbers and factorials.
*
* Example:
SELECT * from udf_Num_FactorialTAB (20)
****************************************************************/
AS BEGIN

DECLARE @I int, @F bigint

SELECT @I = 1, @F = CONVERT(bigint, 1)

WHILE @I < = @N  BEGIN
    SET @F = CONVERT(bigint, @I) * @F
    INSERT INTO @Factorials (Number, Factorial) VALUES (@I, @F)
    SET @I = @I + 1
END -- WHILE

RETURN
END
```

This query tries it out:

```
-- How quickly do factorials grow?
SELECT * FROM dbo.udf_Num_FactorialTAB (20)
GO

(Results - abridged)

Number      Factorial
----------- --------------------
          1                    1
          2                    2
          3                    6
          4                   24
...
         18     6402373705728000
         19   121645100408832000
         20  2432902008176640000
```

The Factorial column is a bigint. Twenty factorial is as high as we can go without switching to a data type that holds larger numbers than a bigint, such as numeric and float.

The primary reason for using a multistatement UDF instead of an inline UDF is the need for the program logic in the function body. Listing 8.2 has `udf_Category_BigCategoryProductsTAB`, a UDF created to illustrate some of the things that can be done with multistatement UDFs. The hypothetical requirement for the UDF is that it returns product information for all products where there are `@MinProducts` products in the category.

Listing 8.2: `udf_Category_BigCategoryProductsTAB`

```
CREATE FUNCTION dbo.udf_Category_BigCategoryProductsTAB (

    @MinProducts int -- Minimum Num of products to include in the category

) RETURNS @Products TABLE (
        CategoryName     nvarchar(15)
      , ProductID        int
      , ProductName      nvarchar(40)
      , QuantityPerUnit  nvarchar(20)
      , UnitsInStock     smallint
      , Discontinued     BIT
      , PRIMARY KEY (CategoryName, ProductName)
                         )
/*
* Returns a table of product information for all products in
* all categories with at least @MinProducts products.
*
* Example:
SELECT * FROM dbo.udf_Category_BigCategoryProductsTAB (9)
**************************************************************/
AS BEGIN

DECLARE CategoryCursor CURSOR FAST_FORWARD FOR
    SELECT CategoryID, CategoryName
       FROM dbo.udf_Category_ProductCountTAB (@MinProducts)
       ORDER BY CategoryName

DECLARE @CategoryID int
      , @CategoryName nvarchar(15)

OPEN CategoryCursor
FETCH CategoryCursor INTO @CategoryID, @CategoryName

WHILE @@Fetch_status = 0  BEGIN

    -- Loop contents
    INSERT INTO @Products (CategoryName, ProductID, ProductName
                 , QuantityPerUnit, UnitsInStock, Discontinued)
        SELECT @CategoryName, ProductID, ProductName
                 , QuantityPerUnit, UnitsInStock, Discontinued
            FROM dbo.udf_Category_ProductsTAB (@CategoryName)

    FETCH CategoryCursor INTO @CategoryID, @CategoryName
END -- WHILE LOOP

-- Clean up the cursor
CLOSE CategoryCursor
DEALLOCATE CategoryCursor

RETURN -- The @Products TABLE is returned by this function
END
```

If you recall from Chapter 7, udf_Category_ProductCountTAB was constructed to return the list of categories with at least @MinProducts products. The TSQLUDFS database has the UDF udf_Category_ProductsTAB, which is not listed. It returns a list of the products in any particular category. The data that we're seeking can be obtained by a combination of information from the two UDFs. What we need is the union of the results of running udf_Category_ProductsTAB once for each category that is returned by udf_Category_ProductsCountTAB. But there's no way to combine the two in a join because a column name can't be used as a parameter to a UDF. It doesn't work.

The answer is to use a cursor. The cursor returns one category ID and category name at a time. Then a call is made to udf_Category_ProductsTAB supplying @CategoryName from the cursor, and the results are stored in the @Products TABLE variable that is ultimately returned as the UDF's resultset. When we've looped through all the categories that satisfy our criteria, @Products has the union of the rows from those categories. Here's a sample query:

```
-- User our cursor based multistatement UDF
SELECT CategoryName as Category, ProductName, QuantityPerUnit
     , UnitsInStock as Stock, Discontinued as Disc
   FROM dbo.udf_Category_BigCategoryProductsTAB(9)
GO
```

(Results - abridged)

```
Category    ProductName          QuantityPerUnit      Stock  Disc
----------- -------------------- -------------------- ------ ----
Beverages   Chai                 10 boxes x 20 bags       39    0
Beverages   Chang                24 - 12 oz bottles       17    0
...
Condiments  Sirop d'érable       24 - 500 ml bottles     113    0
Condiments  Vegie-spread         15 - 625 g jars          24    0
Confections Chocolade            10 pkgs.                 15    0
Confections Gumbär Gummibärchen  100 - 250 g bags         15    0
Confections Maxilaku             24 - 50 g pkgs.          10    0
...
Seafood     Rogede sild          1k pkg.                   5    0
Seafood     Spegesild            4 - 450 g glasses        95    0

(57 row(s) affected)
```

The scenario is a bit contrived. If you examine the two UDFs that udf_Category_BigCategoryProductsTAB calls, it's possible to combine them into a single SQL statement and do away with the cursor. The point is to illustrate some of the features of multistatement UDFs.

The results of the query are returned—sorted first by CategoryName and then by ProductName. That's due to the use of a primary key. The table-level primary key declaration in a multistatement UDF uses only the limited primary key syntax. It can't use the more elaborate CONSTRAINT syntax that's available when using CREATE TABLE. The key created is a unique clustered index on the table.

The rows of the previous query are returned in the order in which they're stored in the UDF's temporary table. Although I've never seen the results returned in any other order, SQL Server is a relational database and it doesn't guarantee the order in which rows are returned. If you want a specific order, be sure to put an ORDER BY clause on the SELECT statement that calls the UDF.

Another way to access data across databases is represented by udf_Category_ProductCountTAB. It's a UDF in TSQLUDFS that reads data from Northwind with explicit database references to its tables. The only limitation on a UDF that references data in another database is that it can't be created using the WITH SCHEMABINDING option.

Cursors can be used in either scalar or multistatement UDFs. They're included in this chapter because it's more common to find them in a multistatement function. The code for a cursor follows a very predictable pattern and creating them is easier with a template. Before we get to that, let's take a look at a template for creating multistatement UDFs.

Template for Multistatement UDFs

Listing 8.3 has a template for creating multistatement UDFs. This template has the following features, which the template distributed with SQL Server doesn't:

- SET QUOTED_IDENTIFIER ON and SET ANSI_NULLS ON start the file to be sure that they're set for every UDF.
- **dbo** always owns the UDF. I recommend that **dbo** own all database objects.
- No DROP statement for the UDF. If the UDF already exists, change CREATE FUNCTION to ALTER FUNCTION.
- Inclusion of a comment block with a place for a description, an example, test cases, and modification history.
- The WITH SCHEMABINDING clause is already in the template. I suggest that you either use WITH SCHEMABINDING or have a comment that says why not.
- The file has a GRANT statement for giving the SELECT permission to PUBLIC.

Listing 8.3: Template for creating multistatement UDFs

```
SET QUOTED_IDENTIFIER ON
GO
SET ANSI_NULLS ON
GO

CREATE FUNCTION dbo.<table_function_name, sysname, udf_> (

    <parm1, sysname, @p1> <parm1_data_type, , int> -- <parm1_description, ,>
  , <parm2, sysname, @p2> <parm2_data_type, , int> -- <parm2_description, ,>
  , <parm3, sysname, @p3> <parm3_data_type, , int> -- <parm3_description, ,>
)   RETURNS TABLE (
         <col1_Name, , [ID]>   <col1_Type, ,int>-- <col1_description, ,>
       , <col2_Name, , [Desc]> <col2_Type, ,int>-- <col2_description, ,>
       , <col3_Name, , [xxxx]> <col3_Type, ,int>-- <col3_description, ,>
       , PRIMARY KEY (<col1_Name, , [ID]>)
                 )
    WITH SCHEMABINDING -- Or comment about why not
/*
* description goes here
*
* Related Functions:
* Attribution: Based on xxx by yyy found in zzzzzzzzzzzz
* Maintenance Notes:
* Example:
SELECT * FROM dbo.<table_function_name, sysname, udf_>(<value_for_@param1, , 1>,
<value_for_@param2, , 2>, <value_for_@param3, , 3>)
* Test Script: TEST_<table_function_name, sysname, udf_>
* History:
* When          Who     Description
* ------------- ------- -----------------------------------------
* <date created,smalldatetime, mm/dd/yy>          <your initials,char(8), XXX>
Initial Coding
****************************************************************/
AS BEGIN

DECLARE

RETURN
END
GO

GRANT SELECT ON [dbo].[<table_function_name, sysname, udf_>]
                    TO [PUBLIC]
GO
```

The template reflects choices that I usually make about what to include or exclude from a multistatement UDF. I've never granted REFERENCES permission on a multistatement UDF, so I don't include it in the template. A PRIMARY KEY clause is included in the template to encourage its use. If you don't need it, comment it out or delete it.

You're not limited to one template. If you have different styles of UDFs, you may have several templates for any of the UDF types. You can also include templates with partial code. The section that follows is about using cursors; it includes a template that makes writing them a snap.

Using Cursors in UDFs with a Template

Scalar and multistatement UDFs may use cursors in their code body. Of course, cursors aren't exclusive to UDFs. Other T-SQL scripts, such as triggers and batches, can run cursors.

In most ways, cursors are a step back from a declarative/relational approach to code to an older procedural/navigational type of code. The cursor code navigates the rows of data in the requested order and acts on each row, one at a time.

For most problems, cursor-based solutions are slower than relational solutions to the same problem. However, sometimes it's not clear how to code a problem into a relational alternative, and it's better to go ahead with the cursor. There are times when cursor-based solutions work faster than any alternatives.

There are even times when some operations can only be completed with a cursor. This happens when you have to do something inside the loop that can't be done with a single relational statement. One example is to execute an extended stored procedure. Chapter 10 is about extended stored procedures and shows one way to get around that limit by creating a UDF.

Listing 8.4 on the following page shows a template that has most of the code needed to create and use a cursor. It isn't an entire UDF. It's intended to be pulled into the UDF body after the header and other structural syntax is in place. You'll find it in the file Cursor Template.tql in the Templates directory of the download.

There's no limit on using the cursor template in a UDF. You could pull it into any procedural code such as a stored procedure, trigger, or batch.

After you've used Query Analyzer's Edit ➤ Replace Template Parameters menu command to fill in the template, there's still work to be done. For starters, you've got to complete the `SELECT` statement for the cursor. You may also need to adjust the number of variables declared and fetched. I put in four, but you may need some other number. Finally, there's the body of the loop to write. What did you really want to do with the cursor anyway?

Once the multistatement UDF is created, it's ready to be used. Multistatement UDFs are used the same way that inline UDFs are—in the `FROM` clause of a `SELECT`. That's been demonstrated several times in previous chapters. So rather than beat a dead horse, I've decided that the best way to illustrate using multistatement UDFs is by using a real problem—list management.

Listing 8.4: Template for a cursor

```
DECLARE <CursorName,varchar(128), myCursor> CURSOR FAST_FORWARD FOR
    SELECT
       FROM
       WHERE
       ORDER BY

DECLARE @<v1_name, sysname, v1> <v1_data_type, ,int> -- <v1_description,,>
      , @<v2_name, sysname, v2> <v2_data_type, ,int> -- <v2_description,,>
      , @<v3_name, sysname, v3> <v3_data_type, ,int> -- <v3_description,,>
      , @<v4_name, sysname, v4> <v4_data_type, ,int> -- <v4_description,,>

OPEN <CursorName,varchar(128), myCursor>
FETCH <CursorName,varchar(128), myCursor> INTO
             @<v1_name, sysname, v1>
           , @<v2_name, sysname, v2>
           , @<v3_name, sysname, v3>
           , @<v4_name, sysname, v4>


WHILE @@Fetch_status = 0  BEGIN

    -- Loop contents

    FETCH <CursorName,varchar(128), myCursor> INTO
                 @<v1_name, sysname, v1>
               , @<v2_name, sysname, v2>
               , @<v3_name, sysname, v3>
               , @<v4_name, sysname, v4>

END -- WHILE LOOP

-- Clean up the cursor
CLOSE <CursorName,varchar(128), myCursor>
DEALLOCATE <CursorName,varchar(128), myCursor>
```

List Management

Data doesn't always come in neat relational tables. Sometimes it comes in delimiter-separated text. One of the most asked-for tasks that can be performed with a multistatement UDF is to convert delimited text into a table. Similarly, when reporting data, the neat relational table isn't always the best way to show a list, particularly when it has few entries. Sometimes it's best to combine the list with a delimiter prior to display.

Code tables are another type of list that many applications use for data validation and drop-down data entry fields. Sometimes shipping a code table as a UDF can simplify the installation process for an application.

This section shows how to handle delimited text and code tables with multistatement UDFs. These are hardly the only tasks suitable for these UDFs, but they are tasks that were previously more difficult in T-SQL.

Creating Tables from Delimited Text

Listing 8.5 shows udf_Txt_SplitTAB, a UDF that takes a delimited list and turns it into a table. Since the delimiter isn't usually a space, the function trims extra spaces from the sides of each item before it's returned.

Listing 8.5: udf_Txt_SplitTAB

```
CREATE FUNCTION dbo.udf_Txt_SplitTAB (

    @sInputList varchar(8000) -- List of delimited items
  , @Delimiter char(1) = ',' -- delimiter that separates items
)   RETURNS @List TABLE (Item varchar(8000))
    WITH SCHEMABINDING
/*
* Returns a table of strings that have been split by a delimiter.
* Similar to the Visual Basic (or VBA) SPLIT function. The
* strings are trimmed before being returned.  Null items are not
* returned so if there are multiple separators between items,
* only the non-null items are returned.
* Space is not a valid delimiter.
*
* Example:
select * FROM dbo.udf_Txt_SplitTAB('abcd,123, 456, efh,,hi', ',')
*
* Test:
DECLARE @Count int, @Delim char(10), @Input varchar(128)
SELECT @Count = Count(*)
    FROM dbo.udf_Txt_SplitTAB('abcd,123, 456', ',')
PRINT 'TEST 1 3 lines:' + CASE WHEN @Count=3
              THEN 'Worked' ELSE 'ERROR' END
SELECT @DELIM=CHAR(10)
     , @INPUT = 'Line 1' + @delim + 'line 2' + @Delim
SELECT @Count = Count(*)
    FROM dbo.udf_Txt_SplitTAB(@Input, @Delim)
PRINT 'TEST 2  LF    :' + CASE WHEN @Count=2

              THEN 'Worked' ELSE 'ERROR' END
***************************************************************/
AS BEGIN

DECLARE @Item Varchar(8000)
DECLARE @Pos int -- current starting position
      , @NextPos int -- position of next delimiter
      , @LenInput int -- length of input
      , @LenNext int -- length of next item
      , @DelimLen int -- length of the delimiter

SELECT @Pos = 1
     , @DelimLen = LEN(@Delimiter) --  usually 1
     , @LenInput = LEN(@sInputList)
     , @NextPos = CharIndex(@Delimiter, @sInputList, 1)

-- Doesn't work for space as a delimiter
IF @Delimiter = ' ' BEGIN
   INSERT INTO @List
       SELECT 'ERROR: Blank is not a valid delimiter'
   RETURN
END
```

```
-- loop over the input, until the last delimiter.
While @Pos <= @LenInput and @NextPos > 0 BEGIN

    IF @NextPos > @Pos BEGIN -- another delimiter found
       SET @LenNext = @NextPos - @Pos
       SET @Item = LTrim(RTrim(
                           substring(@sInputList
                                  , @Pos
                                 , @LenNext)
                              )
                         )
       IF LEN(@Item) > 0
           Insert Into @List Select @Item
       -- ENDIF

    END -- IF

    -- Position over the next item
    SELECT @Pos = @NextPos + @DelimLen
         , @NextPos = CharIndex(@Delimiter
                              , @sInputList
                              , @Pos)
END

-- Now there might be one more item left
SET @Item = LTrim(RTrim(
                     SUBSTRING(@sInputList
                              , @Pos
                              , @LenInput-@Pos + 1)
                     )
                )

IF Len(@Item) > 0 -- Put the last item in, if found
   INSERT INTO @List SELECT @Item

RETURN
END
```

This UDF is pretty easy to use. Just supply the delimited text and the delimiter. This query demonstrates:

```
-- trial use of udf_Txt_SplitTAB
SELECT '->' + Item + '<-' as [->Item<-]
    FROM udf_Txt_SplitTAB (
         'Kaleigh, Phil IV, Ben, Kara, Eric, Tommy , Christine', default)
GO
```

(Results)

```
->Item<-
---------------------------
->Kaleigh<-
->Phil IV<-
->Ben<-
->Kara<-
->Eric<-
->Tommy<-
->Christine<-
```

Notice that the embedded space in the name "Phil IV" is preserved, but the extra space after "Tommy" is removed. Both choices are by design and could have been coded differently. There isn't much more to using the UDF than that.

An awkward situation occurs when you have a table that has a column of delimited text and you want to combine the items from all the rows. As you may recall from Chapter 1, you can't use a column name as the parameter to a multistatement UDF.

To illustrate, let's use the `BBTeams` table that served as an example in Chapter 7. The table has a column, `Players`, that is a comma-separated list of names. The objective is to get a resultset with the list of all players in the league. The table is already in the TSQLUDFS database populated with a few teams. Here's a quick look at what's in it:

```
-- The teams...
SELECT Top 2 * from BBTeams
GO

(Results – truncated on the right)

ID          Name         Players
----------- ------------ -----------------------------------------
          1 Dodgers      Eric, Nick, Patrick, David, Billy, Alex, Matt, Gaven,...
          2 Yankees      Ulli, Tommy, Christine, Rika, Violet, Ken, Pat, Kenny,...
```

What I'd like to do is write a query that executes `udf_Txt_SplitTAB` on every row and `UNION`s the result. Something like the following:

```
-- The query that I'd like to write.
SELECT item as Player
    FROM udf_Txt_Lst2TrimTAB (Players)
        JOIN BBTeams
GO

(Results)

Server: Msg 155, Level 15, State 1, Line 2
'Players' is not a recognized OPTIMIZER LOCK HINTS option.
```

I'm not sure what type of join could possibly make this work. In any case, SQL Server doesn't have any way to let you specify this type of query. There are several possible solutions. One solution is to write code that creates a dynamic SQL string that `UNION`s the result of parsing each row. That solution is limited by the size of a string variable and would require its own cursor. Another solution would be to concatenate the `Players` columns and parse the result. Once again, that's limited by the size of a string variable, and it stops working when the list gets to 8,000 characters. The solution that we're going to try here is to write a UDF that uses a cursor to traverse the `BBTeams` table and split each list of players. Listing 8.6

shows the function udf_BBTeam_AllPlayers with the CURSOR statement. As each list is generated, it's inserted into the function's return TABLE variable, @PlayerList.

Listing 8.6: udf_BBTeam_AllPlayers, a sample UDF with a cursor

```
CREATE FUNCTION dbo.udf_BBTeam_AllPlayers (

)   RETURNS @PlayerList TABLE ([Player] varchar(16)
                              )
/*
* Returns a list of all players on all BBTeams
*
* Example:
SELECT Player FROM dbo.udf_BBTeam_AllPlayers() ORDER BY Player
*****************************************************************/
AS BEGIN

DECLARE @Players varchar(255) -- Holds one team's Player list
DECLARE TeamCURSOR CURSOR FAST_FORWARD FOR
    SELECT Players
        FROM BBTeams
        ORDER BY [Name]

OPEN TeamCURSOR
FETCH TeamCURSOR INTO @Players

WHILE @@Fetch_status = 0 BEGIN
    INSERT INTO @PlayerList (Player)
        SELECT Item
            FROM udf_Txt_SplitTAB (@Players, default)
    FETCH TeamCURSOR INTO @Players -- next team
END -- WHILE

-- Clean up the cursor
CLOSE TeamCURSOR
DEALLOCATE TeamCURSOR

RETURN
END
```

Now all one has to do is select from the UDF:

```
-- Roster of all players
SELECT Player
    FROM udf_BBTeam_AllPlayers()
    ORDER BY Player desc
GO
```

(Results - abridged)

```
Player
----------------
Violet
Vicky
Ulli
Tommy
Thea
Stephen
Shea
Rika
...
```

Although `udf_BBTeam_AllPlayers` solves the problem, it does so at cursor speed. If you lurk on certain database-related newsgroups, you will often see certain people railing against any code that uses a cursor. And there can be a problem. In Chapter 11 you'll see the magnitude of the performance problem that can be caused when that code processes its results row by row.

Before we elaborate on the evils of row-by-row processing, let's attack a problem that's the opposite of parsing delimited text into individual items. The next section turns a column into a delimited text string.

Turning Tables into Delimited Text

The world isn't relational. It's not divided into rows and columns. Sometimes when there's a list associated with a row, it's better to show the list as comma-separated text rather than try to preserve a relational presentation. I use this technique on reports and sometimes on online grids. The UDFs that implement this technique are not multistatement but scalar. I've put this section here because the function performs the inverse operation of the functions that create tables from delimited text, such as `udf_Txt_SplitTAB`.

To illustrate how this works, we'll work in the pubs database and create a list of authors, their books, and the collaborators on the book. The collaborators are the other authors who have worked on the same book. These also come from the `Authors` table.

Like the previous problem of combining the players from many baseball teams, this one isn't amenable to a general-purpose solution using UDFs. Because the UDF must mention specific tables and columns, it works in only one situation. I find myself rewriting this one again and again.

The solution is pretty simple: Use a cursor to traverse the list of authors for this title and concatenate them together as they're found. Listing 8.7 shows `udf_Titles_AuthorList`, which uses the cursor to make the list. That's the basic approach. Stay tuned for an alternative solution that will follow shortly.

Listing 8.7: udf_Titles_AuthorList

```
CREATE  FUNCTION udf_Titles_AuthorList (

    @title_id char(6) -- title ID from pubs database
)   RETURNS varchar(255) -- List of authors
   -- No SCHEMABINDING reads data from another DB
/*
* Returns a comma-separated list of the last name of all
* authors for a title.
*
* Example:
Select Title, dbo.udf_Titles_AuthorList(title_id) as [Authors]

   FROM pubs..titles ORDER by Title
****************************************************************/
AS BEGIN

DECLARE @lname varchar(40)  -- one last name.
     , @sList varchar(255) -- working list

SET @sList = ''

DECLARE BookAuthors CURSOR FAST_FORWARD FOR
    SELECT au_lname
        FROM pubs..Authors A
            INNER JOIN pubs..titleAuthor ta
                ON A.au_id = ta.au_id
        WHERE ta.title_ID = @Title_ID
      ORDER BY au_lname

OPEN BookAuthors
FETCH BookAuthors INTO @lname
WHILE @@Fetch_status = 0 BEGIN
    SET @sList = CASE WHEN LEN(@sList) > 0
                      THEN @sList + ', ' + @lname
                      ELSE @lname
                      END
    FETCH BookAuthors INTO @lname
END

CLOSE BookAuthors
DEALLOCATE BookAuthors

RETURN @sList
END
```

Using it is a cinch:

```
-- Titles and Authors
SELECT Title, dbo.udf_Titles_AuthorList(title_id) as [Authors]
   FROM pubs..titles ORDER by Title
GO

(Results – with selected rows reformatted)

Title                               Authors
----------------------------------- ----------------------------
But Is It User Friendly?            Carson
Computer Phobic AND Non-Phobic I... Karsen, MacFeather
Cooking with Computers: Surrepti... MacFeather, O'Leary
Secrets of Silicon Valley           Dull, Hunter
Sushi, Anyone?                      Gringlesby, O'Leary, Yokomoto
```

It turns out that the cursor isn't necessary. In Listing 8.8, `udf_Titles_AuthorList2` has an alternate implementation that accomplishes the same result. It does this by concatenating each row's `au_lname` to a local variable.

Listing 8.8: `udf_Titles_AuthorList2`, an alternate to `udf_Titles_AuthorList`

```
CREATE FUNCTION dbo.udf_Titles_AuthorList2 (

    @Title_id char(6) -- title ID from pubs database
)   RETURNS varchar(255) -- List of authors
/*
* Returns a comma-separated list of the last name of all
* authors for a title. Illustrates a technique for an aggregate
* concatenation.
*
* Example:
Select Title, dbo.udf_Titles_AuthorList2(title_id) as [Authors]
   FROM pubs..titles ORDER by Title
****************************************************************/
AS BEGIN

DECLARE @lname varchar(40)  -- one last name.
     , @sList varchar(255) -- working list

SET @sList = ''

SELECT @sList = CASE WHEN LEN(@sList) > 0
                     THEN @sList + ', ' + au_lname
                     ELSE au_lname END

    FROM pubs..Authors A
        INNER JOIN pubs..titleAuthor ta
            ON A.au_id = ta.au_id
    WHERE ta.title_ID = @Title_ID
  ORDER BY au_lname

RETURN @sList
END
```

The shaded lines of Listing 8.8 show the key difference from the original function. By concatenating each `au_lname` to the local variable `@sList`, we achieve the same result as using a cursor. With the exception of the "2" at the end of the UDF name, the query to invoke the UDF and the results are the same as those for `udf_Titles_AuthorList`. I won't repeat them.

Although I haven't tested it, my understanding is that because the second query doesn't have a cursor, it's much faster than the version with the cursor. You might have a case where there's enough data where that matters, but for the one to three authors found in most books, you'll never know the difference. Remember, because this UDF is used for display or reporting purposes, you're unlikely to use it on more than a few thousand rows.

Another use of a multistatement UDF to produce a list is the technique of shipping UDFs instead of code tables. This can make the software update process somewhat simpler.

Using UDFs to Replace Code Tables

To retain flexibility, applications are often designed to be "table driven." Instead of writing specific values (also called codes) into the programs, the values come from a table, which is usually referred to as a code table. The table must be maintained as the application evolves. As a new version of the software handles new codes, moving new values into code tables in synchronization with the software distribution is a problem that every designer must solve. It doesn't sound like a hard problem. However, it's a problem that in practice tends to create bugs during version upgrades, and a technique that reduces the incidence of problems is welcome.

If the code table is small enough, distributing the code table as a UDF instead of a real table is one possible solution. For this to work, selecting from the UDF has to return the same results as selecting from the table would. Listing 8.9 has a sample code table for a taxability code.

This UDF could also be implemented as an inline UDF. In that case, the `SELECT` statement with all its `UNION ALL SELECT`s would be the body of the UDF. In this case, the only advantage of the multistatement UDF over the inline alternative is the ability to document the return table more clearly in the function header. Other than that, they're equivalent.

Installation of the UDF would replace any installation code that updated or inserted rows into a physical table. One additional advantage of using the UDF instead of the physical table is that it is more difficult for users who have access to the database to change the UDF than to modify the contents of the table.

Listing 8.9: udf_Tax_TaxabilityCD, a UDF to replace a code table

```
CREATE FUNCTION dbo.udf_Tax_TaxabilityCD (

)   RETURNS @TaxabilityCD TABLE (
          [TaxabilityCD] CHAR(3)-- Code for taxability
        , [Description] varchar(30)-- Short description of the code.
        , Exempt BIT-- 1 if the code implies tax exempt
        , PRIMARY KEY (TaxabilityCD)
                              )
    WITH SCHEMABINDING -- Or comment about why not
/*
* Code table for taxabity of the entity.
*
* Example:
SELECT * FROM dbo.udf_Tax_TaxabilityCD()
****************************************************************/
AS BEGIN

INSERT INTO @TaxabilityCD (TaxabilityCD, [Description], Exempt)
           SELECT 'GMT', 'Government', 1
 UNION ALL SELECT 'CRP', 'Corporate' , 0
 UNION ALL SELECT 'IND', 'Individual', 1
 UNION ALL SELECT 'CHR', 'Charity'   , 0
 UNION ALL SELECT 'UNN', 'Union'     , 0

RETURN
END
```

Summary

Multistatement UDFs are the third and final type of UDF. They're very much like a stored procedure that returns one resultset, with the difference being that they're subject to all the restrictions on UDFs that prevent side effects. Side effects are very common in stored procedures. While they can get you out of a jam, they make the design of the code less understandable and less maintainable.

This chapter has shown several sample UDFs and templates to aid in creating them. These examples are fairly simple. Real-world code may be longer because it has to tackle more complex problems.

Sometimes the complexity leads us to use cursors in our UDFs. Cursors are well supported by SQL Server but can lead to slow-running code. SQL Server is optimized for declarative programming. If you have to resort to cursors, consider moving the code to another layer of the application.

Now that you've seen how to create each type of UDF, the aim of the next chapter is to advance your knowledge of techniques to manage your UDFs. After that, we'll move on to topics like using extended stored procedures and techniques to extend the range of possibilities for what UDFs can do for your application.

9

Metadata about UDFs

Metadata is data about data. This chapter discusses information about user-defined functions—information that SQL Server provides in several different forms. The first place to look is at a few system stored procedures, which are written to provide information about all database objects, including functions. In addition, SQL Server has several ways to give you direct access to metadata in the form of:

- `INFORMATION_SCHEMA` views
- Built-in metadata functions
- System tables

This chapter shows you the best place to look for information about UDFs in each of these sources.

Once the sources of information are defined, the information they provide can be combined into UDFs that reshape the information into formats that are useful to DBAs and programmers. You may want to retrieve the UDF metadata in a different format, but these functions give you a place to start.

There is one more interface available for working with SQL Server metadata: SQL-DMO. SQL-DMO is a Win32 COM library that is not usually used from inside T-SQL. The best way to work with SQL-DMO is from a language that is good at COM automation such as Visual Basic or VB Script. This book is about T-SQL, so there is just a short introduction to SQL-DMO near the end of the chapter.

`sp_help` and many other system stored procedures provide information about all types of database objects. UDFs are no exception. Since the nature of a UDF is different from other database objects, the way the system procedures treat a UDF is also a little different.

As with all the other chapters, the short queries that appear in the chapter have been collected into the file Chapter 9 Listing 0 Short Queries.sql. You can find it in this chapter's download directory.

System Stored Procedures to Help with UDFs

SQL Server has many stored procedures for retrieving information about UDFs. Most of them have been created to serve SQL Server's own tools. This section highlights four of the most important stored procedures that you can use:

- `sp_help` returns basic information about a UDF.
- `sp_helptext` returns the textual definition of a UDF.
- `sp_rename` is supposed to change the name of a UDF, but it doesn't work completely and shouldn't be used.
- `sp_depends` returns dependency information about a UDF.

System stored procedures are only one of the ways to get metadata about UDFs, but they're the ones that are available for use right out of the box.

sp_help

`sp_help` is a system stored procedure that provides a small amount of basic information about any database object, including UDFs. The syntax of the call is:

```
sp_help [ [ @objname] = name ]
```

The name can be the name of any database object. The resultset(s) returned by `sp_help` differ depending on the object type. Each of the three types of UDFs generate different combinations of resultsets. For multistatement UDFs, the number of resultsets depends on whether the UDF has a `ROWGUID` column or an `IDENTITY` column.

`sp_help` works fine for interactive use in Query Analyzer. It gives you most of the basic information about the UDF. However, because of the variable number of resultsets returned by `sp_help`, it's difficult to use its output in a program. This is especially true of report writers, which don't handle a variable number of resultsets well. To get information about UDFs into programs such as report writers, I've created a group of UDFs that return metadata about functions. You'll find them in the section "Metadata UDFs" later in this chapter.

One important resultset that `sp_help` doesn't return is one that describes the parameters of the UDF. Look for `udf_Func_ParmsTAB` in Listing 9.3. It lists the parameters.

sp_help on a Scalar UDF

When run on a scalar UDF, `sp_help` returns only the most basic information. The fields are listed in Table 9.1. The same table is also returned for inline and multistatement UDFs.

Table 9.1: Fields returned by `sp_help`

Column	Data Type	Description
Name	nvarchar(128)	The function's name
Owner	nvarchar(128)	Function owner
Type	nvarchar(31)	Type of object: scalar function, inline function, or table function
Created_datetime	Datetime	Datetime when the function was created. Altering the UDF does not change this column.

A quick example should give you a picture of what's involved:

```
-- sp_help on a scalar UDF
EXEC sp_help udf_Num_LOGN
GO

(Results)

Name           Owner   Type              Created_datetime
-------------- ------- ----------------- -----------------------
udf_Num_LOGN   dbo     scalar function   2003-02-24 10:35:34.987
```

The same table is also returned for inline and multistatement UDFs. The `Type` column for those UDFs says "inline table" or "table function" for multistatement UDFs. Additional recordsets are returned for these types of UDFs.

sp_help on an Inline UDF

In addition to the basic recordset returned for all UDFs that is described in Table 9.1, a second recordset is returned when `sp_help` is invoked on an inline UDF. That recordset has a row for each of the columns that the UDF returns. Table 9.2 describes the columns.

Table 9.2: Columns returned by `sp_help` on an inline UDF

Column	Data Type	Description
Column_name	nvarchar(128)	Column name.
Type	nvarchar(128)	The base data type of the column. For example: int, varchar

Column	Data Type	Description
Computed	varchar(35)	Are the values in the column computed: yes or no. For inline UDFs, this is always no, even if the column is based on an expression. It can be yes for multistatement UDFs.
Length	int	Column length in bytes.
Prec	char(5)	Column precision. Only for numeric data types.
Scale	char(5)	Column scale. Only for numeric data types.
Nullable	varchar(35)	Are NULL values allowed in the column: yes or no. Not applicable to inline UDFs. Multistatement UDF columns can be nullable.
TrimTrailingBlanks	varchar(35)	Trim the trailing blanks (yes or no). Corresponds to the setting of ANSI_PADDING when the function was created.
FixedLenNullInSource	varchar(35)	For backward compatibility only.
Collation	sysname	Collation of the column. NULL for non-character data types.

Let's try it on an existing inline UDF:

```
-- sp_help on an inline UDF
EXEC sp_help udf_Paging_ProductByUnits_Forward
GO

(Results - first recordset)

Name                              Owner  Type            Created...
--------------------------------- ------ --------------- ----------
udf_Paging_ProductByUnits_Forward dbo    inline function 2003-02...

(Results - second recordset - reformatted and truncated on the right)

Column_name  Type     Computed Length Prec Scale Nullable  TrimTraili...
------------ -------- -------- ------ ---- ----- --------- ------------
ProductID    int      no            4 10   0     no        (n/a)
ProductName  nvarchar no           80             no        (n/a)
UnitsInStock smallint no            2 5    0     yes       (n/a)
Total Sold   int      no            4 10   0     yes       (n/a)
CategoryName nvarchar no           30             no        (n/a)
```

The metadata function udf_Func_ColumnsTAB reports similar information. You'll find it in Listing 9.2 in the section on metadata UDFs. That UDF also works on multistatement UDFs. Since it's a UDF, it's much easier to use from a program than the system stored procedures. You'll see why as they're described.

sp_help on Multistatement UDFs

When invoked on a multistatement UDF, sp_help returns the two recordsets described in Tables 9.1 and 9.2. In addition, it returns a recordset that describes the IDENTITY column and one that describes the ROWGUID column. These are returned even if there are no IDENTITY or ROWGUID columns in the UDF's table definition. There isn't anything to add to the Books Online's description of these two recordsets, so you're referred there if you need the details.

Let's try out sp_help on a UDF that has a computed column and an IDENTITY column so we can see what's returned:

```
-- sp_help on a multistatement UDF
EXEC sp_help udf_Example_Multistatement_WithComputedColumn
GO
```

(Results - first resultset - first column wrapped)

```
Name                    Owner   Type            Created_datetime
----------------------- ------- --------------- -----------------------
udf_Example_Multistatem dbo     table function  2003-02-27 09:54:11.860
_WithComputedColumn
```

(Results - second resultset reformatted and truncated on the right)

```
Column_name Type Computed Length Prec  Scale Nullable TrimTraili...
----------- ---- -------- ------ ----- ----- -------- -----------
ID          int  no            4 10    0     no       (n/a)
Num         int  no            4 10    0     yes      (n/a)
PRODUCT     int  yes           4 10    0     yes      (n/a)
```

(Results - third resultset)

```
Identity      Seed       Increment      Not For Replication
------------- ---------- -------------- -------------------
ID            NULL       NULL                             0
```

(Results - fourth resultset)

```
RowGuidCol
-----------------------------------------------------------------
No rowguidcol column defined.
```

I find that I use sp_help only on rare occasions. Of course, the SQL Server tools, such as Enterprise Manager, use it when they retrieve the information that they show to you.

An item that sp_help doesn't return is the text that defines the UDF. The SQL Server tools retrieve the function definition using sp_helptext. You can also retrieve it directly from syscomments if you join with sysobjects.

sp_helptext

sp_helptext retrieves the textual definition of many types of database objects including UDFs. The syntax of the call is:

```
sp_helptext [ @objname = ] 'name'
```

It's pretty simple to use:

```
-- sp_helptext on udf_Num_LOGN
EXEC sp_helptext udf_Num_LOGN
GO

(Results)

Text
------------------------------------------------------------------------



CREATE  FUNCTION dbo. udf_Num_LOGN(

    @n    float -- Number to take the log of
  , @Base float -- Base of the logarithm, 10, 2, 3.74
)   RETURNS float -- Logarithm (base @base) of @n
    WITH SCHEMABINDING
/*
* The logarithm to the base @Base of @n. Returns NULL for any
* invalid input instead of raising an error.
*
* Example:
SELECT dbo. udf_Num_LOGN(1000, 10), dbo. udf_Num_LOGN(64, 4)
     , dbo. udf_Num_LOGN(0, 3), dbo. udf_Num_LOGN(3, 0)
****************************************************************/
AS BEGIN

    IF @n IS NULL OR @n <= 0 OR
       @Base IS NULL OR @Base <= 0 OR @Base = 1
           RETURN NULL

    RETURN LOG(@n) / LOG(@Base)
END
```

When using sp_helptext from Query Analyzer, be sure that you've set the Maximum characters per column field on the Results tab of the Options dialog to a size that's longer than your longest line of text. Otherwise, the text is truncated on the right.

If this happens to you, use the Tools ➢ Options menu command, select the Results tab, and set Maximum characters per line to 8192. That's the largest number the field allows.

Another way to get the function definition is by querying the ROUTINE_DEFINITION column in INFORMATION_SCHEMA.ROUTINES. There's more about using INFORMATION_SCHEMA in this chapter's "Retrieving Metadata about UDFs" section.

sp_rename

For most object types, sp_rename is used to change the name of SQL objects. *sp_rename does not work for user-defined functions!* There's a bug in the implementation, and you should not use it to change the name of a UDF. Instead, you must drop the old UDF and create a new one.

This can be demonstrated with a pretty simple script that creates a UDF, renames it, and then retrieves the text:

```
-- sp_rename doesn't work
IF EXISTS (select * from dbo.sysobjects
             WHERE id = object_id(N'[dbo].[udf_Test_RenamedToNewName]')
                 AND xtype in (N'FN', N'IF', N'TF')) BEGIN
     DROP FUNCTION [dbo].[udf_Test_RenamedToNewName]
END
IF EXISTS (select *
             FROM dbo.sysobjects
             WHERE id = object_id(N'[dbo].[udf_Test_RenameMe]')
                 AND xtype in (N'FN', N'IF', N'TF')) BEGIN
     DROP FUNCTION [dbo].[udf_Test_RenameMe]
END
GO

CREATE FUNCTION dbo.udf_Test_RenameMe () returns int as begin return 1 end
GO
PRINT 'New udf_Test_RenameMe CREATEd.'
GO
EXEC sp_rename 'udf_Test_RenameMe', 'udf_Test_RenamedToNewName'
GO
EXEC sp_helptext 'udf_Test_RenamedToNewName'
GO
```

(Results from the last batch only)

```
Text
-------------------------------------------------------------------------
CREATE FUNCTION dbo.udf_Test_RenameMe () returns int as begin return 1 end
```

What happens is that although an object is created with the new name and the row in sysobjects is changed, the CREATE FUNCTION script in syscomments is not changed. However, the renamed UDF works. Unfortunately, if the database is ever converted to a script, the old name will remain in the database and any code that invokes the UDF under the new name doesn't compile because the UDF is recreated using the old name. That's the bug. If you try to edit the newly renamed UDF using Enterprise Manager, you'll also run into the original script. If you're not careful, you'll recreate the UDF under its original name.

When analyzing the impact of changes to UDFs, you sometimes want to know which database objects reference a UDF and which ones are referenced by it. That information is available from the system stored procedure sp_depends.

sp_depends

sp_depends returns information about the database objects referenced by a UDF and the database objects that reference the UDF in separate resultsets. Both sets of information can be useful. Here's a simple script that retrieves dependency information for udf_Order_Amount, which was created back in Chapter 2. Note that NWOrderDetails is a table in TSQLUDFS:

```
-- What depends on udf_Order_Amount
EXEC sp_depends udf_Order_Amount
GO

(Results)

In the current database, the specified object references the following:
Name                 Type             Updated Selected Column
-------------------- ---------------- ------- -------- ----------
dbo.NWOrderDetails   user table       no      no       OrderID
dbo.NWOrderDetails   user table       no      no       UnitPrice
dbo.NWOrderDetails   user table       no      no       Quantity

In the current database, the specified object is referenced by the following:
Name                         Type
---------------------------- -----------------------------------
dbo.DEBUG_udf_Order_Amount    stored procedure
```

The two resultsets are returned only when they have rows. If neither resultset has any rows, only a message is returned. If you're trying to work with the results from sp_depends in a program, it could get a little tricky.

Notice that the results include the column Updated, which is always "no" when sp_depends is used on a UDF. The Selected column is only "yes" when the column is in the select list. udf_Order_Amount uses the columns shown in the query results in expressions or in the WHERE clause; they aren't directly used in the select list. That's why they're all "no."

Some limitations of sp_depends are:

- References outside the current database are not reported.
- References to system tables are not reported.
- References to INFORMATION_SCHEMA views are not reported.

You'll have to work within these limitations of sp_depends.

The system stored procedures that have been discussed in this section are adequate for many tasks but not always so easy to work with. There are other ways to get metadata about UDFs. One way is to write UDFs that query data from the system tables. The next section discusses the best ways to get at that data.

Retrieving Metadata about UDFs

SQL Server stores metadata about all database objects in its system tables, the ones that begin with "sys" and occur in every database. UDFs are no different. But your best bet for getting information about UDFs from within T-SQL comes from the INFORMATION_SCHEMA views that are derived from the system tables. Sometimes all the information you want isn't available from INFORMATION_SCHEMA and you have to turn to the built-in metadata functions or the system tables.

This section starts with a discussion of the INFORMATION_SCHEMA views that have information relevant to UDFs: ROUTINES, ROUTINE_COLUMNS, and PARAMETERS. These views should be the first place to look for information about UDFs and other database objects.

When information isn't available in INFORMATION_SCHEMA, it may be found in one of two built-in system metadata functions, OBJECTPROPERTY and COLUMNPROPERTY. These functions let you query information one property at a time. They expose several properties that can't be found in INFORMATION_SCHEMA.

When the first two sources of information don't have what you're looking for, the last place to look is the system tables. System tables should be used with some degree of caution if only because they are subject to change when new SQL versions come out or even when new service packs are released. For example, SQL Server 2000 Service Pack 3 introduced new columns in at least one system table.

Each of the three sources of information is examined in a short section that follows. Most of this chapter's UDFs to retrieve metadata about functions draw on more than one of these sources so we'll put off building any UDFs until we've seen all three. INFORMATION_SCHEMA is the first of the information sources to examine.

Finding out about UDFs in INFORMATION_SCHEMA

There are 20 views owned by the special user INFORMATION_SCHEMA. These views are defined in the SQL Standard, and you'll find an identical set of views in Oracle and other relational database management system (RDBMS) products. Being based on a standard is both a blessing and a curse. The advantage is that any queries that are based on INFORMATION_SCHEMA are portable to other RDBMSs. The disadvantage is that information about features that are specific to SQL Server doesn't appear in any of the views.

Of the 20 views, these three have the most important information about UDFs:

- ROUTINES
- ROUTINE_COLUMNS
- PARAMETERS

There is also a smattering of information in CONSTRAINT_TABLE_USAGE and KEY_COLUMN_USAGE. Those details are only present when a multistatement UDF returns a table that has a primary key, CHECK constraint, or other constraint.

The Books Online has the standard information about each of the views, including a summary of the columns that are returned by each view, so it isn't worth repeating here. The sections that follow about the individual routines concentrate on the aspects of each view that's most relevant to UDFs.

INFORMATION_SCHEMA.ROUTINES

INFORMATION_SCHEMA.ROUTINES has information for both stored procedures and UDFs. Use the ROUTINE_TYPE column to distinguish between the two. It equals 'FUNCTION' for all three types of UDF.

Unfortunately, nothing in ROUTINES tells you which type of UDF it is, so you have to rely on other sources for that information. There is a DATA_TYPE column that helps. For scalar UDFs, it gives the base type that is returned. For inline and multistatement UDFs, it is 'TABLE'.

Here's a quick look at a few fields from ROUTINES:

```
-- The basics from INFORMATION_SCHEMA.ROUTINES
SELECT TOP 7
       ROUTINE_NAME, DATA_TYPE, IS_DETERMINISTIC, SQL_DATA_ACCESS
    FROM INFORMATION_SCHEMA.ROUTINES
    WHERE ROUTINE_TYPE = 'FUNCTION'
    ORDER BY ROUTINE_NAME
GO
```

(Results)

```
ROUTINE_NAME             DATA_TYPE      IS_DETERMINISTIC SQL_DATA_ACCESS
------------------------ -------------- ---------------- ---------------
udf_DT_2Julian           int            YES              READS
udf_DT_Age               int            NO               READS
udf_DT_CurrTime          char           NO               READS
udf_DT_dynamicDATEPART   int            NO               READS
udf_DT_FromYMD           smalldatetime  YES              READS
udf_DT_MonthsTAB         TABLE          NO               READS
udf_DT_NthDayInMon       smalldatetime  NO               READS
```

Functions may have been added to TSQLUDFS by the time you read this, so you may see different results.

When I first saw the SQL_DATA_ACCESS column, I hoped that it would help distinguish UDFs that read from the database from UDFs that have no data access. It turns out that in SQL Server 2000, the SQL_DATA_ACCESS column is always 'READS' for all UDFs.

INFORMATION_SCHEMA.ROUTINE_COLUMNS

ROUTINE_COLUMNS has one row for each column returned by either an inline or a multistatement UDF. This script uses it to show the columns returned by udf_DT_MonthsTAB:

```
-- Column information for udf_DT_MonthsTAB
SELECT TABLE_NAME, COLUMN_NAME, ORDINAL_POSITION, DATA_TYPE
    FROM INFORMATION_SCHEMA.ROUTINE_COLUMNS
    WHERE TABLE_NAME= 'udf_DT_MonthsTAB'
GO
```

(Results)

```
TABLE_NAME        COLUMN_NAME      ORDINAL_POSITION DATA_TYPE
----------------- ---------------- ---------------- ------------
udf_DT_MonthsTAB  Year                            1 smallint
udf_DT_MonthsTAB  Month                           2 smallint
udf_DT_MonthsTAB  Name                            3 varchar
udf_DT_MonthsTAB  Mon                             4 char
udf_DT_MonthsTAB  StartDT                         5 datetime
udf_DT_MonthsTAB  EndDT                           6 datetime
udf_DT_MonthsTAB  End_SOD_DT                      7 datetime
udf_DT_MonthsTAB  StartJulian                     8 int
udf_DT_MonthsTAB  EndJulian                       9 int
udf_DT_MonthsTAB  NextMonStartDT                 10 datetime
```

ROUTINE_COLUMNS is the basis for the udf_Func_ColumnsTAB function that's in the "Metadata UDFs" section.

INFORMATION_SCHEMA.PARAMETERS

INFORMATION_SCHEMA.PARAMETERS has parameters for functions as well as stored procedures. There is one entry for each parameter. For scalar UDFs, there is a row for the result of the function that has an ORDINAL_POSITION of 0. This script shows the parameters for udf_DT_Age, which is scalar:

```
-- parameters, including the result for udf_DT_Age
SELECT SPECIFIC_NAME, ORDINAL_POSITION, PARAMETER_NAME
     , DATA_TYPE, PARAMETER_MODE, IS_RESULT
    FROM INFORMATION_SCHEMA.PARAMETERS
    WHERE SPECIFIC_NAME = 'udf_DT_Age'
GO
```

```
(Results)

Name       Position Parm Name     DATA_TYPE Mode       IS_RESULT
---------- -------- ------------- --------- ---------- ----------
udf_DT_Age        0               int       OUT        YES
udf_DT_Age        1 @DateOfBirth  datetime  IN         NO
udf_DT_Age        2 @AsOfDate     datetime  IN         NO
```

That's the last of the INFORMATION_SCHEMA views that has important information about UDFs. The next information sources are two built-in functions that give information about many object types, UDFs included.

Built-in Metadata Functions

SQL Server 2000 offers a couple dozen built-in metadata functions. The ones that are relevant to UDFs are:

- OBJECT_ID
- OBJECTPROPERTY
- COLUMNPROPERTY
- PERMISSIONS

OBJECT_ID is needed to convert a UDF's name to an ID. The ID is the key to the sysobjects system table. The OBJECT_ID function can be used in metadata queries instead of joining with the sysobjects table.

Both OBJECTPROPERTY and COLUMNPROPERTY return a large number of properties; many of them are relevant to UDFs. These two queries give you a taste of what's available from these functions:

```
-- try OBJECTPROPERTY
DECLARE @Func_ID int
SET @Func_ID = OBJECT_ID ('udf_DT_MonthsTAB')
SELECT OBJECTPROPERTY(@Func_ID, 'IsQuotedIdentOn') as IsQuotedIdentOn
     , OBJECTPROPERTY(@Func_ID, 'IsTableFunction') as IsTable
     , OBJECTPROPERTY(@Func_ID, 'IsScalarFunction') as IsScalar
GO

(Results)

IsQuotedIdentOn IsTable     IsScalar
--------------- ----------- -----------
NULL                      1           0

-- try COLUMNPROPERTY
DECLARE @Func_ID int
SET @Func_ID = OBJECT_ID ('udf_Example_Multistatement_WithComputedColumn')
SELECT COLUMN_NAME
     , COLUMNPROPERTY (@Func_ID, COLUMN_NAME
                , 'IsComputed') as [IsComputed]
     , COLUMNPROPERTY (@Func_ID, COLUMN_NAME
                , 'IsPrimaryKey') as [IsPrimaryKey]
    FROM INFORMATION_SCHEMA.ROUTINE_COLUMNS
    WHERE TABLE_NAME = 'udf_Example_Multistatement_WithComputedColumn'
    ORDER BY ORDINAL_POSITION
GO
```

(Results)

```
COLUMN_NAME  IsComputed  IsPrimaryKey
------------ ----------- ------------
ID                     0 NULL
Num                    0 NULL
PRODUCT                1 NULL
```

Books Online has the complete list of properties that the built-in metadata functions can return. But the previous queries illustrate one of the limitations of these functions: They don't always report the expected information when working with UDFs. For example, `IsPrimaryKey` should be 1 or 0 for all columns, but it returns `NULL`. `IsQuotedIdentOn` should also be reported as 1 or 0 but returns `NULL`. I've listed these as bugs in Appendix C.

`PERMISSIONS` summarizes information that is stored in the `syspermissions` and `sysprotects` system tables. By using `PERMISSIONS` it is possible to check whether the current user has permissions to execute a particular UDF. This query checks to see if the current user can run `udf_Order_Amount`:

```
-- Check permission to execute udf_Order_Amount
SELECT CASE WHEN 0x20 = PERMISSIONS (OBJECT_ID('udf_Order_Amount')) & 0x20
            THEN 'Can execute' ELSE 'Can''t execute' END
      + ' udf_Order_Amount'
GO
```

(Results)

```
Can execute udf_Order_Amount
```

The built-in metadata functions should remain the same as new versions of SQL Server are released. That makes using them preferable to interrogating the system tables. However, sometimes the system tables are the only place to get the answer you want.

Information about UDFs in System Tables

SQL Server stores all its information about database objects in system tables within the database. This information is used by:

- System stored procedures like `sp_help` and `sp_depends`
- `INFORMATION_SCHEMA` views
- Built-in metadata functions such as `OBJECTPROPERTY`
- Some metadata UDFs (as described in the next section)

Books Online has the details of the system tables and a complete list of their columns. Table 9.3 lists system tables with the information most important to UDFs.

Table 9.3: Important systems tables

System Table	Information about UDFs
`sysobjects`	One row for all database objects including each UDF.
`syscolumns`	An entry for every column returned and every parameter.
`sysdepends`	Rows for references by UDF and references to the UDF.
`sysconstraints`	Only used when multistatement UDFs have constraints on their table.
`syscomments`	The `CREATE FUNCTION` script is stored here.
`syspermissions`	Permissions granted on database objects including UDFs.
`sysprotects`	Grants and denies to UDFs and other objects.

Every database object such as a table, view, stored procedure, or UDF has an entry in `sysobjects`. Every object has a unique ID and a unique name. The `sysobjects.type` column differentiates between the different object types. The codes for the three different object types for UDFs are given in Table 9.4.

Table 9.4: Object type codes in `sysobjects` for UDFs

Type	Type of UDF
FN	Scalar
IF	Inline
TF	Multistatement

Now that the sources of metadata have been defined, the next section is devoted to creating some functions to package the information in the most useful ways. Some of the functions that follow use the system tables but only when the information isn't available in either `INFORMATION_SCHEMA` or a built-in system function.

Metadata UDFs

This section explores some of the most useful functions that I've created for packaging metadata about UDFs. The functions here gather their information from the sources described in the previous section.

I group metadata functions about UDFs under the group prefix "udf_Func_." You'll also find more general-purpose metadata UDFs in the "udf_Object_" group.

Creating and Using UDFs

Function Information

Listing 9.1 shows udf_Func_InfoTAB, which returns a table of information about all functions in a database. You might also want to take a look at two related functions in the TSQLUDFS database that are not listed here: udf_Func_Type and udf_Func_COUNT.

Listing 9.1: udf_Func_InfoTAB

```
CREATE   FUNCTION dbo.udf_Func_InfoTAB (

   @function_name_pattern nvarchar(128) = NULL -- NULL for all
    -- or a pattern that works with the LIKE operator
)  RETURNS TABLE -- Information about the function or functions.
/*
* Returns a table of information about all functions in the
* database. Based on INFORMATION_SCHEMA.ROUTINES and on
* OBJECTPROPERTIES.
*
* Example:
select * from udf_Func_InfoTAB(default) -- gets info on all
select * from udf_Func_InfoTAB('%SQL%')
****************************************************************/
AS RETURN
SELECT TOP 100 PERCENT -- So an Order by clause can be used.
       ROUTINE_SCHEMA AS [Owner]  -- The Owner name
     , ROUTINE_NAME AS [FunctionName] -- The function name
     , dbo.udf_SQL_DataTypeString (Data_Type
                 , Character_Maximum_Length
                 , Numeric_Precision, Numeric_Scale) as [DataType]
     , CASE WHEN 1=OBJECTPROPERTY(OBJECT_ID (ROUTINE_NAME)
                 , 'IsScalarFunction') THEN 'SCALAR'
            WHEN 1=OBJECTPROPERTY(OBJECT_ID (ROUTINE_NAME)
                 , 'IsTableFunction') THEN 'TABLE'
            WHEN 1=OBJECTPROPERTY(OBJECT_ID (ROUTINE_NAME)
                 , 'IsInlineFunction')  THEN 'INLINE'
            ELSE 'UNKNOWN' END as [TYPE]
     , IS_DETERMINISTIC   as IsDeterministic
     , OBJECTPROPERTY(OBJECT_ID (ROUTINE_NAME)
          , 'IsSchemaBound')    as IsSchemaBound
     , OBJECTPROPERTY(OBJECT_ID (ROUTINE_NAME)
          , 'IsQuotedIdentOn')    as IsQuotedIdentOn
     , OBJECTPROPERTY(OBJECT_ID (ROUTINE_NAME)
          , 'IsAnsiNullsOn')    as IsAnsiNullsOn
     , CREATED -- Date function is created
        -- , LAST_ALTERED Don't report. It's always the
              -- same as CREATED
      FROM INFORMATION_SCHEMA.ROUTINES
      WHERE ROUTINE_TYPE='FUNCTION'
          AND (@function_name_pattern is NULL
               OR ROUTINE_NAME LIKE @function_name_pattern)
      ORDER BY [FunctionName]
```

The function's parameter, @Function_Name_Pattern, is a LIKE expression used to match the function name and limit the list of functions that are returned. Using default or NULL for the parameter requests information on all functions. The caller is expected to put in any wildcard matching characters for the LIKE expression. That way, the caller has full control to request information about a single UDF or multiple UDFs. A naming convention like the one used for functions in this book makes this type of pattern search very convenient.

The UDFs in the udf_Func group can be listed with this query:

```
-- Functions in the Func group
SELECT FunctionName, DataType, Type, IsDeterministic
    FROM udf_Func_InfoTAB ('udf_Func_%')
GO

(Results – You may see any some additional functions in your results)

FunctionName                 DataType    Type    IsDeterministic
---------------------------- ----------- ------- ---------------
udf_Func_BadUserOptionsTAB   TABLE       INLINE  NO
udf_Func_ColumnsTAB          TABLE       INLINE  NO
udf_Func_COUNT               int         SCALAR  NO
udf_Func_InfoTAB             TABLE       INLINE  NO
udf_Func_Type                varchar(9)  SCALAR  NO
```

The query shows a couple of other interesting UDFs that are investigated next.

What Are the Columns Returned by a UDF?

udf_Func_ColumnsTAB returns a row for each column returned by the UDF or UDFs requested by the function name pattern. Listing 9.2 shows the CREATE FUNCTION script for udf_Func_ColumnsTAB:

Listing 9.2: udf_Func_ColumnsTAB, a function to list a UDF's columns

```
CREATE FUNCTION dbo.udf_Func_ColumnsTAB (

    @Function_Name_pattern as nvarchar(128) = NULL -- NULL for All
            -- or LIKE pattern on the name of the function.
)   RETURNS TABLE
/*
* Returns a TABLE of information about the columns returned by a
* function. Works on both inline and multiline UDFs.
*
* Example:
SELECT * FROM udf_Func_ColumnsTAB (default) -- All functions
SELECT * FROM udf_Func_ColumnsTAB ('udf_Func_ColumnsTAB') -- me
****************************************************************/
AS RETURN

SELECT TOP 100 PERCENT WITH TIES
       TABLE_NAME                                  as [Function]
     , COLUMN_NAME                                 as Column_Name
     , ORDINAL_POSITION                            as [Position]
     , COLUMNPROPERTY(OBJECT_ID(c.TABLE_NAME)
```

```
                , COLUMN_NAME, 'IsComputed') as [IsComputed]
    , dbo.udf_SQL_DataTypeString (DATA_TYPE
                , CHARACTER_MAXIMUM_LENGTH
            , NUMERIC_PRECISION,  NUMERIC_SCALE) as [DataType]
    , DATA_TYPE                              as BaseType
    , CHARACTER_MAXIMUM_LENGTH               as [Character_Maximum_Length]
    , NUMERIC_PRECISION                      as Numeric_Precision
    , NUMERIC_SCALE                          as Numeric_Scale
    , COLUMNPROPERTY(OBJECT_ID(c.TABLE_NAME)
               , COLUMN_NAME, 'AllowsNull')   as [Nullable]
    , COLUMNPROPERTY(OBJECT_ID(c.TABLE_NAME)
               , COLUMN_NAME, 'IsRowGUIDCol') as [IsRowGUIDCol]
  FROM
      INFORMATION_SCHEMA.ROUTINE_COLUMNS c
  WHERE (@Function_Name_pattern is NULL
        OR TABLE_NAME LIKE @Function_Name_pattern)
  ORDER BY TABLE_NAME
        , ORDINAL_POSITION
```

The fact that the parameter is a pattern that works with `LIKE` allows you to request information for one or more UDFs in one query. That might be useful when searching for particular column names. To get the columns for one function, supply the UDF name without any wildcards, as in this query that documents the columns returned by `udf_Func_ColumnsTAB`:

```
-- Columns returned by udf_Func_ColumnsTAB
SELECT Column_Name, Position, DataType, Nullable
   FROM udf_Func_ColumnsTAB ('udf_Func_ColumnsTAB')
GO

(Results)

Column_Name                 Position DataType       Nullable
--------------------------- -------- -------------- -----------
Function                           1 nvarchar(128)            0
Column_Name                        2 nvarchar(128)            0
Position                           3 smallint                 0
IsComputed                         4 int                      1
DataType                           5 nvarchar(128)            1
BaseType                           6 nvarchar(128)            1
Character_Maximum_Length           7 int                      1
Numeric_Precision                  8 tinyint                  0
Numeric_Scale                      9 int                      1
Nullable                          10 int                      1
IsRowGUIDCol                      11 int                      1
```

A very similar set of information is retrievable for parameters to the function. The next section has a UDF that does just that.

What Are the Parameters Used When Invoking a UDF?

You can't call any UDF without supplying all the parameters, so it's important to know what they are. Listing 9.3 shows udf_Func_ParmsTAB, which lists a function's parameters. SQL Server doesn't have a place to store a description for the parameter. That makes it important that they use descriptive names.

Listing 9.3: Listing a function's parameters with udf_Func_ParmsTAB

```
CREATE FUNCTION dbo.udf_Func_ParmsTAB (

    @Function_Name_pattern as nvarchar(128) = NULL -- NULL for All
              -- or LIKE pattern on the name of the function.
)   RETURNS TABLE
/*
* Returns a TABLE of information about the parameters used to
* call any type of UDF. This includes the return type which
* is in Position=0.
*
* Example:
SELECT * FROM udf_Func_ParmsTAB (default) -- All functions
SELECT * FROM udf_Func_ParmsTAB ('udf_Func_ParmsTAB') -- me
****************************************************************/
AS RETURN

SELECT TOP 100 PERCENT WITH TIES
       ROUTINE_NAME                               as [Function]
     , CASE WHEN P.ORDINAL_POSITION = 0
            THEN 'RETURNS' ELSE PARAMETER_NAME END as [Parameter]
     , P.ORDINAL_POSITION                         as [Position]
     , P.PARAMETER_MODE                           AS [Mode]
     , IS_RESULT                                  AS IsResult
     , dbo.udf_SQL_DataTypeString (P.DATA_TYPE
                  , P.CHARACTER_MAXIMUM_LENGTH
          , P.NUMERIC_PRECISION,  P.NUMERIC_SCALE) as [DataType]
     , P.DATA_TYPE                                   as BaseType
     , P.CHARACTER_MAXIMUM_LENGTH   as [Character_Maximum_Length]
     , P.NUMERIC_PRECISION                        as Numeric_Precision
     , P.NUMERIC_SCALE                            as Numeric_Scale
    FROM INFORMATION_SCHEMA.ROUTINES R
        INNER JOIN INFORMATION_SCHEMA.PARAMETERS p
            ON R.SPECIFIC_SCHEMA = P.SPECIFIC_SCHEMA
               AND R.SPECIFIC_NAME = P.SPECIFIC_NAME
    WHERE R.ROUTINE_TYPE = 'FUNCTION'
       AND (@Function_Name_pattern is NULL
            OR ROUTINE_NAME LIKE @Function_Name_pattern)
    ORDER BY ROUTINE_NAME, ORDINAL_POSITION
```

INFORMATION_SCHEMA.PARAMETERS has a row for the return type, and I've left it in the results. It can always be filtered out of the results by adding a POSITION!=0 expression in the WHERE clause to any query that doesn't need the return type.

In keeping with the pattern of self reporting, this query gets the list of parameters to all the udf_Func group functions:

```
-- Parameters to all Func group functions
SELECT [Function], Parameter, Position, Mode, DataType
    FROM udf_Func_ParmsTAB ('udf_Func%')
GO

(Results)

Function            Parameter              Position Mode DataType
------------------- ---------------------- -------- ---- -------------
udf_Func_ColumnsTAB @Function_Name_pattern        1 IN   nvarchar(128)
udf_Func_COUNT      RETURNS                       0 OUT  int
udf_Func_COUNT      @function_name_pattern        1 IN   nvarchar(128)
udf_Func_InfoTAB    @function_name_pattern        1 IN   nvarchar(128)
udf_Func_ParmsTAB   @Function_Name_pattern        1 IN   nvarchar(128)
udf_Func_Type       RETURNS                       0 OUT  varchar(9)
udf_Func_Type       @FunctionName                 1 IN   nvarchar(128)
```

As you can see, most of these functions take the same `@Function_name_pattern` parameter. Any multistatement or inline UDF that doesn't have any parameters won't show up in the results.

That's the last of the functions that is specific to UDFs. The next section discusses a couple of functions that work on all objects.

Metadata Functions that Work on All Objects

The functions `udf_Object_Size` and `udf_Object_SearchTAB` both work on the `syscomments` system table. The scripts to create many types of objects, UDFs included, are stored in `syscomments`. In the case of UDFs, that's the `CREATE FUNCTION` script. It is possible for the script to be larger than the `syscomments.text (nvarchar(4000))` field. When that happens, multiple records are used for the object. Table 9.5 lists the object types that have entries in `syscomments`. The type code is the `sysobjects.type` field for the object.

Table 9.5: Object types that have entries in `syscomments`

Type Code	Type Name
C	CHECK constraint
D	DEFAULT constraint
FN	Scalar function
IF	Inline function
P	Stored procedure
R	Rules
TF	Multiline function (table valued)
TR	Trigger
V	View

udf_Object_Size returns the number of bytes taken up by the textual definition of the object by summing the DATALENGTH of the text field for all rows used for the object. It's not listed here, but you can get the definition from the TSQLUDFS database.

Listing 9.4 shows udf_Object_SearchTAB, which is used to search the text of syscomments for a character string. It can be used for all objects in the database or for only objects of a particular type. The @Just4Type parameter is either one of the entries in Table 9.5, NULL for all types, or 'F' for any type of UDF.

Listing 9.4: udf_Object_SearchTAB

```
CREATE   FUNCTION udf_Object_SearchTAB (

    @SearchFor sysname = NULL -- String to search for
  , @Just4Type varchar(2) = NULL -- Object type to search
        -- NULL for all, or
        -- F  = Any function
        -- C  = CHECK constraint
        -- D  = Default or DEFAULT constraint
        -- FN = Scalar function
        -- IF = Inline table function
        -- P  = Stored procedure
        -- R  = Rule
        -- TF = Table function
        -- TR = Trigger
        -- V  = View

) RETURNS TABLE
/*
* Searches the text of SQL objects for the string @SearchFor.
* Returns the object type and name as a table.
*
* Example:
SELECT * from udf_Object_SearchTAB('xp_cmdshell', NULL)
****************************************************************/
AS RETURN

SELECT TOP 100 PERCENT WITH TIES -- TOP clause makes Order by OK
       CASE xtype WHEN 'C'  THEN 'Check Constraint'
                  WHEN 'D'  THEN 'DEFAULT Constraint'
                  WHEN 'FN' THEN 'Function/Scalar'
                  WHEN 'IF' THEN 'Function/Inline'
                  WHEN 'P'  THEN 'Stored Procedure'
                  WHEN 'R'  THEN 'Rule'
                  WHEN 'TF' THEN 'Function/Table'
                  WHEN 'TR' THEN 'Trigger'
                  WHEN 'V'  THEN 'View'
                  ELSE 'Unknown'
                  END as [Object Type]
     , OBJECT_NAME(o.[id]) as [Name]
    FROM syscomments c
        INNER JOIN sysobjects o
            ON c.[id] = o.[id]
    WHERE (@Just4Type IS NULL
             OR (o.xtype = @Just4Type
```

```
                AND o.status >= 0)
          OR (@Just4Type = 'F' -- F works for all functions
                AND o.xtype in ('FN', 'TF', 'IF')
                AND o.status >= 0)
        )
       AND [text] LIKE '%'+@SearchFor+'%'
 GROUP BY xtype, o.[id]
 ORDER BY CASE xtype WHEN 'C'  THEN 'Check Constraint'
               WHEN 'D'  THEN 'DEFAULT Constraint'
               WHEN 'FN' THEN 'Function/Scalar'
               WHEN 'IF' THEN 'Function/Inline'
               WHEN 'P'  THEN 'Stored Procedure'
               WHEN 'R'  THEN 'Rule'
               WHEN 'TF' THEN 'Function/Table'
               WHEN 'TR' THEN 'Trigger'
               WHEN 'V'  THEN 'View'
               ELSE 'Unknown'
               END          , OBJECT_NAME(o.[id])
```

Here's a query that searches for all functions that have a reference to objects in the master database:

```
-- Find all functions that might reference the master database
SELECT * from udf_Object_SearchTAB('master.', 'F')
GO

(Result)

Object Type        Name
------------------ -------------------------------
Function/Inline    udf_SQL_InstanceSummaryTAB
Function/Inline    udf_SQL_UserMessagesTAB
Function/Scalar    udf_Example_User_Event_Attempt
Function/Scalar    udf_SQL_LogMsgBIT
Function/Scalar    udf_SQL_StartDT
```

Of course, this is a text search, and any function or other object that contained the sentence "A dog will always listen to its master" also shows up in the results. Text search is not a perfect technique, but it's often the fastest way to find references to objects.

That's the last of the functions for this chapter. The TSQLUDFS database has other metadata functions that work on other types of database objects, such as tables, views, and stored procedures.

Throughout the book we've been using T-SQL to do all our work with functions. Sometimes working in a compiled language makes the job of coding a solution much easier. SQL-DMO is a COM library that facilitates working with SQL Server objects including UDFs.

SQL-DMO

SQL-DMO is a Win32 COM interface to SQL Server objects. The objects can be used either from compiled programs written in C++, Visual Basic, or any .NET language or from a scripting language such as VBScript. Scripting languages are available in SQL Server's DTS, in ASP pages, and in VBS files executed by Windows Scripting Host.

Enterprise Manager does all its work through SQL-DMO, so you know it has to be pretty complete. A related COM library that is also used by Enterprise Manager is the SQL Namespace library or SQL-NS. This library has the dialog boxes and other user interface elements from Enterprise Manager.

If you want to base any programs on these COM libraries, check on licensing issues. As far as I know SQL-DMO is redistributable with any of your applications, but SQL-NS requires a SQL Server client access license to use at run time, so I don't think that it's okay to distribute it.

An explanation of how to use SQL-DMO to work with UDFs is beyond the scope of this book. However, I thought that I would bring it to your attention because of the robustness of its interface, and the ease of working with COM objects make SQL-DMO a logical choice when trying to program code to manipulate SQL Server objects.

Summary

SQL Server offers a variety of ways to retrieve information about UDFs. This chapter has discussed these possibilities:

- System stored procedures such as `sp_help`, `sp_depends`, and `sp_helptext`
- Querying `INFORMATION_SCHEMA` views
- From built-in metadata functions `OBJECTPROPERTY` and `COLUMNPROPERTY`
- Directly from system tables
- Through SQL-DOM's COM interface

All of these methods have their own advantages and disadvantages. You'll have to match the method to your needs.

Along the way, several functions that package information about UDFs into convenient forms were created. The UDFs package the information in a form that's easy to use in a program, another SQL statement, or a report writer. That's their advantage. Now that you know where to look for the information, you can write your own functions to retrieve the information the way that you want to see it.

10

Using Extended Stored Procedures in UDFs

Extended stored procedures (xp_s) are functions written in C/C++ or another language can create a DLL to use a specific interface that SQL Server supports, named ODS. The names of most extended stored procedures begin with the characters X and P, followed by an underscore. Hence, they are often referred to as xp_s. As we'll see shortly, the xp_ prefix is a convention that even Microsoft breaks; it's not a rule. xp_s reside in DLL files.

SQL Server invokes extended stored procedures in the SQL Server database engine's process. This is the heart of SQL Server. Any untrapped errors in an xp_ can destabilize SQL Server. They shouldn't be created without careful testing. But because of the direct nature of the ODS call interface, xp_s can be very fast. Plus, they have access to resources, such as disk files, network interfaces, and devices that are inaccessible from T-SQL. They can participate in the current connection or open a new one, giving them a great deal of flexibility.

I won't describe how to write your own extended stored procedures. If you're interested, I suggest that you take a look at Books Online and the examples provided with SQL Server. If you'd like to read more, the best explanation of how to create extended stored procedures that I've read is in Ken Henderson's book *The Guru's Guide to SQL Server Stored Procedures, XML and HTML* (Addison-Wesley, 2002).

xp_s can't be created with standard Visual Basic 6.0 because VB can't export functions in the conventional Windows sense. Functions and object interfaces exported by VB are exported through COM. As a programmer who's used Visual Basic intensely for the last six years, I find this somewhat disappointing. However, there's another way: The sp_OA* procedures allow the T-SQL programmer to create and manipulate COM objects through the standard OLE automation interface. This technique is covered extensively in this chapter.

Before getting to OLE, let's start by taking a look at which xp_s are candidates for use within UDFs and which ones cannot be used in a UDF. We'll turn a couple of them into useful UDFs.

Which xp_s Can Be Used in a UDF?

You may recall that UDFs aren't supposed to modify data in SQL Server. They also can't use objects in tempdb or execute stored procedures. In addition, the following syntax is not allowed anywhere in a UDF:

```
INSERT INTO @TableVariable
EXEC anything
```

That doesn't leave many options for working with the output of an xp_.

The only xp_s that can be used are those that return their results in OUTPUT parameters and the return code. Table 10.1 lists all the xp_s documented in the BOL with a column that says whether they can be used in a UDF and either the reason they can't be used in a UDF or a description.

Table 10.1: Documented extended stored procedures that can be used in UDFs

Extended Procedure	Can It Be Used in a UDF?	Summary or Why It Can't Be Used
sp_OA*	YES	This is a group of extended stored procedures that all begin with sp_OA. Although their names begin with sp_, they're extended stored procedures. They create, destroy, and communicate with COM objects. See the sections on OLE automation later in this chapter.
xp_cmdshell	NO	Returns a resultset.
xp_deletemail	YES	Deletes an item from a SQL Mail inbox.
xp_enumgroups	NO	Returns a resultset.
xp_findnextmsg	YES	Possible. Returns a message ID, used with sp_processmail.
xp_gettable_dblib	NO	This is an extended stored procedure that is delivered in the sample code. It can't be used because it returns a resultset. However, OPENROWSET or OPENQUERY can achieve the same functionality.
xp_grantlogin	NO	Although its name begins with "xp_," it's now a stored procedure that is provided for backward compatibility.

Extended Procedure	Can It Be Used in a UDF?	Summary or Why It Can't Be Used
xp_hello	YES	A stored procedure that is delivered as source code. It returns a single output parameter that gets the string 'Hello World'.
xp_logevent	YES	Logs a user-defined message to the SQL Server log file and the NT application event log.
xp_loginconfig	NO	Returns a resultset.
xp_logininfo	NO	Returns a resultset.
xp_msver	NO	Returns a resultset.
xp_readmail	YES	Reads a mail message from the SQL Server Mail inbox. This procedure is used by sp_processmail. It may only be used by including a specific message number.
xp_revokelogin	NO	Although its name begins with "xp_," it's now a stored procedure that is provided for backward compatibility. For uses outside a function, use sp_revokelogin.
xp_sendmail	YES	Sends a mail message.
xp_snmp_getstate	NO	No longer available in SQL Server 2000.
xp_snmp_raisetrap	NO	No longer available in SQL Server 2000.
xp_sprintf	YES	See the discussion on udf_Txt_SPrintF in this chapter.
xp_sqlmant	YES	Executes a maintenance operation on one or more databases. Probably not appropriate for a UDF.
xp_sscanf	YES	Extracts substrings that appear in specific parts of a string pattern. Works the same as the sscanf function of the C computer language. This could be written in T-SQL.
xp_startmail	YES	Starts a SQL Mail client session.
xp_stopmail	YES	Stops a SQL Mail client session.
xp_trace_*	NO	These SQL Server 7 extended stored procedures are not in SQL Server. They have been replaced with the fn_trace_* system UDFs and the sp_trace_* stored procedures. The fn_trace_* functions are discussed in Chapter 17.

xp_logevent

xp_logevent writes a user-defined message to both the SQL Server log file and the Windows NT application event log. The SQL Server log in question is the information log maintained by SQL Server, not its transaction log. The syntax to the call is:

```
exec @RC =  master..xp_logevent   @MessageNumber
                                , @MessageText
                                [, @Severity]
```

The return code, @RC, is either 0 for success or 1 for failure.

@MessageNumber is an int. It's the number of a user-defined message. All user-defined messages must be greater than 50000.

@MessageText is the text of the message. For example, 'Now is the time for all good men to come to the aid of the party.'

@Severity is the severity of the message. This parameter is optional. If not provided, the severity is set to 10.

Let's add a simple message:

```
-- write a simple message to the log and the NT event log.
DECLARE @RC int -- return code
EXEC @rc = master..xp_logevent 60000,
                'The quick brown fox jumped over the lazy dog.'
PRINT 'Return Code = ' + convert (varchar, @rc)
GO

(Results)

Return Code = 0
```

Note:

Before demonstrating xp_logevent, I used the sp_cycle_errorlog stored procedure to create a new SQL Server log. It makes the displays that follow somewhat easier to read. Don't do this unless you're sure it's okay on your system.

Now take a look at what's produced in the SQL Server log. Figure 10.1 shows the log as it appears in Enterprise Manager.

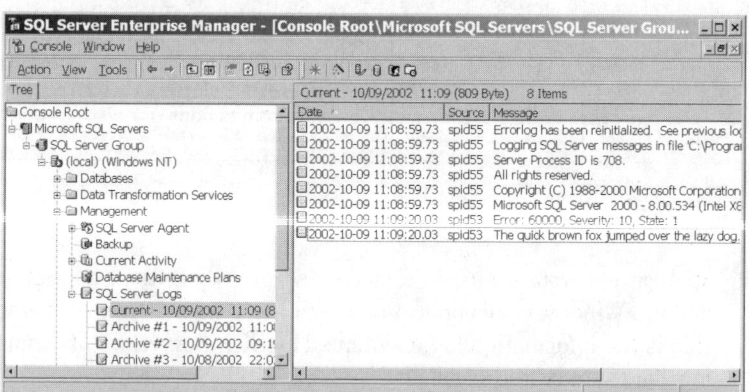

Figure 10.1: The result of xp_logevent as seen in Enterprise Manager

The error log can also be queried using the undocumented extended stored procedure xp_readerrorlog. It's shown in this query:

```
-- Read the current error log
EXEC master..xp_readerrorlog
GO

(Results truncated on the right to fit the page)

ERRORLOG
--------------------------------------------------------------------------------
2002-10-09 11:08:59.73 spid55    Microsoft SQL Server  2000 - 8.00.534 (Intel X8
   Nov 19 2001 13:23:50
   Copyright (c) 1988-2000 Microsoft Corporation
   Developer Edition on Windows NT 5.0 (Build 2195: Service Pack 3)
2002-10-09 11:08:59.73 spid55    Copyright (C) 1988-2000 Microsoft Corporation.
2002-10-09 11:08:59.73 spid55    All rights reserved.
2002-10-09 11:08:59.73 spid55    Server Process ID is 708.
2002-10-09 11:08:59.73 spid55    Logging SQL Server messages in file 'C:\Program
2002-10-09 11:08:59.73 spid55    Errorlog has been reinitialized.  See previous
2002-10-09 11:09:20.03 spid53    Error: 60000, Severity: 10, State: 1
2002-10-09 11:09:20.03 spid53    The quick brown fox jumped over the lazy dog..
```

The log grows quickly, so you'll want to use xp_readerrorlog with care. But it's a valuable tool for seeing what's going on during development. It's so valuable that I wrote a stored procedure, usp_SQL_MyLogRpt, that uses its output to show any messages added by the current process within the last 60 minutes. The most recent messages are displayed first. Listing 10.1 on the following page shows the stored procedure. It has to read the entire SQL log into a temporary table, so use it with care on production servers that may have very long log files. Here's a sample invocation:

```
-- Show just my messages
EXEC usp_SQL_MyLogRpt
GO

(Results)

When                   Message
---------------------- ---------------------------------------------------------
2002-10-09 11:09:20.03 The quick brown fox jumped over the lazy dog..
2002-10-09 11:09:20.03 Error: 60000, Severity: 10, State:
```

The output of xp_logevent is also written to the NT event log. Figure 10.2 shows the NT Event Viewer's Application Log. It contains one message for each invocation of xp_logevent. Our sample message is shown in detail in Figure 10.3.

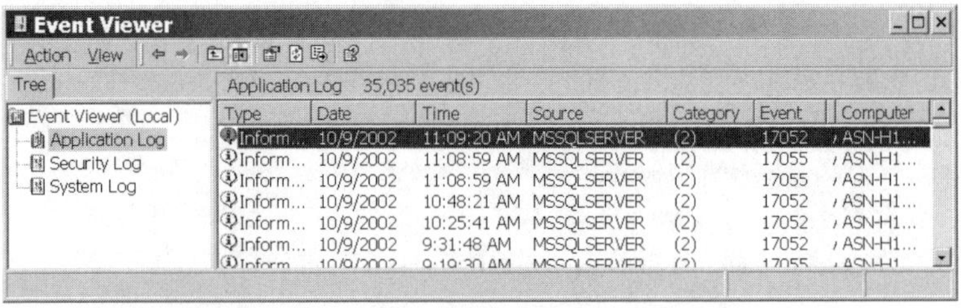

Figure 10.2: The event log with a message from xp_logevent

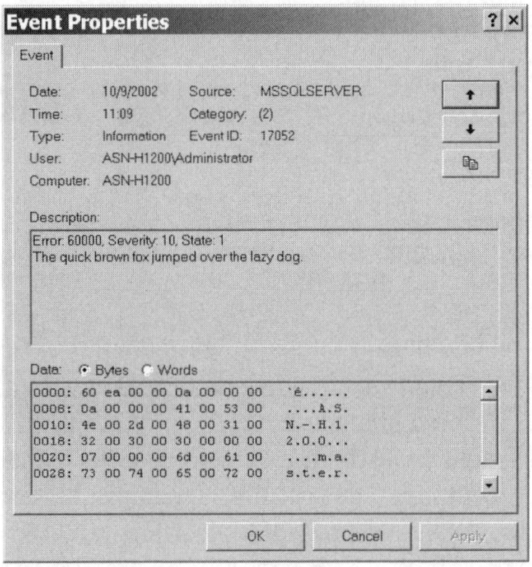

Figure 10.3: The Event Properties window with the details of a message

Listing 10.1: usp_SQL_MyLogRpt

```
CREATE PROCEDURE usp_SQL_MyLogRpt
/*
* Returns a report of the most recent events added to the system log
* by this process within the last 60 minutes with the most recent
* shown first.
*
* Example:
exec usp_SQL_myLogRpt
***************************************************************************/
AS BEGIN

    DECLARE @RC INT -- return code
          , @SPID varchar(9) -- text representation of @@SPID for searching

    CREATE TABLE #ErrorLog (
                    ERRORLOG varchar(1000) --
                  , ContinuationRow int -- Is this a continuation row
                  , SequenceNumber int identity (1,1)
                  )

    INSERT INTO #ErrorLog (ErrorLog, ContinuationRow)
        EXEC  master..xp_readerrorlog
```

```
    SET @spid = 'spid' + convert(varchar, @@spid)

    SELECT
           left(ErrorLog, 22) as [When]
         , dbo.udf_TxtWrapDelimiters(SUBSTRING (ErrorLog, 34, 1000), 80, N' '
                    , N' ', NCHAR(10), 23, 23)  as [Message]
        FROM #ErrorLog
        WHERE LEFT (ErrorLog, 1) <> CHAR(9) -- Lines don't start with a TAB
           AND @spid = CAST (RTRIM(SUBSTRING (ErrorLog, 24, 9)) as varchar(9))
                    -- From my process
           AND 1=ISDATE(LEFT(ErrorLog, 22)) -- Date found on the line
           AND 61 > DATEDIFF (n, CASE WHEN 1=ISDATE(LEFT(ErrorLog, 22))
                                      THEN CONVERT(datetime, LEFT(ErrorLog, 22))
                                      ELSE 0
                                      END
                             , GETDATE()) -- within the last 60 minutes
        ORDER BY SequenceNumber DESC

    DROP TABLE #ErrorLog

END
```

Listing 10.2: udf_SQL_LogMsgBIT

```
CREATE   FUNCTION dbo.udf_SQL_LogMsgBIT (

    @nMessageNumber int = 50001 -- User-defined message >= 50000
  , @sMessage varchar(8000) -- The message to be logged
  , @sSeverity varchar(16) = NULL -- The severity of the message
      -- may be 'INFORMATIONAL', 'WARNING', OR 'ERROR'
)   RETURNS BIT -- 1 for success or 0 for failure
/*
* Adds a message to the SQL Server log and the NT application
* Event log. Uses xp_logevent. xp_log event can be used whenever
* in place of this function.
* One potential use of this UDF is to cause the logging of a
* message in a place where xp_logevent cannot be executed
* such as in the definition of a view.
*
* Example:
select dbo.udf_SQL_LogMsgBIT(default,
                    'Now that''s what I call a message!', NULL)
****************************************************************/
AS BEGIN

DECLARE @WorkingVariable BIT

IF @sSeverity is NULL
    EXEC @WorkingVariable = master..xp_logevent @nMessageNumber
                                              , @sMessage
ELSE
    EXEC @WorkingVariable = master..xp_logevent @nMessageNumber
                                              , @sMessage
                                              , @sSeverity

-- xp_logevent has it backwards
RETURN CASE WHEN @WorkingVariable=1 THEN 0 ELSE 1 END
END
```

xp_logevent can be used in a UDF. The function udf_SQL_LogMsgBIT uses xp_logevent to write a message to the logs. It's shown in Listing 10.2. This query executes it once:

```
-- use udf_SQL_LogMsgBIT
Declare @rcBIT BIT -- return code
SELECT @rcBIT = dbo.udf_SQL_LogMsgBIT (default,
                          'Now that''s what I call a message!', null)
PRINT 'Return Code is ' + convert(varchar, @rcBIT)
GO

(Result)

Return Code is 1
```

Now show the new message:

```
-- Show the new message
EXEC usp_SQL_MyLogRpt
GO

(Result – truncated on the right)

When                   Message
---------------------- ----------------------------------------------------------
2002-10-09 11:32:31.92 Now that's what I call a message!.
2002-10-09 11:32:31.92 Error: 50001, Severity: 10, State:
2002-10-09 11:09:20.03 The quick brown fox jumped over the lazy dog..
2002-10-09 11:09:20.03 Error: 60000, Severity: 10, State:
```

That's interesting enough. But where would you ever use the function? After all, in almost all circumstances where you want to add a message to the log, you can just use xp_logevent. The only circumstance that I know of for using it is when you want to log an event in the middle of a query, such as for each row in a query as the query is processed. This might occur in the select list or in the middle of the WHERE clause. Of course, I wouldn't want to do that in a production system, but I've done it during development as a debugging tool. The following view definition makes use of the technique:

```
CREATE view ExampleViewThatLogsAMessage
AS
   SELECT *
        , CASE WHEN 1=dbo.udf_SQL_LogMsgBIT(default
                              , 'Executing for Customer ' + CompanyName
                              , NULL)
               THEN 'Message Logged'
               ELSE 'logevent failed'
               END as [Event Logged]
       FROM Cust

GO
```

The view does a SELECT on the sample Cust table in the TSQLUDFS database. If we SELECT from the view, one event is added for every row in the table.

```
-- Select that adds log messages for each row.
SELECT * FROM ExampleViewThatLogsAMessage
GO

(Results)

CustomerID  CompanyName          City                 Event Logged
----------- -------------------- -------------------- ---------------
1           Novick Software      Sudbury              Message Logged
2           Wordware             Dallas               Message Logged
```

Now let's look at the log:

```
-- Show the new message
EXEC usp_SQL_MyLogRpt
GO

(Results)

When                   Message
---------------------- -------------------------------------------------------
2002-10-09 11:46:01.72 Executing for Customer Wordware.
2002-10-09 11:46:01.72 Error: 50001, Severity: 10, State:
2002-10-09 11:46:01.72 Executing for Customer Novick Software.
2002-10-09 11:46:01.72 Error: 50001, Severity: 10, State:
2002-10-09 11:32:31.92 Now that's what I call a message..
2002-10-09 11:32:31.92 Error: 50001, Severity: 10, State:
2002-10-09 11:09:20.03 The quick brown fox jumped over the lazy dog..
2002-10-09 11:09:20.03 Error: 60000, Severity: 10, State:
```

That's pretty powerful. Creating a debug message from the middle of a SELECT statement isn't easy. Although you can always add another column to a select list with whatever information you want, you could never do it before in the WHERE clause. This query illustrates it a little better:

```
-- Create a log message from the middle of a WHERE clause.
SELECT *
     FROM Cust
     WHERE Left (CompanyName, 1) > 'N'
        AND 1=dbo.udf_SQL_LogMsgBIT(65000
                                 , 'Message In WHERE Clause for Customer '
                                    + CompanyName
                                 , NULL)
GO

(Results)

CustomerID  CompanyName          City
----------- -------------------- --------------------
2           Wordware             Dallas
```

Show the results from the SQL log:

```
-- Show the new message
EXEC usp_SQL_MyLogRpt
GO

(Results)

When                    Message
----------------------- -----------------------------------------------------------
2002-10-09 11:55:35.88 Message In WHERE Clause for  Customer Wordware.
2002-10-09 11:55:35.88 Error: 65000, Severity: 10, State:
2002-10-09 11:46:01.72 Executing for Customer Wordware.
2002-10-09 11:46:01.72 Error: 50001, Severity: 10, State:
2002-10-09 11:46:01.72 Executing for Customer Novick Software.
2002-10-09 11:46:01.72 Error: 50001, Severity: 10, State:
2002-10-09 11:32:31.92 Now that's what I call a message!.
2002-10-09 11:32:31.92 Error: 50001, Severity: 10, State:
2002-10-09 11:09:20.03 The quick brown fox jumped over the lazy dog..
2002-10-09 11:09:20.03 Error: 60000, Severity: 10, State:
```

The `Left (CompanyName, 1) > 'N'` clause filters out Novick Software, so Wordware is the only company left. Although two rows are processed by the `WHERE` clause, there was only one invocation of `udf_SQL_LogMsgBIT`. That's because once the Novick Software row was excluded by the `Left (CompanyName, 1) > 'N'` clause, there was no reason to execute the test on the other side of the `AND`. This is called expression short-circuiting, and it's a technique that SQL Server uses to speed the evaluation of queries.

Switching the clause that invokes `udf_SQL_LogMsgBIT` to one that always returns false doesn't help either. It would read:

```
     WHERE Left (CompanyName, 1) > 'N'
         OR     0=dbo.udf_SQL_LogMsgBIT(65000
                                      , 'Message In WHERE Clause for Customer '
                                         + CompanyName
                                      , NULL) -- Always false
```

However, I found that switching both the order of the clauses and using an `OR` operator between them does the trick. Here's the query:

```
-- Create a log message from the middle of a WHERE clause using OR
SELECT *
     FROM Cust
     WHERE
           0=dbo.udf_SQL_LogMsgBIT(65000
                                      , 'Message In WHERE Clause for Customer '
                                         + CompanyName
                                      , NULL) -- Always false
        OR Left (CompanyName, 1) > 'N'
GO
```

```
(Results)

CustomerID  CompanyName          City
----------- -------------------- --------------------
2           Wordware             Dallas
```

Here are the log messages:

```
-- Show the new message
EXEC usp_SQL_MyLogRpt
GO

(Results - abridged)

When                   Message
---------------------- --------------------------------------------------------
2002-10-09 12:06:25.83 Message In WHERE Clause for  Customer Wordware.
2002-10-09 12:06:25.83 Error: 65000, Severity: 10, State:
2002-10-09 12:06:25.82 Message In WHERE Clause for  Customer Novick Software.
2002-10-09 12:06:25.82 Error: 65000, Severity: 10, State:
2002-10-09 11:55:35.88 Message In WHERE Clause for  Customer Wordware.
2002-10-09 11:55:35.88 Error: 65000, Severity: 10, State:
2002-10-09 11:46:01.72 Executing for Customer Wordware.
2002-10-09 11:46:01.72 Error: 50001, Severity: 10, State:
```

That did it. The results are consistent. According to SQL Server Books Online, they should be repeatable. In the article on search conditions, Books Online says this about predicate order:

> The order of precedence for the logical operators is NOT (highest), followed by AND, followed by OR. **The order of evaluation at the same precedence level is from left to right.** Parentheses can be used to override this order in a search condition.

Net has a similar behavior, and therefore it's likely that future versions of SQL Server will continue to short-circuit expressions.

Message text and severity levels in sysmessages are ignored by xp_logevent and hence by udf_SQL_LogMsgBIT. To use one of the messages in sysmessages, use the FORMATMESSAGE built-in function to create the message before calling udf_SQL_LogMsgBIT.

That's all for xp_logevent. As you can see from the log, it's time for lunch. Today it's cucumber salad and leftover meatloaf.

xp_sprintf

This extended stored procedure is similar to the C language function sprintf. However, it's a very limited version of that function because it only supports the insertion of strings with the %s format. The syntax of the call is:

```
xp_sprintf    @Result OUTPUT
              @Format
              [, @Argument1 [,..n]]
```

@Result is a varchar variable to receive the output.

@Format is a varchar with the text of the output message and embedded %s symbols where substitution should take place.

@Argument1, @Argument2... are varchar arguments to @Format. There should be as many of these as %s insertion points in @Format.

As an extended stored procedure, xp_sprintf is used to format textual messages by substituting several arguments into the correct position of a format string. However, it suffers from two limitations:

- It can only be used in circumstances where an xp_ can be invoked.
- It only accepts strings for substitution.

These limitations can be overcome with the UDF shown in Listing 10.3. Because it's a UDF, it can be invoked in additional circumstances, such as a select list, where xp_s couldn't be used. udf_Txt_Sprintf uses xp_sprintf to perform the substitution but takes care of the conversion to character string. Its limitations are that it only handles input and output strings up to 254 characters, and it always expects exactly three parameters.

Listing 10.3: udf_Txt_Sprintf

```
CREATE FUNCTION dbo.udf_Txt_Sprintf (

    @Format varchar(254) -- The format with embedded %s insertion chars
  , @var1 sql_variant = NULL -- The first substitution string
  , @var2 sql_variant = NULL -- Second substitution string
  , @var3 sql_variant = NULL -- Third substitution string
)   RETURNS varchar(8000) -- Format string with replacements performed.
    -- No SCHEMABIND due to use of EXEC
/*
* Uses xp_sprintf to format a string with up to three insertion
* arguments.
*
* Example:
select dbo.udf_Txt_Sprintf('Insertion 1>%s 2>%s, 3>%s', 1, 2, null)
*
* Test:
```

```
PRINT 'Test 1    ' + CASE WHEN '123.0'=
                     dbo.udf_Txt_Sprintf ('%s%s%s', 1,'2', 3.0)
                     THEN 'Worked' ELSE 'ERROR' END
PRINT 'Test 2    ' + CASE WHEN
             dbo.udf_Txt_Sprintf ('%s%s%s', NULL,NULL, NULL) is NULL
                     THEN 'Worked' ELSE 'ERROR' END
PRINT 'Test 3    ' + CASE WHEN 'Jan  1 2002 12:00AM' =
dbo.udf_Txt_Sprintf ('%s%s%s', CONVERT(datetime, '2002-01-01', 121)
                     ,NULL, NULL)
                     THEN 'Worked' ELSE 'ERROR' END
* History:
* When          Who     Description
* ------------- ------- -----------------------------------------
* 2003-06-14    ASN        Initial Coding
***************************************************************/
AS BEGIN

    DECLARE @Result varchar(254)

    DECLARE @Parm1 varchar(254)
          , @Parm2 varchar(254)
          , @Parm3 varchar(254)

    SELECT @Parm1 = CAST (@var1 as varchar(254))
         , @Parm2 = CAST (@var2 as varchar(254))
         , @Parm3 = CAST (@var3 as varchar(254))

    EXEC master.dbo.xp_sprintf
                     @Result OUTPUT
                   , @Format
                   , @Parm1
                   , @Parm2
                   , @Parm3

    RETURN @Result
END
```

Using the function is pretty simple. The easiest location to use it is in the select list, as shown by this query:

```
-- Print authors and contract value, which has a BIT data type.
SELECT TOP 4
       dbo.udf_Txt_Sprintf ('%s %s Contract Value = %s'
                          , au_fname, au_lname, contract)
              as [Author and Contract]
    FROM pubs..authors
GO
```

(Results)

```
Author and Contract
----------------------------------------------------------------------
Johnson White Contract Value = 1
Marjorie Green Contract Value = 1
Cheryl Carson Contract Value = 1
Michael O'Leary Contract Value = 1
```

Of course, you could use it in any context that you prefer.

The set of documented xp_s that can be used in UDFs is actually pretty limited. However, the next group allows the extension of T-SQL scripts by creating and using COM objects. This has the potential to vastly expand what can be done from a UDF.

sp_OA* and OLE Automation: The Keys to the Vault

OLE née OLE2 née ActiveX née COM has lived through almost as many name changes as true versions. It's the component technology in Windows. It's also been used to construct many Windows programs. But you know that already.

SQL Server can tap into OLE components through a group of extended stored procedures. Although their names begin with sp_, they're not stored procedures. They're extended stored procedures and can be used from inside UDFs. Table 10.2 lists them.

Table 10.2: sp_OA* extended stored procedures

XP Name	Description
sp_OACreate	Creates an instance of an OLE object.
sp_OADestroy	Destroys an OLE object.
sp_OAGetErrorInfo	Obtains error information after another sp_OA* call.
sp_OAGetProperty	Retrieves the value of a property from an OLE object.
sp_OAMethod	Calls a method of an OLE object.
sp_AOSetProperty	Sets the value of a property of an OLE object.
sp_OAStop	Stops the environment used to run all OLE objects in the instance of SQL Server.

The COM objects that you automate can be objects in an existing program or in a new program that you create. There are no restrictions on what they can do beyond the restrictions placed on the account that executes SQL Server.

Permissions to Use sp_OA*

There is an important restriction on who can use these extended stored procedures. By default, EXECUTE permission on all the sp_OA* xp_s is restricted to users who have the sysadmin role. Granting EXECUTE permission on a stored procedure or UDF that invokes them *does not override the restriction*. So if you want users to be able to execute a UDF that uses one of these xp_s, they either have to have the sysadmin role, or you have to

GRANT EXECUTE permission on the sp_OA* procedures to all users who will use UDFs that invoke them.

Granting permission to the sp_OA* extended stored procedures may meet your needs, but doing so means that users with permission to execute them can write their own SQL script to execute other COM objects. This presents an opportunity for serious accidents. It also presents an opportunity for hacking. Anyone with access to the sp_OA* procedures can wreak havoc on your server. For example, the Windows Scripting Runtime DLL includes the FileSystemObject, which allows disk access to the entire server on which SQL Server runs. This access would be in the security context of the account that's running SQL Server, possibly LocalSystem or a local administrator account, not the user that originated the query. This type of vulnerability is called a privilege elevation. It's a security hole big enough to drive a truck through.

Hopefully, you're now reluctant to hand out privileges to use the sp_OA* xp_s. My opinion is that the risks presented by giving out EXECUTE permission on these objects is pretty high. Having said that, I do think there is a place for using these procedures by users with the sysadmin role. In particular, it can be a big aid in automating administrative procedures on your servers.

Picking the Best Uses of OLE Automation

Don't forget, COM has never been known for its great efficiency. Each time you create an object, you're using memory, CPU, disk accesses, and other resources from inside the Windows kernel. It all doesn't come cheap. But it's a foundation technology for Windows, so it's usually worth the cost in resources.

Am I sending mixed messages? Let me clarify. In my opinion, OLE Automation is best for:

- Repetitive or administrative tasks that occur less frequently than once every few minutes. For example, a daily disk space analysis.
- Occasional tasks that recur but only when specific conditions warrant. For example, an analysis that occurs when performance falls below the desired service level.
- Proof-of-concept experiments. A development experiment where sometimes you just want to find any way that works so you can demonstrate a concept.

OLE Automation is not good for:

- Embedding in T-SQL that is used as part of a production application to respond to very frequent requests, such as web page displays, reports, or user screens.

- Ad hoc script writing. There are other languages better suited to ad hoc tasks than T-SQL. For example, both VBScript and Jscript are available in DTS and Windows Scripting Host.

For high-volume production work, consider executing the OLE objects in some other layer, or tier, of the application. If the output of the OLE object needs to be integrated with a query, consider providing the results of the object execution as XML. The XML can be integrated into a query through the use of the `OPENXML` syntax.

If you need OLE Automation for administrative purposes, consider some alternatives that invoke `COM` objects from within T-SQL scripts:

- SQLAgent Jobs can have steps that execute ActiveX scripts or execute Windows programs.
- DTS packages can also have ActiveX scripts or execute Windows programs.

Neither of these solutions are executed from within the SQL engine and don't entail either putting it at risk from failed objects or the potential for excessive locking caused by long running OLE methods. Either one of these alternatives should be considered for any OLE Automation task that runs for anything longer than a second.

Now that you're all warned, let's go do it.

Invoking a COM Object

The first script uses the `FileSystemObject` from the Microsoft Scripting Runtime. It's contained in the file scrrun.dll that you'll find in the Windows\System32 directory and is usually distributed with Internet Explorer and other programs from Microsoft. `FileSystemObject` is an OLE object that provides access to disk and network resources.

About the simplest method of `FileSystemObject` is `DriveExists`. Given the letter of a disk drive, it returns `True` when the drive exists or `False` when it does not. The following batch shows how it can be used. I've left it as a batch instead of a function so we can get into a discussion of how to handle the error conditions.

I was talking to a colleague who was having some difficulty handling errors in a stored procedure and had to remind him that the return code of each and every statement that could generate an error must be checked. Since the `sp_OA*` extended stored procedures return an HRESULT return code, that's the code that must be checked. *It must be checked after every* `sp_OA*` *call.*

All that error checking makes for awkward scripts. To make them slightly simpler, I've resorted to coding with a few `GOTO` statements. This is the only place in the book that you'll find any `GOTO`s. Although I learned programming with languages like BASIC, FORTRAN, and COBOL, by the mid-1970s when I went to college, the evils of GOTO were very apparent to the leading edge of the programming community. In college, I learned PL/1 and *structured programming* and removed all GOTO statements from my coding style. But language limitations in T-SQL and Visual Basic make the use of a few GOTOs (particularly in error handling) almost essential. Since their occasional use makes the code more readable, I think they're worthwhile.

In the next script, the stored procedure used for displaying error information, sp_displayoaerrorinfo, and its companion, sp_hexadecimal, come straight from Books Online, so they won't be reproduced here. You'll find them in the article "OLE Automation Return Codes and Error Information." They've already been added to the TSQLUDFS database.

Note:

Some of the scripts in this chapter produce long results that wrap over several lines. To see them properly, you should send output to text by using Query Analyzer's Query ➤ Results in Text (Ctrl+T) menu command. In addition, set the maximum characters per column to 8192 in the Results tab of the Options dialog. You can reach it using the Tools ➤ Options menu command.

Here's the script:

```
-- Script to test for the existence of a drive letter.
   DECLARE
        @driveLetter char (1) -- Check the existence of this drive

SET @DriveLetter = 'C' -- Check for Drive
DECLARE @hResult1 int -- return code
      , @hFSO int -- Handle to the File System Object
      , @hResult2 int -- return code from error handling call.
      , @errSource varchar (255) -- Source of the error
      , @errDesc varchar(255) -- Description of the error
      , @DriveExists BIT -- result of does it exist
      , @msg varchar(1000)

EXEC @hResult1 = sp_OACreate 'SCRIPTING.FileSystemObject' -- The ProgID
                       , @hFSO OUTPUT -- object token
                       , 5 -- allow in-process server

IF @hResult1 != 0 GOTO Automation_Error

EXEC @hResult1 = sp_OAMethod @hFSO
                           , 'DriveExists'
                           , @DriveExists Output
                           , @DriveSpec = @DriveLetter

IF @hResult1 != 0 GOTO Automation_Error

PRINT 'Drive Exists = ' +  convert(varchar, @DriveExists)
```

```
GOTO BypassErrorHandling

Automation_Error:

   EXEC sp_displayoaerrorinfo @hFso, @hResult1

ByPassErrorHandling:

   -- Destroy the object if we created it
   IF @hFSO is not NULL
       EXEC @hResult1 = sp_OADestroy @hFSO

   PRINT 'done'
GO

(Results)

Drive Exists = 1
Done
```

If I change the fifth line from:

```
SET @DriveLetter = 'C' -- Check for Drive
```

to:

```
SET @DriveLetter = 'R' -- Check for Drive
```

Then the results are:

```
Drive Exists = 0
done
```

There is no R drive on my system. Your system might have drive R, so if you're running the code as you go, use a drive letter that doesn't exist on your system.

If the `Scripting.FileSystemObject` is registered on your system, you shouldn't get an error from the script. Since error handling is one of the more time-consuming tasks when using the `sp_OA*` routines, showing one error is instructive. To generate an error, I've changed the call to `sp_OAMethod` so that the method name is commented out. The full revised script is in Listing 0 for this chapter:

```
-- Script to show how errors are handled in sp_OAMethod
...
EXEC @hResult1 = sp_OAMethod @hFSO
                --        , 'DriveExists'
                          , @DriveExists Output
                          , @DriveSpec = @DriveLetter

...
GO
```

(Results - with some line wrapping)

```
OLE Automation Error Information
  HRESULT: 0x80042725
  Source: ODSOLE Extended Procedure
  Description: sp_OAMethod usage:  ObjPointer int IN
               , MethodName varchar IN [, @returnval <any> OUT
               [, additional IN, OUT, or BOTH params]]
done
```

As you can see, the error is handled and `sp_displayoaerrorinfo`, from Books Online, prints out the HRESULT and the correct calling sequence, which is the error message. The error number can be broken down further and turned into a more understandable message.

Breaking Down an HRESULT

The Books Online page on `sp_OAGetErrorInfo` lists several common HRESULTS and their meaning. Additional information can be gleaned from the C++ file WINERROR.H, which documents the format of HRESULT return codes. Here's the top of that file:

```
//
//  Values are 32-bit values laid out as follows:
//
//   3 3 2 2 2 2 2 2 2 2 2 2 1 1 1 1 1 1 1 1 1 1
//   1 0 9 8 7 6 5 4 3 2 1 0 9 8 7 6 5 4 3 2 1 0 9 8 7 6 5 4 3 2 1 0
//  +---+-+-+-----------------------+-------------------------------+
//  |Sev|C|R|     Facility          |               Code            |
//  +---+-+-+-----------------------+-------------------------------+
//
//  where
//
//      Sev - is the severity code
//
//          00 - Success
//          01 - Informational
//          10 - Warning
//          11 - Error
//
//      C - is the Customer code flag
//
//      R - is a reserved bit
//
//      Facility - is the facility code
//
//      Code - is the facility's status code
//
//
// Define the facility codes
//
#define FACILITY_WINDOWS                 8
#define FACILITY_STORAGE                 3
#define FACILITY_SSPI                    9
#define FACILITY_SETUPAPI                15
```

```
#define FACILITY_RPC                    1
#define FACILITY_WIN32                  7
#define FACILITY_CONTROL                10
#define FACILITY_NULL                   0
#define FACILITY_MSMQ                   14
#define FACILITY_MEDIASERVER            13
#define FACILITY_INTERNET               12
#define FACILITY_ITF                    4
#define FACILITY_DISPATCH               2
#define FACILITY_CERT                   11
```

The three parts of the code that are most useful are:

- The Severity Code in bits 31 and 30
- The Facility Code in bits 27-16
- The Facility Status Code in bits 15-0

The remainder of WINERROR.H lists error codes. The file is part of Visual C++ and Visual Studio, so you'll need one of those products to get the complete file.

sp_displayoaerrorinfo uses sp_hexadecimal to display the error code in hex. It's the hex codes that are listed in Books Online. The function udf_BitS_FromInt shows the bits in full detail.

Note:

You should be running with SQL Server 2000 Service Pack 2 or above to execute the next script. For security reasons, all SQL Servers should have at least Service Pack 3.

udf_BitS_FromInt, which relies on an undocumented system function, is discussed more fully in Chapter 18, "Undocumented System UDFs." Here's a query that breaks down the error code from above, 0x80042725, into its bits:

```
-- Break down the HRESULT into its bits
SELECT N' 3 3 2 2 2 2 2 2 2 2 2 2 1 1 1 1 1 1 1 1 1 1 '
     + NCHAR(10)
     + N' 1 0 9 8 7 6 5 4 3 2 1 0 9 8 7 6 5 4 3 2 1 0 9 8 7 6 5 4 3 2 1 0'
     + NCHAR(10)
     + N'+---+-+-+-----------------------+-------------------------------+'
     + NCHAR(10)
     + N'|Sev|C|R|        Facility       |              Code             |'
     + NCHAR(10)
     + N'+---+-+-+-----------------------+-------------------------------+'
     + NCHAR(10)
     + N' '
     + dbo.udf_TxtNSpreadChars (dbo.udf_NumIntToBITSTRING (0x80042725, 0)
                              , 1, ' ')
GO
```

(Results)

```
Breakdown of error code 0x80042725
-------------------------------------------------------------------------------
 3 3 2 2 2 2 2 2 2 2 2 2 1 1 1 1 1 1 1 1 1 1
 1 0 9 8 7 6 5 4 3 2 1 0 9 8 7 6 5 4 3 2 1 0 9 8 7 6 5 4 3 2 1 0
+---+-+-+-----------------------+-------------------------------+
|Sev|C|R|        Facility       |              Code             |
+---+-+-+-----------------------+-------------------------------+
 1 0 0 0 0 0 0 0 0 0 0 0 0 1 0 0 0 0 1 0 0 1 1 1 0 0 1 0 0 1 0 1
```

The HRESULT code breaks down as:

- Severity = Warning
- Facility = 4 meaning `Facility_ITF`
- Code = 10021 (Nope, it's not in WINERROR.h.)

A more useful error handling routine would produce a similar breakdown and use the known error information from Books Online to let the programmer know as much as possible. Function `udf_OA_ErrorInfo` does just that. It's shown in Listing 10.4.

Listing 10.4: `udf_OA_ErrorInfo`

```
CREATE FUNCTION dbo.udf_OA_ErrorInfo (

    @hObject int -- Handle to the object
  , @HRESULT int -- Return code from the sp_OA* call
)   RETURNS varchar(255) -- Descriptive error message
/*
* Consolidates information about an error from the sp_OA* routines
* into a single error message.
*
* Example:
DECLARE @HRESULT int, @hObject int
EXEC @HRESULT = sp_OACREATE  'BADPROGID', @hObject OUTPUT, 5
select dbo.udf_OA_ErrorInfo(@hObject, @HRESULT)
EXEC @HRESULT = sp_OADestroy @hObject
****************************************************************/
AS BEGIN

    DECLARE @FacilityCode int -- numeric facility
          , @FacilityName varchar(16) -- name of the facility from WINERROR.h
          , @Code int -- the error code.
          , @CommonError varchar(128) -- A common error code
          , @ErrorMsg varchar(255) -- the full message we're producing
          , @ErrSource varchar(128) -- source of msg from sp_OAGetErrorInfo
          , @ErrDesc varchar(255) -- description from sp_OAGetErrorInfo
          , @HelpFile varchar(128) -- help file (Ususally not returned)
          , @Helpid int -- Help ID in @HelpFile
          , @HRESULTfromGetErrorInfo int -- return code from get error info

    EXEC @HRESULTfromGetErrorInfo = sp_OAGetErrorInfo @hObject
                                                    , @ErrSource OUTPUT
                                                    , @ErrDesc OUTPUT
                                                    , @HelpFile OUTPUT
                                                    , @HelpID OUTPUT
```

```
    IF @HRESULTfromGetErrorInfo != 0 BEGIN
        SELECT @ErrorMsg = 'Call to GetErrorInfo failed. Suggest stopping '
                         + 'ODSOLE with sp_OAStop. '
                         + ' HRESULT from sp_OAGetErrorInfo = '
                         + master.dbo.fn_varbintohexstr(@HRESULTfromGetErrorInfo)
                         + ' Original HRESULT = '
                         + master.dbo.fn_varbintohexstr(@HRESULT)
        RETURN @ErrorMsg
    END -- end if

    -- Extract the correct bits to get the facility code and error code
    SELECT @FacilityCode = (@HRESULT & 0x0FFF0000)  -- first mask
                          / POWER(2, 16) -- then shift right 16 bits
         , @Code = @HRESULT & 0X0000FFFF -- Just mask

    SELECT @FacilityName = CASE @FacilityCode
                             WHEN 0 THEN 'NULL'
                             WHEN 1 THEN 'RPC'
                             WHEN 2 THEN 'DISPATCH'
                             WHEN 3 THEN 'STORAGE'
                             WHEN 4 THEN 'ITF'
                             WHEN 7 THEN 'WIN32'
                             WHEN 8 THEN 'WINDOWS'
                             WHEN 9 THEN 'SSPI'
                             WHEN 10 THEN 'CONTROL'
                             WHEN 11 THEN 'CERT'
                             WHEN 12 THEN 'INTERNET'
                             WHEN 13 THEN 'MEDIASERVER'
                             WHEN 14 THEN 'MSMQ'
                             WHEN 15 THEN 'SETUPAPI'
                             ELSE 'UNKNOWN ' + CONVERT(varchar, @FacilityCode)
                             END
          , @CommonError = CASE @HRESULT
                WHEN 0x80020008 THEN 'Bad variable type or NULL'
                WHEN 0x80020006 THEN 'Property or Method Unknown'
                WHEN 0x800401F3 THEN 'PROGID or CLSID not registered'
                WHEN 0x80080005 THEN 'Registered EXE not found'
                WHEN 0x8007007E THEN 'Registered DLL not found'
                WHEN 0x80020005 THEN 'Type mismatch in return value.'
                WHEN 0x8004275B THEN 'Context parm invalid. Must be 1, 4, or 5'
                ELSE ''
                END

    -- Combine what we know into a complete message
    SELECT @ErrorMsg = 'HRESULT=' + master.dbo.fn_varbintohexstr(@HRESULT) + ' '
                  + 'Facility:' + @FacilityName + ' '
                  + 'Src:' + @ErrSource + CHAR(10)
                  + 'Desc:' + CASE WHEN LEN(@CommonError) > 0
                                   THEN '(' + @CommonError + ') '
                                   ELSE ''
                                   END
                  + @ErrDesc

    RETURN @ErrorMsg

END
```

To test `udf_OA_ErrorInfo`, you have to create an error. Here's a query that uses a bad PROGID to be sure to create one:

```
-- Create a common sp_OA* error
DECLARE @HRESULT int, @hObject int
EXEC @HRESULT = sp_OACreate 'BADPROGID', @hObject OUTPUT, 5
SELECT dbo.udf_OA_ErrorInfo(@hObject, @HRESULT) as [Error Message]
EXEC @HRESULT = sp_OADestroy @hObject
GO

(Results)

Error Message
------------------------------------------------------------------------------
HRESULT=0x800401f3 Facility:ITF Src:ODSOLE Extended Procedure
Desc:(PROGID or CLSID not registered)  Invalid class string
```

That gives us a better error message. But if we're going to use it inside a function, we have to decide what to do with the message. If the function is going to return a string, the error message could be used for the return value. All functions don't return strings, so that doesn't always work. Besides, it greatly complicates using the function. The next section has an alternative solution that's pretty powerful.

Logging OLE Automation Errors

Based on a few factors, I've decided to use `udf_SQL_LogMsgBIT` to send the message to the SQL log. I think that it's okay for the following reasons:

- Most of these errors occur during development.
- The `sp_OA*` procedures are best used for administrative functions, not high-volume queries.
- Getting the error message from one of these routines is very important. You don't want to allow unhandled errors in these routines to accumulate without being addressed. The side effects could slow or bring down the server.

If the messages are going to go into the SQL log and NT event log, there's another gap in the process that needs to be closed. There is only one SQL log in use for writing at any time. Messages from all code that uses `udf_SQL_LogMsgBIT` is intermixed in the log. We'd better identify precisely what code produced the message, the call that is being made, and which call it was. Otherwise, it will become very difficult to identify which code created the message.

`udf_OA_LogError` is a UDF that creates an error message about a problem with OA automation and sends it to the log. Having this routine around makes it easier to handle errors encountered when writing functions that use the `sp_OA*` procedures. Listing 10.5 shows the code for `udf_OA_LogError`.

Listing 10.5: udf_OA_LogError

```
CREATE FUNCTION dbo.udf_OA_LogError (

    @hObject int -- Handle to the object
  , @HRESULT int -- Return code from the sp_OA* call
  , @CallerName sysname -- name of the caller
  , @spName sysname -- Name of the procedure being called.
  , @ContextOfCall varchar(64) -- Description of the call.
)   RETURNS varchar(255) -- Error message that was logged.
/*
* Creates an error message about an OA error and logs it to the
* SQL log and NT event log.
*
* Example:
DECLARE @HRESULT int, @hObject int
EXEC @HRESULT = sp_OAALTER  'BADPROGID', @hObject OUTPUT, 5
SELECT dbo.udf_OA_LogError(@hObject, @HRESULT, 'Common Usage'
            , 'sp_OACreate', 'BADPRODID') as [Error Message]
EXEC @HRESULT = sp_OADestroy @hObject
****************************************************************************/
AS BEGIN

    DECLARE @FullMsg varchar(255) -- The full message being sent
          , @ErrMsg varchar(255)
          , @MessageLogged BIT -- temporary bit

    SELECT @ErrMsg=dbo.udf_OA_ErrorInfo (@hObject, @HRESULT)

    SELECT @FullMsg = 'OA error in ''' + @CallerName
                    + ''' Invoking:' + @spName
                    + ' (' + @ContextOfCall + ')' + CHAR(10)
                    + @ErrMsg

    -- Write the message to the log, should always succeed
    IF NOT 1=dbo.udf_SQL_LogMsgBIT (50002, @FullMsg, default)
       SELECT @FullMsg = 'Logging Process Failed for message:' + @FullMsg

    RETURN @FullMsg
END
```

Next is a script that uses udf_OA_LogError instead of udf_OA_ErrorInfo:

```
-- Log an error message to the SQL log and NT event log using udf_OA_LogError
DECLARE @HRESULT int, @hObject int
EXEC @HRESULT = sp_OACreate 'BADPROGID', @hObject OUTPUT, 5
SELECT dbo.udf_OA_LogError(@hObject, @HRESULT, 'Chapter 10 Listing 0'
            , 'sp_OACreate', 'BADPRODID') as [Error Message]
EXEC @HRESULT = sp_OADestroy @hObject
GO
```

(Results)

```
Error Message
--------------------------------------------------------------------------------
OA error in 'Chapter 10 Listing 0' Invoking:sp_OACreate (BADPRODID)
HRESULT=0x800401f3 Facility:ITF Src:ODSOLE Extended Procedure
Desc:(PROGID or CLSID not registered)  Invalid class string
```

Warning:

The text for this script, along with all the others in the chapter, are in the file Chapter 10 Listing 0 Short Queries.sql, which you'll find in the download directory. Because it logs a message to the SQL log and NT event log on the server, don't execute it unless you're sure it's okay on the SQL Server (for example, if you're using a development server).

Now that we have a way to handle OLE Automation errors and a way to log them efficiently, it's time to create a UDF that does something useful. The following example builds on a script shown above. It's a simple example of what can be done.

Creating a Useful OLE Automation UDF

Based on the approach just outlined, `udf_SYS_DriveExistsBIT` turns the script that checks for a drive into a UDF that returns a bit that tells if the drive is available on this system. It's shown in Listing 10.6.

Listing 10.6: `udf_SYS_DriveExistsBIT`

```
CREATE FUNCTION dbo.udf_SYS_DriveExistsBIT (

    @DriveLetter char(1) -- The letter of the drive
)   RETURNS BIT -- 1 if drive exists, else 0, Null for OLE Error
/*
* Uses OLE Automation to check if a drive exists.
*
* Example:
select dbo.udf_SYS_DriveExistsBIT('C')  as [Drive C Exists]
******************************************************************/
AS BEGIN

    DECLARE @HRESULT int -- return code
          , @hFSO int -- Handle to the File System Object
          , @DriveExists BIT -- result of does it exist
          , @Msg varchar(1000)
          , @TempBIT BIT -- temp for assignment

    EXEC @HRESULT = sp_OACreate 'SCRIPTING.FileSystemObject'
                        , @hFSO OUTPUT -- object token
                        , 5 -- allow in-process server
```

```
    IF @HRESULT != 0 BEGIN
        SELECT @msg = dbo.udf_OA_LogError (
                            'udf_SYS_DriveExistsBIT'
                          , 'sp_OACreate'
                          , 'FileSystemObject'
                          , @HRESULT, @hFSO)
        GOTO Function_Cleanup
    END

    EXEC @HRESULT = sp_OAMethod @hFSO
                              , 'DriveExists'
                              , @DriveExists Output
                              , @DriveSpec = @DriveLetter

    IF @HRESULT != 0 BEGIN
        SELECT @msg = dbo.udf_OA_LogError (
                            'udf_SYS_DriveExistsBIT'
                          , 'sp_OAMethod'
                          , 'DriveExists'
                          , @HRESULT, @hFSO)
        SET @DriveExists = NULL -- In case it had been set by the call
    END

Function_Cleanup:

   -- Destroy the object if we created it
   IF @hFSO is not NULL
       EXEC @HRESULT = sp_OADestroy @hFSO

   RETURN @DriveExists
END
```

Here udf_SYS_DriveExistsBIT is used to check for an R drive. My server doesn't have an R drive, so the result is 0.

```
-- Does Drive R exist?
SELECT dbo.udf_SYS_DriveExistsBIT ('R') as [Drive R Exists]
GO

(Results)

Drive R Exists
--------------
0
```

Be careful how you interpret the results of the function. The UDF is run on the computer that's running SQL Server. That might not be the same computer that Query Analyzer is running on. The results returned are for the server machine.

As you can see from Listing 10.6, every method call to an sp_OA* extended stored procedure is accompanied by a group of statements that handle and log the error, such as this code:

```
IF @HRESULT != 0 BEGIN
    SELECT @msg = dbo.udf_OA_LogError (
                       'udf_SYS_DriveExistsBIT'
                     , 'sp_OACreate'
                     , 'FileSystemObject'
                     , @HRESULT, @hFSO)
    GOTO Function_Cleanup
END
```

Each message must identify exactly which call caused the problem so that it can be tracked down efficiently. Without this kind of detail, you'll be left to speculate about the origin of the error.

Encapsulating Properties and Methods with UDFs

Objects don't have to be created, used, and destroyed within a single UDF. If you're making multiple method calls or property invocations on a single object, you could pass in the handle to the object. In fact you could make a UDF for each property and method that the object exposes.

In my opinion, this is going further than is really appropriate inside of T-SQL. If you're going to make a series of calls to properties and methods, the best approach isn't to code a lengthy T-SQL script. You're better off creating your own OLE object that encapsulates all the logic needed to accomplish your task. Alternatively, you might already have OLE objects available. The next section discusses creating and using your own OLE objects.

Invoking Your Own OLE Objects

The previous section used OLE objects that are part of Windows. It's also possible to create your own OLE objects and use them from T-SQL user-defined functions. In fact, it's very easy. You just need the right tool.

For creating OLE objects, the easiest tool around is Visual Basic 6. If you read through the documentation for the sp_OA* extended stored procedures, you'll see Visual Basic mentioned several times. It's the tool that the authors of the sp_OA* documentation assumed you'd use to create OLE objects.

Note:

If at all possible, use Visual Basic 6.0 and the latest service pack for creating OLE objects. Versions of Visual Basic before Version 5.0 Service Pack 3 shouldn't be used for creating COM objects to use with SQL Server. VB .NET doesn't use COM by default. The way to create an object with the .NET framework and use it from SQL Server is through COM interop.

The VB project TSQLUDFVB is in the subdirectory TSQLUDFVBDemo in this chapter's download directory. It creates the object cTSQL-UDFVBDemo, which is sort of a Hello World application. Listing 10.7 shows the text of the VB class that becomes the OLE object when compiled. It is the contents of the file TSQLUDFVBDemo.cls.

Listing 10.7: OLE object `TSQLUDFVB.cTSQLUDFVBDemo`

```
Option Explicit

Private m_sMyName As String

Public Property Get myName() As Variant

    myName = m_sMyName

End Property

Public Property Let myName(ByVal vNewValue As Variant)

    m_sMyName = vNewValue

End Property

Public Function SayHello() As String

    SayHello = "Hello " + m_sMyName

End Function
```

The object has one property, `myName`, and one method, `sayHello`. The example script below does the following:

- Creates the object
- Sets the `myName` property to my name
- Invokes the `sayHello` method to produce our message

Before you try to execute the script, you must create and register the DLL that has the OLE object. You can do that in one of two ways:

- Open the project TDSQLUDFVB with VB 6.0 and make the DLL on your system.
- Register the DLL with the command-line utility regsvr32.exe. To do that, open a command window and navigate to the directory with TDSQLUDFVB.DLL. Then execute the command: `regsvr32.exe TDSQLUDFVB.DLL`.

You should see a dialog box like the one shown in Figure 10.4.

Figure 10.4: Successful registration of the DLL

Be sure that you register the DLL or make it on the machine where SQL Server is running. That's the machine where the OLE object is going to be executed.

Listing 10.8 shows `udf_Example_OAhello`, a short example UDF to exercise the new OLE object by creating a Hello string. There are only three OLE calls necessary to use the demonstration object:

- `sp_OACreate` — To create the object
- `sp_OASetProperty` — To set the name property of the object
- `sp_OAMethod` — To execute the `SayHello` method of the object

Listing 10.8: `udf_Example_OAhello`

```
CREATE FUNCTION dbo.udf_Example_OAhello (

    @Name varchar(64) -- Name to say hello to
)   RETURNS varchar(128) -- Returns a greeting using an OA call
/*
* Example UDF to exercise the TSQLUDFVB.cTSQLUDFVBDemo OLE
* automation object.
*
* Example:
select dbo.udf_Example_OAhello ('Andy')
****************************************************************/
AS BEGIN

DECLARE @HRESULT int -- RETURN VALUE from OA calls
      , @hObject int -- handle to object
      , @sMessage varchar(128) -- the message returned by the object.
      , @ErrMsg varchar(255) -- an error message

    EXEC @HRESULT = sp_OACreate 'TSQLUDFVB.cTSQLUDFVBDemo'
                              , @hObject OUTPUT -- object token
                              , 5 -- allow in-process server

    IF @HRESULT != 0 BEGIN
        SELECT @sMessage = dbo.udf_OA_LogError (
                             @hObject, @HRESULT
                           , 'udf_ExampleOAhello'
                           , 'sp_OACreate'
                           , 'TSQLUDFVB.cTSQLUDFVBDemo'
                            )
        GOTO Function_Cleanup
    END
```

```
    -- Set the MyName Property
    EXEC @HRESULT = sp_OASetProperty @hObject
                              , 'MyName'
                              , @Name

    IF @HRESULT != 0 BEGIN
        SELECT @sMessage = dbo.udf_OA_LogError (
                           @hObject, @HRESULT
                         , 'udf_ExampleOAhello'
                         , 'sp_OASetProperty'
                         , 'TSQLUDFVB.cTSQLUDFVBDemo'
                         )
        GOTO Function_Cleanup
    END

    EXEC @HRESULT = sp_OAMethod @hObject
                              , 'SayHello'
                              , @sMessage Output
    IF @HRESULT != 0 BEGIN
        SELECT @sMessage = dbo.udf_OA_LogError (
                           @hObject, @HRESULT
                         , 'udf_ExampleOAhello'
                         , 'sp_OAMethod '
                         , 'TSQLUDFVB.cTSQLUDFVBDemo'
                           )
        GOTO Function_Cleanup
    END

Function_Cleanup:

   -- Destroy the object if we created it
   IF @hObject is not NULL
       EXEC @HRESULT = sp_OADestroy @hObject

    RETURN @sMessage

END
```

Now, let's execute the UDF:

```
-- Run the Hello UDF
SELECT dbo.udf_Example_OAhello('Andy') as [Now that's what I call a message.]
GO
```

(Results)

```
Now that's what I call a message.
-------------------------------------------------------------------------------
Hello Andy
```

There's a useful technique for debugging the object that you ought to know about. It's possible to debug your object while it is called from SQL Server. If you're trying to track down a problem and can't reproduce the problem any other way, this might work for you. However, don't use this technique on any computer except a development machine that's not being used by anyone else. To debug your object, do the following:

- Start your Visual Basic project in the integrated development environment and use the Run ➢ Start menu command to start up your project.
- Set breakpoints where you want to stop.
- Execute the T-SQL that uses the object. I usually do this in Query Analyzer.

The Visual Basic debugger stops if it hits one of your breakpoints. To demonstrate this, I first started the TSQLUDFVB project and set breakpoints in the Let procedure for the property `myName` and in the `SayHello` method. Then I ran the previous query, `SELECT * from dbo.udf_Example_OAHello('Andy')`, using Query Analyzer.

Query Analyzer seemed to hang and the Visual Basic debugger was stopped at the assignment statement in the Let procedure. Figure 10.5 shows how the VB debugger looked at this point.

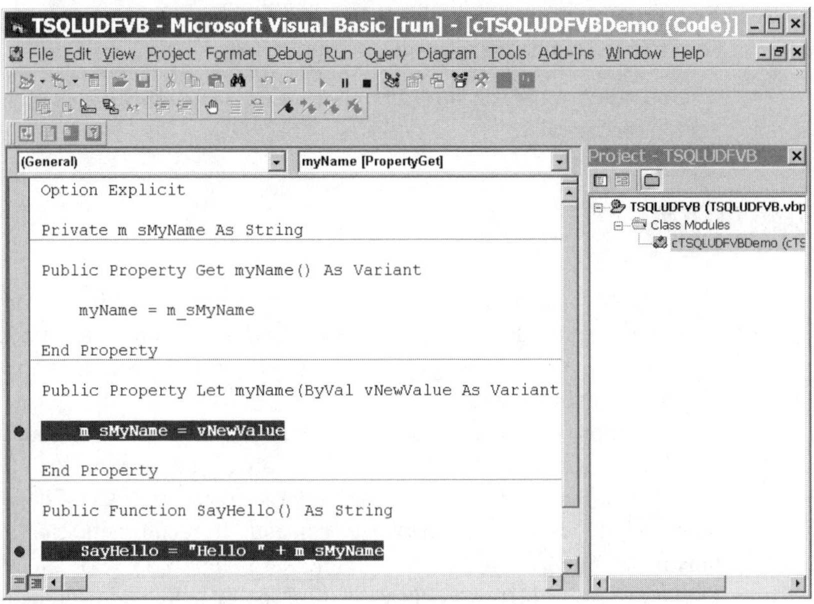

Figure 10.5: Visual Basic debugger at a breakpoint

At that point, I could do any of the normal VB debugger functions such as examining or changing the value of a variable or even changing the code. By using VB's Run ➢ Continue menu command, execution continues until the next breakpoint or until the UDF completes execution and the object is destroyed. This technique can even be combined with debugging the UDF using one of the techniques described earlier in Chapter 3.

Warning:

Just in case this isn't obvious, let me make this very clear: This is a technique that could bring down a SQL Server. I recommend that it only be used on dedicated development machines, such as a programmer's computer with the SQL Server Developer edition installed.

The OLE object presented here is a trivial one. But there are many OLE objects in the Windows world. Many of them can be used constructively from within SQL Server. Some of them are suitable for use within a UDF. A few suggestions are:

- The SQL-DMO interface to SQL Server
- The WMI interface to manage Windows objects
- Cryptography libraries
- Collaboration Data Objects for interacting with mail systems
- MSXML for manipulating XML documents
- The COM interface to Visual SourceSafe

The usefulness of OLE objects to you will depend on the tasks that you seek to accomplish.

Summary

This chapter has discussed using extended stored procedures from UDFs. SQL Server provides a long list of xp_s, both documented and undocumented. I've tried to show you the few that are most useful as a way to illustrate what can be done.

The most powerful of the xp_s are those that enable OLE Automation. COM is the backbone for most Windows programs created since the mid-1990s. The ability to tap into that large resource of COM code is a powerful but dangerous capability. I continue to recommend that it be used only for administrative tasks. If you need to employ a COM object in a high activity production application, it probably belongs in some other application tier, such as the user interface or the application server.

Throughout this book I've shown small tests of how one function or another should work. Most UDFs in the listings have one or more tests in the program's header. The next chapter is about testing UDFs with header tests and more extensive test scripts.

11

Testing UDFs for Correctness and Performance

Everyone who loves to write code to unit test other code, please take two steps forward!

What, no volunteers?

I don't blame you. Writing code to test other code isn't my idea of fun. Most programmers avoid it like the plague. But sometimes writing code to test individual functions is important to the success of an application.

Although I'll admit that I don't write a full test for every UDF, I try to write one for any UDF that is either critically important or when it's difficult to be sure that it's correct. Like all other resource allocation decisions, the cost of testing has to be a consideration. However, the immediate cost of writing the test today isn't the only cost to consider. If it's any good, a UDF will be around for a while and used in multiple databases. Over the long run, getting it right pays off.

UDFs are components. They're building blocks or small pieces of an application. They're not the application. Most of the time, there's no way for an end user or even a software quality assurance (SQA) department to test them in isolation. The most appropriate person to write the test for each UDF is the programmer or DBA who writes the UDF in the first place. The next best choice is the programmer who is going to have to use the UDF first. These people have an interest in ensuring that the UDF is usable. While they're testing, they're learning the functionality of the UDF.

In most of the UDFs that I write, you'll find a few tests down at the bottom of the comment block. Having the tests right there in the definition of the function makes it as easy as I can make it to perform the tests every time the UDF changes, even if the change is small. This chapter starts with a brief discussion of embedded tests.

These two- or three-line tests are much better than no test at all, but they're not the only testing that should be done on a UDF. Test scripts are appropriate when the importance or complexity of the UDF warrant one. That leaves a lot of room for judgment. It'll have to be up to the project manager to decide. I like to put my complete test scripts into stored procedures. After discussing embedded tests, I'll show you a complete test embedded in an SP.

Once the UDF works, you may or may not be done with testing it. Performance evaluation is important to improving your applications. In this regard, UDFs can pose a problem. Depending on how they're used, they can introduce noticeable performance problems. It's important that you watch out for this. After discussing test scripts, we'll look at evaluating the speed of a UDF and comparing it to an equivalent SQL expression.

If you want to execute the scripts as you read the chapter, the short queries used in this chapter are stored in the file Chapter 11 Listing 0 Short Queries.sql. You'll find it in this chapter's download directory. The UDFs and stored procedures used here are in the TSQLUDFS database.

Embedding Tests in the Header of the UDF

Throughout this book there are tests embedded in the comment block that I always place near the top of the UDF. These tests are ready to run whenever the UDF is turned into a `CREATE FUNCTION` or `ALTER FUNCTION` script. That's what makes them so easy to execute.

The testing section begins with a line reading "* Test:". It's followed with the actual test or tests in T-SQL. These lines don't have the leading asterisk, making it easy to select the tests in SQL Query Analyzer and execute them. Here's an example of the tests for `udf_DT_dynamicDATEPART`:

```
* Test:
PRINT 'Test 1 year  ' + case when DATEPART(yy, Getdate())
                    =dbo.udf_DT_dynamicDATEPART ('yy', GetDate())
                    THEN 'Worked' ELSE 'ERROR' END
PRINT 'Test 2 month ' + case when DATEPART(mm, Getdate())
                    =dbo.udf_DT_dynamicDATEPART ('mm', GetDate())
                    THEN 'Worked' ELSE 'ERROR' END

DECLARE @dtTest DATETIME -- Time used for the test
SELECT @dtTest = Getdate()
PRINT 'Test 3 ms    ' + case when DATEPART(ms, @dtTest)
                    =dbo.udf_DT_dynamicDATEPART ('ms', @dtTest)
                    THEN 'Worked' ELSE 'ERROR' END
*
```

As shown in Figure 11.1, you select the code of the test in Query Analyzer and use the F5 button, use the green execute arrow, or press Ctrl+E to run the tests. The results print out in the results window, and you can quickly evaluate if they worked.

One of the important aspects of the tests is that they check their own answers. An embedded test should print out either "Worked" or "ERROR." It shouldn't print out the result of executing the function.

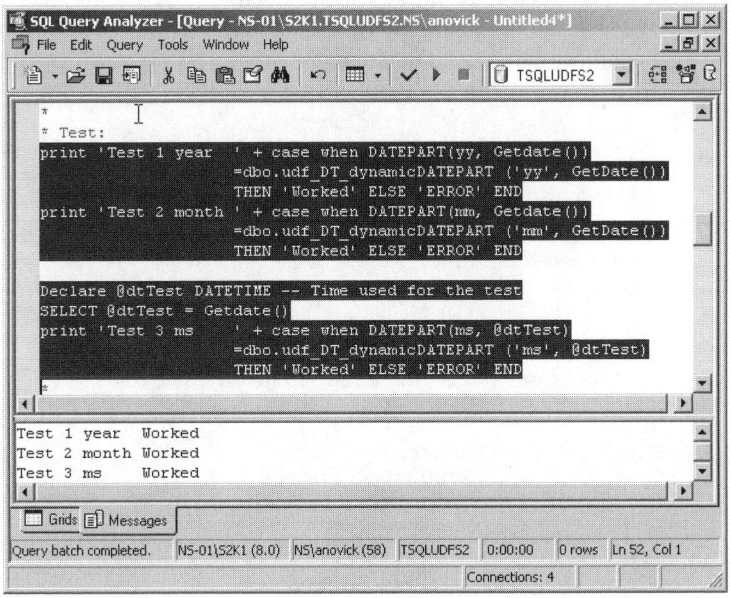

Figure 11.1: Embedded tests on udf_DT_dynamicDATEPART

The day after you write the UDF code you may know what results to expect. A few months later or when someone else has to test the code, the tester has to spend time figuring out what to expect from the function. The practice of printing only a confirmation message makes it nearly trivial to run a quick test and know that the UDF is still, probably, okay.

The inline tests work really well. But unless the UDF is trivial, they don't do a complete job of testing the functionality of the routine. That job falls to the test script.

Test Scripts

There are many ways that tests can be written. They can be textual scripts with instructions on what queries to run and what results to expect. They can be programs written in a client-side development tool such as VB .NET. They can also be a script in an automated testing tool. I prefer to write tests for UDFs in a T-SQL stored procedure.

Stored procedures are backed up with the database. That makes them your best bet for having the test around for the long term. Separate scripts are too easy to lose. SPs also have the advantage of being in a programming language that is certain to always be available when the time comes to test. If you rely on having a VB compiler or even Windows Scripting Host available in the field, you may be caught short in a critical situation.

By convention, I name my testing stored procedures with a prefix of TEST_ followed by the UDF's name. Listing 11.1 shows `TEST_udf_DT_WeekdayNext`. You'll find `udf_DT_WeekdayNext` in the TSQLUDFS database.

Listing 11.1: `TEST_udf_DT_WeekdayNext`

```
CREATE PROC dbo.TEST_udf_DT_WeekdayNext

    @AllWorked BIT OUTPUT -- 1 when all tests worked.
  , @PrintSuccessMsgs BIT = 0
AS
/*
* Test driver for udf_DT_WeekdayNext. A year's worth of dates
* are tested with every possible value of @@DATEFIRST.
* It always assumes that Sat and Sun are not weekdays.
*
* Test:
DECLARE @AllWorked BIT, @RC int
EXEC @RC = TEST_udf_DT_WeekdayNext @AllWorked OUTPUT, 1
PRINT 'Test udf_DT_WeekdayNext @RC = ' + CONVERT(char(10), @RC)
      + '  @AllWorked = ' + CONVERT(VARCHAR(1), @ALLWORKED)
*************************************************************/

DECLARE @TestDate datetime -- the date being tested
      , @Answer   datetime -- known answer
      , @TestDayName varchar(9) -- name of the test day
      , @AnswerName  varchar(9) -- name of the answer
      , @FuncSays datetime -- The function says
      , @df       int      -- value for DATEFIRST
      , @TestNo   int      -- Test Number
      , @Worked   BIT      -- Did the test work.
      , @SaveDF   int      -- Save DATEFIRST

SET @SaveDF = @@DATEFIRST
SET @AllWorked = 1 -- Assume the best

-- First some hard-coded cases
SET DATEFIRST 7
IF 'Monday'!=DATENAME (dw,dbo.udf_DT_WeekdayNext('2003-03-21'))
  OR 'Monday'!=DATENAME (dw,dbo.udf_DT_WeekdayNext('2003-03-22 9:34:03'))
  OR 'Monday'!=DATENAME (dw,dbo.udf_DT_WeekdayNext('2003-03-23'))
  OR 'Friday'!=DATENAME (dw,dbo.udf_DT_WeekdayNext('2003-03-20'))
   BEGIN
   SET @AllWorked = 0
   PRINT 'Hard-coded tests failed.'
   END
ELSE BEGIN
```

```
    IF @PrintSuccessMsgs=1 PRINT 'Hard-coded tests worked.'
END

SELECT @TestNo =  1
     , @TestDate = '2003-01-01'

WHILE @TestDate < '2004-01-10' BEGIN
    SET @TestNo = @TestNo + 1

    SET DATEFIRST 7 -- This is the default. Has to be this way
                    -- to get the answer correct.

    SET @TestDayName = DATENAME(dw, @TestDate)
    SET @Answer = CASE @TestDayName
               WHEN 'Sunday' THEN DATEADD(day, 1, @TestDate)
               WHEN 'Monday' THEN DATEADD(day, 1, @TestDate)
               WHEN 'Tuesday' THEN DATEADD(day, 1, @TestDate)
               WHEN 'Wednesday' THEN DATEADD(day, 1, @TestDate)
               WHEN 'Thursday' THEN DATEADD(day, 1, @TestDate)
               WHEN 'Friday' THEN DATEADD(day, 3, @TestDate)
               WHEN 'Saturday' THEN DATEADD(day, 2, @TestDate)
               END
    SET @AnswerName = DATENAME (dw, @Answer)

    SET @DF = 1 -- test DATEFIRST FROM 1 TO 7
    WHILE @DF <= 7 BEGIN
       SET DATEFIRST @DF

       SELECT @FuncSays = dbo.udf_DT_WeekDayNext (@TestDate)
       SET @Worked = CASE WHEN @Answer = @FuncSays
                          THEN 1 ELSE 0 END
       IF 0=@Worked  SET @AllWorked = 0

       -- Print on request or failure
       IF @PrintSuccessMsgs=1 or 0=@Worked BEGIN
           PRINT 'Test ' + CONVERT(char(6), @TestNo) + '  '
             + ' DATEFIRST=' + CONVERT(VARCHAR(10), @@DATEFIRST)
             + ' TestDate='
                   + CONVERT (varchar(22), @TestDate, 120)
                   + ' ' + @TestDayName
           PRINT SPACE(28)
             + 'Answer=' + CONVERT(varchar(22), @Answer, 120)
             + ' ' + @AnswerName
           PRINT SPACE(26)
             +'Function=' + convert(varchar(22), @FuncSays, 120)
             + CASE WHEN 1=@Worked
                    THEN ' Worked' Else ' Error' END
        END -- ENDIF

        SET @TestNo = @TestNo + 1
        SET @DF = @DF + 1
    END -- WHILE

    SELECT @TestDate = DATEADD(DAY, 1, @Testdate)
END -- WHILE

SET DATEFIRST @SaveDF -- Restore the incoming value

IF @PrintSuccessMsgs=1
    PRINT 'TEST_udf_DT_WeekdayNext Done. ' + CASE WHEN 1=@AllWorked
        THEN ' All tests worked.' ELSE ' Some tests failed!' END
```

The first thing that you should do with the test procedure is run it. This test is embedded in the comment block near the top of the procedure. It's kept there so that it's always accessible and difficult to lose:

```
-- Testing UDFs
DECLARE @AllWorked BIT, @RC int
EXEC @RC = TEST_udf_DT_WeekdayNext @AllWorked OUTPUT, 1
PRINT 'Test udf_DT_WeekdayNext @RC = ' + CONVERT(char(10), @RC)
GO
```

(Results - abridged)

```
Hard coded tests worked.
Test 2         DATEFIRST=1 TestDate=2003-01-01 00:00:00 Wednesday
                             Answer=2003-01-02 00:00:00 Thursday
                           Function=2003-01-02 00:00:00 Worked
Test 3         DATEFIRST=2 TestDate=2003-01-01 00:00:00 Wednesday
                             Answer=2003-01-02 00:00:00 Thursday
                           Function=2003-01-02 00:00:00 Worked
...
Test 2991      DATEFIRST=6 TestDate=2004-01-09 00:00:00 Friday
                             Answer=2004-01-12 00:00:00 Monday
                           Function=2004-01-12 00:00:00 Worked
Test 2992      DATEFIRST=7 TestDate=2004-01-09 00:00:00 Friday
                             Answer=2004-01-12 00:00:00 Monday
                           Function=2004-01-12 00:00:00 Worked
TEST_udf_DT_WeekdayNext Done.  All tests worked.
Test udf_DT_WeekdayNext @RC = 0
```

The proc has a mixture of a few hard-coded tests and a double loop of tests that test every day for a year under every possible value for `@@DATEFIRST`. `@@DATEFIRST` governs the numbering of days. Changing it, with `SET DATEFIRST`, changes the result from the `DATEPART` function when requesting the day of the week.

Usually, it's trivial for a human to decide what's the next weekday. Under most circumstances, it's also easy to code. However, `udf_DT_WeekdayNext` is sensitive to the value of `@@DATEFIRST`. That's the reason for the double loop.

The most important part of any test procedure is that it's correct. In addition, if attention is paid to a few mechanical items, the long-term value of the procedure is improved.

The parameter `@AllWorked` should be part of every test procedure. I haven't written it yet, but I'm moving toward having a regression test procedure that runs all my testing stored procedures. That could be run a few times a day during any heavy-duty development to be sure that nothing is broken. Once development slows down, it could be run once a day or when needed.

The parameter `@PrintSuccessMsgs` is there to suppress the 9,000 lines of output from the procedure most of the time. While I'm developing the test, I want to see all the output. Once UDF is no longer in active development, I don't want to see the messages unless there's a problem.

Just as UDFs contain examples and tests in their comment block, I put a short script that runs the procedure in the procedure's comments. This makes it easy to run the test. The easier it is to run, the easier it is to avoid the temptation of assuming that the procedure is fine and that you don't have to run the test one last time.

There are many variations on how to perform testing. The most important thing is that the tests get written in the first place. Coding the unit tests for UDFs in stored procedures keeps them nearby at all times.

Once testing for correctness is complete, it may be important to test for performance. Whether it's necessary to conduct performance testing on a UDF depends on how the UDF is used. The next section shows that under the right circumstances, a UDF can have very negative consequences for performance.

Drilling Down into the Performance Problem

The problem of inadequate performance is the primary reason not to use scalar UDFs. There can be a big difference in the performance of a query that employs UDFs and one that replaces them with equivalent expressions.

Using UDFs gives your query the same performance as if you implemented the query using a cursor instead of relational SQL. That's because the SQL Server query engine has to address every row and invoke the UDF. It creates a loop very much like a cursor.

Using UDFs is great! Most of the time. But there are times when the extra overhead of UDF execution is more than you can tolerate. Eliminating the UDF, where possible, is a strategy that usually produces dramatically faster query execution times. By "dramatically" I mean two to 500 times faster (enough to make a real difference in the response time of your application).

This section demonstrates and documents the performance problem in detail by constructing an experiment that compares the performance of a UDF-based solution with one that replaces the UDF with an expression. The first step is to pick a suitable UDF for the experiment—one that can be replaced by an expression. Secondly, to make the results dramatic enough, we'll build a table with a sufficient number of rows to show the difference between the UDF and the expression. Finally, we'll run the experiment.

The Function and the Template for Testing Performance

The function that we're going to use is udf_Txt_CharIndexRev, which is shown in Listing 11.2. It works just like the built-in CHARINDEX function except that it works from the back of the string. Like CHARINDEX, the position it reports is relative to the beginning of the string that's searched. I use udf_Txt_CharIndexRev for tasks like finding the slash that separates a file name from the rest of a file path.

Listing 11.2: udf_Txt_CharIndexRev

```
CREATE FUNCTION dbo.udf_Txt_CharIndexRev (

    @SearchFor varchar(255) -- Sequence to be found
  , @SearchIn varchar(8000) -- The string to be searched
)  RETURNS int -- Position from the back of the string where
               -- @SearchFor is found in @SearchIn
    WITH SCHEMABINDING
/*
* Searches for a string in another string working from the back.
* It reports the position (relative to the front) of the first
* such expression it finds. If the expression is not found, it
* returns zero.
*
* Equivalent Template:
       CASE
         WHEN CHARINDEX(<search_for, varchar(255), ''>
                     , <search_in, varchar(8000), ''>) > 0
         THEN LEN(<search_in, varchar(8000), ''>)
              - CHARINDEX(REVERSE(<search_for, varchar(255), ''>)
                  , REVERSE (<search_in, varchar(8000), ''>)) + 1
         ELSE 0 END
* Example:
select dbo.udf_Txt_CharIndexRev('\', 'C:\temp\abcd.txt')
*
* Test:
PRINT 'Test 1    ' + CASE WHEN 8=
           dbo.udf_Txt_CharIndexRev ('\', 'C:\temp\abcd.txt')
                     THEN 'Worked' ELSE 'ERROR' END
PRINT 'Test 2    ' + CASE WHEN 0=
           dbo.udf_TxtCharIndexRev ('*', 'C:\tmp\d.txt')
                     THEN 'Worked' ELSE 'ERROR' END
****************************************************************/
AS BEGIN

    DECLARE @Result int
          , @StringLen int
          , @ReverseIn varchar(8000)
          , @ReverseFor varchar(255)

    SELECT @ReverseIn = REVERSE (@SearchIn)
         , @ReverseFor = REVERSE(@SearchFor)
         , @StringLen = LEN(@SearchIn)
```

```
    SELECT @Result = CHARINDEX(@ReverseFor, @ReverseIn)

    -- return the position from the front of the string
    IF @Result > 0
        SET @Result = @StringLen - @Result + 1
    -- ENDIF

    RETURN @Result
END
```

Before we get to the experiment, let's try out a few simple cases with this test query:

```
-- Demonstrate udf_Txt_CharIndexRev
SELECT dbo.udf_Txt_CharIndexRev('fdf', 'f123 asdasfdfdfddfjas  ')
            as [Middle]
     , dbo.udf_Txt_CharIndexRev('C', 'C:\temp\ab.txt') as [start]
     , dbo.udf_Txt_CharIndexRev('X', '123456789X') as [end]
     , dbo.udf_Txt_CharIndexRev('AB', '12347') as [missing]

GO

(Results)

Middle      start       end         missing
----------- ----------- ----------- -----------
         13           1          10           0
```

`udf_Txt_CharIndexRev` is simple enough that it's possible to replace it with an expression. The section in the comment block labeled "Equivalent Template" tells how to achieve the same result as the UDF without using the UDF. Here's the template:

```
        CASE
          WHEN CHARINDEX(<search_for, varchar(255), ''>
                       , <search_in, varchar(8000), ''>) > 0
          THEN LEN(<search_in, varchar(8000), ''>)
               - CHARINDEX(REVERSE(<search_for, varchar(255), ''>)
                   , REVERSE (<search_in, varchar(8000), ''>)) + 1
          ELSE 0 END
```

Why bother having the UDF at all if it can be replaced with an expression? As you may recall, my philosophy about writing efficient code is that coding is an economic activity with trade-offs between the cost of writing code and the cost of running it. In my opinion, the best course of action is to write good, easy-to-maintain code and use a basic concern for performance to eliminate any obvious performance problem. The overhead of using a UDF to parse the extension from one file name isn't ever going to show up on the performance radar screen. It's when a UDF is used on large numbers of rows that it becomes a problem. In situations with few rows, having the UDF helps by making the code easier to write.

The Equivalent Template section of the comment block is used to replace a function call to `udf_Txt_CharIndexRev` with the text in the template and then, using SQL Query Analyzer's menu item Edit ➤ Replace Template Parameters, put the function parameters into the revised SQL at the locations where they belong. The Query Analyzer template facility comes in handy because the parameters have to be inserted in more than one place.

So that we don't have to perform the replacement process four times, let's convert this query that does just one call to `udf_Txt_CharIndexRev` into an equivalent query using the template:

```
-- Query to translate
SELECT dbo.udf_Txt_CharIndexRev('fad', 'f123 asdasfdfdfddfjas  ')
          as [Middle]
GO
```

The first step is to replace the function call with the Equivalent Template, and we get:

```
SELECT CASE
        WHEN CHARINDEX(<search_for, varchar(255), ''>
                     , <search_in, varchar(8000), ''>) > 0
        THEN LEN(<search_in, varchar(8000), ''>)
             - CHARINDEX(REVERSE(<search_for, varchar(255), ''>)
                 , REVERSE (<search_in, varchar(8000), ''>)) + 1
        ELSE 0 END
           as [Middle]
```

Next we use the Edit ➤ Replace Template Parameters menu item and enter the two parameters. Figure 11.2 shows the Replace Template Parameters dialog box with the replacement text entered.

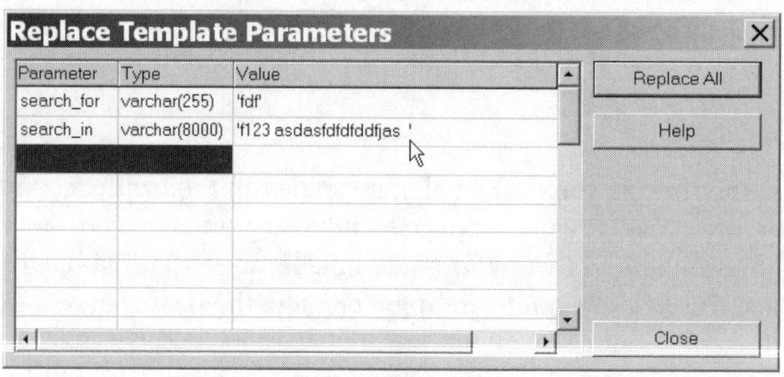

Figure 11.2: Replacing an equivalent template

After pressing the Replace All button, the result looks like this:

```
-- Translated query
SELECT CASE
         WHEN CHARINDEX('fdf'
                       , 'f123 asdasfdfdfddfjas  ') > 0
         THEN LEN('f123 asdasfdfdfddfjas  ')
              - CHARINDEX(REVERSE('fad')
                  , REVERSE ('f123 asdasfdfdfddfjas  ')) + 1
         ELSE 0 END
            as [Middle]
GO

(Results)

Middle
-----------
         13
```

As you can see, replacing the call to the UDF with the equivalent expression results in a much longer and messier query. Simplification, with a corresponding reduction in maintenance effort, is a benefit of using UDFs that is lost when you replace them with complex expressions.

Now that we have a function and can replace it with an expression, we need some data that helps show us the difference in performance between the two. Pubs and Northwind are useful for learning but they don't contain very much data; at best they have a few hundred rows in any one table. I like to run tests on a million-row table. SQL Server doesn't come with any tables that large, so we'll have to construct one.

Constructing a Large Test Table

To test the difference between the UDF and the equivalent expression, we need a table with a large number of rows. Figure 11.3 shows a database diagram for the `ExampleNumberString` table that will be used for the experiment. The `NumberString` column is a 20- to 23-digit numeric string that we can use for experimentation on `udf_Txt_CharIndexRev`.

ExampleNumberString

Column Name	Data Type	Length	Allow Nulls
ID	int	4	
BigNum	numeric	17	✓
NumberString	varchar	128	✓

Figure 11.3: ExampleNumberString table fields

The table hasn't been added to your TSQLUDFS database because there is a stored procedure in the database to create the table and populate it with plenty of rows. `usp_CreateExampleNumberString` is shown in Listing

11.3. Its parameter is the number of times to double the number of rows in ExampleNumberString.

Listing 11.3: usp_CreateExampleNumberString

```
CREATE  PROC usp_CreateExampleNumberString

    @Loops int = 20 -- creates POWER (2, @Loops) Rows
                    -- 20 Creates 1,000,000 rows
AS

    DECLARE @LC int -- Loop counter

    -- delete an existing ExampleNumberString table
    if exists (select * from dbo.sysobjects
                where id = object_id(N'dbo.ExampleNumberString')
                     and OBJECTPROPERTY(id, N'IsUserTable') = 1)
        DROP TABLE dbo.ExampleNumberString

   CREATE TABLE ExampleNumberString (
                ID int identity (1,1)
              , BigNum Numeric (38, 0)
              , NumberString varchar(128) NULL
                )

    INSERT INTO ExampleNumberString  (BigNum, NumberString)
          VALUES(CONVERT (numeric(38,0), rand() * 9999999999999)
                , '                              ') -- preallocate


    SELECT @LC = 0
    WHILE @LC < @Loops BEGIN

        INSERT INTO ExampleNumberString (BigNum, NumberString)
            SELECT BigNum * RAND(@LC + 1) * 2
                , '                              '
                FROM ExampleNumberString

        SELECT @LC = @LC + 1
    END -- WHILE

   UPDATE ExampleNumberString
        SET NumberString = convert(varchar(128)
                       , convert(numeric(38,0), 9834311) * bignum)
```

Before running usp_CreateExampleNumberString, check to be sure you have enough disk space. Adding one million rows takes about 70 megabytes. With the size of today's disks, that shouldn't be a problem, but check anyway. To add the million rows, run the query as is. If you can't spare the 70 megabytes, reduce the parameter from 20 to just 10, which will add only about 1,000 rows. Now create the table:

```
-- Create and populate the table
DECLARE @RC int
EXEC @RC = usp_CreateExampleNumberString 20
GO
```

usp_CreateExampleNumberString does a reasonable job of producing a different large NumberString for each row. There is usually about one percent duplication of numbers, which seems acceptable for most testing scenarios. With a parameter of 20, the procedure takes about 55 seconds to run on my desktop development system.

Since we're going to run multiple queries against the NumberString column to test the time it takes to use a UDF on a large number of rows, we should try to make the circumstances for all queries as similar as possible. One way to do that is to force all the rows that are going to be queried into memory, SQL Server's page cache, and keep them there. If we don't have all the desired rows in memory, then we might be comparing one query that reads a million rows from disk with another query that reads the same million rows from SQL Server's page cache. It wouldn't be a fair comparison.

SQL Server provides the DBCC PINTABLE statement to force all pages from a table to remain in the cache once they've been read the first time. *Use it with caution!* It can fill SQL Server's cache and cause the query engine to lock up to the point where you have to shut it down and restart it. Only do this if you have adequate RAM available, not just virtual memory. There's no point in using virtual memory as a substitute for RAM in this situation. That just substitutes one form of disk I/O (paging) for the one we're trying to eliminate (reading pages from disk).

This next script pins ExampleNumberString in memory. On my desktop development system with a million-row table, pinning the table forced SQL Server to consume 82 additional megabytes of RAM. The system has 512 megabytes of RAM, and I used Task Manager to see that memory isn't full. If your system has less available RAM, reduce the number of rows in the test to eliminate paging.

```
-- Pin ExampleNumberString into memory. You must change the database name, if
-- you're not going to run it in TSQLUDFS
-- Be sure that you have enough memory available before you do
-- this.  My SQL Server Process grew to 82 megabytes when I ran
-- this script.
DECLARE @db_id int, @tbl_id int
SET @db_id = DB_ID('TSQLUDFS') --  DB_ID('<your database name goes here>')
SET @tbl_id = OBJECT_ID('ExampleNumberString')
DBCC PINTABLE (@db_id, @tbl_id)
GO
```

(Results)

```
Warning: Pinning tables should be carefully considered. If a pinned table is larger,
or grows larger, than the available data cache, the server may need to be restarted
and the table unpinned.
DBCC execution completed. If DBCC printed error messages, contact your system
administrator.
```

Pinning the table only tells SQL Server to never remove the table's pages from the page cache. It doesn't read them into the cache. The next query does:

```
-- Read all the rows to force the pages into the cache
SELECT * from ExampleNumberString
GO
```

With a million-row table in memory, the stage is set for comparing the UDF and the equivalent template. Ladies and gentleman, place your bets.

Experimenting with UDF vs. Expression Performance

Let's start by constructing a query that uses `udf_Txt_CharIndexRev` to search for the string `'83'` from the back of the `NumberString` column and then replace the UDF with the equivalent expression. The two queries are:

```
SELECT dbo.udf_Txt_CharIndexRev ('83', NumberString)
                as [Index of 83 from the string end]
    FROM ExampleNumberString

SELECT CASE WHEN CHARINDEX('83', NumberString) > 0
         THEN LEN(NumberString)
              - CHARINDEX(REVERSE('83')
                  , REVERSE (NumberString)) + 1
         ELSE 0 END as [Index of 83 from the string end]
    FROM ExampleNumberString
```

Don't run them yet. I have a few more wrinkles to throw into the experiment.

Any query that returns a million rows to SQL Query Analyzer's results window is going to do a lot of work on sending, receiving, and displaying the results. To eliminate most of that work, using an aggregate function, such as `MAX`, forces the UDF or expression to be evaluated without returning much data as the result.

For comparison purposes, I've also included a third query, labeled Query #0, that just takes the `MAX` of the `LEN` function. This query represents the minimum time it might take to just read the million rows of data.

The `SET STATISTICS TIME ON` command tells SQL Server to measure the time to parse and compile the query and the time to execute the query and report them back with the query results.

Making these three changes to the queries gives us our experiment. If you run them, be patient. Query #1 took over four minutes on my system. The three queries with their results from my desktop development system are:

```
-- Query #0:  The minimum time for an operation that scans the whole table.
SET STATISTICS TIME ON
SELECT MAX(LEN(NumberString)) as [Max Len]
    FROM ExampleNumberString
GO
```

(Results)

```
SQL Server parse and compile time:
   CPU time = 2 ms, elapsed time = 2 ms.Max Length
-----------
         23

SQL Server Execution Times:
   CPU time = 991 ms,  elapsed time = 991 ms.
```

(End of Results for Query #0)

```
-- Query #1: The UDF.  Note execution time is incorrect.
SET STATISTICS TIME ON
SELECT MAX (dbo.udf_Txt_CharIndexRev ('83', NumberString))
             as [Right Most Position]
    FROM ExampleNumberString
GO
```

(Results)

```
SQL Server parse and compile time:
   CPU time = 2 ms, elapsed time = 2 ms.
Right Most Position
-------------------
                 23

SQL Server Execution Times:
   CPU time = 0 ms,  elapsed time = 0 ms.
```

(End of Results for Query #1 - It took 4 minutes 38 seconds)
(- CPU was working at 100% during that time)

```
-- Query #2: The equivalent expression
SET STATISTICS TIME ON
SELECT MAX (CASE WHEN CHARINDEX('83', NumberString) > 0
         THEN LEN(NumberString) - CHARINDEX(REVERSE('83')
                  , REVERSE (NumberString)) + 1
         ELSE 0 END
        ) [Right Most Position]
    FROM ExampleNumberString
GO
```

(Results)

```
SQL Server parse and compile time:
   CPU time = 3 ms, elapsed time = 3 ms.
Right Most Position
-------------------
                 23

SQL Server Execution Times:
   CPU time = 2934 ms,  elapsed time = 2954 ms.
```

(End of Results for Query #2)

Query #1, the UDF, didn't report its execution times correctly. It seems that `SET STATISTICS TIME` is limited in the duration that it can measure. I used the Windows Task Manager to watch what was happening on my system, and the CPU time for Query #1 is very close to the elapsed time. For our comparison, we'll have to use the elapsed time.

Table 11.1 has the comparison in run time of the queries. The Net column subtracts the time it took to run Query #0, the very simplest expression on the same set of strings, from the other queries. I think that the Net column has the numbers that should be compared because it isolates just the effect of running the UDF or the replacement expression.

Table 11.1: Query timings for the experiment

Query	Description	Time (milliseconds)	Net
#0	Simple expression	991	N/A
#1	UDF	278000	277009
#2	UDF replaced by expression	2954	1963

The difference in time is dramatic. The UDF takes about 140 times longer to run as an equivalent expression. Wow! Four-plus minutes versus three seconds is the kind of difference users really notice.

Of course, the difference isn't going to be perceivable when the query is run on 1, 5, or even 100 rows. Only when the number of rows grows into the thousands does the difference begin to be noticeable.

The lesson that I draw from this experiment is that UDFs must be used with care in performance-sensitive situations. They're a great tool for simplifying code and promoting code reuse, but they can have a dramatically negative effect on performance.

Summary

This chapter described issues about testing UDFs for correctness and performance that didn't belong in the earlier chapters. I wanted to wait until you had seen all the basic material before delving into these topics.

I know that few programmers really love to write test programs for their production programs. In the case of UDFs, writing a program in the form of a stored procedure appears to be the best way to test it and be able to continue to test it over time. Like all other code writing, the amount of testing applied depends on the economics of the situation. A partial solution that should be included with most scalar UDFs is the test inside the comment block. Having a quick and easy-to-execute test available increases the likelihood that at least some tests will be run after any change to the function.

Through experimentation, this chapter has shown that the difference in performance between a SQL query that uses UDFs and the equivalent query that eliminates the UDF can be over 100 times. That's a big enough difference to give you second thoughts about using a UDF at all. However, there are many times when you're not working with a thousand or a million rows and the performance implications are outweighed by the ease of coding, readability, and maintainability that UDFs provide.

Now that we've covered the technology for creating UDFs, the next two chapters turn to specific problems and how to solve them with UDFs. Both are data conversion problems. The first one is the Metric-to-Imperial units conversion problem that sparked my interest in UDFs in the first place. The second problem is currency conversion where a table-driven solution is required.

12

Converting between Unit Systems

The Introduction described how I originally encountered the lack of functions in T-SQL back in 1996 while designing the Pavement Management System (PMS) for the Mississippi Department of Transportation (MDOT). The database used for the project was Sybase SQL Server System 11, which also uses the Transact-SQL (T-SQL) dialect of SQL used by Microsoft SQL Server. Of course, a solution was found that didn't require UDFs, but I was never happy with the lack of functions in T-SQL. The pain was particularly acute because the two other databases that I use often, Oracle and Access, both have user-defined functions. My prayers were answered when SQL Server 2000 arrived.

Converting distances and areas from the metric system to the system of feet and miles that is commonly used in the United States is a problem in the MDOT PMS that would have benefited from the availability of UDFs. This chapter discusses UDFs that implement the conversion between unit systems.

There are many ways that a conversion function can be constructed. The variations all produce the same result, but they reflect choices about what parameters to give to the function and when certain parameters, such as the unit system of the result, must be specified. This chapter shows three alternative methods for constructing the conversion UDF. Each alternative represents a different balance between flexibility, complexity, and performance. There are many other alternatives that you might also construct based on the needs of your application.

Of particular importance in any system to convert between unit systems is maintaining numeric precision and showing the results to the correct number of significant digits. This chapter reviews the use of SQL Server built-in functions for rounding and data type conversion and shows how they're applied in the context of unit conversion.

The measurements that might require conversion are often stored or handled in floating-point data types. Floating-point data can be particularly tricky to work with because it represents numbers by an approximation. Comparing and aggregating floating-point numbers can lead to unnecessary bug reports for your application. Once the conversion functions are constructed, these issues are hashed out and some solutions are demonstrated.

All the functions in this chapter are in the TSQLUDFS database. As with the other chapters, short queries that do not have listing numbers are saved in the file Chapter 12 Listing 0 Short Queries.sql. The file is in the download directory for this chapter.

Before performing any conversions, we need the conversion factors. I'll bet you know a few of them off the top of your head, but there are actually hundreds of factors that might be used. Let's start with a little history of the metric system in the U.S. and locate a good source for the conversion factors.

Getting Conversion Factors for the Metric System

The metric system, also known as the International System of Units and abbreviated SI from the French *Système International d'Unités*, was created by the French near the turn of the 19th century. Along with their fries, their toast, and their kiss, it's one of their greatest creations. The SI system was established by a treaty known as the *Convention du Mètere* and is now managed by the *Bureau International des Poids et Mesures*.

In the United States we still use what used to be called the Imperial system of measures. With the decline of the empire and the United Kingdom's adoption of the metric system, it's now often referred to as the U.S. Standard system or the English system. I'll use U.S. Standard for the rest of this chapter.

Much of the world laughs or groans at Americans when it comes to units. Two hundred years of exposure to a system that is simpler, easier to learn, and more precise hasn't been enough to persuade us to switch. Since the 1860s, when the metric system was made legal in the U.S., there have been efforts to convert from the U.S. Standard system. I've noticed serious attempts to convert the U.S. about once every ten years. The Metric Conversion Act of 1975, as revised in the '80s, attempted to make SI the "preferred system of weights and measures for United States trade and commerce." It hasn't happened.

It's not that some people haven't tried. Many of us Americans old enough to remember the 1970s may recall gas pumps that measured liters instead of gallons and dual miles/kilometers distance measurements on interstate highways. I still see one lonely sign on I-95 between Boston and Providence touting "Providence 28km." Whether metric ever gains wide adoption in the United States or not, it's the system used by the rest of the world, in science, and in some industries. Until the United States switches, American programmers often have to work in both systems.

The MDOT PMS was partially paid for with funds from the United States Department of Transportation (USDOT). In alignment with a general policy to migrate to the metric system, USDOT mandated that the database be stored in metric measurements. However, almost all of the instruments, such as tape measures, owned by MDOT and its engineers in the field are calibrated in U.S. Standard units. Although their engineers are trained in both systems, most are more comfortable with the U.S. Standard system. MDOT management requested that, although the database was to be in metric units, the system's user interface work in either system based on user preference.

Converting from one system of measures to another is easy, isn't it? Yes, once you've decided on the conversion factor and how to handle issues of precision. Many books on math and science contain the most important conversion factors, but there's no law that dictates them. A reliable, up-to-date source must be found because there have been small adjustments to the conversion factors over time, based on new science.

For comprehensive coverage of the metric conversion, I use the Washington State Department of Transportation, or WSDOT. WSDOT maintains a very useful web site at http://www.wsdot.wa.gov/Metrics/factors.htm that is relied on by the transportation industry. It also makes available for download a Windows program, convert.exe, by Josh Madison, that implements the conversion factors. You'll find convert.exe in the download directory for this chapter. The WSDOT conversion factors have been used for the conversion functions that accompany this book.

In addition to converting between systems of units, it is sometimes necessary to convert between measures within the same system. For example, one foot is 12 inches. Since conversions within the same system are defined by the system, there is no issue about which conversion factor to use; it's a matter of getting the definitions correct. Of course, in the metric system, this is almost trivial because all intra-system conversions are based on a factor of 10.

Conversions don't have to be performed in the database engine. It would be perfectly legitimate for an application designer to decide that conversions take place in the client application or some other application layer. Although some programming tools have unit conversion functions in their libraries, Access, VBA, VB Script, Visual Basic, and T-SQL do *not* have such functions and can't be used as sites for conversion without writing the functions in their language.

Performing conversion in the database has the advantage of centralization. If done properly, there is only one place to get conversion factors, and the DBA can be responsible for managing unit system conversions in both directions. Considering that a database may be accessed by several client applications, such as report writers, web pages, and Windows applications, centralization in the database has substantial advantages.

Stand-alone report writers, such as Crystal Reports, make it particularly important that conversion functions be centralized. While report writers can perform the conversions, it's often necessary to code the conversion into every field. This becomes tedious and error prone. It's difficult to make sure that every field is converted correctly, using the same conversion factor and rules for managing precision. Keeping the conversion in the database engine promotes consistency.

If you're not sure that care in making consistent conversions is really so important, recall that NASA's Mars Climate Orbiter was lost due to a conversion error between one program that worked in U.S. Standard units and another that worked in the metric system. Noel Hemmers, the spokesman for Lockheed Martin, the primary contractor, was quoted as saying, "It was, frankly, just overlooked." See http://abcnews.go.com/sections/science/DailyNews/climateorbiter991110.html for more information on this conversion error.

Now that we have a way to get good conversion factors, the other design issues that affect the construction of unit conversion functions should be discussed. Most important among them is the preservation of measurement precision.

Design Issues for Unit Conversions

The design for unit conversion functions needs to take the following issues into account:

- **Data storage** — What data type should be used to store the dimensional data?
- **Data type** — What data type should be returned as the result of the unit conversion functions?
- **Presentation** — How is the data presented?
- **Precision** — How accurate are the results of conversion? Is that accuracy preserved when the data is presented?
- **Performance** — How fast do the functions execute?

- **Programmer productivity** — How easily can the functions be incorporated into a program?
- **Development time** — How long will it take to develop the functions?

The ones that have proven to be of most importance when converting between unit systems are precision and performance. These get the lion's share of the attention in this section, but the others won't be ignored.

SQL Server can't provide any more numeric precision after a conversion than the original measurements contain. If data is accurate to two digits of precision to the right of the decimal place, the result of a conversion doesn't gain any accuracy even though the result may gain digits.

To take an example from pavement management, let's say a road is measured with an odometer that is known to have precision to a hundredth of a mile. The measurement is 1.27 miles. Multiplying by the miles-to-kilometer conversion factor of 1.609344 gives a result of 2.04386688 kilometers. While there are eight digits to the right of the decimal and nine digits in the answer, the distance isn't known to nine significant digits. The distance is still only known to the three significant digits in the original measurement. Here's a query that shows the results of this calculation in Query Analyzer:

```
-- A simple conversion
SELECT 1.27 * 1.609344 as [km]
GO

(Results)

Km
-------------
2.04386688
```

SQL Server returned eight digits to the right of the decimal. Multiplication by hand, as I was taught in third grade by Mrs. Eidelhoch♥, as implemented by my desktop calculator, a TI-503SV, and as implemented by Microsoft Excel, all return eight digits to the right of the decimal, which shows meaningless precision. Therefore, precision must be handled in ways that go beyond straightforward multiplication.

To manage numeric precision, SQL Server has the `ROUND`, `CAST`, and `CONVERT` functions. `ROUND` changes a number to have the requested digits of precision. This query shows how applying `ROUND` changes the previous calculation. The expression requests two digits to the right of the decimal:

```
-- Demonstrate ROUND
SELECT ROUND(1.27 * 1.609344, 2) as Km
GO

(Results)

Km
-------------
2.04000000
```

Interestingly enough, SQL Server continues to return eight digits to the right of the decimal place, even after applying the ROUND function. However, the result has been rounded to the second decimal place, and all the digits after that are always 0.

To get the result shown to the desired precision, use the CAST or CONVERT function to convert the answer to the numeric data type.

numeric is a data type that stores numbers with an exact amount of precision. It can be used instead of float or real, which store approximations. However, numeric stores a smaller range of numbers than float. Also, float has better support from the hardware of modern microprocessors and is thus faster. decimal can be used as a synonym for numeric, and you'll find both used interchangeably in the sample code. The next query shows how to use CAST to get an exact number of digits:

```
-- Casting a conversion to two digits
SELECT CAST (1.27 * 1.609344 as numeric(18,2) ) as [Km Cast to 2 digits]
GO

(Results)

Km Cast to 2 digits
----------------------------------------
2.04
```

When the CAST function is applied, its argument is rounded using the same algorithm used by ROUND.

Note:

CAST and CONVERT usually do the same job, but CAST is part of the SQL-92 specification and CONVERT is not. If you want your SQL to be portable between databases, use CAST when possible. The only difference between the two is that CAST doesn't accept the date conversion parameter that CONVERT can use to format dates as strings.

Preserving the proper amount of precision during a conversion involves more than just the number of significant digits in the measurement. When the conversion factors are large enough, the measurement is scaled. This should be taken into consideration.

Scaling the Results

The miles-to-kilometers conversion factor (1.609344) is near one. After the conversion, the kilometer measurement is in the same decimal order of magnitude as the original measurement in miles. Some conversions change the order of magnitude of the measurement. For instance, if we convert the measurement in miles to meters, multiplying 1.27 by 1609.344, the result is 2043.867 meters. The third digit after the decimal place represents millimeters. Do we know the answer to within a millimeter? Of course not. We also don't know the answer to within two digits to the right of the decimal place, or centimeters, which was the precision of the original measurement. Since the original measurement has three significant digits, our results in meters should show the same precision.

The `length` parameter from the `ROUND` function works well for expressing precision. It's the number of digits to the right of the decimal place to keep after rounding is performed. When the precision of a number is less than the number of digits to the left of the decimal place, use a negative number. Thus, this query rounds to the hundreds place:

```
-- Round to hundreds place
SELECT ROUND (12345.67, -2) as [Round To Hundreds]
GO

(Result)

Round To Hundreds
-----------------
12300.00
```

The precision of a measurement is often different from the precision of the database data type used to store it. Since SQL Server doesn't know the precision of the measurement from the data type, the database designer or SQL programmer must provide it. That makes it necessary to use the precision as a parameter in all conversion functions.

Combining Scale and Precision

The solution to keeping the correct amount of precision is to round by a number that combines the known precision of the measurement and the scale change of the conversion factor. The algorithm to combine precision and scale is: Take the number of digits of precision to the right of the decimal from the input measurement and subtract the Log^{10} of the scale factor. The result of the Log^{10} must be rounded to an integer before being used. For the conversion from miles to meters from the example above, there are two digits of precision to the left of the decimal place, and our conversion factor is 1609.344. This code shows how they're combined:

```
-- Formula for the correct parameter to the ROUND function to preserve precision
SELECT 2 - ROUND(Log10 (1609.344), 0) as [Combined Rounding]
GO

(Results)

Combined Rounding
-----------------------------------------------------
-1.0
```

The answer, –1, says to round to one digit to the left of the decimal, the tens place. In other words, if a measurement is known to an accuracy of hundredths of miles, the measurement is known to tens of meters. It's not a perfect answer. A hundredth of a mile is 52.8 feet and 10 meters is 32.8 feet, so we're claiming somewhat increased precision. However, the alternative of claiming hundreds of meters of precision is further from the truth. The TSQLUDFS database has the function `udf_Unit_Rounding-Precision` that implements the algorithm. Listing 12.1 creates a similar function, `udf_Unit_Rounding4Factor`, with just the scale computation. It's used in the next section as an aid when writing conversion functions.

Listing 12.1: udf_Unit_Rounding4Factor

```
CREATE FUNCTION dbo.udf_Unit_Rounding4Factor (

    @fConversionFactor float -- Conversion factor (must be >= 0)
)   RETURNS int -- Use to adjust length parm of ROUND function
/*
*  Returns the number of digits of precision that a
*  units conversion is performed on a measurement with
*  @nDigits2RtofDecimal of precision and a conversion factor
*  of @fConversionFactor.  The result is intended to be used as
*  input into the ROUND function as the length parameter.
*
* Example:
select dbo.udf_Unit_Rounding4Factor (1609.344) -- Miles to meters
*
* Test:
print 'Test 1 Mi to Meters   ' +
      case when -3 = dbo.udf_Unit_Rounding4Factor (1609.344)
           then 'Worked' else 'ERROR' end
print 'Test 2 Zero Parm      ' +
      case when dbo.udf_Unit_Rounding4Factor (0.0) is NULL
           then 'Worked' else 'ERROR' end
print 'Test 3 Negative Parm ' +
      case when dbo.udf_Unit_Rounding4Factor (-1.2321) is NULL
           then 'Worked' else 'ERROR' end
*************************************************************************/
AS BEGIN

   -- LOG10 won't take a zero or negative parameter.
      -- the result is undefined, return null instead.
   IF @fConversionFactor <= 0 BEGIN
      RETURN NULL
   END
```

```
    RETURN - ROUND(LOG10 (@fConversionFactor), 0)

END
```

The issues about precision and scale are important. Without addressing them, we're liable to produce results that show more or less precision than can be truly assigned to the data. This section has created tools to handle these issues; the next section uses the tools to create unit conversion UDFs in a variety of ways.

Writing the Conversion Functions

Now that we've covered some of the design issues about maintaining precision and scaling data, it's time to get down to the business of writing unit conversion functions. Depending on how the functions are going to be used, there are different ways to organize the parameters. This section shows three different approaches to creating conversion UDFs. The differences between the approaches isn't going to change the result or handle precision very differently. Instead, the differences arise from practical considerations about how the functions will be integrated into the application's SQL code.

The three approaches are:

- Convert from one specific unit directly to another specific unit.
- Add a parameter that makes the conversion optional.
- Create a function that converts from any unit to any other unit in the same dimension.

These three choices are hardly the only choices available. They illustrate some of the possible trade-offs that seem to make sense to me, particularly when they are applied to pavement management. Your application or development environment may dictate other variations that work better for you.

Converting Measurements the Simple Way

The first approach to conversion functions is simple. It accepts the measurement and the number of digits of precision and produces a floating-point result that performs the conversion and rounds it to preserve the precision of the original measurement. Listing 12.2 shows the first one, `udf_Unit_mi2m`.

Listing 12.2: udf_Unit_mi2m

```
01 CREATE FUNCTION udf_Unit_mi2m (
02
03    @fInput Float -- Miles to convert to meters
04  , @nDigits2RtOfDecimal int = 0 -- Precision to right of decimal
05       -- negative for left of decimal, like length parm of ROUND
06 )   RETURNS float -- use for the length parameter of the ROUND function
07     WITH SCHEMABINDING
08 /*
09 *  Converts Miles to Meters
10 *
11 * Example:
12 select dbo.udf_Unit_mi2m (1.27, 2) -- Mi to m
13 *
14 * Test:
15 print 'Test 1 1.27 Mi to m  ' +
16      case when 2040.00 = dbo.udf_Unit_mi2m (1.27, 2)
17           then 'Worked' else 'ERROR' end
18 print 'Test 2 0 Parm        ' +
19      case when 0 = dbo.udf_Unit_mi2m (0, 0)
20           then 'Worked' else 'ERROR' end
21 print 'Test 3 Negative Parm ' +
22      case when 198680000.0 = dbo.udf_Unit_mi2m (123456.18934, -1)
23           then 'Worked' else 'ERROR' end
24 **********************************************************************/
25 AS BEGIN
26
27  DECLARE  @nRound2Digits int -- Digits to round
28         , @fConversionFactor float -- factor used for conversion
29
30  SET @fConversionFactor = 1609.344
31
32  -- SELECT dbo.udf_Unit_Rounding4Factor (@fConversionFactor) As Adjustment
33  SET @nRound2Digits = @nDigits2RtOfDecimal + -3 -- <put adjustment here
34
35  RETURN ROUND(@fInput * @fConversionFactor, @nRound2Digits)
36
37 END
```

The function has been designed to execute quickly, but a few extra statements have been left in for ease of editing. In the middle of the function at line 32 is the line:

```
-- SELECT dbo.udf_Unit_Rounding4Factor (@fConversionFactor) As Adjustment
```

that is commented out. It calculates the number of digits required to scale the input as it is rounded. Like the Example and Test sections of the header comment, this line is intended for selection and execution while writing the function, not when the function runs. To execute this line, perform the following steps from inside Query Analyzer:

1. Remove the double dashes from line 32.
2. Select the code from the `DECLARE` at line 27 down to and including line 32.

3. Press F5 to execute this code fragment, and you'll get the adjustment factor.
4. Put the adjustment factor into line 33.
5. Put the double dashes back on line 32.

Figure 12.1 shows Query Analyzer at the end of step 3 where we get the result. The commented line is left in the function to be used when the function is altered. Since the factor used to adjust precision never changes, it doesn't have to be recalculated each time the function is executed. It's just hard coded into the function.

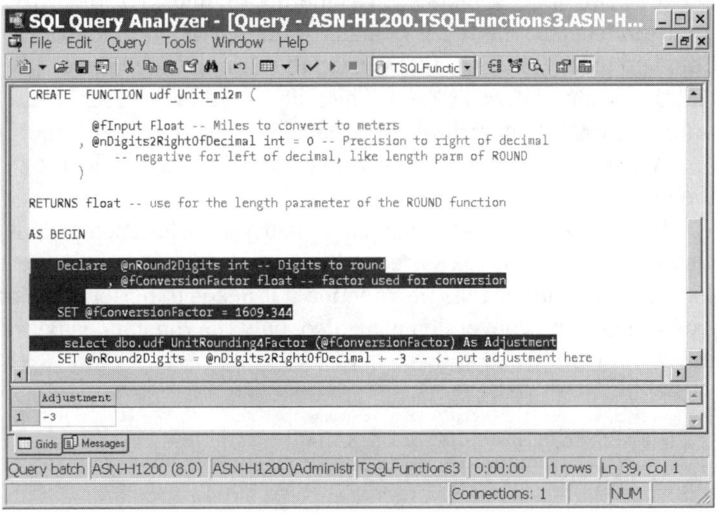

Figure 12.1: Getting the adjustment factor for a units conversion function

Here's our example conversion performed by `udf_Unit_mi2m`:

```
-- Use udf_Unit_mi2m to convert 1.27 miles
SELECT dbo.udf_Unit_mi2m (1.27, 2) as [Meters]
GO

(Results)

1.27 miles converted to Meters
-----------------------------------------------------
2040.0
```

Functions that perform a single unit-to-unit conversion have the advantage that they execute quickly. All they're really doing is one multiplication and a rounding operation. When necessary, they could even be consolidated into a single expression to avoid the extra overhead of splitting the code into a few statements.

The downside to such simple conversion functions is that when you use them in a SQL statement, you must be sure of exactly which units are being converted to which other units. There isn't any flexibility in the function. The next alternative adds some flexibility so that they can be used in situations, such as the MDOT PMS, where the user's choice of unit system isn't known when the SQL is written.

Adding the Choice of Output Units

The unit conversion functions shown in the previous section translate between two specific units such as meters to miles. For the MDOT PMS, the user decides whether he wants to see the output in metric or U.S. Standard units. The SQL that is used to communicate between the client and the database doesn't know which unit system the user wants until run time. Since the unit system of the database data was always metric, it's pretty easy to write a UDF that converts any kilometer field to the system the user has chosen.

Listing 12.3 shows the `udf_Unit_Km2Distance` function to convert a distance measure that is stored in kilometers. The input parameter `@UnitSystemOfOutput` tells the function if it needs to perform the conversion or not. If no conversion is needed, only the rounding is performed and the result is returned in these lines:

```
-- Check to see if any conversion is needed.
IF @UnitSystemOfOutput = 'M' COLLATE Latin1_General_CI_AI
     RETURN ROUND(@fInputKM, @nDigits2RightOfDecimal)
```

When the conversion is requested, it's done the same way as in `udf_Unit_mi2m`. Notice that the clause `COLLATE Latin1_General_CI_AI` is used in case the function is executed within a case-sensitive database and the caller supplies a lowercase m.

Listing 12.3: udf_Unit_Km2Distance

```
CREATE FUNCTION dbo.udf_Unit_Km2Distance (

    @UnitSystemOfOutput  char(1) = 'M' -- M for metric, U for US Std.
  , @fInputKM            float -- Kilometers to convert to miles
  , @nDigits2RtOfDecimal int = 0 -- Precision to right of decimal
        -- negative for left of decimal, like length parm of ROUND
)   RETURNS float -- use for the length parameter of the ROUND function
    WITH SCHEMABINDING
/*
*  Returns a distance measure whose input is a kilometer measurement.
*  The parameter @UnitSystemOfOutput requests that the output be left
*  as Kilometers 'M' or converted to the US Standard system unit miles
*  signified by a 'U'.
*
```

```
* Example:
select dbo.udf_Unit_Km2Distance ('U', 2.04, 2) -- Km to Mi
*
* Test:
print 'Test 1 2.04 Km to Mi ' +
      case when 1.27 = dbo.udf_Unit_Km2Distance ('U', 2.04, 2)
           then 'Worked' else 'ERROR' end
print 'Test 2 1.27 Km to Km ' +
      case when 1.27 = dbo.udf_Unit_Km2Distance ('M', 1.27, 2)
           then 'Worked' else 'ERROR' end
print 'Test 3 Negative Parm ' +
      case when 123450 = dbo.udf_Unit_Km2Distance ('U', 198680.321, -1)
           then 'Worked' else 'ERROR' end
*********************************************************************/
AS BEGIN

   DECLARE  @nRound2Digits int -- Digits to round
          , @fConversionFactor float -- factor used for conversion

    -- Check to see if any conversion is needed.
    IF @UnitSystemOfOutput = 'M' COLLATE Latin1_General_CI_AI
        RETURN ROUND(@fInputKM, @nDigits2RtOfDecimal)

   SET @fConversionFactor = 0.6213711922

   -- select dbo.udf_UnitRounding4Factor (@fConversionFactor) As Adjustment
   SET @nRound2Digits = @nDigits2RtOfDecimal + 0 -- <-- put adjustment here

   RETURN ROUND(@fInputKM * @fConversionFactor, @nRound2Digits)

END
```

The advantage to writing functions that include both the conversion and a choice about whether a conversion is necessary is that simple SELECT statements can be used to retrieve data from the database and supply the user's choice of unit system at run time. This batch illustrates how it might have worked:

```
-- Using udf_km2Distance
DECLARE @UnitSystem char(1)
SET @UnitSystem = 'U' -- For US Standard system

SELECT TOP 3 route_name
     , dbo.udf_Unit_Km2Distance (@UnitSystem,  begin_km, 3) as begin_mi
     , dbo.udf_unit_Km2Distance (@UnitSystem,  end_km, 3) as end_mi
    FROM pms_analysis_section
GO
```

(Results)

```
route_name          begin_mi             end_mi
------------------- -------------------- ---------------------
SR1                 4.4320000000000004   4.6079999999999997
SR1                 4.6079999999999997   8.0630000000000006
SR1                 8.0630000000000006   9.9179999999999993
```

For the MDOT PMS, this would have been particularly useful because the front end was built using Sybase's PowerBuilder product. Its DataWindow control makes good use of the SELECT statement, and it would have shortened the time needed to develop the application.

udf_Unit_Km2Distance is still pretty restrictive. It requires that the input be in kilometers and assumes that the only choices for the result are either kilometers or miles. That works well in a pavement management system but not in other applications.

Anything-to-Anything Conversions

The conversion functions written so far translate from one particular unit to another particular unit. This only works well when you know in advance what type of conversion is required. The benefit of using them is that the functions are short and efficient.

Sometimes you don't know what units need to be converted when the code is written, so a function that can convert between any two units is required. For example, suppose your database is in meters, but your users might like to see the measurement in centimeters, meters, kilometers, inches, feet, yards, or miles. A more flexible function is required in such a situation.

Excel's function for converting units, CONVERT, is an any-unit-to-any-unit conversion function. It's part of Excel's Analysis ToolPak add-in. Load that add-in before using the function or trying the spreadsheet Unit Conversions.xls provided in this chapter's download.

The function udf_Unit_CONVERT_Distance is similar to Excel's CONVERT but works only with units that measure distance. It's shown in Listing 12.4. One potential way to code this function is to use a large CASE statement that has every possible combination of conversion. I considered it but decided on a different approach.

Listing 12.4: udf_Unit_CONVERT_Distance

```
CREATE   FUNCTION dbo.udf_Unit_CONVERT_Distance (

    @fMeasurement float -- Measurement to convert
  , @MeasuredUnitCD  varchar(12) -- UNITCD Unit code of the measurement.
  , @ToUnitCD        varchar(12) -- UNITCD Units to convert to.
  , @nDigits2RtOfDecimal int = 0 -- like length parm of ROUND
)   RETURNS numeric(18,9) -- @fMeasurement converted to new type
    WITH SCHEMABINDING
/*
*  Converts a distance measurement from any unit to any other unit.
*
* Example:
select dbo.udf_Unit_CONVERT_Distance (3.14159, 'mi', 'km', 3) as [km]
* Test:
print 'Test 1 1.27 Mi to KM  ' + case when 2.04 =
```

```
            dbo.udf_Unit_CONVERT_Distance (1.27, 'mi', 'km', 2)
            THEN 'Worked' ELSE 'ERROR' END
print 'Test 2 0 Parm         ' + case when 0 =
            dbo.udf_Unit_CONVERT_Distance (0, 'ft', 'mm', 2)
            THEN 'Worked' ELSE 'ERROR' END
print 'Test 3 Negative Parm  ' +  case when 198680 =
            dbo.udf_Unit_CONVERT_Distance (123456.789, 'mi', 'km', -1)
            THEN 'Worked' ELSE 'ERROR' END
print 'Test 4 Same to same   ' +  case when 1 =
                     dbo.udf_Unit_CONVERT_Distance (1.0, 'mi', 'mi', 0)
             and 1 = dbo.udf_Unit_CONVERT_Distance (1.0, 'm', 'm', 0)
             and 1 = dbo.udf_Unit_CONVERT_Distance (1.0, 'ft', 'ft', 0)
             and 1 = dbo.udf_Unit_CONVERT_Distance (1.0, 'NM', 'nm', 0)
             THEN 'Worked' ELSE 'ERROR' END
**********************************************************************/
AS BEGIN

DECLARE @fCvt2Base float -- factor from measurement to the base system.
      , @fCvt2Target float -- factor from base to the target system.
      , @bMeasureIsMetric BIT -- Is the measurement metric
      , @bTargetIsMetric BIT -- Is the target metric
      , @fCvtSystems float -- to convert between systems
-- metric base unit is the meter.  Every unit is converted to meters.
SELECT @fcvt2Base = CASE @MeasuredUnitCD COLLATE Latin1_General_CI_AI
        WHEN 'cm' THEN .01         WHEN 'dm' THEN 10.0
        WHEN 'hm' THEN 100.0       WHEN 'km' THEN 1000.0
        WHEN 'm'  THEN 1.0         WHEN 'mm' THEN 0.001
        WHEN 'NM' THEN 1852.0      ELSE 0    END
       , @bMeasureIsMetric = 1 -- Assume, it's metric
IF @fcvt2base = 0 -- Wasn't a metric unit
    SELECT @fCvt2Base = CASE @MeasuredUnitCD collate Latin1_General_CI_AI
        WHEN 'ft' THEN 1.0          WHEN 'furlong' THEN 660.0
        WHEN 'in' THEN 0.083333333 WHEN 'mi'      THEN 5280.0
        WHEN 'yd' THEN 3.0          ELSE 0        END
      , @bMeasureIsMetric = 0 -- no, not metric
-- Try to convert target to a base unit is the meter.
SELECT @fcvt2Target =
    CASE @ToUnitCD COLLATE Latin1_General_CI_AI
        WHEN 'cm' THEN 100.0        WHEN 'dm' THEN 0.1
        WHEN 'hm' THEN 0.01         WHEN 'km' THEN 0.001
        WHEN 'm'  THEN 1.0          WHEN 'mm' THEN 1000.0
        WHEN 'NM' THEN 0.0005399568035  ELSE 0  END
       , @bTargetIsMetric = 1 -- Assume it's metric
IF @fcvt2Target = 0 -- Wasn't a metric unit
    SELECT @fCvt2Target =
        CASE @ToUnitCD COLLATE Latin1_General_CI_AI
           WHEN 'ft' THEN 1.0   WHEN 'furlong' THEN 0.001515151515
           WHEN 'in' THEN 12    WHEN 'mi' THEN 0.000189394
           WHEN 'yd' THEN 0.33333333333333333333 ELSE 0   END
        , @bTargetIsMetric = 0 -- no, not metric
-- If base and target systems differ, convert between the two bases.
SET @fCvtSystems =
    CASE WHEN @bMeasureIsMetric=1 and @bTargetIsMetric=0 THEN 3.28083
         WHEN @bMeasureIsMetric=0 and @bTargetIsMetric=1 THEN 0.3048
         ELSE 1.0 END

RETURN round(@fcvt2Base * @fCvtSystems * @fcvt2Target * @fMeasurement
           , @nDigits2RtOfDecimal)
END
```

Instead, a base unit for each system of units is chosen. For the metric system, the meter is the base. For the U.S. Standard system, the foot is the base. Then two conversion factors are looked up in `CASE` statements. `@fCvtToBase` is the conversion factor from the measurement-to-base in the unit system of the measurement. Next, `@fCvtToTarget` is looked up. It's the conversion factor from the base-to-target units. The conversion factors for base-to-target conversion are the reciprocals of the measurement-to-base factors.

That works fine if the measurement and the target are from the same unit system. However, if they're from different unit systems, a third conversion factor is used, `@fCvtSystems`. It converts between the base units of the two systems.

`udf_Unit_CONVERT_Distance` returns a `numeric (18,9)` type. The type was chosen so that rounding shows the amount of precision. However, double precision floating-point computations (data type `float`) are used internally. Returning `numeric (18,9)` limits the range of values that can be used to $\pm 10^9$. That range represents the most common real-world conversions. While there might be a reason to convert miles to nanometers using a factor of 1.609344e+12, that sort of high-magnitude conversion is the exception. It is not handled by this function in favor of avoiding some issues of numerical rounding. Of course, your application may need a larger range of possible values in its result, and you might want to return `float` or `numeric (38,9)` instead.

`udf_Unit_CONVERT_Distance` is the last of the three methods for converting units. Each fits a slightly different situation, and I might choose between them based on the application design. However, it's worthwhile to check their performance. How much might they slow the application? Is it enough to make you want to switch conversion methods?

Putting the Unit Conversion Functions to Work

Now that alternative functions for performing conversions are written, it's time to put them to work and see how they perform. This section builds tests based on pavement management data to compare their performance characteristics. The conclusion won't surprise you: The shorter and simpler the function, the quicker it executes.

The experiment shown is based on a fictionalized pavement table, `pms_analysis_section`, in the TSQLUDFS database. Each row represents a segment of road. To provide a sufficient amount of data for performance differences to show up, I've populated it with 4000 mythical analysis sections. Each section includes the columns `route_name`, `begin_km`, and `end_km` that define the section. In addition, there are columns for a variety of measurements that are used in economic analysis of pavement.

Each of the three conversion methods created previously used a slightly different calling convention, but they can each be counted on to produce a correct result. The first method is represented by udf_Unit_Km2mi, which is shown in Listing 12.5. The second conversion method is based on udf_Unit_Km2Distance, and the third is based on udf_Unit_CONVERT_Distance.

Listing 12.5: udf_Unit_Km2mi

```
CREATE   FUNCTION dbo.udf_Unit_Km2mi (

    @fInput Float -- Kilometers to convert to miles
  , @nDigits2RightOfDecimal int = 0 -- Precision to right of decimal
         -- negative for left of decimal, like length parm of ROUND
)   RETURNS float -- Equivalent distance in miles
    WITH SCHEMABINDING
/*
*  Converts Kilometers to Miles
*
* Example:
select dbo.udf_Unit_Km2mi (2.04, 2) -- Km to Mi
*
* Test:
print 'Test 1 2.04 1.27 Km to Mi   ' +
        case when 1.27 = dbo.udf_Unit_Km2mi (2.04, 2)
             then 'Worked' else 'ERROR' end
print 'Test 2 0 Parm       ' +
        case when 0 = dbo.udf_Unit_Km2mi (0, 0)
             then 'Worked' else 'ERROR' end
print 'Test 3 Negative Parm ' +
        case when 123450 = dbo.udf_Unit_Km2mi (198680.321, -1)
             then 'Worked' else 'ERROR' end
***********************************************************************/
AS BEGIN

    DECLARE  @nRound2Digits int -- Digits to round
           , @fConversionFactor float -- factor used for conversion

    SET @fConversionFactor = 0.6213711922

    -- select dbo.udf_UnitRounding4Factor (@fConversionFactor) As Adjustment
    SET @nRound2Digits = @nDigits2RightOfDecimal + 0 -- < put adjustment here

    RETURN ROUND(@fInput * @fConversionFactor, @nRound2Digits)
END
```

All three methods produce the same results with slightly different calling sequences. Here's a query that converts the begin_km markers to miles. The conversion is performed first using an expression that doesn't require a UDF and then using each of the three types of conversion functions:

```
-- A sample of the data and conversion functions
SELECT top 5
       route_name
     , begin_km
     , begin_km * 0.6213711922 [Begin Expression]
     , dbo.udf_Unit_Km2mi(begin_km, 3) [Begin Km2mi]
     , dbo.udf_Unit_Km2Distance ('U', begin_km, 3) [Begin Km2Dist]
     , dbo.udf_Unit_CONVERT_Distance (begin_km, 'km', 'mi', 3) [Begin CONVERT]
   FROM pms_analysis_section
GO
```

(Results)

```
begin_km Begin Expression  Begin Km2mi         Begin Km2Dist       Begin CONVERT
-------- ----------------- ------------------- -------------------------------
7.132    4.4316193427704   4.4320000000000004  4.4320000000000004 4.432000000
7.416    4.6080887613552   4.6079999999999997  4.6079999999999997 4.608000000
12.976   8.0629125899872   8.0630000000000006  8.0630000000000006 8.063000000
15.962   9.9183269698964   9.9179999999999993  9.9179999999999993 9.918000000
28.773   17.8787133131706  17.879000000000001  17.879000000000001 17.879000000
```

All of the results are very close. The only differences are due to the rounding performed by each of the functions.

To compare the time that it takes to execute each of the functions, let's set up a simple experiment. The script that follows uses a technique for measuring performance similar to the one used in Chapter 11. The table in question is first pinned into memory. Then each of the functions gets their chance to convert two of the columns in the test table. To prevent the time needed to display thousands of rows of data from becoming a factor in the experiment, the results are summed instead of displayed. Here's the script:

```
-- Experiment into the performance of differing unit conversion functions

-- Create variables to hold the start time and duration in ms for each query
DECLARE @Start_Expr datetime      , @Start_Km2mi datetime
      , @Start_Km2Dist datetime   , @Start_CONVERT datetime
      , @ms_Expr int, @ms_Km2mi int, @ms_Km2Dist int, @ms_CONVERT int

PRINT 'Pinning the pms_analysis_section table'
DECLARE @db_id int, @tbl_id int
SELECT @db_id = DB_ID(), @tbl_id = OBJECT_ID('pms_analysis_section')
DBCC PINTABLE(@db_id, @tbl_id)

PRINT 'SUM of Begin_km column. Used to force all pages into memory'
SELECT SUM(begin_km) as [Sum in km]
    FROM pms_analysis_Section

PRINT 'SUM of the conversion performed in an expression'
SELECT @Start_Expr = getdate()
SELECT sum(begin_km * 0.6213711922) [Begin Expression]
     , sum(end_km * 0.6213711922) [End Expression]
   FROM pms_analysis_section
SET @ms_Expr = DATEDIFF(ms, @Start_Expr, getdate())

PRINT 'SUM of the conversion performed by udf_Unit_Km2mi'
```

```
SELECT @Start_Km2mi = getdate()
SELECT  sum(dbo.udf_Unit_Km2mi(begin_km, 3)) [Begin Km2mi]
      , sum(dbo.udf_Unit_Km2mi(end_km, 3)) [End Km2mi]
   FROM pms_analysis_section
SET @ms_Km2mi = DATEDIFF(ms , @start_Km2mi, getdate())

PRINT 'SUM of the conversion performed by udf_Unit_Km2Distance'
SELECT @Start_Km2Dist = getdate()
SELECT  sum(dbo.udf_Unit_Km2Distance ('U', begin_km, 3)) [Begin Km2Distance]
      , sum(dbo.udf_Unit_Km2Distance ('U', end_km, 3)) [End Km2Distance]
   FROM pms_analysis_section
SET @ms_Km2Dist = DATEDIFF(ms , @start_Km2Dist, getdate())

PRINT 'SUM of the conversion performed by udf_Unit_CONVERT_Distance'
SELECT @Start_CONVERT = getdate()
SELECT  sum(dbo.udf_Unit_CONVERT_Distance (begin_km, 'km', 'mi', 3))
                                                    as [Begin Km2Distance]
      , sum(dbo.udf_Unit_CONVERT_Distance ( end_km, 'km', 'mi', 3))
                                                    as [End Km2Distance]
   FROM pms_analysis_section
SET @ms_CONVERT = DATEDIFF(ms , @start_CONVERT, getdate())

PRINT 'Compare the duration of each query'
SELECT @ms_Expr as [Using Expression]
     , @ms_Km2mi as [udf_Unit_Km2mi]
     , @ms_Km2dist as [udf_Unit_Km2Distance]
     , @ms_Convert as [udf_Unit_CONVERT_Distance]

PRINT 'Unpinning the pms_analysis_section table'
DBCC UNPINTABLE(@db_id, @tbl_id)
GO
```

(Results – Reformatted for readability)

```
Pinning the pms_analysis_section table
Warning: Pinning tables should be carefully considered. If a pinned table is
larger, or grows larger, than the available data cache, the server may need
to be restarted and the table unpinned.
DBCC execution completed. If DBCC printed error messages, contact your system
administrator.

SUM of Begin_km column. Used to force all pages into memory
Sum in km
----------------------------------------
61743.138

SUM of the conversion performed in an expression
Begin Expression                         End Expression
---------------------------------------- ------------------------------------
38365.4072692291236                      49081.2554651175328

SUM of the conversion performed by udf_Unit_Km2mi
Begin Km2mi                                           End Km2mi
----------------------------------------------------- -------------------------
38365.417000000059                                    49081.259000000086

SUM of the conversion performed by udf_Unit_Km2Distance
Begin Km2Distance                                     End Km2Distance
----------------------------------------------------- -------------------------
38365.417000000059                                    49081.259000000086
```

```
SUM of the conversion performed by udf_Unit_CONVERT_Distance
Begin Km2Distance                        End Km2Distance
---------------------------------------- ----------------------------------------
38365.310000000                          49081.135000000

Compare the duration of each query
Using Expression udf_Unit_Km2mi udf_Unit_Km2Distance udf_Unit_CONVERT_Distance
---------------- -------------- -------------------- -------------------------
16               93             123                  453

Unpinning the pms_analysis_section table
DBCC execution completed. If DBCC printed error messages, contact your system
administrator.
```

It's obvious that using a UDF has a substantial cost. Using the simplest UDF takes almost six times as long as using the equivalent expression. The difference between `udf_Unit_Km2mi` and `udf_Unit_Km2Distance` is noticeable but pretty small. There's a big jump when using `udf_Unit_CONVERT_Distance`. That must be accounted for by the complexity of this longer UDF.

There are other ways to write the functions, but there's no point to endless variations. I suggest that after reading this chapter, you pick a way that works well in your application. It might be one of the alternatives shown here, but it may just as well be some other variation. It should be efficient, easy to code, and easy to maintain. With UDFs there's always a trade-off.

In the course of the conversion we've paid a lot of attention to numeric precision and issues caused by rounding. One of the most important of these issues occurs when numbers are compared. This is addressed in the next section.

What Is Equal?

Listing 12.6 has a function, `udf_Unit_lb2kg` that illustrates another issue about working with floating-point data in UDFs. If you execute the example you see what can happen when SQL Server stores floating-point data:

```
-- Example from udf_Unit_lb2kg
SELECT dbo.udf_Unit_lb2kg (185.4, 1) as [Weight lb to kg]
GO

(Results)

Weight lb to kg
-----------------------------------------------------
84.099999999999994
```

The series of 13 9s and a 4 are SQL Server's way of storing floating-point data that approximates 84.1. Now, try the first test in the function header:

```
-- Test 1 from header comment of udf_Unit_lb2kg
PRINT 'Test 1 185.4 lb to kg  ' +
        case when 84.10 = dbo.udf_Unit_lb2kg (185.4, 2)
        then 'Worked' else 'ERROR' end
GO
```

(Results)

```
Test 1 185.4 lb to kg  Worked
```

Why did it work? Is 84.10 equal to 84.099999999999994? The answer is yes when SQL Server converts it to floating point. This is illustrated by executing the following query:

```
-- Floating-point approximation
SELECT CAST (84.10 AS FLOAT) as [Show floating-point approximation]
GO
```

(Results)

```
Show floating-point approximation
-----------------------------------------------------
84.099999999999994
```

Before performing the comparison in Test 1, SQL Server has converted 84.10 to a floating-point representation of 84.09999999999994 and arrived at the same answer as the udf_Unit_lb2kg function.

Listing 12.6: udf_Unit_lb2kg

```
CREATE   FUNCTION udf_Unit_lb2kg (

    @fInput Float -- Pounds to convert to Kilograms
  , @nDigits2RightOfDecimal int = 0 -- Precision to right of decimal
       -- negative for left of decimal, like length parm of ROUND
)   RETURNS float -- use for the length parameter of the ROUND function
    WITH SCHEMABINDING
/*
*  Converts Pounds (advp) to kilograms (kg)
*
* Example:
select dbo.udf_Unit_lb2kg (185.4, 1) -- lb to kg
*
* Test:
print 'Test 1 185.4 lb to kg  ' +
        case when 84.10 = dbo.udf_Unit_lb2kg (185.4, 2)
             then 'Worked' else 'ERROR' end
print 'Test 2 0 Parm          ' +
        case when 0 = dbo.udf_Unit_lb2kg (0, 0)
             then 'Worked' else 'ERROR' end
print 'Test 3 Negative Parm   ' +
        case when 56000 =  dbo.udf_Unit_lb2kg (123456.789, -1)
             then 'Worked' else 'ERROR' end
*********************************************************************/
```

```
AS BEGIN

    DECLARE  @nRound2Digits int -- Digits to round
          , @fConversionFactor float -- factor used for conversion

    SET @fConversionFactor = 0.45359237

    -- SELECT dbo.udf_UnitRounding4Factor (@fConversionFactor) As Adjustment
    SET @nRound2Digits = @nDigits2RightOfDecimal + 0 -- < put adjustment here

    RETURN ROUND(@fInput * @fConversionFactor, @nRound2Digits)
END
```

The issue of when two numbers are equal is very important. Making good choices about how to compare numbers can make a big difference in the number of bugs reports made about your application. This is especially important when your application uses floating-point numbers or when UDFs convert numbers to floating point.

Testing Numbers for Equality

I've often heard the warning not to use equality comparisons of floating-point columns in WHERE clauses. The warning is sound because although the data is stored as an approximation, SQL Server compares floating-point numbers exactly. The comparison of other data types that represent numbers is also exact, but fewer problems occur because the representations are precise. This section is about the problems that occur due to rounding and floating-point approximation.

To illustrate, start by executing this simple query:

```
-- Simple comparison of numeric equality
SELECT CASE when 84.01 + 0.01 = 84.02
            then 'Equal' else 'Not Equal' end as [Are they equal?]
     , dbo.udf_SQL_VariantToDatatypeName(84.01) as [Data Type for 84.01]
GO

(Results)

Are they equal? Data Type for 84.01
--------------- --------------------
Equal           numeric(4, 2)
```

The result is equal because SQL Server uses numeric data types to perform the addition and comparison. Now CAST the numbers to float, and we get a different answer:

```
-- Simple comparison of equality using floating-point numbers
SELECT CASE when CAST(84.01 as FLOAT) + CAST(0.01 as FLOAT)
                 = CAST(84.02 as FLOAT)
            then 'Equal' else 'Not Equal' end as [Are they equal?]
GO
```

(Results)

```
Are they equal?
---------------
Not Equal
```

Listing 12.7 gives the function udf_Unit_EqualFpBIT, which encapsulates a test for equality between two floating-point numbers to within a specific degree of precision. It does this by taking the difference between the two numbers. If the difference is less than half of the desired amount of precision, then the numbers are considered equal.

Listing 12.7: udf_Unit_EqualFpBIT

```
CREATE FUNCTION dbo.udf_Unit_EqualFpBIT (

    @fArg1 float -- 1st number
  , @fArg2 float -- 2nd number
  , @nDigits2RtOfDecimal int = 0 -- Precision to Rt of decimal
       -- negative for left of decimal, like length parm of ROUND
)  RETURNS BIT -- 1 when equal else 0
   WITH SCHEMABINDING
/*
* Checks for equality of two floating-point numbers within a
* specific number of digits and returns 1 if equal, otherwise 0
*
* Example:
select dbo.udf_Unit_EqualFpBIT (1.23456, 1234555, 3) as [Equal]
* Test:
PRINT 'Test 1 3 digits ' + case when 1=
          dbo.udf_Unit_EqualFpBIT (1.23456, 1.234555, 3)
             THEN 'WORKED' ELSE 'ERROR' END
PRINT 'Test 2 6 digits '  + case when 0=
           dbo.udf_Unit_EqualFpBIT (1.23456, 1.234555, 6)
           THEN 'WORKED' ELSE 'ERROR' END
*********************************************************************/
AS BEGIN

   DECLARE @fDiff float    -- abs of difference between the two parms
         , @fEpsilon float -- small number, the amount considered equal
         , @bEqual BIT     -- result

    SET @fDiff = ABS(@fArg1 - @fArg2)
    SET @fEpsilon =  0.499999999999999
        * POWER (CAST(10 as float), -1 *  @nDigits2RtOfDecimal)
    SET @bEqual = CASE WHEN @fDiff < @fEpsilon THEN 1 ELSE 0 END

    RETURN @bEqual
END
```

When deciding on a return code for udf_Unit_EqualFpBIT, we run into SQL Server's lack of a Boolean data type. The data type available in SQL Server that is closest to Boolean is BIT. Because BIT is the return type, the function returns 1 when the arguments are equal or 0 otherwise.

Let's try out the udf_Unit_EqualFpBIT function to see how it works. Here's a simple test:

```
-- Exercise udf_Unit_EqualFpBIT
SELECT dbo.udf_Unit_EqualFpBIT (1.1234567890, 1.1230000000, 1) as [To 1 Digit]
     , dbo.udf_Unit_EqualFpBIT (1.1234567890, 1.1230000000, 2) as [To 2 Digits]
     , dbo.udf_Unit_EqualFpBIT (1.1234567890, 1.1230000000, 3) as [To 3 Digits]
     , dbo.udf_Unit_EqualFpBIT (1.1234567890, 1.1230000000, 4) as [To 4 Digits]
     , dbo.udf_Unit_EqualFpBIT (1.1234567890, 1.1230000000, 5) as [To 5 Digits]
GO

To 1 Digit To 2 Digits To 3 Digits To 4 Digits To 5 Digits
---------- ----------- ----------- ----------- -----------
1          1           1           0           0
```

Everything looks okay there. What if the numbers are really close?

```
-- Comparison of very close numbers to different number of digits
SELECT dbo.udf_Unit_EqualFpBIT (1.12500000000001, 1.12499999999999, 1)
                                as [To 1 Digit]
     , dbo.udf_Unit_EqualFpBIT (1.12500000000001, 1.12499999999999, 2)
                                as [To 2 Digits]
     , dbo.udf_Unit_EqualFpBIT (1.12500000000001, 1.12499999999999, 3)
                                as [To 3 Digits]
     , dbo.udf_Unit_EqualFpBIT (1.12500000000001, 1.12499999999999, 4)
                                as [To 4 Digits]
     , dbo.udf_Unit_EqualFpBIT (1.12500000000001, 1.12499999999999, 13)
                               as [To 13 Digits]
     , dbo.udf_Unit_EqualFpBIT (1.12500000000001, 1.12499999999999, 14)
                               as [To 14 Digits]
GO
To 1 Digit To 2 Digits To 3 Digits To 4 Digits To 13 Digits To 14 Digits
---------- ----------- ----------- ----------- ------------ ------------
1          1           1           1           1            0
```

Still okay? Does 1.12500000000001 equal 1.12499999999999 to two decimal places? For all intents and purposes, it does. But the word "all" is not quite right. For the purpose of most scientific or economic analysis, the two numbers are equal. But how about for accounting, billing, or cost allocation? What happens when 1.12500000000001 and 1.12499999999999 represent dollar amounts and they're shown on a report to two decimal places? The next query uses the CAST function to perform the rounding:

```
-- Rounding your bill and his bill
SELECT CAST(1.12500000000001 as numeric (18,2)) as [Your Bill]
     , CAST(1.1249999999999 as numeric (18,2)) as [His Bill]
     , dbo.udf_Unit_EqualFpBIT (1.12500000000001, 1.1249999999999, 2)
                                  as  [udf_Unit_EqualFpBit Says]
GO

(Results)
Your Bill            His Bill             udf_Unit_EqualFpBit Says
-------------------- -------------------- ------------------------
1.13                 1.12                 1
```

So udf_Unit_EqualFpBIT says that the numbers are equal, but your bill is one cent higher than his bill. Why are you charged more than him? The answer is that even though the numbers are very close, they round to different pennies. When compared as floating-point numbers by udf_Unit_EqualFpBIT, they're equal.

To a programmer, there are two groups of people to whom the interpretation of number equality matters: the Software Quality Assurance (SQA) team and the users of the application. Do they think a bill of $1.12 equals a bill of $1.13? Experience shows that they don't. When rounding results in one-cent differences, both SQA and users report the discrepancy as a bug. Both groups can be educated and might accept a reasonable explanation when appropriate. But the importance of the one-cent difference is going to depend on the application in which it appears and on the people involved. If hundreds, thousands, or millions of occurrences multiply the one-cent difference, sooner or later it's going to add up to enough money to matter to someone. For some users, the one-cent difference is always going to matter, regardless of the context and even if it never costs anyone a single cent.

To avoid issues caused by rounding, it's better to compare numbers in exactly the same way that they are shown to the user. Doing this results in fewer bug reports and arguably a better system. The function udf_Unit_EqualNumBIT in Listing 12.8 checks numbers for equality by converting to a numeric data type. Since this method of comparison uses numbers in the way they are presented to the user, the function's answers are more acceptable in most applications than other methods of comparison.

Listing 12.8: udf_Unit_EqualNumBIT

```
CREATE   FUNCTION dbo.udf_Unit_EqualNumBIT (

    @fArg1 FLOAT -- 1st number
  , @fArg2 FLOAT -- 2nd number
  , @nDigits2RtOfDecimal int = 0 -- like length parm of ROUND
            -- must be between +9 and -9, otherwise we use 9
)   RETURNS BIT -- 1 when equal else 0
    WITH SCHEMABINDING
/* Checks for equality of two floating-point numbers within a specific
* number of digits by converting to numeric and comparing those digits.
*
* Example:
select dbo.udf_Unit_EqualNumBIT (1.23456, 1234555, 3) as [Equal]
* Test:
PRINT 'Test 1 3 digits ' + case when 1 =
dbo.udf_Unit_EqualNumBIT (1.23456, 1.234555, 3) THEN 'Works' ELSE 'ERROR' END
PRINT 'Test 2 6 digits ' + case when 0 =
dbo.udf_Unit_EqualNumBIT (1.23456, 1.234555, 6) THEN 'Works' ELSE 'ERROR' END
***********************************************************************/
AS BEGIN

DECLARE @bEqual BIT -- result
```

```
if @nDigits2RtOfDecimal > 0
    SELECT @bEqual =
        CASE @nDigits2RtOfDecimal
           WHEN 1 THEN CASE WHEN CAST(@fArg1 AS NUMERIC (38, 1))
                        = CAST(@fArg2 AS NUMERIC (38, 1)) THEN 1 ELSE 0 END
            WHEN 2 THEN CASE WHEN CAST(@fArg1 AS NUMERIC (38, 2))
                        = CAST(@fArg2 AS NUMERIC (38, 2)) THEN 1 ELSE 0 END
            WHEN 3 THEN CASE WHEN CAST(@fArg1 AS NUMERIC (38, 3))
                        = CAST(@fArg2 AS NUMERIC (38, 3)) THEN 1 ELSE 0 END
            WHEN 4 THEN CASE WHEN CAST(@fArg1 AS NUMERIC (38, 4))
                        = CAST(@fArg2 AS NUMERIC (38, 4)) THEN 1 ELSE 0 END
            WHEN 5 THEN CASE WHEN CAST(@fArg1 AS NUMERIC (38, 5))
                        = CAST(@fArg2 AS NUMERIC (38, 5)) THEN 1 ELSE 0 END
            WHEN 6 THEN CASE WHEN CAST(@fArg1 AS NUMERIC (38, 6))
                        = CAST(@fArg2 AS NUMERIC (38, 6)) THEN 1 ELSE 0 END
            WHEN 7 THEN CASE WHEN CAST(@fArg1 AS NUMERIC (38, 7))
                        = CAST(@fArg2 AS NUMERIC (38, 7)) THEN 1 ELSE 0 END
            WHEN 8 THEN CASE WHEN CAST(@fArg1 AS NUMERIC (38, 8))
                        = CAST(@fArg2 AS NUMERIC (38, 8))  THEN 1 ELSE 0 END
            ELSE -- Only supports up to 9 digits of precision
                CASE WHEN CAST(@fArg1 AS NUMERIC (38, 9))
                        = CAST(@fArg2 AS NUMERIC (38, 9))  THEN 1 ELSE 0 END
            END
ELSE
    -- Negative numbers of digits implies to the left of the decimal
    -- ROUND takes a parameter for the length so we don't need a CASE.
    -- After ROUNDing the numbers are CAST to INT to insure INT comparison.
    SELECT @bEqual =
            CASE WHEN CAST(ROUND (@fArg1, @nDigits2RtOfDecimal) AS INT)
                    = CAST(ROUND (@fArg2, @nDigits2RtOfDecimal) AS INT)
                 THEN 1 ELSE 0 END
-- ENDIF

RETURN @bEqual
END
```

Neither the CAST nor CONVERT functions accept a variable or expression in the length parameter. To get around this limitation, a large CASE expression is used to first CAST the arguments to the specified precision and then compare them. Let's try the previous query again, but this time we add a test using udf_Unit_EqualNumBIT:

```
-- Comparison of Bills using udf_Unit_EqualNumBIT
SELECT CAST(1.12500000000001 as numeric (18,2)) as [Your Bill]
     , CAST(1.1249999999999 as numeric (18,2)) as [His Bill]
     , dbo.udf_Unit_EqualFPBIT (1.12500000000001, 1.1249999999999, 2)
                                 as  [udf_UnitEqualFPBIT Says]
     , dbo.udf_Unit_EqualNumBIT (1.12500000000001, 1.1249999999999, 2)
                                 as  [udf_UnitEqualNumBIT Says]
GO

(Results)

Your Bill          His Bill           udf_Unit_EqualFpBIT udf_Unit_EqualNumBIT
------------------ ------------------ ------------------- --------------------
1.13               1.12               1                   0
```

udf_Unit_EqualNumBIT tells us that the numbers are not equal, while the floating-point comparison method in udf_Unit_EqualFpBIT says that the numbers are equal.

The strong point about the udf_Unit_EqualNumBIT function is that numbers are considered equal only when they will be displayed the same way. That strength is also a weakness because asking for more digits to the right of the decimal can change the result from not equal back to equal. The next query shows the problem case:

```
-- Demonstrate the problem with numeric rounding as a comparison method
SELECT  dbo.udf_Unit_EqualFpBIT (1.12500000000001, 1.1249999999999, 2) [EqualFP]
 , dbo.udf_Unit_EqualNumBIT (1.12500000000001, 1.1249999999999, 1) [To 1 Digit]
 , dbo.udf_Unit_EqualNumBIT (1.12500000000001, 1.1249999999999, 2) [To 2 Digits]
 , dbo.udf_Unit_EqualNumBIT (1.12500000000001, 1.1249999999999, 3) [To 3 Digits]
 , dbo.udf_Unit_EqualNumBIT (1.12500000000001, 1.1249999999999, 4) [To 4 Digits]
GO
```

(Results)

```
EqualFP To 1 Digit  To 2 Digits  To 3 Digits  To 4 Digits
------- ----------- ------------ ------------ -----------
1       1           0            1            1
```

As you can see, when the comparison is done to one digit of precision, udf_Unit_EqualNumBIT says they're equal. When compared to two digits, they're not equal, but when compared to three and four digits they're equal again. That's called a discontinuity in the result of the function. Mathematicians don't like discontinuous functions. In this case, living with the discontinuity is a choice that you might make to satisfy application requirements.

In my book (oh, this is my book!), the choice of numeric comparison methods depends on the application. For the pavement application, floating point works well. That's partially because the users of the application are engineers who have an appreciation of measurement inaccuracies and rounding errors. For other applications, I lean toward whichever method the users consider correct, usually the CAST to numeric method as implemented by udf_Unit_EqualNumBIT.

Reducing Bug Reports Due to Numeric Rounding

To reduce bug reports and the number of times that you have to explain how rounding works, it's often better to convert floating-point data to a precise data type, such as `numeric` or `int`, before performing an aggregation operation such as `SUM`. In financial contexts, it's often essential that reporting is done this way. While summing before rounding may be better in some scientific contexts, the user who takes the time to add the numbers in the column and check it against the total is rarely happy when his manually calculated total doesn't match the reported total. Of course, the SQA person who discovers such a discrepancy is very happy; it means he found another bug in your code! Let's take a look at an example cost allocation query. Notice that I'm using SQL Server's `COMPUTE` clause to perform the sums. I find that `COMPUTE` is rarely useful and summation is usually done in the client application or report writer. But SQL Server sums the same way that most client applications and report writers do, so it's used here:

```
-- -- Alternate methods of summing
SELECT CostAllocation as [CostAllocation as float]
     , CAST (CostAllocation as numeric (18,2)) as
                 [CostAllocation as numeric with 2 digits]
FROM examplefloatdata
COMPUTE sum (CostAllocation), sum(CAST(CostAllocation as numeric (18,2)))
GO
```

(Results)

```
CostAllocation as float              CostAllocation as numeric with 2 digits
----------------------------------- ---------------------------------------
1.2344999999999999                          1.23
3.1223000000000001                          3.12
6.2342000000000004                          6.23
7.3444000000000003                          7.34
9.7893000000000008                          9.79
2.3420000000000001                          2.34
5.9800000000000004                          5.98

sum
===================================
36.046700000000001
                                     sum
                                     ========================================
                                     36.03
```

The `COMPUTE` clause doesn't allow a function to be applied to the sum, so I couldn't write `COMPUTE CAST(SUM(CostAllocation) as Numeric (18,2))`. You'll have to imagine what happens when the client application shows the sum of the floating-point data rounded to the nearest cent as \$36.05. When the data is rounded before being summed, the answer is \$36.03. Which one is correct? It depends on the context in which the numbers are used. Rounding before summing makes the numbers in the column add up to the total, and you'll get fewer bug reports. If there is an accounting system involved, the same rounding system should be used when reporting, as when the charges are allocated in the accounting system.

If you decide to do the sum before rounding, as in the first column, and if you want to avoid the appearance of a discrepancy between the data and the sum, it is necessary to show more than just two digits of precision in the data points. It may be necessary to show four or five digits (that is, change the report so it shows more of each value so the reader will understand how the sum was derived).

Summary

This chapter has created T-SQL UDFs to solve the problem of converting between unit systems. As it turned out, most of the chapter focused on ways to maintain the proper amount of numeric precision as functions are created.

Centralization of the conversion process in the database has some distinct advantages, of which the most important is consistency. If the conversion process is moved to a higher level, such as the client application, every type of client code becomes responsible for performing the correct conversion. Particularly when working with report writers, this can lead to inconsistency and error.

Key points to remember from this chapter are:

- Managing numeric precision is the responsibility of the database designer and should be given careful consideration based on the requirements of the application.
- Choice of data type and careful use of the `CONVERT`, `CAST`, and `ROUND` functions are essential to accurate results and maintaining the correct amount of precision.
- Care in comparing and aggregating of numeric data can cut down on bug reports.

The chapter contains several functions that perform unit conversion in a variety of ways. The sample database TSQLUDFS contains several more unit conversion functions.

The next chapter addresses a similar problem, currency conversion. The key difference is that conversion rates change frequently—so frequently that the conversion rates must be stored in a table.

13

Currency Conversion

Currency conversion has many similarities with unit conversion, but there are some important differences. It's different on these counts:

- The precision of amounts and rates is well known and presents less of an issue than the precision of measurements of length, volume, or time.
- It's the conversion factor, or exchange rate, that creates the complexity when changing money. The exchange rate changes over time, almost continuously.
- There are different rates depending on the relationship of the parties making the exchange.

Like the unit conversion functions, a currency conversion function should return a scalar value. However, instead of being based on a fixed conversion rate, the rate changes frequently and must be looked up in a table. We'll design a table to hold the rates and a few support tables to go along with it.

Since the rate is stored in a table, the possibility that the rate is missing could come up. The example UDFs show two alternative approaches for handling that situation.

Before getting into the design issues, it's best to start with some background material. I find that knowing a little bit about the history of any subject makes it easier to understand design choices, some of which may have historical origins.

Background on Variable Exchange Rates

When I was a kid, the conversion rate between currencies was fixed. Rates were fixed because back in the 1930s, when my father was a kid, the U.S. Congress and President Roosevelt, on behalf of the United States, and other governments fixed the rate of exchange of their currencies to gold. Americans weren't even allowed to own gold except in jewelry and teeth. No gold coins circulated. They were purchased by the government and sent to Fort Knox. Governments bought and sold gold to each other for $35 an ounce.

Fixed exchange rates collapsed under the pressure of inflation in the early 1970s during the Nixon administration. The $35 price for an ounce of gold was adjusted a few times and then set free to float with the market. With it went fixed exchange rates for currencies.

In the open markets, currency exchange rates change by the minute. Some applications need minute-by-minute accuracy and must store conversion rates at very short time intervals. For most purposes, particularly when looking back at historical rates, knowing the rate every minute isn't necessary. The `CurrencyXchange` table, used by the currency conversion functions presented in this chapter, stores only a single end-of-day price for each currency.

There are different rates depending on the relationship of the parties doing the conversion. Although rates for the same currency on the same day are close, they're not identical. The difference is important to anyone making a substantial exchange. For example, banks that buy currency from other banks purchase large quantities and expect to get the best possible rate. When a consumer uses his credit card to purchase a sweater in a store while on vacation in another country, he is charged the credit card exchange rate by his bank. It's a few percentage points higher than a bank would pay. The `CurrencyRateTypeCD` table has the codes for rate type.

For economic analysis, a useful rate is the Interbank rate, which summarizes the rate that banks charge each other. Many rates, including the Interbank rate, can have both a bid and an ask price. Other rates, such as the credit card rate, have only one rate. That's because there is no negotiation between the parties when the credit card rate is used. Consumers never get a chance to sell foreign currencies to their credit card issuer. The sample data in `CurrencyXchange` contains only a single Interbank rate that is a combination of the bid and ask prices.

I've already mentioned a few of the sample tables that we'll need for currency conversion. Let's take a closer look at them and other design issues before basing functions on the data they contain.

Design Issues for Currency Conversion

Because of the changing nature of currency exchange rates, we'll have to have a table for storing the exchange rate. We'll also need a few tables to provide documentation and enable foreign key constraints to validate the codes used in the table that holds the rates.

Table design is the first issue to tackle. As with unit conversion, we'll also have to be sure of the data types. Unlike unit conversion, we have to handle situations in which the rate information in the table isn't available.

Creating the Schema to Support the Functions

Figure 13.1 diagrams the tables that we'll use for currency conversion. There is also a full schema creation script that includes extended properties in the download directory for this chapter in the file Currency Schema.sql. The tables, rules, relationships, and functions have already been created and populated in the TSQLUDFS database. You don't have to run the schema creation script to use them.

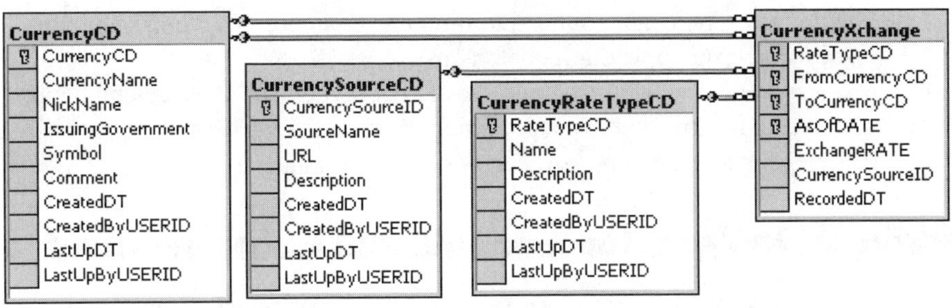

Figure 13.1: CurrencyXchange and the tables that support it

The sample data in the `CurrencyXchange` table is fictionalized but based on real data found on the web. The table includes Interbank rates for four currencies and gold during the period from January 1, 2002, to June 19, 2002. Each currency is convertible to U.S. dollars and back. The exchange rates have been changed by small random amounts so that they cannot be used in real calculations.

Notice that gold is included in the list of currencies. Precious metals are often traded using the same systems as currencies. However, they trade in units of ounces, which makes them a little different.

The `CurrencyCD` table is for maintaining the integrity of the `CurrencyCD` columns in other tables. It also has columns for storing various names and symbols for the currencies. The table is loaded with most of the currencies from the ISO 4217 standard for three-character currency symbols. I strongly encourage you to use standards where they're available instead of making up your own codes. This query lists the currencies that appear in CurrencyXchange:

```
-- List currency codes in CurrencyXchange
SELECT CurrencyCD, CurrencyName, IssuingGovernment
    FROM CurrencyCD
    WHERE CurrencyCD in (Select Distinct(FromCurrencyCD) from CurrencyXchange)
    ORDER BY CurrencyCD
GO
```

(Results)

```
CurrencyCD CurrencyName                          IssuingGovernment
---------- ------------------------------------- --------------------------
ALL        Lek                                   Albania
EUR        Euro                                  European Union
ISK        Krona                                 Iceland
JPY        Yen                                   Japan
USD        Dollar                                United States of America
XAU        Gold                                  None
```

The CurrencySourceCD table has a CurrencySourceCD column. The CurrencySourceCD is used to record the origin of each conversion rate. Knowing where a data point came from can be important when resolving issues that crop up when the data is used.

As we discussed in Chapter 12, the data type used to store and manipulate units is important to maintaining precision. Selecting data types is a little easier when it comes to currency conversion.

Picking Data Types for Amounts and Exchange Rates

Once you know the currency, the precision of a monetary value is well known. Many currencies use two digits of precision after the decimal to denote hundredths of a unit, or cents. There are a few currencies, particularly in the Arab world, that use four digits to the right of the decimal. SQL Server's money type stores that much precision. money is used for the data type of currency amounts when stored in a table.

It turns out that money isn't really a built-in data type in SQL Server. It appears to be a user-defined type (UDT) that's been shipped with the system. Because it's a UDT, using it is incompatible with the use of the WITH SCHEMABINDING clause on UDF definitions. Since I favor use of WITH SCHEMABINDING, you'll see numeric (18,4) substituted for money in the currency-related UDFs. However, you can still use it for any database column that holds an amount.

Precious metals such as gold (XAU) and platinum (XPT) are often traded using the same systems as used for currency conversion. Metals are a case where the digits of precision for a monetary quantity are not well known. They're usually traded by the ounce, but the required precision could be anything. Four digits to the right of the decimal provide enough precision for economic analysis, and that's what's used in the TSQLUDFS database. With four digits, a column can represent one-ten-thousandth of an ounce. Even for platinum selling at $550 U.S. per ounce, the value of the smallest quantity that can be represented is worth $0.055. That might be too large for you, and you'll have to increase the number of digits of precision.

While the `money` type works well for amounts, it's too imprecise for rates. When exchange rates are in the same order of magnitude, such as the U.S. dollar and the euro or the United Kingdom's pound, four digits of precision will suffice. However, there are many currencies where the exchange rate can be 100 or more to one, and the exchange rate must be stored at least six digits to the right of the decimal. For example, as I write this, one U.S. dollar is trading for 120.159 Japanese yen (JPY). That gives a yen to dollar change rate of 0.008323 dollars for each yen. The examples in this book use `decimal(18,8)` for storing exchange rates as given in this type definition:

```
EXEC sp_addtype N'CurrencyExchangeRate', N'decimal(18,8)', N'null'
```

As with other UDTs, because of the use of `WITH SCHEMABINDING`, columns in tables can be coded with the type, but it isn't used in UDFs. You'll see the `decimal(18,8)` data type coded into any function with a variable that holds a rate.

With the tables in place, it's time to face some of the other design issues. For example, what do you do when a desired rate isn't in the conversion table?

Returning a Meaningful Result When Data Is Missing

Since the currency conversion rate is in a table, there is a possibility that a rate could be missing. Therefore, before writing the code, an important decision must be made. What do you do when the data requested isn't in the table? The choices that I know of are:

- Raise an error condition
- Return a `NULL` value
- Return a special value
- Interpolate between known values

As shown in Chapter 5, it's impossible to use the `RAISERROR` statement inside a UDF. It is possible to cause an unrelated error, such as divide-by-zero, to stop execution of the program. That's a messy solution that would confuse anyone who came along and used the function without knowledge of this unusual behavior, and I recommend against it. This technique was also covered back in Chapter 5.

Returning NULL has a lot of benefits when used in the currency conversion functions. When push comes to shove, it's the choice that I've chosen most often. NULLs have the advantage that they are easily detected and can be handled with standard SQL expressions such as the IS NULL operator and the COALESCE function. They also propagate themselves to the result of an expression. The result of any mathematical operation performed on NULL always gives a NULL result.

Returning a special value to represent a missing exchange rate could be a viable technique in some circumstances. This was discussed in Chapter 5, and I understand that SAS, a statistical analysis package, has always made extensive use of this technique. It works in statistics because many statistical variables are positive by their definition. Any negative number used in this context is obviously a special value instead of a valid data point.

Currency conversion is a candidate for using special values because the range of values stored by the data type (numeric) include some that are not legitimate exchange rates. Specifically, 0 and negative numbers are not valid conversion rates.

The database rule CurrencyExchangeRatePositive on the CurrencyExchangeRate user-defined type enforces this restriction. If this rule is modified, it's possible to use 0 or a particular negative number to indicate that the value was in some way missing or defective. Here's an alternative rule that does just that:

```
CREATE rule [CurrencyExchangeRatePositiveAlternate] as
        @Rate > 0 -- Must be a positive number
     or @Rate = -1 -- Indicates a missing value
```

There are some problems with the return-a-special-value approach when applied to currency conversion. This is due to the way programmers typically use conversion rates. For starters, it's sometimes necessary to divide by a rate. That pretty much rules out the use of 0 to indicate a missing value. There's no sense setting everyone up for any extra divide-by-zero errors. Also, on occasion, two rates might be multiplied. If both are special values and if proper checking isn't performed, the negative signs cancel each other, and the information that there was missing data, or some other error, would be lost. For these reasons, I've ruled out the special value approach when working with currencies and stick with NULL. However, the "Returning Special Values" section in Chapter 5 discusses a project where the missing value technique is used successfully.

Writing the Functions for Currency Conversion

The basic currency conversion function is udf_Currency_XlateOnDate, which is shown in Listing 13.1. It accommodates different rate type codes and a from/to pair of currency codes. The user-defined types have been removed due to the use of the WITH SCHEMABINDING clause.

Listing 13.1: udf_Currency_XlateOnDate

```
CREATE  FUNCTION dbo.udf_Currency_XlateOnDate (

    @RateTypeCD      CHAR(3) = 'IBR' -- rate type
  , @mAmount   numeric(18,4) -- amount to convert
  , @FromCurrencyCD char(3) = 'USD'
  , @ToCurrencyCD   char(3) = 'USD'
  , @AsOfDATE SMALLDATETIME -- What Date?  Will use SOD.
)   RETURNS numeric(18,4) -- Resulting amount in the To currency.
    WITH SCHEMABINDING
/*
*  Converts from one currency to another on a specific date.
*  The date must be in the database or the result is NULL.
*
* Example:
SELECT dbo.udf_Currency_XlateOnDate (DEFAULT, 1000.00, 'USD', 'EUR'
        , '2002-06-01' ) -- Convert $1000 to Euros on June 6, 2002
*
* Test: (These depend on the sample data in CurrencyXchange)
PRINT 'Test 1 $1000.00 To Euro   ' + CASE when 1070.9000
            = dbo.udf_Currency_XlateOnDate (DEFAULT, 1000, DEFAULT,
                'EUR', '2002-06-01') then 'Worked' else 'ERROR' end
PRINT 'Test 2 Missing date       ' + CASE when
            dbo.udf_Currency_XlateOnDate (DEFAULT, 1000, DEFAULT,
        'EUR', '1998-01-01') is NULL then 'Worked' else 'ERROR' end
*******************************************************************/
AS BEGIN

    DECLARE @Rate numeric(18,8)
        , @nMyError int -- local for error code
        , @nMyRowCount int -- local for row count
        , @mResult money

    SELECT TOP 1 @Rate = ExchangeRATE
        FROM dbo.CurrencyXchange WITH(NOLOCK)
        WHERE RateTypeCD = @RateTypeCD
            AND FromCurrencyCd = @FromCurrencyCD
            AND ToCurrencyCD = @ToCurrencyCD
            and AsOfDate = dbo.udf_DT_SOD (@AsOfDate)

    SET @mResult = @Rate * @mAmount

    RETURN @mResult
END
```

Using the function is a matter of supplying the required parameters, such as rate, date, from and to currencies, and, of course, the amount to be converted. Here's a sample query that requests the conversion of $1000 on every day from December 30, 2001 to January 14, 2002:

```
-- Select some sample rates:
SELECT convert(varchar(12), D.date) as [Date]
     , dbo.udf_Currency_XlateOnDate ('IBR' -- TYPE OF RATE
                                   , 1000.000 -- amount
                                   , 'USD', 'EUR'  -- $ to yen
                                   , D.date) as [$1000 to EUR]
    FROM udf_DT_DaysTAB ('2001-12-30', '2002-01-14') D
GO
```

(Results)

```
Date         $1000 To EUR
------------ ------------
Dec 30 2001  NULL
Dec 31 2001  NULL
Jan  1 2002  1121.8000
Jan  2 2002  1124.7000
Jan  3 2002  1107.1000
Jan  4 2002  1111.9000
Jan  5 2002  1117.9000
Jan  6 2002  1117.7000
Jan  7 2002  1116.2000
Jan  8 2002  1119.4000
Jan  9 2002  1120.0000
Jan 10 2002  1122.0000
Jan 11 2002  1122.4000
Jan 12 2002  NULL
Jan 13 2002  NULL
Jan 14 2002  1119.8000
```

udf_Currency_XlateOnDate returns NULL for any date for which there is no entry in the CurrencyXchange table. If you're exchanging money, then a missing rate is an important enough event to cause you to abort the transaction. However, for many applications such as economic analysis or even accounting, an interpolated result might be acceptable.

The next UDF takes the interpolation approach. Listing 13.2 shows udf_Currency_XlateNearDate. When it encounters a missing rate, it attempts to interpolate. However, it will only use data points that are within 30 days of @AsOfDate. If @AsOfDate is earlier than the first rate or later than the last rate, it uses the closest rate available, but only if it's within the 30-day window. If no rate close enough to @AsOfDate can be found, udf_Currency_XlateNearDate resorts to returning NULL.

Listing 13.2: udf_Currency_XlateNearDate

```
CREATE FUNCTION dbo.udf_Currency_XlateNearDate (

    @RateTypeCD char(3)  = 'IBR' -- Which rate
  , @mAmount numeric(18,4) -- amount to convert
  , @FromCurrencyCD char(3)  = 'USD'
  , @ToCurrencyCD char(3)  = 'USD'
  , @AsOfDate SMALLDATETIME -- What Date?  Will use SOD
)   RETURNS numeric(18,4) -- Resulting amount in the To currency.
    WITH SCHEMABINDING
/*
* Converts from one currency to another using a rate that's on or
* near the specified date.  If the date is not found in the table
* an approximate result is returned. If AsOfDate is:
*  - Matched, the rate from that date is used.
*  - Less than the first available date but within 30 days of it,
*     the rate from the first date is used.
*  - Greater than the last available date but within 30 days of it,
*     the rate from the last date is used.
*  - between two available dates but within 30 days of both,
*    straight line interpolation is performed between the nearest dates.
* Example:
select dbo.udf_Currency_XlateNearDate ('IBR', 1000.00, 'USD',
       'EUR', '2002-06-01' ) -- Convert $1000 to Euros,  June 1, 02
* Maintenance Note: must be maintained in sync with
*      udf_Currency_XlateOnDate they use same logic for dates.
* Test: (Depend on the sample currency data in CurrencyXchange)
print 'Test 1 $1000.00 To Euro  ' +
        CASE when 1070.9000 = dbo.udf_Currency_XlateNearDate ('IBR',
    1000, 'USD', 'EUR','2002-06-01') then 'Worked' else 'ERROR' end
print 'Test 2 Missing date      ' +
        CASE when dbo.udf_Currency_XlateNearDate ('IBR', 1000, 'USD',
        'EUR', '1998-01-01') is NULL then 'Worked' else 'ERROR' end
print 'Test 3 Interpolation     ' +
        CASE when 1120.6667 = dbo.udf_Currency_XlateNearDate ('IBR',
    1000, 'USD', 'EUR', '2002-01-12') then 'Worked' else 'ERROR' end
print 'Test 4 Before 1st date   ' + CASE when
        dbo.udf_Currency_XlateNearDate ('IBR', 1000, 'USD', 'EUR',
        '1956-07-10') is null then 'Worked' else 'Error' end
***************************************************************/
AS BEGIN
DECLARE @Rate numeric (18,8)
    , @EarlierExchangeRate numeric (18,8)
    , @EarlierDATE SMALLDATETIME
    , @EarlierDaysDiff int -- # days Earlier
    , @EarlierFactor float -- Weight for Earlier Rate
    , @LaterExchangeRate numeric (18,8)
    , @LaterDATE SMALLDATETIME
    , @LaterDaysDiff int -- # days for next later rate
    , @LaterFactor float -- Weight for LaterRate

-- Truncate the time from @AsOfDate
SET @AsOfDate = dbo.udf_DT_SOD (@AsOfDate) -- Its call by Value

-- First try for an exact hit
SELECT Top 1 @Rate = ExchangeRATE
    FROM dbo.CurrencyXchange WITH(NOLOCK)
    WHERE RateTypeCD = @RateTypeCD AND AsOfDate = @AsOfDate
```

```
        AND FromCurrencyCd = @FromCurrencyCD AND ToCurrencyCD = @ToCurrencyCD

-- Did we get a hit
IF @Rate IS NOT NULL RETURN @Rate * @mAmount

-- Get nearest result that is earlier than the date
SELECT Top 1 @EarlierExchangeRate = ExchangeRATE
         , @EarlierDate = AsOfDate
    FROM dbo.CurrencyXchange WITH(NOLOCK)
    WHERE RateTypeCD = @RateTypeCD AND AsOfDate < @AsOfDate
        AND FromCurrencyCd = @FromCurrencyCD AND ToCurrencyCD = @ToCurrencyCD
    ORDER BY AsOfDate desc

IF @EarlierExchangeRate is not Null
    SET @EarlierDaysDiff
             = ABS(datediff (d, @EarlierDate, @AsOfDate))

-- Get nearest result that is later than the date
SELECT Top 1 @LaterExchangeRate = ExchangeRATE
         , @LaterDate = AsOfDate
    FROM dbo.CurrencyXchange WITH(NOLOCK)
    WHERE RateTypeCD = @RateTypeCD AND AsOfDate > @AsOfDate
        AND FromCurrencyCd = @FromCurrencyCD AND ToCurrencyCD = @ToCurrencyCD
    ORDER BY AsOfDate asc

IF @EarlierExchangeRate IS NULL -- If no rate was found return null
   AND @LaterExchangeRate Is NULL    RETURN NULL

IF @LaterExchangeRate is not Null
    SET @LaterDaysDiff = ABS(datediff (d, @LaterDate, @AsOfDate))

-- Decide if one of the edges can be used.
-- We're later than the earliest date, try and use the later date
IF @EarlierExchangeRate is Null
    AND @LaterExchangeRate Is Not Null
    AND @LaterDaysDiff <= 30
    -- Use the rate from the first date
    RETURN @LaterExchangeRate * @mAmount

IF @LaterExchangeRate Is NULL
    AND @EarlierExchangeRate is Not Null
    AND @EarlierDaysDiff <= 30
    RETURN @EarlierExchangeRate * @mAmount

-- Return the interpolated result
SELECT @EarlierFactor = CAST (@EarlierDaysDiff as float)
        / CAST(@EarlierDaysDiff + @LaterDaysDiff as float)
     , @LaterFactor = CAST (@LaterDaysDiff as float)
        / CAST(@EarlierDaysDiff + @LaterDaysDiff as float)
SELECT @Rate = (@EarlierFactor * @EarlierExchangeRate )
             + (@LaterFactor * @LaterExchangeRate)
RETURN @Rate * @mAmount
END
```

Let's rerun the query on a dollar to euro exchange, adding a column that calls `udf_Currency_XlateOnDate` for possible interpolation:

```
-- Sample rates with possible interpolation
SELECT convert(char(10), D.date, 120) as [Date]
     , dbo.udf_Currency_XlateOnDate ('IBR' -- TYPE OF RATE
                                    , 1000.000 -- amount
                                    , 'USD', 'EUR'  -- $ to euro
                                    , D.date) as [$1000 To EUR]
     , dbo.udf_Currency_XlateNearDate ('IBR' -- TYPE OF RATE
                                    , 1000.000 -- amount
                                    , 'USD', 'EUR'  -- $ to euros
                                    , D.date) as [$1000 To EUR with interpolation]
    FROM udf_DT_DaysTAB ('2001-12-30', '2002-01-14') D
    ORDER BY d.Date
GO
```

(Results)

```
Date         $1000 To EUR         $1000 To EUR with interpolation
------------ -------------------- --------------------------------
Dec 30 2001  NULL                 1121.8000
Dec 31 2001  NULL                 1121.8000
Jan  1 2002  1121.8000            1121.8000
Jan  2 2002  1124.7000            1124.7000
Jan  3 2002  1107.1000            1107.1000
Jan  4 2002  1111.9000            1111.9000
Jan  5 2002  1117.9000            1117.9000
Jan  6 2002  1117.7000            1117.7000
Jan  7 2002  1116.2000            1116.2000
Jan  8 2002  1119.4000            1119.4000
Jan  9 2002  1120.0000            1120.0000
Jan 10 2002  1122.0000            1122.0000
Jan 11 2002  1122.4000            1122.4000
Jan 12 2002  NULL                 1121.5333
Jan 13 2002  NULL                 1120.6667
Jan 14 2002  1119.8000            1119.8000
```

As you can see, from December 30 to 31, when the `@AsOfDate` is earlier than the available rates, the nearest good rate is used. When a rate is missing but there are rates on both sides of `@AsOfDate` (for instance, on January 12), linear interpolation is performed to produce the most usable rate.

Actually, you can't really see what happened by looking at the result. When a conversion is made, you don't know if the rate was available in the table or interpolated. Sometimes that's okay, and sometimes the user really has to know how the rate was derived.

A scalar UDF can't return both the rate and a code to say how the rate was derived. To make up for that, I've written a companion function, `udf_Currency_DateStatus`, that returns a status code indicating how the result of `udf_Currency_XlateNearDate` is determined. The logic is very similar to `udf_Currency_XlateNearDate`, and both functions must be maintained in parallel. The UDF is in Listing 13.3. The most common use for it is to footnote the results of a currency conversion. The 30-day window is arbitrary, and you might want to adjust it for your application.

Listing 13.3: udf_Currency_DateStatus

```
CREATE   FUNCTION dbo.udf_Currency_DateStatus (

    @RateTypeCD      CHAR(3) = 'IBR' -- Which rate
  , @FromCurrencyCD CHAR(3) = 'USD'
  , @ToCurrencyCD   CHAR(3) = 'USD'
  , @AsOfDATE SMALLDATETIME -- What date?  Will use SOD.
)   RETURNS INT -- Status code, see description above.
    WITH SCHEMABINDING
/*
* Used together with udf_Currency_XchangeNearDate to understand the
* status of the exchange rate. The returned status codes are:
*
*   1   Exact date match found
*  -1   Date Missing. Interpolation performed.
*  -2   Date Missing. Earliest data point used.
*  -3   Date Missing. Last data point used
*  -4   Date Missing. Null returned
*
* Example:
SELECT dbo.udf_Currency_DateStatus (DEFAULT, 'USD', 'EUR',
        '2002-06-01') -- Status of converting dollars to euros on 6/1/02
* Maintenance Note: maintain in sync with
          udf_CurrencyXlateNearDate, same logic for handling dates.
* Test: (depend on the sample currency data in CurrencyXchange)
PRINT 'Test 1 exact hit        ' +
        CASE when 1 = dbo.udf_Currency_DateStatus (DEFAULT, 'USD',
                'EUR', '2002-06-01') then 'Worked' else 'ERROR' end
PRINT 'Test 2 Missing data     ' +
        CASE when -4 = dbo.udf_Currency_DateStatus ('IBR','USD',
                   'ABR', '1998-01-01') then 'Worked' else 'ERROR' end
PRINT 'Test 3 Interpolation    ' + CASE when -1 =
                   dbo.udf_Currency_DateStatus ('IBR','USD','EUR',
                   '2002-01-12') then 'Worked' else 'ERROR' end
**********************************************************************/
AS BEGIN
DECLARE @Rate as decimal (18, 8)
    , @EarlierExchangeRate decimal (18,8)
    , @EarlierDATE SMALLDATETIME
    , @EarlierDaysDiff int -- # days Earlier
    , @LaterExchangeRate decimal (18,8)
    , @LaterDATE SMALLDATETIME
    , @LaterDaysDiff int -- # days for next later rate

-- Truncate the time from @AsOfDate
SET @AsOfDate = dbo.udf_DT_SOD (@AsOfDate) -- Its call by value

-- First try for an exact hit
SELECT Top 1 @Rate = ExchangeRATE
    FROM dbo.CurrencyXchange WITH(NOLOCK)
    WHERE RateTypeCD = @RateTypeCD AND AsOfDate = @AsOfDate
        AND FromCurrencyCd = @FromCurrencyCD AND ToCurrencyCD = @ToCurrencyCD

IF @Rate IS NOT NULL RETURN 1 -- Return for a direct hit
```

```
-- Get nearest result that is earlier than @AsOfDate
SELECT Top 1 @EarlierExchangeRate = ExchangeRATE
         , @EarlierDate = AsOfDate
    FROM dbo.CurrencyXchange WITH(NOLOCK)
    WHERE RateTypeCD = @RateTypeCD AND AsOfDate < @AsOfDate
        AND FromCurrencyCd = @FromCurrencyCD
        AND ToCurrencyCD = @ToCurrencyCD
    ORDER BY AsOfDate desc

IF @EarlierExchangeRate is not Null
    SET @EarlierDaysDiff
                 = ABS(datediff (d, @EarlierDate, @AsOfDate))

-- Get nearest result that is later than the date
SELECT TOP 1 @LaterExchangeRate = ExchangeRATE
         , @LaterDate = AsOfDate
    FROM dbo.CurrencyXchange WITH(NOLOCK)
    WHERE RateTypeCD = @RateTypeCD AND AsOfDate > @AsOfDate
        AND FromCurrencyCd = @FromCurrencyCD AND ToCurrencyCD = @ToCurrencyCD
    ORDER BY AsOfDate asc

IF @LaterExchangeRate is not Null
    SET @LaterDaysDiff = ABS(datediff (d, @LaterDate, @AsOfDate))

-- Decide if one of the edges was used
-- We're later than the earliest date, try to use the later date
IF @EarlierExchangeRate is Null
    AND @LaterExchangeRate is not Null
    AND @LaterDaysDiff <= 30
     RETURN -2     -- Use the rate from the first date in the table

IF @LaterExchangeRate is NULL
   AND @EarlierExchangeRate is not Null
   AND @EarlierDaysDiff <= 30
    RETURN -3     -- Use the rate from the last date in the table

-- If no rate was found return null
if (@EarlierExchangeRate IS NULL OR COALESCE(@EarlierDaysDiff,31) > 30)
   AND (@LaterExchangeRate Is NULL OR COALESCE(@LaterDaysDiff, 31)  > 30)
    RETURN -4

RETURN -1 -- The result was interpolated
END
```

udf_Currency_DateStatus is used in the next section. It constructs a scenario where reporting the status of the exchange rate conversion is important.

Using Currency Conversion Functions

The currency conversion function udf_Currency_XlateNearDate returns either a conversion based on a rate found in CurrencyXchange or an approximation. Approximations like this aren't suitable for offering products for sale on a web site. They're better for economic analysis or casual reporting. In either case it would be a sound design decision to tell the caller if any approximations were used.

So let's say that an imaginary publishing company, which once stored its data in the sample database pubs, has been swallowed up by a German publishing giant. The new owners want a report of orders, but they want the amounts to be translated to their own currency, the euro. To make the example work, I've copied the `Sales` table from pubs into TSQLUDFS under the name `ExampleSales`. I've updated the dates to match the available data in the `CurrencyXchange`, which contains data from July 1, 2002 through June 19, 2002. This situation is arranged so that the `udf_Currency_DateStatus` function can help us out by showing how the conversion rate was obtained. Here's the query:

```
-- Script to Report on Sales in Euros
SELECT  CONVERT(char(10), S.ord_date, 120)  as [Date]
      , LEFT(t.Title, 24)
      , CAST(dbo.udf_Txt_FmtAmt(
              dbo.udf_Currency_XlateNearDate ('IBR',
                  t.price * s.qty, 'USD', 'EUR', s.ord_date)
             , 12, ' ') as char(12)) as [Euro Sales]
      , dbo.udf_Currency_StatusName (
                        dbo.udf_Currency_DateStatus ('IBR', 'USD',
                                      'EUR', s.Ord_Date)
            ) as [Currency OK?]
    FROM ExampleSales S
        INNER JOIN pubs..Titles T
            ON S.Title_id = t.Title_id
    ORDER BY S.ord_date
GO
```

(Results – reformatted)

```
Date                                    Euro Sales   Currency OK?
---------- ------------------------ ------------ -------------
2002-01-13 The Gourmet Microwave           50.30 Interpolation
2002-02-21 You Can Combat Computer        120.36 Available
2002-03-11 Cooking with Computers:        341.68 Available
2002-05-22 But Is It User Friendly?       748.61 Available
2002-05-24 Secrets of Silicon Valle      1085.40 Available
2002-05-29 Computer Phobic AND Non-       464.96 Available
2002-05-29 Life Without Fear              188.44 Available
2002-05-29 Prolonged Data Deprivati       322.88 Available
2002-05-29 Emotional Security: A Ne       215.09 Available
2002-06-15 Onions, Leeks, and Garli       886.44 Available
2002-06-15 Fifty Years in Buckingha       252.81 Available
2002-06-15 Sushi, Anyone?                 317.13 Available
2002-07-04 Is Anger the Enemy?             34.51 Extension
2002-09-13 Is Anger the Enemy?      NULL         Unavailable
2002-09-14 Is Anger the Enemy?      NULL         Unavailable
2002-09-14 The Busy Executive's Dat NULL         Unavailable
2002-09-14 Is Anger the Enemy?      NULL         Unavailable
2002-09-14 The Gourmet Microwave    NULL         Unavailable
2002-09-14 The Busy Executive's Dat NULL         Unavailable
2002-10-28 Straight Talk About Comp NULL         Unavailable
2002-12-12 Silicon Valley Gastronom NULL         Unavailable
```

The `Currency OK?` column reports on the availability of the conversion rates. Another UDF, `udf_Currency_StatusName`, is used to translate from the numeric status that `udf_Currency_DateStatus` returns to a name that is more meaningful to you and me.

Summary

This chapter has put T-SQL functions to work to solve the problem of currency conversion. Along the way, we've run into new issues about numeric precision and error handling. The key points to remember from this chapter are:

- Managing numeric precision of currency conversion is more straightforward than with units of measure but still important.
- Because functions can't raise errors, designing a clever solution to handling missing data and numeric errors is essential to good function writing. The use of `NULL` works well in many situations. Returning a special value or interpolation was also discussed.

Currency conversion requires that the ever-changing conversion rate be stored in a table. This chapter demonstrates a group of tables to store currency conversion information and several functions that perform the currency conversion. They give you a place to start when you have to code a conversion based on a table in your application. Most importantly, they illustrate another type of problem that UDFs can solve.

Showing the two versions of the currency conversion function, `udf_Currency_XlateOnDate` and `udf_Currency_XlateNearDate`, illustrates another important dividing line. I can conceive of ways to get by without `udf_Currency_XlateOnDate`. Any query that uses it could be modified to use an outer join that coupled the proper rate with the amount instead. I can't conceive of similar ways to get by without `udf_Currency_XlateNearDate`. Even if the logic it contains could be rewritten in a declarative syntax, the result would be so complex as to be unmaintainable. Writing new queries that also handled the same logic would be time consuming and very error prone. This isn't where I want my development time to go.

This chapter concludes Part I of the book, which was about the creation and use of UDFs. There is a group of UDFs that come with SQL Server that expose real-time information from inside the SQL Server database engine and can be very useful at times. You'll see these in Part II.

Part II

System User-Defined Functions

14

Introduction to System UDFs

The addition of UDFs to SQL Server 2000 created the opportunity for the SQL Server development team to use them to implement features of SQL Server itself. They've taken advantage of that opportunity in a couple of ways. This chapter and the next four are devoted to system UDFs.

System UDFs aren't just normal UDFs that happened to be shipped with SQL Server. They're a distinct entity that can run in any database and reference the tables in that database instead of the tables in the database in which they are defined. They can also use T-SQL syntax that's reserved for them and for system stored procedures.

There are three groups of system UDFs to discuss:

- The ten system UDFs that are supplied with SQL Server and documented in Books Online. We'll start the discussion of them in this chapter. The next three chapters cover the most useful documented system UDFs in depth.
- The numerous undocumented system UDFs. These are supplied as source code and compiled into SQL Server during installation. Chapter 18 documents several of the more interesting of these and shows how to find them and view their source code.
- Your own system UDFs. Chapter 19 describes how to create your own system UDFs as well as the pros and cons of doing so.

System UDFs are different from both normal UDFs, the ones we create in a user database, and the functions that are built into the SQL Server engine, such as `DATEPART`. The first task of this chapter is to define what sets system UDFs apart from other functions.

Special factors distinguish system UDFs from normal UDFs. Most importantly, the naming rules and the place where they are defined serve to give them their status. That status allows them to be referenced from all databases and to use SQL syntax that is reserved for system UDFs and system stored procedures.

Because of their special status, the syntax for referencing system UDFs is different from the syntax for referencing normal UDFs. For the system UDFs that return tables, which includes all the documented system UDFs, a special syntax exists. In Chapters 18 and 19 we'll see the syntax to invoke scalar system UDFs.

This chapter shows the details of four of the documented system UDFs. This group isn't particularly interesting, except possibly for `fn_get_sql`, which lets you see the SQL that is being executed by any SQL process.

As with the other chapters, this one is accompanied by a single file with all the short queries. Loading it into Query Analyzer is an easy way to execute the chapter's queries as you read. You'll find it in this chapter's download directory as file Chapter 14 Listing 0 Short Queries.sql.

Distinguishing System UDFs from Other Functions

There are several characteristics that set system UDFs apart from other functions. In particular:

- They are UDFs and not built into the SQL Server engine.
- They must follow a specific naming convention to be system UDFs.
- They are defined in master and owned by `system_function_schema`.
- They have a special syntax that is used to refer to them.
- Their use of undocumented T-SQL syntax is reserved for system UDFs and system stored procedures.

Although system UDFs may have been written by the SQL Server development team, shipped with SQL Server, and updated in service packs, they're not a part of the core functionality of SQL Server the way that built-in functions such as `DATEDIFF`, `SUBSTRING`, and `@@ERROR` are implemented inside the SQL engine. System UDFs are written in T-SQL and use the T-SQL execution engine just like other UDFs. They're very much like system stored procedures, which are also shipped as part of SQL Server.

Normal UDFs can have any name that follows the T-SQL rules for identifiers including upper and lowercase characters, digits, and the special characters underscore, ampersand (@), and pound sign (#). System UDFs must follow narrower rules, which are detailed in the next subsection.

Naming Requirements for System UDFs

For starters, the name of a system UDF must satisfy the normal rules for a T-SQL object name. In addition, system UDFs must follow these naming rules:

- The name must begin with the characters `fn_`.
- The name must be all lowercase characters, and can include digits and underscores.

The system UDFs shipped with SQL Server already follow these rules. When we discuss creating your own system UDFs in Chapter 19, the naming rules are an important requirement. SQL Server won't create a system UDF with a name that doesn't follow these conventions.

In addition to the name, the database and owner where the system UDFs are defined is key to giving them their status as system UDFs. As the adage goes, "What are the three most important factors in being a system UDF?"

Location, Location, Location

System UDFs are defined in the master database and owned by the pseudo-user `system_function_schema`. There is no user named `system_function_schema`; it's a special case handled by SQL Server for the sole purpose of owning system UDFs.

It's possible to have a UDF in master that's owned by **dbo** or some other user. In fact, SQL Server creates several functions owned by **dbo** in the master database. However, they're not system UDFs. A function in master is only a system UDF if it's owned by `system_function_schema`.

System stored procedures can be used in any database, even though they're defined in master. System UDFs have the same characteristic. They can be used in any database, even though they're only defined in master. Unlike stored procedures that are invoked with the same `EXECUTE` statement whether they're system stored procedures or user stored procedures, system UDFs must be invoked with a special syntax.

Referencing System UDFs

As it happens, the ten system UDFs that are documented in Books Online all return tables and require a special syntax to be invoked or referenced. The reference uses a double colon and no owner name before the function name. Here's an example call to `fn_helpcollations`, a system UDF that returns the list of collations available in SQL Server:

```
-- Sample call to fn_helpcollations
SELECT * FROM ::fn_helpcollations()
GO

(Results - abridged and reformatted)

name                      description
------------------------- ----------------------------------------------------
Albanian_BIN              Albanian, binary sort
Albanian_CI_AI            Albanian, case-insensitive, accent-insensitive, kanat
Albanian_CI_AI_WS         Albanian, case-insensitive, accent-insensitive, kanat
...
```

The double colon is required to use the system UDFs that return tables. Using the `database.owner.functionname` syntax doesn't work, as seen in this attempt:

```
-- Attempt database.owner.functionname reference to system UDF
SELECT * from master.system_function_schema.fn_helpcollations()
GO

(Results)

Server: Msg 208, Level 16, State 1, Line 2
Invalid object name 'master.system_function_schema.fn_helpcollations'.
```

You'll see the double colon used for all the documented system UDFs that are discussed in this chapter.

There is no documented scalar system UDF. However, there are a few undocumented scalar system UDFs, and it's also possible to create your own. Scalar system UDFs can be referenced without the database or owner name qualification. There are also a few scalar non-system UDFs defined in master. These are referenced with the three-part name `master.dbo.functionname` since **dbo** is their owner.

Due to the special status of system UDFs, they can invoke special syntax that you and I can't use in our T-SQL. What's more, the text of the system UDFs is hidden from view behind a little smoke and a flimsy curtain (that is, until Toto pulls the curtain aside).

Pay No Attention to the Man Behind the UDF Curtain

So you want to see what that system UDF is doing? For normal UDFs, sp_helptext prints the script. But it doesn't work on system UDFs, as seen in this attempt to retrieve the text of fn_helpcollations:

```
-- Try sp_helptext on a system UDF
USE master
GO

EXEC sp_helptext 'fn_helpcollations'
EXEC sp_helptext 'system_function_schema.fn_helpcollations'
GO
```

(Results)

```
Server: Msg 15009, Level 16, State 1, Procedure sp_helptext, Line 53
The object 'fn_helpcollations' does not exist in database 'master'.
Server: Msg 15009, Level 16, State 1, Procedure sp_helptext, Line 53
The object 'system_function_schema.fn_helpcollations' does not exist in database
'master'.
```

The way to see the text of the documented system UDFs is to query master..syscomments. It's a table that stores the text of all stored procedures and UDFs.

Be sure you set the Maximum characters per column field on the Results tab of the Tools ➢ Options menu command statement to 8192 so long output from Query Analyzer isn't truncated. Here's a query that retrieves the text of fn_helpcollations:

```
USE master
GO

-- Retrieve the text of fn_helpcollations
SELECT text
    FROM syscomments
    WHERE text like '%system_function_schema.fn_helpcollations%'
GO
```

(Results)

```
text
------------------------------------------------------------------------------
create function system_function_schema.fn_helpcollations
    (
    )

returns @tab table(name sysname NOT NULL,
    description   nvarchar(1000) NOT NULL)
as
begin
    insert @tab
    select * from OpenRowset(collations)

    return
end -- fn_helpcollations
```

System UDFs

The unusual syntax, `OpenRowset(collations)`, doesn't appear anywhere in Books Online, nor can you use it in normal T-SQL code, as demonstrated by this script:

```
USE TSQLFUDFS
GO

-- Try to use the OpenRowset (collations) clause used by in fn_helpcollations
SELECT * from OpenRowset (collations)
GO

(Results)

Server: Msg 156, Level 15, State 17, Line 3
Incorrect syntax near the keyword 'OPENROWSET'.
```

This special syntax is reserved for system UDFs and system stored procedures. The rowset `collations` is created inside the SQL Server engine. Other system UDFs use similar undocumented syntax.

SQL Server knows to allow the reserved syntax based on the requirements for system UDFs that we've been discussing in this chapter: the naming of the function with `fn_` followed by lowercase characters and the location of the function in `master.system_function_schema`.

We've seen one system UDF, `fn_helpcollations`. There are nine more documented system UDFs, which are introduced in the next section.

Documented System UDFs

SQL Server 2000 comes with ten system UDFs that are documented and available in all databases. The documented system UDFs are listed alphabetically in Table 14.1. I've separated them into four groups based on how they'll be covered in the next few chapters.

Table 14.1: Alphabetic list of documented system UDFs

Function Name	Group	Description
fn_get_sql	Special Purpose	Returns the SQL statement just executed by a connection. Added in SP3.
fn_helpcollations	Special Purpose	Returns a table of collation names.
fn_listextendedproperty	fn_listextendedproperty	Returns a table of the extended properties of a database object.
fn_servershareddrives	Special Purpose	Returns information on shared drives that could be used in clustering.

Function Name	Group	Description
fn_trace_geteventinfo	fn_trace_*	Returns a table of the events monitored by a trace.
fn_trace_getfilterinfo	fn_trace_*	Returns a table of the filter expressions defined for a trace.
fn_trace_getinfo	fn_trace_*	Returns a table of information about all running traces such as those used by SQL Profiler.
fn_trace_gettable	fn_trace_*	Returns a table of trace data from a trace file.
fn_virtualfilestats	fn_virtualfilestats	Returns a table of I/O statistics since startup.
fn_virtualservernodes	Special Purpose	Used for fallover clustering, this function returns a table with a list of nodes on which the virtual server can run.

The documented system UDFs return tables of raw information from inside the SQL Server database engine. On its own, this raw information isn't very useful or particularly interesting. In the course of discussing the documented system UDFs, we'll develop a set of UDFs that build on them to create useful information from the raw data.

fn_listextendedproperty retrieves extended properties that have been associated with various objects in a database. Extended properties are used by Enterprise Manager to store information such as the description of tables and columns. You can also use extended properties to document your database or store other information that you want to associate with database objects such as tables, views, and stored procedures. We'll build several functions that aid in documenting a database in Chapter 15, which is devoted to fn_listextendedproperty.

fn_virtualfilestats returns raw information about file input/output operations throughout the SQL Server instance. When troubleshooting performance problems, it can be an important diagnostic tool. The raw data can be sliced and diced a few different ways, and we'll create functions to summarize it by disk drive, by database, or for the instance as a whole. fn_virtualfilestats is covered in Chapter 16.

SQL Server traces are the foundation behind the SQL Profiler. Four functions whose names begin with the characters fn_trace return tables of information about the traces that are running on the SQL Server instance. I'll refer to them as the fn_trace_* group. They can be used either with traces that are started by the SQL Profiler or with traces that are created by stored procedures. In Chapter 17 we'll use the fn_trace_* group to build UDFs that describe running traces in terms that we humans can understand. Then we'll pull them together to produce a function, udf_Trc_RPT, that shows all the running traces and what they're tracing.

The remaining four system UDFs are used in limited, special-purpose situations. I've called this group the special-purpose group. Unless you're running a SQL Server cluster, the only two of these that you might use are `fn_helpcollations` and `fn_get_sql`. The special-purpose group is covered in the next section.

Special-purpose System UDFs

These system UDFs don't fall into any particular category, but you should at least be aware that they're around. They handle situations that most of us won't run into very frequently, except for `fn_get_sql`, which can help with locking situations and performance analysis.

The last and most interesting of these functions, `fn_get_sql`, was released in a hotfix between SQL Server Service Packs 2 and 3. Once you install Service Pack 3 or later, you'll have the function in your system. Due to security flaws in earlier versions, all SQL Server 2000 instances should be upgraded to Service Pack 3 or above.

Let's start with `fn_helpcollations`, which enumerates all the collations available in our system. Collations encapsulate the rules that apply to character comparisons.

fn_helpcollations

This function returns a list of the collations supported by SQL Server. The syntax of the call is:

```
::fn_helpcollations()
```

It doesn't have any arguments. The resultset returned has the two columns described in Table 14.2.

Table 14.2: Columns returned by `fn_helpcollations`

Column Name	Data Type	Description
`name`	`sysname`	The collation name. Names are coded with suffixes such as _BIN for binary or _AS for accent sensitive. This makes it possible to search for a particular type of collation using the `LIKE` operator.
`description`	`nvarchar(1000)`	A textual description of the collation. This column is useful when searching for a particular type of collation. The characteristics of the collation are spelled out for easier searching.

Try this simple query on your system:

```
-- See all the collations
SELECT * FROM ::fn_helpcollations()
GO
```

(Results - abridged and truncated on the right)

```
name                             description
-------------------------------- ----------------------------------------------
Albanian_BIN                     Albanian, binary sort
Albanian_CI_AI                   Albanian, case-insensitive, accent-insensitive,
...
SQL_Latin1_General_CP1253_CI_AI  Latin1-General, case-insensitive, accent-insens
SQL_Latin1_General_CP1253_CI_AS  Latin1-General, case-insensitive, accent-sensit
SQL_Latin1_General_CP1253_CS_AS  Latin1-General, case-sensitive, accent-sensitiv
...
SQL_Latin1_General_CP850_BIN     Latin1-General, binary sort for Unicode Data, S
SQL_Latin1_General_CP850_CI_AI   Latin1-General, case-insensitive, accent-insens
SQL_Latvian_CP1257_CI_AS         Latvian, case-insensitive, accent-sensitive, ka
...
SQL_Ukrainian_CP1251_CS_AS       Ukrainian, case-sensitive, accent-sensitive, ka
As of SQL Server 2000 Service Pack 2 there are 753 of them.
```

You don't have to see all the collations at once. If you're searching for a binary collation, you can ask for just the collations that have `_BIN` in their name with the following query:

```
-- All the binary collations
SELECT *
    FROM ::fn_helpcollations()
    WHERE [name] like '%_BIN%'
    ORDER BY [name]
GO
```

(Results - abridged and truncated on the right)

```
name                             description
-------------------------------- ----------------------------------------------
Albanian_BIN                     Albanian, binary sort
Arabic_BIN                       Arabic, binary sort
Chinese_PRC_BIN                  Chinese-PRC, binary sort
...
Slovenian_BIN                    Slovenian, binary sort
SQL_Latin1_General_CP437_BIN     Latin1-General, binary sort for Unicode Data, S
SQL_Latin1_General_CP850_BIN     Latin1-General, binary sort for Unicode Data, S
Thai_BIN                         Thai, binary sort
...
Vietnamese_BIN                   Vietnamese, binary sort
```

Most of the time you'll only use your database's default collation. But if you're working with multiple languages, where text might or might not have Unicode characters or accent marks, collations can be important.

fn_virtualservernodes

This function is used for fallover clustering. It returns a table with a list of nodes on which the virtual server can run. The syntax of the call is:

`::fn_virtualservernodes()`

The function takes no arguments, and there is only one column in the result set, `NodeName`. When you're not running on a clustered server, `fn_virtualservernodes` returns an empty table. I don't have a cluster so the results to this sample query are made up:

```
-- get the list of nodes that the server can run on
SELECT NodeName FROM ::fn_virtualservernodes()
GO

(Results - simulated)

NodeName
--------
Moe
Larry
Curly
```

fn_servershareddrives

This function returns a table with a row for each shared drive used by the clustered server. The syntax of the call is:

`::fn_servershareddrives()`

This function has no arguments, and there's only one column in the result table, `DriveName`, which is an `nchar(1)` column. If the current server is not a clustered server, `fn_servershareddrives` returns an empty table. I'm not running a cluster, so the results shown in this query are made up. But if you're running in a cluster, give it a try:

```
-- get the list of shared drives in the cluster
SELECT DriveName from ::fn_servershareddrives()
GO

(Results - simulated)

DriveName
---------
p
q
```

The next UDF is a bit more interesting. It lets us take a look into the SQL statements that are being executed by any user of the system. It's particularly useful when deadlocks have occurred.

fn_get_sql

SQL Server 2000 Service Pack 3 (SP3) includes a new system user-defined function, `fn_get_sql`. It was actually in an earlier hotfix, but SP3 is the best way to get it. (See Microsoft Knowledge Base article 325607 for details.) Throughout this section, I'm going to assume that you've installed SP3, including the updated documentation.

Based on a conversation that I had with a gentleman representing a vendor of SQL performance tools, I suspect that `fn_get_sql` was added primarily to make it possible for such vendors to produce more robust tools. But the motivation for creating the function doesn't matter. It's available to us all.

`fn_get_sql` retrieves the text of the SQL being executed by active SQL processes. This is a technique commonly used when diagnosing a deadlock or other blocking problem. Diagnostic tools that monitor activity inside the database engine can also use it.

Prior to the availability of `fn_get_sql`, the only way to see the SQL being used by a SQL process was by executing the `DBCC INPUTBUFFER` command. Let's take a look at that first.

Viewing a Connection's SQL the Old Way

`DBCC INPUTBUFFER` takes a SPID as its argument and shows the first 255 characters of the statement that the connection is executing. SPIDs are integers that uniquely identify a database connection. A connection can retrieve its own SPID by using the `@@SPID` built-in function.

When invoked, `DBCC INPUTBUFFER` returns a rowset consisting of the columns listed in Table 14.3. Notice that the data type of the `EventInfo` column is `nvarchar(255)`. The size of the column has proven to be an annoying limitation because it restricts the results to the first 255 characters of any SQL statement. While that might be enough when the statement is executing a stored procedure, it's often insufficient when a complex `SELECT` or `UPDATE` is involved.

Table 14.3: Columns returned by `DBCC INPUTBUFFER`

Column Name	Data Type	Description
`EventType`	`nvarchar(30)`	Language, EventNo, or EventRPC
`Parameters`	`int`	0=text 1–n=parameters
`EventInfo`	`nvarchar(255)`	For an RPC (stored procedure), it contains the procedure name. For a language event, it contains the text of the SQL being executed.

This query gives you an idea of how `DBCC INPUTBUFFER` works by showing you its own text:

System UDFs

```
DBCC INPUTBUFFER (@@SPID)
GO

(Results)

EventType      Parameters EventInfo
-------------- ---------- ---------------------------
Language Event          0 DBCC INPUTBUFFER (@@SPID)
```

DBCC INPUTBUFFER continues to work after Service Pack 3 is installed. You may even want to use it during any initial diagnosis of a locking problem. fn_get_sql overcomes the length limitation of DBCC INPUTBUFFER, so let's turn to it.

Calling fn_get_sql

The syntax of the call to fn_get_sql is:

::fn_get_sql (@HandleVariable)

@HandleVariable is a sql_handle, which is a new BINARY(20) column in the sysprocesses table that resides in master. Two more columns, stmt_start and stmt_end, were also added to sysprocesses to support fn_get_sql.

fn_get_sql returns a rowset with the columns listed in Table 14.4. In spite of the fact that the text column is of data type text, the design of SQL Server's internal cache limits the size of the statement to 8,000 bytes.

Table 14.4: Columns returned by fn_get_sql

Column Name	Data Type	Description
dbid	smallint	Database ID
objectid	int	ID of the database object. NULL for ad hoc statements.
number	smallint	The number of the group, if the procedures are grouped.
encrypted	bit	1=Encrypted 0=Not encrypted
text	text	Text of the statement. NULL if the object is encrypted. Will only return 8,000 characters.

Before trying to run fn_get_sql, it's important to understand a little about the SQL cache. SQL Server stores the execution plan for stored procedures, UDFs, triggers, and scripts in the SQL cache for potential reuse. It turns out that if a plan has zero cost, it normally isn't cached.

Scripts that don't do any I/O have zero cost, so a simple script isn't usually in the cache. Since fn_get_sql uses the cache, it often won't find the zero cost scripts. This can appear very mysterious because it causes fn_get_sql to return a script in some cases but return nothing in other cases.

SQL Server has a remedy to this situation in the form of a new trace flag, 2861. Once it is turned on, zero cost plans are cached and they show up as the result of fn_get_sql. Trace flags are turned on with the DBCC TRACEON statement such as the following:

```
-- Turn on caching of zero cost plans
DBCC TRACEON (2861)
GO

(Results)

DBCC execution completed. If DBCC printed error messages, contact your system
administrator.
```

Trace flags are turned off with the DBCC TRACEOFF command. The Listing 0 file has a script that uses DBCC TRACEOFF after the other scripts that use fn_get_sql are done.

Query Analyzer can truncate the output of any column to a specific size. Be sure you set the Maximum characters per column field on the Results tab of the Tools ➢ Options menu command to 8192 so the output isn't truncated. Then, with trace flag 2861 on, the following script shows itself:

```
-- Retrieve the sql of this connection
DECLARE @handle binary(20)

SELECT @handle = sql_handle
    FROM master..sysprocesses
    WHERE spid = @@SPID

SELECT [text]
    FROM ::fn_get_sql(@handle)
GO

(Results)

text
----------------------------------------------------------------
-- Retrieve the sql of this connection
DECLARE @handle binary(20)

SELECT @handle = sql_handle
    FROM master..sysprocesses
    WHERE spid = @@SPID

SELECT [text]
    FROM ::fn_get_sql(@handle)
```

Don't get confused by the fact that the output is identical to the query. It's supposed to be the same. It even includes the comment line that starts the batch.

Handles expire very quickly and must be used immediately. If you pass in a handle that is no longer in the cache, `fn_get_sql` returns an empty resultset. Remember, on a highly active, memory-constrained system, statements might be aged out of the cache almost instantly.

One of the most common situations for using `DBCC INPUTBUFFER`, and now `fn_get_sql`, involve situations where a process can't run because of resources locked by another process. The most severe of these situations is a deadlock.

An Example of Using fn_get_sql

A truly real-world example of using `fn_get_sql` might involve creating a deadlock, using `sp_lock` to find out which processes are blocked and then using `fn_get_sql` to retrieve the text of the SQL that the blocked and blocking processes were executing. The thought of publishing code that deliberately created a deadlock somehow struck me as overly risky so I've decided to use a simpler example—a case of simple blocking due to a long running transaction.

The following example uses two Query Analyzer windows to run Script A and Script B. Both should be run in the pubs sample database. The scripts include six batches, which should be run in numerical order. In the text that follows, I execute each batch in order and show you the results. The two script files are in the download directory for this chapter.

Open a new Query Analyzer connection using the File ➢ Connect menu command and load Script A.sql from this chapter's download directory. Start by executing Batch A-1. It turns on trace 2861 and moves the connection into the pubs database.

```
-- Batch A-1  Moves to the pubs sample database
PRINT 'Batch A-1  Script A''s SPID = ' + CAST (@@SPID as varchar)
DBCC TRACEON(2861)
USE pubs
GO
```

(Results)

```
Batch A-1  Script A's SPID = 53
DBCC execution completed. If DBCC printed error messages, contact your system
administrator.
```

Next, run Script A Batch A-2. This batch begins a transaction and deletes a row in the `Authors` table. I've deliberately chosen an author who hasn't written any books, so there are no referential integrity issues. Don't worry about losing the row, we'll roll back the transaction in Batch A-6. Here's Batch A-2:

```
-- Batch A-2
PRINT 'Batch A-2 Begin a transaction and create the blockage'
BEGIN TRAN -- the transaction will cause an exclusive lock
   DELETE FROM authors WHERE au_id = '527-72-3246'
GO
-- Stop Batch A-2 here
```

(Results)

```
Batch A-2 Begin a transaction and create the blockage

(1 row(s) affected)
```

Batch A-2 leaves open a transaction, which isn't closed until Batch A-6. In Script A-5, we'll see that the open transaction causes the SPID to hold several locks, including an exclusive lock on the row being deleted.

The next step is to open a new Query Analyzer connection using the File ➢ Connect menu command and load file Script B.sql. The first batch in script B is B-3, which prints the SPID of the connection for Script B. We'll use that SPID in Batch A-5. Here's Batch B-3 with the results of running it on my system:

```
-- Batch B-3   Moves to the pubs sample database
--             And prints the SPID
PRINT 'Batch B-3 Printing the SPID and Using pubs'
PRINT 'Script B -- Has SPID ' + CAST(@@SPID as varchar)
USE pubs
GO
```

(Results)

```
Batch B-3 Printing the SPID and Using pubs
Script B -- Has SPID 55
```

You will probably get a different number for the SPID. Once again, take note of the SPID because it's needed later in Batch A-6.

Batch B-4 selects from the Authors table. Here's the batch:

```
-- Batch B-4
PRINT 'Batch B-4 SELECT a blocked resource.'
SELECT * from authors
GO
```

There are no results because the batch can't run due to the open transaction left by Batch A-2. Figure 14.1 shows what my Query Analyzer window looks like after I execute B-4.

System UDFs

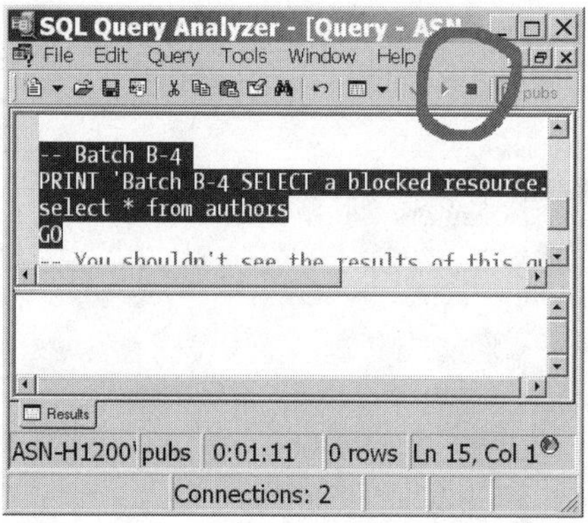

Figure 14.1: Script B Batch B-4 is blocked.

I've circled the red execution flag to highlight the fact that the batch is running. If you look down in the information bar near the bottom of the figure, you'll see that it had been running for one minute and 11 seconds by the time I took the screen shot.

Leave Batch B-4 running and switch back to the connection with Script A. Batch A-5 uses the `sp_lock` system stored procedure to show the locks being held by the system. The exclusive locks (Mode = X) held by Script A and the shared lock (Mode = S) are shaded in the result.

```
-- Batch A-5  sp_lock shows who's waiting and who's locking
PRINT 'Batch A-5 -- Output of sp_lock'
EXEC sp_lock
GO
```

(Results)

```
Batch A-5 -- Output of sp_lock
spid   dbid   ObjId       IndId  Type Resource         Mode     Status
------ ------ ----------- ------ ---- ---------------- -------- ------
    53      5  1977058079      0 TAB                   IX       GRANT
    53      5  1977058079      1 PAG  1:127            IX       GRANT
    53      5  1977058079      1 KEY  (0801c4f7a625)   X        GRANT
    53      5           0      0 DB                    S        GRANT
    53      5  1977058079      1 PAG  1:239            IX       GRANT
    53      5  1977058079      2 KEY  (1f048d178a34)   X        GRANT
    53      1    85575343      0 TAB                   IS       GRANT
    54     14           0      0 DB                    S        GRANT
    55      5  1977058079      1 PAG  1:127            IS       GRANT
    55      5           0      0 DB                    S        GRANT
    55      5  1977058079      0 TAB                   IS       GRANT
    55      5  1977058079      1 KEY  (0801c4f7a625)   S        WAIT
```

SPID 55, which is running Batch B-4, is waiting for a shared lock on Key 0801c4f7a625. But SPID 53 was granted an exclusive lock on that key. Had we set the transaction isolation level in Batch B-4 to `READ UNCOMMITTED`,

Batch B-4 wouldn't have requested the shared lock and would not have to wait.

Finally, it's time to use fn_get_sql to examine the SQL that Batch B-4 is running. This is done with Batch A-6. Before you can run A-6, you must change the line WHERE spid=55 to replace the 55 with the SPID that was printed by Batch B-3. Here's Batch A-6 with its results on my system:

```
-- Batch A-6  You must change the SPID number in this batch
--            before executing this step!
PRINT 'Batch A-6 -- Get the text of the blocked connection'
DECLARE @Handle binary(20)
SELECT @handle=sql_handle
     FROM master..sysprocesses
     WHERE spid= 55 -- <<<<<< Change 55 to the SPID of Script B

SELECT * FROM ::fn_get_sql(@handle)

ROLLBACK TRAN -- Releases the lock on authors
GO
```

(Results)

```
Batch A-6 -- Get the text of the blocked connection
dbid   objectid    number encrypted text
------ ----------- ------ --------- ------------------
NULL   NULL        NULL           0 -- Batch B-4
PRINT 'Batch B-4 SELECT a blocked resource.'
select * from authors

(1 row(s) affected)
```

The text column has carriage returns in it that show up in the output. To make it easier to see the results, I've shaded the output of the text column. Since there were three lines in the batch, it wraps onto a second and third line of output.

The last line of A-6 is a ROLLBACK TRAN statement. This undoes the effect of the DELETE done earlier. It also has the effect of releasing the exclusive locks that are held by Script A's connection. If you flip back to Script B, you'll see that it has run and sent its output to the results window.

fn_get_sql is a new function to aid the DBA and programmer in the diagnosis of blocking problems. It's going to be used by diagnostic and performance-monitoring tools to monitor the SQL by continually sampling the SQL of all processes to discover the statements that are executed most often. I'm aware of at least one tool on the market that's using it in this way. But you don't need an expensive tool to put fn_get_sql to good use. A simple script, like the one in Batch A-6 that gets a sql_handle and uses it, is all you need.

Summary

This chapter introduced system UDFs. While they're written in T-SQL, they are different from other UDFs that we've seen previously in this book. They're distinguished by:

- Their name, which must begin with `fn_` and contain only lowercase characters, digits, and underscores.
- Their location, which must be in the master database, under the ownership of a special-purpose owner, `system_function_schema`.
- Their use of reserved T-SQL syntax.

You may or may not ever use the system UDFs shown in this chapter, at least not directly. However, they're worth knowing.

The next three chapters are devoted to putting system UDFs to work in useful ways:

- Chapter 15 discusses `fn_listextendedproperty`, which retrieves extended properties, a new feature in SQL Server 2000.
- Chapter 16 discusses `fn_virtualfilestats`, which returns a table of input/output statistics about database files. It'll be put to use to create performance diagnostic UDFs.
- Chapter 17 discusses the `fn_trace_*` functions and how to use them on SQL Server traces, both those created by SQL Profiler and those that are created with stored procedures.

After we've discussed the documented system UDFs, the last two chapters in this part of the book go further:

- Chapter 18 discusses the undocumented system UDFs and when you might choose to use them.
- Chapter 19 shows you how to make your own system UDFs and why you might create them.

Enterprise Manager uses extended properties to store descriptions for tables and columns, but there are actually several ways to add extended properties to your database. The next chapter shows you how they're associated with database objects and retrieved with `fn_listextendedproperty`.

15

Documenting DB Objects with fn_listextendedproperty

Extended properties are user-defined or application-defined information about a database object. They're new in SQL Server 2000. This chapter describes and then builds on the fn_listextendedproperty system UDF to create functions useful for managing extended properties.

Enterprise Manager uses extended properties to store its description fields in the MS_Description extended property for tables, views, and columns. Extended properties can also be added using stored procedures or through an interface provided by Query Analyzer.

Once they're entered, fn_listextendedproperty is used to retrieve them. Its seven parameters tell fn_listextendedproperty which extended properties to return and for which set of database objects to return them. While there are many possibilities, we'll narrow the choices down and create these *task-oriented* UDFs:

- udf_Tbl_DescriptionsTAB — Returns a table of the descriptions for all user tables in a database
- udf_Tbl_ColDescriptionsTAB — Returns a table of the descriptions for all columns in all user tables
- udf_Tbl_MissingDescrTAB — Returns a table listing any table that does not have a description. It's used to locate tables that need more attention to their documentation.
- udf_Tbl_RptW — Returns a table with information about a table; some of it comes from the extended properties

I call them task-oriented because they accomplish a task that I consider worthwhile. Additional helper functions are created along the way.

Before the functions are developed, the next section has some information to expand your knowledge of extended properties and how to create them. That's followed by a description of the ins and outs of invoking `fn_listextendedproperty`.

Note:

As with other chapters, the short queries that appear without listing numbers are in the file Chapter 15 Listing 0 Short Queries.sql in the chapter's download directory.

Understanding and Creating Extended Properties

Extended properties are metadata. That is, they're data that describes other data. In the case of extended properties, they describe SQL Server database objects such as tables, columns, procedures, functions, users, and the database itself.

There are many ways to store metadata. One distinguishing feature of extended properties is that they are stored within the database. When a database's files are moved, the extended properties come along with the file. When you generate a script for a database object using SQL Server's script generation tools, you can optionally request that the script to create the extended properties is also generated. This makes them a particularly robust method of storing metadata.

Maintaining Extended Properties

`fn_listextendedproperty` retrieves extended properties. That's all. Extended properties are added, updated, and deleted by using three system stored procedures:

- `sp_addextendedproperty` — Adds an extended property
- `sp_updateextendedproperty` — Changes the value of an extended property
- `sp_dropextendedproperty` — Deletes an extended property

Books Online has the complete documentation for these procedures, so I won't repeat it here. Let's just take a look at a sample script that adds the `'ShortCaption'` extended property to the `Cust.CompanyName` column:

```
-- Add a caption to the Cust table
EXEC sp_addextendedproperty 'ShortCaption' -- Name of the property
                          , 'Cpny'     -- Value of the property
                          , 'USER'    -- level 0 object type
                          , 'dbo'     -- level 0 object name
                          , 'TABLE'   -- level 1 object type
                          , 'Cust'    -- level 1 object name
                          , 'COLUMN'  -- level 2 object name
                          , 'CompanyName' -- L 2 object type
GO

(Results)

The command(s) completed successfully.
```

`fn_listextendedproperty` hasn't been property described yet, but let's take a quick look at how it can be used to retrieve the extended property just added:

```
-- Retrieve the ShortCaption caption just added
SELECT value
    FROM ::fn_listextendedproperty('ShortCaption'
          , 'USER', 'dbo', 'TABLE', 'Cust', 'COLUMN', 'CompanyName')
GO

(Results)

value
----------------
Cpny
```

Now let's delete the extended property so it doesn't get retrieved in any of the other queries:

```
-- Remove an extended property
EXEC sp_dropextendedproperty 'ShortCaption' -- Name of the property
                          , 'USER'    -- level 0 object type
                          , 'dbo'     -- level 0 object name
                          , 'TABLE'   -- level 1 object type
                          , 'Cust'    -- level 1 object name
                          , 'COLUMN'  -- level 2 object name
                          , 'CompanyName' -- L 2 object type
GO

(Results)

The command(s) completed successfully.
```

It isn't necessary to use these system stored procedures directly. Enterprise Manager uses them when you edit a description field, and Query Analyzer has a graphical user interface that's convenient for entering extended properties on functions. It can also be used for maintaining extended properties on most other types of database objects. When you use it for this purpose, Query Analyzer uses the system stored procedures to add, update, and delete extended properties. Figure 15.1 shows the Query Analyzer editing the extended properties for the TSQLUDFS database.

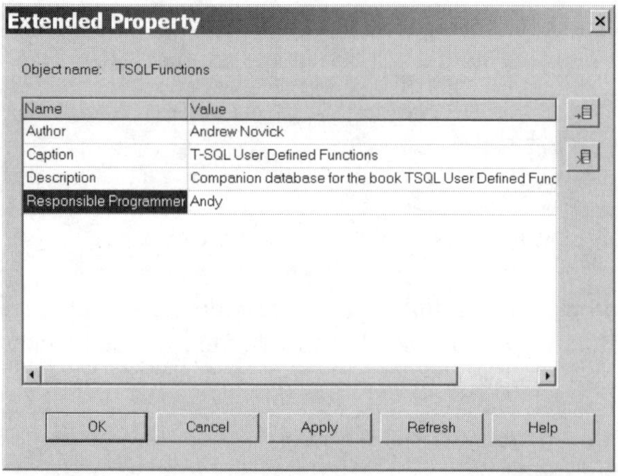

Figure 15.1: Maintaining extended properties on a database with Query Analyzer

Query Analyzer lets you enter any name for the extended property, whereas Enterprise Manager uses only one name: `MS_Description`.

Maintaining MS_Description Using Enterprise Manager

Enterprise Manager uses an extended property to store descriptions that are entered for tables and columns. The user interface for this capability is in the Design Table dialog boxes. Figure 15.2 shows Enterprise Manager while editing the description for the `CustomerID` column in the `Cust` table of the TSQLUDFS database.

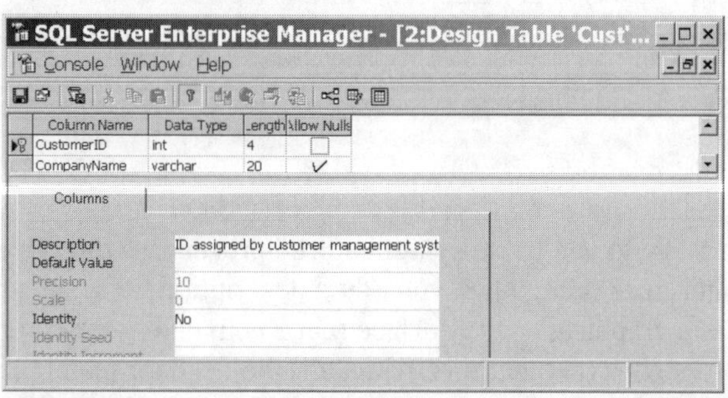

Figure 15.2: Editing the description for an extended property of a column

Enterprise Manager stores the description field in an extended property named MS_Description. It uses the same name for descriptions on both tables and columns.

I've come to rely on the MS_Description extended property precisely because Enterprise Manager (EM) maintains it. Since everyone on the development team has EM on their desktop and knows how to use it, there's no excuse for not documenting a table. Nobody that I work with can say, "I can't document the tables I create because I don't have (or know to use) such and such a tool." Another advantage is that it's available at every site that has SQL Server. Although I enjoy learning new tools, they take time.

While EM and a few reports are hardly a complete database documentation solution, it does fit Pareto's law: It gets 80 percent of the job done at 20 percent of the cost of the alternatives. However, in this case, it's more like 80 percent of the benefit for 1 percent of the cost.

Using fn_listextendedproperty

I find the description of fn_listextendedproperty's arguments in Books Online to be confusing, so I'll try to be clearer. The function definition is:

```
fn_listextendedproperty (
    { default | [ @name = ] 'property_name' | NULL }
  , { default | [ @level0type = ] 'level0_object_type' | NULL }
  , { default | [ @level0name = ] 'level0_object_name' | NULL }
  , { default | [ @level1type = ] 'level1_object_type' | NULL }
  , { default | [ @level1name = ] 'level1_object_name' | NULL }
  , { default | [ @level2type = ] 'level2_object_type' | NULL }
  , { default | [ @level2name = ] 'level2_object_name' | NULL }
  )
```

All seven arguments are required for every call.

The first argument, **@name**, gives the name of the property. Next come three groups of arguments for three levels in the object hierarchy—level 0, level 1, and level 2. Each group consists of an object type and an object name. I'll discuss the case where the arguments are strings and discuss later what happens when they are NULL or default. Table 15.1 describes the arguments.

Table 15.1: Arguments for `fn_listextendedproperty`

Argument Name	Data Type	Description
@name	sysname	The name of the property given when it was created. There is no fixed set of names. The SQL Server tools create properties with names that begin with the letters MS. Names may contain embedded spaces.
@level0type	varchar(128)	The top-level object to be searched for. Table 15.2 has the list of valid entries for this level.
@level0name	sysname	Name of the Level 0 object. It must be either NULL or an object of the type given in @level0type. NULL means that extended properties associated with all the objects of @level0type should be returned, such as all USER objects.
@level1type	varchar(128)	The Level 1 object to be searched for. Table 15.3 has the list of valid entries for this level.
@level1name	sysname	Name of the Level 1 object. It must be either NULL or an object of the type given in @level1type. NULL means that extended properties associated with all the objects of @level1type should be returned, such as all TABLE objects.
@level2type	varchar(128)	The bottom-level object to be searched for. The @level2type arguments allowed for each @level1type are listed in Table 15.3.
@level2name	sysname	Name of the Level 2 object. It must be either NULL or an object of the type given in @level2type. NULL means that extended properties associated with all the objects of @level2type should be returned, such as all COLUMN objects.

Let's try an example. This query retrieves the `MS_Description` for the `Cust.CustomerID` column using `fn_listextendedproperty`:

```
-- Query to get the MS_Description property from Cust.CustomerID
SELECT *
    FROM ::fn_listextendedproperty ('MS_Description'
               , 'USER', 'dbo'
               , 'TABLE', 'Cust'
               , 'COLUMN' , 'CustomerID')
GO

(Results - reformatted)

objtype objname    name            value
------- ---------- --------------- -------------------------------------------
COLUMN  CustomerID MS_Description  ID assigned by customer management system.
```

The valid object types depend on the level. In the query above, the `@level0type` is `USER`, the `@level1type` is `TABLE`, and the `@level2type` is `COLUMN`.

Table 15.2: Valid entries for Level 0 extended properties

Level 0 Object	Valid Level 1 Objects	Description
NULL	NULL	Used for database-wide properties
USER	NULL, TABLE, VIEW, PROCEDURE, FUNCTION, DEFAULT, RULE	Used for objects related to a user, including dbo
TYPE	NULL	Used for properties related to a user-defined type

Level 0 has three possible object types, which are shown in Table 15.2. `USER` can have various entries at Level 1, which are shown in Table 15.3 along with the Level 2 objects that are paired with them. `NULL` and `TYPE` have no valid entries at the lower levels.

Table 15.3: Level 1 objects and the Level 2 objects that go with them

Level 1 Objects	Valid Level 2 Objects
TABLE	NULL, COLUMN, INDEX, CONSTRAINT, TRIGGER
PROCEDURE	NULL, PARAMETER
VIEW	NULL, COLUMN, TRIGGER, INDEX*
FUNCTION	NULL, COLUMN, PARAMETER
DEFAULT	NULL
RULE	NULL

*Note: Only schema-bound views can have properties on `INDEX`.

The output of `fn_listextendedproperty` is a table with the columns shown in Table 15.4.

Table 15.4: Result columns from `fn_listextendedproperty`

Column Name	Data Type	Description
object_type	varchar(128)	The type of object such as TABLE, COLUMN, or USER
object_name	sysname	Name of the object such as Cust, CustomerID, or dbo
name	sysname	Name of the property such as MS_Description
value	sql_variant	The value of the property

The simple query that retrieved `MS_Description` for `Cust.CustomerID` worked nicely. That's because all seven parameters to `fn_listextended-property` were string constants. Once `NULL` arguments are introduced, things get a little trickier.

System UDFs

The Problem with NULL Arguments to fn_listextendedproperty

Let's try the sample query from Books Online. You'll think it works only if you anticipate its behavior correctly. It certainly baffled me for a while. Here's the query:

```
-- The BOL says this should return all the extended properties in the database
-- but it does not.  What it does is return all extended properties at the
-- database level. That is, those with all null levels.
SELECT * FROM ::fn_listextendedproperty (NULL, NULL, NULL, NULL
                                       , NULL, NULL, NULL)
GO

(Results)

objtype objname    name           value
------- ---------- -------------- --------------------------------------------
```

It returns nothing. Where is the `MS_Description` property that was returned above? Where are the other `MS_Description` properties in the database? The confusion arises because specifying `NULL` for an object type at any level doesn't mean, "Give me all the extended properties that have anything to do with the higher level object types." Instead, it means, "Give me all extended properties for objects at a higher level that are not associated with any specific object." So the Books Online query doesn't show all extended properties for all objects in the database. It shows only properties that are tied to the database but to no other object.

This next batch creates the extended property `'Responsible Developer'` at the database level and assigns the value `'Andy'` to it.

```
-- Make Josiah Carberry the responsible developer for this database.
EXEC sp_addextendedproperty 'Responsible Developer', 'Josiah Carberry'
          , NULL, NULL, NULL, NULL, NULL, NULL
GO

(Results)

The command(s) completed successfully.
```

After running that batch, the following query shows that we have an extended property defined at the database level. `Default` has been substituted for `NULL`. They work identically.

```
-- Get all properties that are at the database level only.
SELECT *
    FROM ::fn_listextendedproperty (default, default, default, default
                                   , default, default, default)
GO
```

(Results)

```
objtype objname name                   value
------- ------- ---------------------- --------------------
NULL    NULL    Responsible Developer  Josiah Carberry
```

Of course, the query could have requested just the one property that we're interested in:

```
-- Get the Responsible Developer property
SELECT *
    FROM ::fn_listextendedproperty ('Responsible Developer', default, default, default
                                   , default, default, default)
GO
```

If you want to leave your database in its original state, delete the `'Responsible Developer'` extended property with this script:

```
-- Get rid of Responsible Developer property.
DECLARE @rc int -- return code
EXEC @rc = sp_dropextendedproperty 'Responsible Developer'
                                   , NULL, NULL, NULL, NULL, NULL, NULL
IF @rc = 1 -- 1 means failure
    PRINT 'Extended property not dropped, please check out.'
ELSE
    PRINT 'Extended property Responsible Developer dropped.'
GO
```

(Results)

```
Extended property Responsible Developer dropped.
```

To better demonstrate the use of extended properties in the next few sections, the following script adds several extended properties to the database. If you're executing the scripts as you're reading this chapter, run this script now:

```
-- Add the demonstration properties to the database.
EXEC sp_addextendedproperty 'Caption', 'Customer List'
                , 'USER', 'dbo', 'TABLE', 'cust', NULL, NULL
EXEC sp_addextendedproperty 'Caption', 'Currency Exchange Rates'
                , 'USER', 'dbo', 'TABLE', 'CurrencyXchange', NULL, NULL
EXEC sp_addextendedproperty 'Caption', 'Customer ID'
                , 'USER', 'dbo', 'TABLE', 'CUST', 'COLUMN', 'CustomerID'
EXEC sp_addextendedproperty 'Caption', 'Name'
                , 'USER', 'dbo', 'TABLE', 'CUST', 'COLUMN', 'CompanyName'
EXEC sp_addextendedproperty 'Caption', 'City'
                , 'USER', 'dbo', 'TABLE', 'CUST', 'COLUMN', 'City'
```

```
EXEC sp_addextendedproperty 'Pager', 'XXX-555-1212'
                , 'USER', 'LimitedUser', NULL, NULL, NULL, NULL
GO
```

(Results)

```
The command(s) completed successfully.
```

The key to understanding how to call `fn_listextendedproperty` is focusing on the use of `NULL`. It's worth spending time on because Books Online is pretty confusing about this point.

Understanding NULL Arguments to fn_listextendedproperty

`NULL` can be used for any of the seven arguments to `fn_listextended-property`. When used for the extended property name, it means, "Return all extended properties for the objects selected." The other six arguments determine which objects are selected.

The meaning of `NULL` is different when it's used for a `@levelNtype` argument than when it's used for a `@levelNname` argument. When `NULL` is used as a `@levelNtype` argument, it's applied to the higher level object as a whole. So when `NULL` is used for `@level0type` argument, it means, "To the database as a whole." When it's used as the `@level1type` argument, it implies, "Get extended properties for the object that is specified for Level 0." When it's used as the `@Level2type`, it means, "Get extended properties for the object at Level 1." However, when `NULL` is used for a `@levelNname` argument, it means, "All the objects at this level."

This next query gets all the properties that are defined at the `TABLE` level (`@level1type='TABLE'`) for all tables (`@level1name=NULL`). At the time I wrote this chapter, I only had the few properties shown here, but I may have added a few more as the database evolved. You may see slightly different results.

```
-- Get all the extended properties on all the tables.
SELECT * from ::fn_listextendedproperty (NULL,
                                                    'USER', 'dbo',
                                                    'TABLE', NULL,
                                                     NULL, NULL)
            ORDER BY objname, name
GO
```

```
(Result - reformatted)

objtype objname           name            value
------- ----------------- --------------- -----------------------------------
TABLE   CurrencySourceCD  MS_Description  Defines the known currency sourc...
TABLE   CurrencyXchange   Caption         Currency Exchange Rates
TABLE   CurrencyXchange   MS_Description  Exchange rates between currencies.
TABLE   Cust              Caption         Customer List
TABLE   ExampleNames      MS_Description  Sample Names
```

As you can see, none of the properties for any of the columns are in the results. That's because using NULL for @level2type requests results for extended properties that are defined for @level1@type (in this case TABLE). Since the @level1name is NULL, results are produced for all tables. If a specific table is used for the @level1name argument, only properties for the given table are in the result, as in this query:

```
-- Get all the extended properties on the CurrencyXchange table
SELECT * from ::fn_listextendedproperty (NULL, 'USER', 'dbo',
                                          'TABLE', 'CurrencyXchange',
                                           NULL, NULL)
GO

(Results - reformatted)

objtype  objname           name            value
-------- ----------------- --------------- -----------------------------------
TABLE    CurrencyXchange   Caption         Currency Exchange Rates
TABLE    CurrencyXchange   MS_Description  Exchange rates between currencies.
```

Another combination of arguments that I would like to work, but doesn't, is a request for the 'Caption' extended property for all COLUMN objects in all TABLE objects. Here's the query that I would like to work:

```
-- This query doesn't return anything because it doesn't work the way that
-- I imagine it should work.
SELECT * from ::fn_listextendedproperty ('Caption', 'USER', 'dbo',
                                          'TABLE', NULL,
                                           'COLUMN', NULL)
GO

(Results)

objtype  objname           name            value
-------- ----------------- --------------- -----------------------------------
```

If the query is modified to include a table name, the new query produces results for just that table, as seen here:

```
-- Specifying the table name gets results.
SELECT * from ::fn_listextendedproperty ('Caption', 'USER', 'dbo',
                                          'TABLE', 'CUST',
                                           'COLUMN', NULL)
GO
```

System UDFs

```
(Results - reformatted)

objtype objname          name             value
------- ---------------- ---------------- -----------------------------------
COLUMN  City             Caption          City
COLUMN  CompanyName      Caption          Name
COLUMN  CustomerID       Caption          Customer ID
```

However, we can't use `fn_listextendedproperty` alone to meet our need to find the `MS_Description` for every column of every table. Also, we don't have a solution for the task of retrieving extended properties across all entries of a Level 1 object, like `TABLE`. That is, I also want to see all the `MS_Description` extended properties for all tables in the database. Providing the correct group of `NULL` arguments isn't going to be sufficient for this task; it's going to take a cursor. While there are other solutions to this problem using stored procedures and dynamic SQL, they're not available in functions.

The next group of functions consolidates data provided by `fn_listextendedproperty` and other sources into more useful information about the objects in a database. They perform tasks that anyone responsible for a SQL Server database might be interested in.

Task-oriented UDFs that Use fn_listextendedproperty

The UDFs in this section are targeted at specific tasks instead of being more general purpose. If you want to create reports on your database objects and include information about extended properties, these UDFs should prove useful. They don't do everything that can be done with `fn_listextendedproperty`, but they illustrate what can be achieved by using it.

Fetching an Extended Property for All Tables

The function `udf_Tbl_DescriptionsTAB` completes the task of showing the description of all tables in the database. I've generally used this as input to a report writer as part of database documentation. It's shown in Listing 15.1. As you can see, it's just a `SELECT` on another function that does the bulk of the work.

Listing 15.1: `udf_Tbl_DescriptionsTAB`

```
CREATE  FUNCTION udf_Tbl_DescriptionsTAB ()

    RETURNS TABLE
/*
* Returns the description extended property for all user tables
* in the database.
*
* Example:
select * from udf_Tbl_DescriptionsTAB()
****************************************************************/
AS RETURN
    SELECT Owner as [Owner]
         , objname as [TableName]
         , OBJECT_ID(objname) as [ID]
         , CAST(value as nvarchar(255)) as [Description]

        FROM dbo.udf_EP_AllUsersEPsTAB('MS_Description'
                                      , 'TABLE'
                                      , default)
```

Let's use `udf_Tbl_DescriptionsTAB` and then go on to examine how it works. It doesn't have any arguments, so the query is very simple:

```
-- Get all MS_Description extended properties for all TABLES in the database.
SELECT * from udf_Tbl_DescriptionsTAB() ORDER BY TableName
GO

(Results - reformatted and truncated on the right)

User      TableName                                 Description
-----     ----------------------------------------- ----------------------------
dbo       A Table to Show the Length of MS_Descrip 123456789 123456789 12345678
dbo       Broker                                    Has all the information for
dbo       CurrencySourceCD                          Defines the known currency s
dbo       CurrencyXchange                           Exchange rates between curre
dbo       ExampleNames                              Sample Names
dbo       ExampleTableWithKeywordColumnNames        This table has column names
```

Note:

This query was run in TSQLUDFS. By the time that database reaches you, there may be a different result.

Now that we've seen the output, let's turn to how the function accomplishes its task. Most of the work is turned over to the function `udf_EP_AllUsersEPsTAB`, which does the job of searching for an extended property associated with all tables for all users. It does it in a general-purpose way. I've made it general purpose so that it can be the foundation for several functions. Listing 15.2 shows its `CREATE FUNCTION` script.

There is a warning produced when the CREATE FUNCTION script for udf_EP_AllUsersEPsTAB is executed:

> Warning: The table '@EP' has been created, but its maximum row size (9,201) exceeds the maximum number of bytes per row (8,060). INSERT or UPDATE of a row in this table will fail if the resulting row length exceeds 8,060 bytes.

The warning is issued by SQL Server because of the value column. It's a sql_variant that makes it possible to insert 8,000 bytes of data into the value column and might push the total column length beyond the maximum allowed, 8,060. MS_Description columns are limited to 255 Unicode characters, so they'll never extend the row anywhere near the limit. However, you might store your own extended property that is 8,000 bytes long. If you do, be aware that it could cause an error in this function and other udf_EP_* functions created in this chapter.

Listing 15.2: udf_EP_AllUsersEPsTAB

```
CREATE   FUNCTION dbo.udf_EP_AllUsersEPsTAB (

    @epname sysname = NULL -- name of EP desired, NULL for all
  , @level1_object_type varchar(128) = NULL -- Sub objects
        -- NULL is for EPs associated with the USER or
        -- or TABLE, VIEW, PROCEDURE, FUNCTION, DEFAULT, RULE
  , @level1_object_name sysname = NULL -- or, Null for all.
)   RETURNS @EP TABLE (
         [Owner] sysname -- the user/Owner/Schema name
       , objtype varchar(128) -- The type of object such as TABLE
       , objname sysname -- Name of the object
       , [name] sysname -- name of the extended property
       , value sql_variant -- Value of the extended property
       )
    -- No SCHEMABINDING DUE TO USE OF SYSTEM TABLES
/*
* Returns the extended property value for a property (or null for
* all properties) on all USERS in the database.  The Level 1
* object type must be specified. Useful for finding a property
* for all TABLES, VIEWS, etc. The cursor is needed because it does
* not assume that every object is owned by dbo.
*
* Example:
select * from udf_EP_AllUsersEPsTAB('MS_Description'
                                    , 'TABLE', default)
* © Copyright 2002 Andrew Novick http://www.NovickSoftware.com
* You may use this function in any of your SQL Server databases
* including databases that you sell, so long as they contain
* other unrelated database objects. You may not publish this
* UDF either in print or electronically.
****************************************************************/
AS BEGIN
    DECLARE @user_name sysname -- holds a user name
```

```
    DECLARE UserCursor CURSOR  FAST_FORWARD FOR
        SELECT [name] as [User]
            FROM sysusers
            WHERE issqlrole = 0 -- NOT A SQL ROLE
              AND isapprole = 0 -- NOT AN APPLICATION ROLE

    -- Open the cursor and fetch the first result
    OPEN UserCursor
    FETCH UserCursor INTO @user_name

    WHILE @@Fetch_status = 0  BEGIN

        INSERT INTO @EP
            SELECT @user_name, objtype, objname, [name], value
                FROM  ::fn_listextendedproperty (@epname
                              , 'USER', @user_name
                              , @level1_object_type
                              , @level1_object_name
                              , NULL, NULL)

        FETCH UserCursor INTO @user_name -- retrieve next USER
    END -- of the WHILE LOOP

    -- Clean up the cursor
    CLOSE UserCursor
    DEALLOCATE UserCursor

    RETURN
END
```

udf_EP_AllUsersEPsTAB starts by creating a cursor for all users. There isn't an INFORMATION_SCHEMA view on users, so UserCursor selects from the sysusers system table. Here's the cursor declaration:

```
    DECLARE UserCursor CURSOR  FAST_FORWARD FOR
        SELECT [name] as [User]
            FROM sysusers
            WHERE issqlrole = 0 -- NOT A SQL ROLE
              AND isapprole = 0 -- NOT AN APPLICATION ROLE
```

Once the user name is fetched into @user_name, a SELECT from fn_listextendedproperty gets the requested extended properties and inserts them into the @EP result table variable:

```
        INSERT INTO @EP
            SELECT @user_name, objtype, objname, [name], value
                FROM  ::fn_listextendedproperty (@epname
                              , 'USER', @user_name
                              , @level1_object_type, @level1_object_name
                              , NULL, NULL)
```

The rest of the function is the looping structure for the cursor.

In addition to USER, the other Level 1 objects that could have extended properties are NULL and TYPE. They could get a similar treatment if there were extended properties associated with them. Outside of writing this chapter, I've never created extended properties for those objects, so our effort is better expended moving down a level in the hierarchy. Level 2 has the COLUMN, INDEX, and TRIGGER objects. The columns are of greatest interest, and a function for retrieving all column descriptions would fit in nicely to a report giving the details of a table.

Fetching an Extended Property for All Columns

Fetching extended properties at Level 2 is similar to Level 1 with a few different details. COLUMN is a Level 2 object. Our task is to get the MS_Description extended property for all columns in a table or for all columns in all tables. Function udf_Tbl_ColDescriptionsTAB does the job. It's shown in Listing 15.3.

Listing 15.3: udf_Tbl_ColDescriptionsTAB

```
CREATE  FUNCTION dbo.udf_Tbl_ColDescriptionsTAB (

    @TableOwner sysname = NULL -- Onwer to search for
  , @TableName sysname = NULL -- Table to query or NULL for all tables
)   RETURNS TABLE -- EPs for all COLUMNS in the table(s)
   -- NO SCHEMABINDING, using User Defined Variables (sysname)
/*
* Returns the description extended property for all columns of
* user tables in the database.  A specific Owner or table can
* be named. If @TableOwner is null, extended properties for all
* owners is returned. If @TableName is NULL, columns for all
* tables are returned.
*
* Example:
select * from udf_Tbl_ColDescriptionsTAB(NULL, NULL)
   -- Descriptions for all columns in all tables.
*****************************************************************/
AS RETURN SELECT [Owner]
               , [TableName]
               , objname as [ColumnName]
               , CAST(Value as nvarchar(255)) as [Description]
             FROM udf_EP_AllTableLevel2EPsTAB
                                 ('MS_Description'
                                 , @TableOwner
                                 , @TableName
                                 , 'COLUMN'
                                 , NULL
                                 )
```

As you can see, the work is done by udf_EP_AllTableLevel2EPsTAB, which is shown in Listing 15.4. Running its CREATE FUNCTION script gives the same warning that we saw previously with udf_EP_AllUsersEPsTAB.

Listing 15.4: udf_EP_AllTableLevel2EPsTAB

```
CREATE    FUNCTION dbo.udf_EP_AllTableLevel2EPsTAB (

    @epname sysname = NULL -- name of the EP desired, NULL for all.
  , @InputTableOwner sysname = NULL -- name of schema, NULL for all.
  , @InputTableName sysname = NULL -- Table to SELECT or NULL for all.
  , @level2_object_type varchar(128) = NULL -- Which subobjects
          -- NULL is for EPs associated with the table: COLUMN, INDEX
               -- CONSTRAINT, or TRIGGER
      , @level2_object_name sysname = NULL -- level 2 object, NULL for all.
      )

    RETURNS @EP TABLE ( Owner sysname -- The owner/user/schema name
                      , TableName sysname -- the Table Name
                      , objtype varchar(128)
                      , objname sysname
                      , [name] sysname -- name of the extended property
                      , value sql_variant
                      )
    -- No SCHEMABINDING when using INFORMATION SCHEMA
/*
* Returns a table of extended properties for a property (or null for all),
* for an owner (or null for all), for a table (or null for all) in the
* database.  The Level 2 object name must be specifid (Null means on the
* table itself).  The Level 2 object name may be given to get info
* specific Level 2 object, or use NULL for all Level 2 objects.
*
* Example: to get all extended properties on columns for all tables.
select * from udf_EP_AllTableLevel2EPsTAB('MS_Description'
                                          , NULL -- All Owners/Users/Schema
                                          , NULL -- All Table Names
                                          , 'COLUMN' -- The Level 2 Object
                                          , default -- All columns
                                          )
****************************************************************************/
AS BEGIN

    DECLARE @TableName sysname -- holds a table name
          , @TableOwner sysname -- holds the owner/user/schema

    DECLARE TableCursor CURSOR  FAST_FORWARD FOR
        SELECT TABLE_NAME, TABLE_SCHEMA
            FROM INFORMATION_SCHEMA.TABLES
            WHERE TABLE_TYPE = 'BASE TABLE'
              and (@InputTableOwner is NULL
                   or TABLE_SCHEMA = @InputTableOwner)
              and (@InputTableName is NULL
                   or TABLE_NAME = @InputTableName)
            ORDER BY TABLE_SCHEMA, TABLE_NAME

    -- Open the cursor and fetch the first result
    OPEN TableCursor
    FETCH TableCursor INTO @TableName, @TableOwner

    WHILE @@Fetch_status = 0  BEGIN
        -- Get All EPs for this table and user
```

System UDFs

```
        INSERT INTO @EP
            SELECT @TableOwner, @TableName
                   , objtype, objname
                   , [name], value
                FROM ::fn_listextendedproperty (@epname
                              , 'USER', @TableOwner
                              , 'TABLE', @TableName
                              , @level2_object_type, @level2_object_name)

        FETCH TableCursor INTO @TableName, @TableOwner -- retrieve next Table
    END -- of the WHILE LOOP

    -- Clean up the cursor
    CLOSE TableCursor
    DEALLOCATE TableCursor

    RETURN
END
```

udf_EP_AllTableLevel2EPsTAB starts by creating a cursor on the list of all tables in the database. The list of tables in a database is provided by the INFORMATION_SCHEMA.TABLES view. That view has information about both base tables and views. The UDF is only interested in base tables. Here's the cursor definition that asks for the tables:

```
01    DECLARE TableCursor CURSOR  FAST_FORWARD FOR
02        SELECT TABLE_NAME, TABLE_SCHEMA
03            FROM INFORMATION_SCHEMA.TABLES
04            WHERE TABLE_TYPE = 'BASE TABLE'
05              and (@InputTableOwner is NULL
06                   or TABLE_SCHEMA = @InputTableOwner)
07              and (@InputTableName is NULL
08                   or TABLE_NAME = @InputTableName)
09            ORDER BY TABLE_SCHEMA, TABLE_NAME
```

The clause TABLE_SCHEMA = @InputTableOwner on line 06 restricts the cursor to just one owner. Table owners are sometimes referred to as User and sometimes as Schema. In this context, all three terms mean the same thing; I use Owner because it's not a SQL Server keyword. If the owner name isn't supplied, the clause @InputTableOwner is NULL on line 05 takes over and the cursor finds the tables owned by all users that have tables in the database.

Similarly, the clause TABLE_NAME = @InputTableName on line 08 restricts the cursor to just one table, if the caller supplies one. If the table name isn't supplied, the @InputTableName is NULL clause on line 07 takes over and the cursor finds all the tables.

As each TABLE_NAME is read into the @table_name variable, its extended properties are queried and inserted into the results table, @EP, with this statement:

```
            INSERT INTO @EP
               SELECT @TableOwner, @TableName
                      , objtype, objname
                      , [name], value
                   FROM  ::fn_listextendedproperty (@epname
                                  , 'USER', @TableOwner
                                  , 'TABLE', @TableName
                                  , @level2_object_type, @level2_object_name)
```

The rest of the function is the loop that runs the cursor and fetches each row.

So let's get the information that we were after in the first place. Here's a query on udf_Tbl_ColDescriptionsTAB that uses udf_EP_AllTableLevel2EPsTAB to ask for the MS_Description property in every column of every table where it exists:

```
-- Get all MS_Description extended properties for all columns in the database.
SELECT * from udf_Tbl_ColDescriptionsTAB(NULL, NULL)
              ORDER BY TableName, ColumnName
GO

(Results - reformatted and abridged)

TableName          ColumnName           Description
------------------ -------------------- ---------------------------------------
CurrencyCD         Comment              Descriptive comment
CurrencyCD         CurrencyCD           ISO 4217 Currency Code used by Currency
CurrencyCD         CurrencyName         Common Name for the currency.
...
```

I use udf_Tbl_DescriptionsTAB and udf_Tbl_ColDescriptionsTAB as input into reports when documenting databases. Most of the time, the report writer is Crystal Reports, but you can use them with pretty much any report writer.

Almost as useful as functions that retrieve the extended properties is a second group of functions that help manage use of extended properties by finding those that should have been created but are missing.

Finding Missing Table Descriptions

To enforce a requirement that all tables must have a description, it's useful to be able to find out where the requirement hasn't been met. udf_Tbl_MissingDescrTAB is a function that lists all tables that are missing the MS_Description extended property at the TABLE level. It's shown in Listing 15.5. Running it gives a quick list of the tables that need more documentation.

Listing 15.5: udf_Tbl_MissingDescrTAB

```
CREATE   FUNCTION dbo.udf_Tbl_MissingDescrTAB (

)   RETURNS TABLE
  -- No SCHEMABINDING due to use of INFORMATION_SCHEMA
/*
* Returns the schema name and table name for all tables that do
* not have the MS_Description extended property.
*
* Example:
SELECT Owner + '.' + TABLE_NAME as
[Tables without MS_Description] FROM udf_Tbl_MissingDescrTAB()
****************************************************************/
AS RETURN
    SELECT TOP 100 PERCENT WITH TIES
           TABLE_SCHEMA as [Owner]
         , TABLE_NAME
    FROM INFORMATION_SCHEMA.TABLES I
         Left Outer Join udf_Tbl_DescriptionsTAB () F
            On I.TABLE_SCHEMA=F.Owner
               and I.TABLE_NAME = F.TableName
    WHERE TABLE_TYPE = 'BASE TABLE'
          and F.TableName is NULL -- NO description
    ORDER BY I.TABLE_SCHEMA
           , I.TABLE_NAME
```

By the time you get the TSQLUDFS database, there will be a different group of tables without MS_Description, so you'll get a different answer than is shown by this query:

```
-- Find tables that are missing their description.
SELECT Owner + '.' + TABLE_NAME AS [Tables missing MS_Description]
      FROM udf_Tbl_MissingDescrTAB()
GO
```

(Results - abridged. Your results will differ)

```
Tables missing MS_Description
--------------------------------------------------------------------------------
dbo.BBTeams
dbo.CurrencyCD
dbo.CurrencyRateTypeCD
dbo.Cust
dbo.ExampleSales
```

Although I've concentrated on MS_Description since Enterprise Manager maintains it, you may want to make more extensive use of extended properties. I certainly intend to in the future.

The next function goes beyond extended properties by combining MS_Description with other information.

Reporting on All Tables

When starting a project with an existing database, I always want to know about all the tables in the database. With luck, someone's filled in the description on at least a few of the tables. `udf_Tbl_RptW`, shown in Listing 15.6, is a textual report of information on all user tables in a database. It's a wide report (hence `RptW` at the end of its name) and intended for landscape printing. The `udf_TxtN_WrapDelimiters` function that is in the TSQLUDFS database wraps the text from the extended property `MS_Description` so that the report can be sent to a text file and then printed neatly.

Listing 15.6: `udf_Tbl_RptW`

```
CREATE    FUNCTION udf_Tbl_RptW (

    @table_name_pattern sysname = NULL -- Table Desired, NULL for all
                        -- or a pattern that works with the LIKE operator
)   RETURNS TABLE
/*
* Returns a report of information about a table. Information is from
* sysobjects, sysowner, extended properites, and OBJECTPROPERTIES.
* Intended to output from Query Analyzer.  It can be sent to a file
* and then printed from the file with landscape layout.
*
* Example:
select * from udf_Tbl_RptW(default)
***********************************************************************/
AS RETURN
SELECT TOP 100 PERCENT
     dbo.udf_Txt_FixLen( [Owner] + N'.' + [Name], 64, N' ')
     + N' Created: ' +  convert(char(10), [Create Date], 120)
     + N'  RefDT: ' +  convert(char(10), [Reference Date], 120)
     + N'  Rows: ' + dbo.udf_Txt_FmtInt( [Rows], 10, ' ')
     + NCHAR(10) + space(22)
     + N'Indexes: '
         + CASE WHEN ClustIndex = 1 THEN N'Clustered ' ELSE N'' END
         + CASE WHEN NonclustIndex = 1 THEN N'NonClust ' ELSE N'' END
         + CASE WHEN PrimaryKey=1 THEN N'PK ' ELSE N'' END
         + CASE WHEN UniqueCnst=1 THEN N'Unique ' ELSE N'' END
         + CASE WHEN ActiveFulltextIndex=1 THEN N'FullText ' ELSE N'' END
     + N' Triggers: '
         + CASE WHEN AfterTrig=1 THEN N'After ' ELSE N'' END
         + CASE WHEN InsertTrig =1 THEN N'Insert ' ELSE N'' END
         + CASE WHEN InsteadOfTrig =1 THEN N'Instead ' ELSE N'' END
         + CASE WHEN UpdateTrig=1 THEN N'Update ' ELSE N'' END
         + CASE WHEN DeleteTrig=1 THEN N'Delete ' ELSE N'' END
     + N' Misc: '
         + CASE WHEN AnsiNullsOn = 1 THEN N'AnsiNulls ' ELSE N'' END
         + CASE WHEN QuotedIdentOn =1 THEN N'QuotedIdent ' ELSE N'' END
         + CASE WHEN  Pinned = 1 THEN N'Pinned ' ELSE N'' END
     + NCHAR(10) + space(22)
     + dbo.udf_TxtN_WrapDelimiters([Description], 129, N' ', N' ',
                 NCHAR(10), 22, 22)
```

```
     + NCHAR(10) + NCHAR(10)
         as rptline
    FROM udf_Tbl_InfoTAB (@table_name_pattern)
    ORDER BY [Name] -- table name.
          , [Owner] -- owner
```

udf_Tbl_RptW gets its information from udf_Tbl_InfoTAB, which does the job of gathering information. udf_Tbl_InfoTAB is not listed, but you'll find it in the TSQLUDFS database. If you want to send output to a report writer, such as Crystal, Brio, or Access, you're better off using udf_TBL_InfoTAB directly and dispensing with udf_Tbl_RptW.

Be sure to use the Query Analyzer menu commands Query ➢ Results to Text (Ctrl+T) or Query ➢ Results to File (Ctrl+Shift+F) before running any of the Rpt or RptW functions. The output is pretty unreadable in a grid. Here's the script to run udf_Tbl_RptW with a small sample of the output:

```
-- Request a report of table information
SELECT rptline as [TableRpt] from udf_Tbl_RptW(default)
GO

(Results - abridged and reformatted to show more of the output)

TableRpt
------------------------------------------------------------------------------
dbo.Broker            Created: 2002-09-11  RefDT: 2002-09-11  Rows:          0
                      Indexes:  Triggers:  Misc: AnsiNulls QuotedIdent
                      Example table with stock broker names and IDs.


dbo.CurrencyCD        Created: 2002-09-11  RefDT: 2002-09-11  Rows:        172
                      Indexes: Clustered PK  Triggers:  Misc: AnsiNulls QuotedI
```

Although I'd like to run udf_Tbl_RptW on every database as soon as I start working at a site, it isn't always a good idea to come in and say, "Hi, I'd like to start modifying all your databases immediately by adding some of my own code." It's usually a few days before the function library can be added to a database. However, if the information is available, it's worth doing.

That's the last of the task-oriented UDFs in this chapter. You may find them useful in your own work. More importantly, I hope they give you a feel for what can be done using extended properties and UDFs.

Summary

`fn_listextendedproperty` is the tool that SQL Server provides for access to extended properties. We've seen how careful use of its seven arguments gives us access to extended properties for all database objects. Attention to the meaning of `NULL` arguments is particularly important.

Along the way, we've constructed a group of UDFs that are useful for managing extended properties. They've been oriented to the documentation tasks that I've found most important when working with databases:

- Creating reports on tables and columns that include the descriptions maintained in Enterprise Manager
- Ensuring that every table has a description
- Reporting about the characteristics of a table

If you think that you might execute the scripts in this chapter again, it would be a good idea to run the next script. It cleans out the extended properties created for this chapter:

```
-- Remove the demonstration properties from the database.
EXEC sp_dropextendedproperty 'Caption'
                , 'USER', 'dbo', 'TABLE', 'cust', NULL, NULL
EXEC sp_dropextendedproperty 'Caption'
                , 'USER', 'dbo', 'TABLE', 'CurrencyXchange', NULL, NULL
EXEC sp_dropextendedproperty 'Caption'
                , 'USER', 'dbo', 'TABLE', 'CUST', 'COLUMN', 'CustomerID'
EXEC sp_dropextendedproperty 'Caption'
                , 'USER', 'dbo', 'TABLE', 'CUST', 'COLUMN', 'CompanyName'
EXEC sp_dropextendedproperty 'Caption'
                , 'USER', 'dbo', 'TABLE', 'CUST', 'COLUMN', 'City'
EXEC sp_addextendedproperty 'Pager'
                , 'USER', 'LimitedUser', NULL, NULL, NULL, NULL
GO
```

That does it for `fn_listextendedproperty`. On to another useful function, `fn_virtualfilestats`. It tells how much input/output activity has occurred on your system. That information can be useful in locating performance bottlenecks.

16

Using fn_virtualfilestats to Analyze I/O Performance

fn_virtualfilestats returns a table of input/output statistics for database files. They can be used to diagnose performance issues and for capacity planning. This chapter builds on the raw information that fn_virtualfilestats returns to produce UDFs that summarize the I/O statistics in various ways. Specifically, at these levels:

- A single database — udf_Perf_FS_DBTotalsTAB
- For all databases in the SQL Server instance — udf_Perf_FS_ByDbTAB
- By physical file — udf_Perf_FS_ByPhysicalFileTAB
- By disk drive letter — udf_Perf_FS_ByDriveTAB

The data returned by fn_virtualfilestats is pretty raw and almost impossible to use without interpretation. Before we can make use of its results, we're going to have to perform several minor interpretation tasks:

- The DbID and FileID columns have to be converted to a more human-friendly name.
- Logical file names must be translated into physical file names.
- We have to know how long the system has been running to be able to put the numbers into perspective.

We'll start with converting numeric IDs to names that you and I can understand. Then we'll find that fn_virtualfilestats isn't the only way to ask SQL Server for I/O statistics. There is a group of system statistical functions that report similar information.

Warning:

SQL Server 2000 Service Pack 1 fixed a bug in `fn_virtualfilestats`. Prior to the fix, if there are more than four files in the database, `fn_virtualfilestats` fails to return the last file. See Microsoft Knowledge Base article 290916. You should install SQL Server Service Pack 3 or above.

Raw counts of I/O activity aren't very indicative of system performance. The time dimension is necessary to turn counts into rates of I/O operations per second. In the case of `fn_virtualfilestats`, the relevant time is the number of seconds since the instance started. It's in the output of the function, but there are also other ways to get it.

Once we have the basics down, we'll turn to creating a few UDFs that summarize I/O activity in several different ways: by database, by physical file, and by disk drive. Before we get there, let's start with the basic calling sequence for the function and take a look at the data it returns.

Calling fn_virtualfilestats

The format of the function call is:

```
::fn_virtualfilestats ([ @DatabaseID= ] database_id
                      , [ @FileID = ] file_id )
```

@DatabaseID is an integer database ID number, which is the identifying field in the `sysdatabases` system table in the master database. Using –1 for this argument requests statistics for all databases.

@FileID is the ID number for a logical file, which is the identifying field in the `sysfiles` system table that exists in every database. Using –1 for this argument requests statistics for all files in the database.

Here's a very simple example call to `fn_virtualfilestats` and its results when run on my development system. You'll get different results:

```
-- get I/O statistics on database 1, file 1
SELECT * FROM :: fn_virtualfilestats(1, 1)
GO

(Results - reformatted)

DbId FileId TimeStamp NumberReads NumberWrites BytesRead  BytesWritten IoStallMS
---- ------ --------- ----------- ------------ ---------- ------------ ---------
1    1      5427123   115         1            6692864    8192         2434
```

Database 1 happens to be master. File 1 happens to be master.mdf. The columns in the result table are given in Table 16.1.

Table 16.1: Columns in the result table from `fn_virtualfilestats`

Column Name	Data Type	Description
`DbId`	`smallint`	Database ID
`FileId`	`smallint`	File ID
`TimeStamp`	`int`	Time at which the measurement was recorded. Unlike the data type `timestamp`, this time stamp is the number of milliseconds since the SQL Server instance started.
`NumberReads`	`bigint`	Number of reads on the file
`NumberWrites`	`bigint`	Number of writes made to the file
`BytesRead`	`bigint`	Number of bytes read from the file
`BytesWritten`	`bigint`	Number of bytes written to the fil
`IoStallMS`	`bigint`	Time, in milliseconds, that users waited for I/O operations on the file to complete

To make the results of `fn_virtualfilestats` easier to use, we'll need to modify its output by coupling it with some supporting information, such as names that you and I can understand.

Getting Supporting Information

Our I/O analysis needs human-readable names for the database, logical files, and physical files. In addition, we need to know how long the instance has been running. This kind of supporting information is pretty easy to find, once you know where to look. The next few sections lay out where to get it.

Metadata Functions to Get Database and File IDs

The `@DatabaseID` parameter to `fn_virtualfilestats` can be derived from the database name by using the `DB_ID()` metadata function. Similarly, the `DbId` column in the result can be converted back to a database name with the `DB_Name()` metadata function. These functions may be used from any database on the server. Let's try an example:

```
-- Show DB_ID() and DB_Name()
SELECT DB_ID('pubs') as [pubs ID], DB_Name(DB_ID('pubs')) [Should say pubs]
GO

(Results)

pubs ID Should say pubs
------- ------------------------------------------------------------------------
5       pubs
```

Logical file names and file IDs can be converted with the `FILE_ID()` and the `FILE_NAME()` functions. They are similar to the `DB_ID` and `DB_Name` functions. However, they only return information about files in the current database. Run this query from inside TSQLUDFS:

```
-- Run this query from inside TSQLFunctions
USE TSQLUDFS
GO

SELECT File_Name(1) as [ID 1], File_Name(2) as [ID 2]
         , File_ID('TSQLUDFS_Data') as [ID of the Data File]
         , File_ID('TSQLUDFS_Log') as [ID of the Log File]
GO
```

(Results - reformatted)

```
ID 1                 ID 2              ID of the Data File ID of the Log File
-------------------- ----------------- ------------------- ------------------
TSQLUDFS_Data        TSQLUDFS_Log                        1                  2
```

The output of `fn_virtualfilestats` can be made to be more understandable by using the metadata functions to label the files. This script moves to the pubs database to get information about its files:

```
-- Convert IDs to Names

USE pubs
GO

DECLARE @DatabaseID smallint -- holds the database ID
SET @DatabaseID = DB_ID() -- no argument means use the current database

SELECT DB_NAME(DbId) as [Database]
     , FILE_NAME(FileID) as [File Name]
     , NumberReads, NumberWrites, BytesRead, BytesWritten, IoStallMS
    FROM ::fn_virtualfilestats(@DatabaseID, -1)
GO
```

(Results - reformatted)

```
Database Logical File NumberReads NumberWrites BytesRead BytesWritten IoStallMS
-------- ------------ ----------- ------------ --------- ------------ ---------
pubs     pubs                  67           10   1810432        81920       871
pubs     pubs_log               8           18    270336       177152       471
```

As you can see, pubs has two logical files. The file name returned by `fn_virtualfilestats` is the logical file name.

Note:

This chapter contains several queries with numeric results. If you're using Query Analyzer's Output to Text instead of Output to Grid, there's a way to make the numbers line up to be more readable. Use the Results tab of the Tools ➢ Options menu command and check Right Align Numerics (*). I used it for the queries in this chapter.

The logical file name is used within SQL Server. The operating system uses a physical file name that includes the directory path. We'll want that to better understand where the I/O is being performed.

Converting Logical File Names to Physical File Names

To make the statistics for each file meaningful, it's desirable to get the physical file name of a logical file so that it can be matched up with its statistics. The name must be retrieved from one of the two system tables that contain physical file information:

- `sysfiles` — A system file that exists in every database
- `master..sysaltfiles` — Only exists in master

The next two subsections examine what's in these tables. In particular, how should we get the physical file name?

What's in sysfiles?

Every database has its own copy of `sysfiles`. Any query on `sysfiles` must be run from the database in question. Here's a query that shows what's in `sysfiles`. The output was broken into two groups of columns so that the `filename` column could be shown.

```
-- What's in sysfiles
USE TSQLUDFS
GO

SELECT * from sysfiles
GO

(Results - first group of columns)

fileid groupid size     maxsize  growth   status    perf      name
------ ------- -------- -------- -------- --------- --------- -----------------
     1       1 1304           -1       10 1081346           0 TSQLUDFS_Data
     2       0 3688           -1       10 1081410           0 TSQLUDFS_Log

(Results - second group of columns)

filename
-------------------------------------------------------------------------------
C:\BT\Projects\Book T-SQL Functions\Data\TSQLUDFS_Data.MDF
C:\BT\Projects\Book T-SQL Functions\Data\TSQLUDFS_Log.LDF
```

The `name` column is the logical file name.

The next query combines information from `sysfiles` with the output of `fn_virtualfilestats`. It must be run from inside pubs to give meaningful results. The results are too long for a single line and are reformatted with the results split into two sections:

```
USE pubs
GO
-- Join with the sysfiles to get a physical file name
DECLARE @DatabaseID smallint -- holds the database ID
      , @FileID smallint -- holds the file name for pubs
SET @DatabaseID = DB_ID() -- no argument means use the current database
SET @FileID = File_ID('pubs') -- Get ID of the pubs logical file

SELECT DB_NAME(DbId) as [Database]
     , FILE_NAME(vfs.FileID) as [Logical File]
     , RTRIM(s.filename) as [Physical File]
     , NumberReads, NumberWrites, BytesRead, BytesWritten, IoStallMS
    FROM ::fn_virtualfilestats(@DatabaseID, 1) vfs
        Inner Join sysfiles s
             on vfs.FileID = s.FileID
GO
```

(Results - first group of columns)

```
Database Logical File Physical File
-------- ------------ ------------------------------------------------------------
pubs     pubs         C:\Program Files\Microsoft SQL Server\MSSQL\data\pubs.mdf
```

(Results - second group of columns)

```
NumberReads NumberWrites BytesRead BytesWritten IoStallMS
----------- ------------ --------- ------------ ---------
67          10           1810432   81920        871
```

The limitation when using `sysfiles` is that it exists in every database and has information only for that database. That makes it difficult to use from a UDF that isn't created in the database for which you want information. Fortunately, there's another table that consolidates information about all database files used by the instance.

What's in master..sysaltfiles?

The alternative location for information about physical files is `master..sysaltfiles`. There is only one copy of it, and it has information about all the files in all the databases in the SQL Server instance. The next query selects its most interesting columns. Once again, the output is split into two groups of lines so you can see the `filename` column:

```
-- What's in master..sysaltfiles?
SELECT fileid, groupid, [size], growth, [status], dbid, [name], [filename]
    FROM master..sysaltfiles
GO
```

(Results - abridged - first group of columns)

```
fileid groupid size        growth      status      dbid   name
------ ------- ----------- ----------- ----------- ------ -------------------
     1       1        1784          10           0      1 master
     2       0         480          10          66      1 mastlog
     1       1        1024          10     1048578      2 tempdev
     2       0          64          10     1048642      2 templog
...
     1       1         640          10       32770     31 TSQLUDFS_Data
     2       0         640          10       32834     31 TSQLUFDS_Log
```

(Results - abridged - second group of columns)

```
filename
------------------------------------------------------------------------------
C:\Program Files\Microsoft SQL Server\MSSQL\data\master.mdf
C:\Program Files\Microsoft SQL Server\MSSQL\data\mastlog.ldf
C:\Program Files\Microsoft SQL Server\MSSQL\data\tempdb.mdf
C:\Program Files\Microsoft SQL Server\MSSQL\data\templog.ldf
...
C:\BT\Projects\Book T-SQL Functions\Data\TSQLUSDF_Data.mdf
C:\BT\Projects\Book T-SQL Functions\Data\TSQLUDFS_Log.ldf
```

Since `master..sysaltfiles` has both the `dbid` and the `fileid`, it can easily be joined with the output of `fn_virtualfilestats`. This script first moves back to TSQLUDFS and then does the join:

```
-- Join fn_virtualfilestats with master..sysaltfiles
USE TSQLUDFS
GO

SELECT db_name(vfs.dbid) as [database] -- The database name
     , saf.name -- the logical file name
     , saf.filename -- the physical file name
    FROM ::fn_virtualfilestats(-1, -1) vfs -- all files, in all databases
         left outer join master..sysaltfiles saf
           on vfs.dbid = saf.dbid
              and vfs.fileid = saf.fileid
GO
```

(Results - abridged and reformatted)

```
database        name                filename
--------------- ------------------- -----------------------------------------
master          master              C:\Program File...SSQL\data\master.mdf
master          mastlog             C:\Program File...SSQL\data\mastlog.ldf
tempdb          tempdev             C:\Program File...SSQL\data\tempdb.mdf
tempdb          templog             C:\Program File...SSQL\data\templog.ldf
...
TSQLUDFS        TSQLUDFS_Data       C:\BT\Projects\...a\TSQLFunctions5.mdf
TSQLUDFS        TSQLUDFS_Log        C:\BT\Projects\...a\TSQLFunctions5_log.ldf
```

The advantage of using `master..sysaltfiles` is that information on all databases is available. This lets us run functions based on `fn_virtualfilestats` from any database.

The next question to answer is, "How do I know how long the counts have been accumulating?" That's important for converting the raw counts into rates.

How Long Has the Instance Been Up?

`fn_virtualfilestats` returns information about I/O since the system was started. When was that? The SQL Server development team thought of that issue; the third column in the result table, `timestamp`, is the number of milliseconds since the system started. It's returned for every row in the resultset.

The `timestamp` column is the preferred way to get a denominator for computing rates of I/O operations. The UDFs in the second half of this chapter that aggregate I/O statistics all use `timestamp` to convey the number of seconds that they're reporting. However, it's not the only way to get that information.

It's possible to get the number of seconds since the instance started from system tables. The function `udf_SQL_StartDT`, shown in Listing 16.1, begins the process by getting the time that SQL Server started. It turns out that system processes like `LAZY WRITER`, `LOG WRITER`, and several others have entries in `sysprocesses`. As you'd expect, they log in when the system starts, and they stay logged in until the system stops. `udf_SQL_StartDT` queries the `login_time` of the process that's executing the `LAZY WRITER` command, and thus the system start time is known.

Listing 16.1: udf_SQL_StartDT

```
CREATE FUNCTION dbo.udf_SQL_StartDT (

)   RETURNS datetime -- Date/time the SQL Server instance started

/* Returns the date/time that the SQL Server instance was started.
*
* Common Usage:
select dbo.udf_SQL_StartDT() as [System Started AT]
****************************************************************/

AS BEGIN

    DECLARE @WorkingVariable datetime

    SELECT @WorkingVariable = login_time
        FROM master..sysprocesses
        WHERE cmd='LAZY WRITER'

    RETURN @WorkingVariable
END
```

Try out udf_SQL_StartDT with this query:

```
-- Find out when the system started
SELECT dbo.udf_SQL_StartDT() as [SQL Server Started At]
GO

(Results)

SQL Server Started At
------------------------------------------------------
2002-10-26 14:34:53.547
```

Now to figure out how long it's been since SQL Server started, we need to know the current date and time. But we can't use GETDATE in a UDF. udf_Instance_UptimeSEC, shown in Listing 16.2, uses the view Function_Assist_GETDATE that bypasses the prohibition on calling GETDATE. The view and the technique that gets around the restriction were discussed in Chapter 4.

Listing 16.2: udf_Instance_UptimeSEC

```
CREATE  FUNCTION dbo.udf_Instance_UptimeSEC (

)   RETURNS int -- Seconds since SQL Server was started.
/*
* Returns the number of seconds since the instance started.
*
* Example:
select dbo.udf_Instance_UptimeSEC()/3600.0
                                [Hours since SQL Server started]
****************************************************************/
AS BEGIN

DECLARE @Now datetime -- the current date time

SELECT @Now = [GetDATE]
    FROM Function_Assist_GETDATE

RETURN DATEDIFF (s, dbo.udf_SQL_StartDT(), @Now)
END
```

So, to answer our question, "How long has SQL Server been up?" run the query:

```
-- How Long Has SQL Server Been Up?
SELECT dbo.udf_Instance_UptimeSEC()
GO

(Result)

Seconds since SQL Server Started
--------------------------------
                          207694
```

Now that we can improve on the results of fn_virtualfilestats by making it easier for humans to read, it's almost time to create some UDFs that aggregate data. However, at least at the instance level, SQL Server already does the aggregation in its system statistical functions.

Statistics for the SQL Server Instance

Using –1 for both arguments to `fn_virtualfilestats` gives us the statistics of all the files used by the SQL Server instance and a chance to get total statistics for the system.

```
-- information from all files.
SELECT * FROM ::fn_virtualfilestats(-1, -1)
GO

(Results - abridged and reformatted)

  DbId FileId   TimeStamp  NumberReads  NumberWrites  BytesRead  BytesWritten
------ ------ ----------- ------------ ------------- ------------------------
     1      1   172571845         1541            10   30597120         98304
     1      2   172571845           19           790     315392       1270784
     2      1   172571845           21           249     688128       2334720
     2      2   172571845           10          1322     282624      44027392
     3      1   172571845           66             4    1417216         32768
     3      2   172571845           15            87     207360        172032
...
```

Some of the same totals are available as system statistical functions such as `@@Total_Read` and `@@Total_Write`. That group has other functions that measure resource use since the system started, and that can be valuable for analyzing system performance. These are listed in Table 16.2.

Table 16.2: System statistical functions for reporting resource consumption

Function	Description
`@@CPU_BUSY`	Number of milliseconds of CPU time consumed by SQL Server since it started.
`@@IDLE`	Number of milliseconds that SQL Server has been idle since it was started.
`@@IO_WAIT`	Number of milliseconds that SQL Server has spent performing input and output since the system started.
`@@PACK_RECEIVED`	Number of input packets read from the network since SQL Server was started.
`@@PACK_SENT`	Number of output packets sent to the network since SQL Server was started.
`@@TOTAL_READ`	The number of disk reads since the SQL Server instance was started.
`@@TOTAL_WRITE`	The number of disk writes since the SQL Server instance was started.

`@@Total_Read` and `@@Total_Write` are used by the next query, which compares them to the results of `fn_virtualfilestats`:

```
-- Get totals of the virtualfilestats and compare to system statistical funcs.
SELECT  sum(NumberReads) as NumberReads
      , @@Total_Read as [@@Total_Read]
      , sum(NumberWrites) as NumberWrites
      , @@Total_Write as [@@Total_Write]
      , sum(BytesRead) as BytesRead
      , sum(BytesWritten) as BytesWritten
      , sum(IoStallMS) as IoSTallMS
    FROM ::fn_virtualfilestats(-1, -1)
GO
```

(Results - reformatted)

```
NumReads @@Total_Read NumrWrites @@Total_Write BytesRead BytesWritten IoSTallMS
-------- ------------ ---------- ------------- --------- ------------ ---------
    1768         1778       1347          1377  65080832     20875776     32288
```

As you can see, SUM(NumberReads) and SUM(NumberWrites) do not exactly equal @@Total_Read and @@Total_Write. The two statistical functions are close but always more than the SUMs. The statistical functions must be counting writes to files not counted by fn_virtualfilestats, such as writing to the SQL Server log files.

Along with fn_virtualfilestats, the system statistical functions all report on the amount of activity that has occurred since SQL Server started. Now that we've seen how to get the statistics and the corresponding number of seconds that the system has been running, we can turn to creating UDFs that summarize the raw numbers into useful information.

Summarizing the File Statistics with UDFs

Pulling together several of the techniques that were discussed previously, we can build the UDFs that were described in the introduction based on the raw data from fn_virtualfilestats. Each summarizes the statistics at a different level: single database, physical file, or drive letter.

Also in the TSQLUDFS database, but not shown, is udf_Perf_FS_InstanceTAB that aggregates statistics for an entire instance into a single line. Here's a summary of the SQL Server on my laptop:

```
-- Get the Instance statistics
SELECT * FROM udf_Perf_FS_InstanceTAB()
GO
```

(Results – reformatted)

```
Server Files Reads Writes BytesRead BytesWritten IoStallMS    Sec
------ ----- ----- ------ --------- ------------ --------- ------
NSL2      39  1171   1234  61747200     26354688     37795 142309
```

That gives you the big picture, but to locate the cause of any bottleneck, we're going to have to look at more detail. Let's start at the database level.

Getting Statistics for a Single Database

Listing 16.3 shows the function udf_Perf_FS_DBTotalsTAB that returns a single row table of total I/O statistics for a database. It gives you a quick gauge of the amount of I/O that has occurred on the database since the system started.

Listing 16.3: udf_Perf_FS_DBTotalsTAB

```
CREATE  FUNCTION dbo.udf_Perf_FS_DBTotalsTAB (

    @DBName sysname -- name of the database to return stats for
)   RETURNS  @FileStats  TABLE (
          NumberOfFiles int -- Number of files in the database
        , NumberReads bigint -- Number of reads on the database
        , NumberWrites bigint -- Number of writes to the database
        , BytesRead bigint -- Number of bytes read from the database
        , BytesWritten bigint -- Number of bytes written to the database
        , IoStallMS bigint  -- Milliseconds that user waited for I/O ops
        , Sec int -- Seconds since the system started
        )
   -- No SCHEMABINDING due to use of system UDF
/*
* Returns a table of total statistics for one particular database
* by summing the statistics for all of its files.
*
* Example:
select * from dbo.udf_Perf_FS_DBTotalsTAB ('pubs')
****************************************************************/
AS BEGIN

   DECLARE @DatabaseID int -- Database ID from master..sysdatabases
   SET @DatabaseID = DB_ID(@DBName)

    INSERT INTO @FileStats
        SELECT Count(*) -- Number of files
             , Sum(NumberReads)
             , Sum(NumberWrites)
             , Sum(BytesRead)
             , Sum(BytesWritten)
             , Sum(IoStallMS)
             , ROUND(max(timestamp) / 1000.0, 0) as Sec
            FROM ::fn_virtualfilestats(@DatabaseID, -1) -- -1 means all files

     RETURN
END
```

Here's a simple query that uses udf_Perf_FS_DBTotalsTAB to get statistics on the pubs database:

```
-- Get I/O stats on pubs including all files
SELECT NumberOfFiles, NumberReads, NumberWrites
        , BytesRead, BytesWritten, IoStallMS, Sec
    FROM dbo.udf_Perf_FS_DBTotalsTAB ('pubs')
GO
```

(Results - reformatted)

```
NumberOfFiles NumberReads NumberWrites BytesRead BytesWritten IoStallMS  Sec
------------- ----------- ------------ ---------- ------------ --------- -------
2             75          33           2080768    271360       1342       218312
```

On many large systems, there are many databases, and you may want to find the most active one. The next UDF lets you do that.

Getting Statistics by Database

udf_Perf_FS_ByDbTAB returns a table of statistics for all databases in the instance. This is the quick picture of what's going on in the SQL Server. There is always at least a little additional I/O activity for the operating system, but on many dedicated systems, SQL Server does the bulk of the I/O.

Listing 16.4: udf_Perf_FS_ByDbTAB

```
CREATE  FUNCTION dbo.udf_Perf_FS_ByDbTAB (

    @DB_Name_Pattern sysname = NULL -- LIKE name of the database
             -- to get stats for or NULL for ALL
)   RETURNS  TABLE
   -- No SCHEMABINDING due to use of system UDF
/*
* Returns a table of total statistics for one database or
* a group of databases where the name matches a pattern. Null for
* all.  Done by grouping by database.
*
* Example:
select * from dbo.udf_Perf_FS_ByDbTAB ('pubs')
****************************************************************/
AS RETURN

SELECT TOP 100 PERCENT WITH TIES
       DB_Name(DbId) [DatabaseName]-- get the name
     , DbId AS [DBID]-- ID might be useful sometimes
     , Count(DbId) [NumberOfFiles]-- Number of files
     , Sum(NumberReads) as [NumberReads]
     , Sum(NumberWrites) as [NumberWrites]
     , Sum(BytesRead) as [BytesRead]
     , Sum(BytesWritten) as [BytesWritten]
     , Sum(IoStallMS) as [IoStallMS]
     , Avg([TimeStamp] / 1000) as SecondsInMeasurement
    FROM ::fn_virtualfilestats(-1, -1) -- -1 for all db and files
    WHERE (@DB_Name_Pattern IS NULL
          OR db_Name(dbid) LIKE @DB_Name_Pattern)
    GROUP BY DbID
    ORDER BY Sum(NumberReads)
           + Sum(NumberWrites) desc -- Top I/O first
```

System UDFs

Sorting the results makes it easy to spot the databases with the most activity. Here's a sample query run on my rather quiet development system:

```
-- Get the top 5 databases in terms of number of I/O operations since startup
SELECT  Top 5 DatabaseName, NumberOfFiles as [Files]
       , NumberReads as NumReads, NumberWrites as NumWrites
       , SecondsInMeasurement as [Sec]
      FROM dbo.udf_Perf_FS_ByDbTAB (default)
GO
```

(Results - reformatted)

```
DatabaseName     Files  NumReads             NumWrites            Sec
---------------- ------ -------------------- -------------------- -----------
VersqDev1             2                 7367                   29      216915
TESTDB37              3                 2577                   33      216915
Versq2                2                 1676                  640      216915
TSQLWorking           2                  154                  720      216915
msdb                  2                  378                  255      216915
```

Breaking Down the I/O Statistics by Physical File

We might want to know the amount of I/O broken down by physical file. The function udf_Perf_FS_ByPhysicalFileTAB, seen in Listing 16.5, gives us physical file-based statistics. As discussed earlier, the metadata functions FILE_NAME() and FILE_ID() don't work when you want information about a file in a different database. To get the physical file names, the results from fn_virtualfilestats must be joined with information in master..sysaltfiles, which has the physical file names of all database files in the SQL Server instance.

Listing 16.5: udf_Perf_FS_ByPhysicalFileTAB

```
CREATE    FUNCTION dbo.udf_Perf_FS_ByPhysicalFileTAB (

    @File_Name_Pattern sysname = NULL -- LIKE pattern, NULL for ALL
)   RETURNS  TABLE
    -- No SCHEMABINDING due to use of system UDF
/*
* Returns a table of statistics for all files in all databases
* in the server that match the @File_Name_Pattern. NULL for all.
* The results are one row for each file including both data
* flies and log files. Information about physical files is
* taken from master..sysaltfiles which has the physical file
* name needed.
*
* Example:
select * from dbo.udf_Perf_FS_ByPhysicalFileTAB (default) -- All
*****************************************************************/
AS RETURN
```

```
SELECT TOP 100 WITH TIES
       [FileName] as [PhysicalFile]
     , saf.FileID AS [FileID]
     , CAST(saf.[name] as sysname) as LogicalFileName
     , CAST(saf.[size] / 128.0 as numeric (18,3)) as SizeMB
             -- convert to megabytes from 8k pages
     , DB_Name(saf.DbId) as [DatabaseName] -- get the name
     , saf.DbId as DbID -- ID might be useful sometimes
     , NumberReads
     , NumberWrites
     , BytesRead
     , BytesWritten
     , IoStallMS
     , CAST (([TimeStamp] / 1000.0) as int)
                                    as SecondsInMeasurement
    FROM ::fn_virtualfilestats(-1, -1) vfs -- -1 = all db & files
        inner join master..sysaltfiles saf
            on vfs.DbId = saf.DbId and vfs.FileID = saf.FileID
    WHERE (@File_Name_Pattern IS NULL
        OR [FileName] LIKE @File_Name_Pattern)
    ORDER BY NumberReads + NumberWrites desc -- sort by top IO
```

Here's a query on udf_Perf_FS_ByPhysicalFileTAB from my development system. On a production system, you wouldn't expect to see any database files on drive C:

```
-- Physical files with the most I/O
SELECT Top 5 PhysicalFile, SizeMB, NumberReads, NumberWrites
    FROM dbo.udf_Perf_FS_ByPhysicalFileTAB(default)
GO
```

(Results - abridged and reformatted)

```
PhysicalFile                    SizeMB NumberReads NumberWrites
------------------------------- ------ ----------- ------------
C:\MSSQL\data\templog.ldf         .500           9          682
C:\MSSQL\data\msdblog.ldf        2.250          14          622
C:\MSSQL\data\master.mdf        13.938         411           27
C:\MSSQL\data\msdbdata.mdf      12.750         367            2
C:\MSSQL\data\mastlog.ldf        3.750          19          268
...
```

These statistics are even more useful when a database is split into different physical files. For example, by creating indexes on a separate file group, the amount of I/O devoted to the data vs. the amount devoted to indexes would be apparent. That can lead to separating the two file groups on different drives.

The physical file name contains the path to the file. Since that contains the drive letter, we can use it to summarize by drive letter. The drive letters often correspond to physical disks but not always.

I/O Statistics by Disk Drive

Finally, the function udf_Perf_FS_ByDriveTAB summarizes the I/O statistics by drive letter. It's shown in Listing 16.6. Just like udf_Perf_FS_ByPhysicalFileTAB, it uses the physical file information in master..sysaltfiles to aggregate to individual drives.

Listing 16.6: udf_Perf_FS_ByDriveTAB

```
CREATE   FUNCTION dbo.udf_Perf_FS_ByDriveTAB (

    @DriveLetter CHAR(1) = NULL -- Drive or NULL for all
)   RETURNS  TABLE
/*
* Returns a table of statistics by drive letters for all drives
* with database files in this instance. They must match
* @Driveletter (or NULL for all).  Returns one row for each
* drive. Information about physical files is taken from
* master..sysaltfiles which has the physical file name needed.
* Warning: Drive letters do not always correspond to physical
* disk drives.
*
* Example:
select * from dbo.udf_Perf_FS_ByDriveTAB (default)
****************************************************************/
AS RETURN

SELECT TOP 100 PERCENT WITH TIES
       LEFT(saf.[Filename], 1) + ':' as DriveLetter
     , Count(saf.FileID) as NumFiles
     , CAST (Sum(saf.[size] / 128.0) as numeric(18,3)) as SizeMB
              -- convert to megabytes from 8k pages
     , Sum(NumberReads) as NumberReads
     , Sum(NumberWrites) as NumberWrites
     , Sum(BytesRead) as BytesRead
     , Sum(BytesWritten) as BytesWritten
     , SUM(IoStallMS) as IoStallMS
     , Avg(vfs.[TimeStamp]/1000) as SecondsInMeasurement
    FROM ::fn_virtualfilestats(-1, -1) vfs -- -1 = all db & files
         inner join master..sysaltfiles saf
              on vfs.DbId = saf.DbId
                and vfs.FileID = saf.FileID
    WHERE (@DriveLetter is NULL
        OR LEFT(saf.[Filename], 1) = @DriveLetter)
    GROUP BY LEFT(saf.[Filename], 1) + ':'
    ORDER BY DriveLetter asc -- by Drive letter C, D, ....
```

Statistics by drive are particularly important numbers. Over the years, I've found that all drives reach a maximum number of I/O operations per second and can go no further. This number frequently becomes a limiting factor in application performance.

In the mid-1980s when I was working with minicomputers, the maximum number of I/O operations for most drives was around 20 operations per second. That's improved to about 75 to 250 operations per second on some drives today, an improvement of maybe six times. Contrast that with the improvement in CPU speed since the mid-1980s, which is around 100,000 times, and in drive capacity, which is around 1,000 times, and you can see that I/O operations is one performance factor that just hasn't kept pace with other advances in computer technology.

Here's a summary of the I/O performance of my desktop system produced with `udf_Perf_FS_ByDriveTAB`. Obviously, it's not a highly stressed system.

```
-- I/O summary for the drives on a system
SELECT DriveLetter, NumFiles, SizeMb, NumberReads, NumberWrites
          , IoSTallMS, SecondsInMeasurement as Sec
    FROM dbo.udf_Perf_FS_ByDriveTAB (default)
GO

(Results - reformatted)

DriveLetter    NumFiles        SizeMb NumberReads NumberWrites IoSTallMS  Sec
----------- ----------- ------------ ----------- ------------ --------- --------
C:                   47      456.563        2477         3087     33430    70789
D:                    2     5000.000         105           14       702    70789
```

These numbers, particularly at peak usage times, are critical to evaluating bottlenecks in your system. But even the aggregate numbers aren't the whole story. You're going to have to know the I/O structure of your system for these numbers to be meaningful. On most servers, drive letters don't correspond to individual physical disks. For example, when disks are put into a RAID 1, RAID 5, or RAID 10 array, several disks appear as one drive letter. On small systems, one physical drive might be divided into multiple partitions, each with its own drive letter. So be careful.

What I do know from experience is that more disk spindles almost always give better drive performance. Making the most of the spindles is a matter of spreading the I/O as uniformly as possible. For a more thorough description of the analysis of I/O, including a description of RAID performance, I use Microsoft Press's *SQL Server 2000 Administrator's Companion*.

Summary

I've found the four functions that use `fn_virtualfilestats` to be pretty useful in giving a quick impression of the I/O on a system. Often, the quick impression is going to point out an obvious problem. However, they're not a complete solution to monitoring system I/O performance.

A more complete solution that would help isolate bottlenecks in system performance would monitor I/O along with memory use, CPU use, and network traffic as it varied over time. Most importantly, it would have to record this information at periods of peak activity. `fn_virtualfilestats` returns information from the time that the SQL Server instance started. That includes both peak and non-peak periods.

`sp_monitor`, which is provided as a system stored procedure, does a similar job and reports performance statistics since the last time it was run. If used alone during a time when the performance problem is present, it can also give you a quick impression of what part of the system is the performance bottleneck. However, it only works at the level of the entire system. `fn_virtualfilestats` is much finer grained.

If you're interested in gathering I/O statistics over time, check out an article titled "Examining SQL Server's I/O Statistics." You'll find a link to it on my articles page at: http://www.NovickSoftware.com/Articles.htm. The article has code to gather I/O statistics and keep them around for more thorough analysis.

Another, more detailed, way to analyze performance is with a trace, the technology behind the SQL Profiler. The next chapter is about a group of system functions that return information about the traces running on a SQL Server.

17

fn_trace_* and How to Create and Monitor System Traces

Chapter 3 shows the SQL Profiler in action as it captures output from a trace. But SQL Profiler isn't the only way to run a trace. Traces can also be created with a T-SQL script that uses a group of system stored procedures that I'll refer to collectively as sp_trace_*. Under the hood, the SQL Profiler uses these procedures to create and manipulate traces.

This chapter discuss four system functions that I'll refer to collectively as the fn_trace_* UDFs. It relates them to the sp_trace_* procedures that create traces. The UDFs retrieve information about traces that are running in the SQL Server instance. Before discussing how to use them, we need some background information on tracing and the SQL Profiler.

One of the goals of the SQL Server 2000 development team was reaching the C2 level of security. In order to achieve the C2 security designation, SQL Server had to be able to provide a complete audit of all successful and unsuccessful statements and attempts to access database objects. The mechanism chosen to fulfill this requirement is the trace.

The trace facility originated in SQL Server Version 6.5 where its purpose was to enable the SQL Trace program that has evolved into the SQL Profiler. In versions of SQL Server before 2000, it was known and accepted that in times of high system load, events might get lost. When profiling is used during software development or performance analysis, the loss of events is annoying but acceptable. For C2 security compliance, the SQL Server engine has to guarantee that no events are lost. Traces can be written to three different places:

- To a disk file — This is the fastest option.
- To a SQL table
- To a rowset as the trace events are generated — This is the way that SQL Profiler gets trace information.

In SQL Server 2000, the trace facility is more robust than in earlier versions, and it can make the guarantee that no events are lost, at least when writing to a disk file. It might still lose events when sending trace events to the SQL Profiler or saving them in a table. That's a trade-off we'll have to accept for performance reasons.

The first section of this chapter starts with an explanation of creating traces with the `sp_trace_*` system stored procedures. That section also shows you how to get SQL Profiler to write the script for you.

Once there are traces running on your system, the SQL `fn_trace_*` functions become relevant. The functions are listed in Table 17.1 in the order in which they're presented in the rest of the chapter.

Table 17.1: System trace UDFs

Function Name	Description
`fn_trace_getinfo`	Returns a table of information about all running traces such as those used by SQL Profiler
`fn_trace_gettable`	Returns a table of trace data from a trace file
`fn_trace_geteventinfo`	Returns a table of the events monitored by a trace
`fn_trace_getfilterinfo`	Returns a table of the filter expressions defined for a trace

These functions return tables that consist mostly of coded numeric fields that are difficult to read. The purpose of the UDFs created in this chapter is to turn the raw information from the `fn_trace_*` functions into something meaningful to DBAs and programmers.

The task-oriented functions and stored procedures built in this chapter are:

- `udf_Trc_InfoTAB` — Produces a short summary of the traces running on the SQL Server
- `udf_Trc_RPT` — Produces a very readable summary of every trace that's running on the system with the details of its columns, events, and filter definitions
- `usp_Admin_TraceStop` — Stops a trace or all traces. It's a stored procedure because it does things that UDFs can't do.

Along the way, a dozen other functions are created to build `udf_Trc_RPT`. Most do mundane jobs like translating numeric codes into character strings, but a few are more interesting than that.

udf_Trc_RPT is the most robust way to see what traces are running in a SQL Server instance, and it's the ultimate goal of this chapter. To give you some perspective about where we're headed, take a look at its results. I was running one SQL Profiler trace, with traceid=1, when I ran this query:

```
-- Show a report of all running traces
SELECT * from udf_Trc_Rpt(default)
GO

(Results)

rptline
--------------------------------------------------------------------------------
Trace: 1  RUNNING Rowset:YES Rollover:NO ShutOnErr:NO BlckBx:NO  MaxSize:5
 Stop At: NULL  Filename:NULL
  Events: RPC:Completed, SQL:BatchCompleted, Login, Logout, ExistingConnection,
          SQL:StmtStarting, SQL:StmtCompleted
 Columns: TextData, NTUserName, ClientProcessID, ApplicationName,
          SQLSecurityLoginName, SPID, Duration, StartTime, Reads, Writes, CPU,
          Success
  Filter: ApplicationName NOT LIKE N'SQL Profiler' AND NOT LIKE N'sqla%
```

I find that pretty readable. If you're familiar with the SQL Profiler, I think you will also.

As with most other chapters, the download directory has a file with the short queries that are interspersed within the chapter's text: Chapter 17 Listing 0 Short Queries.sql. You won't get exactly the same results shown in this chapter unless you happen to be running exactly the same set of traces. Also, if you're on a shared server, traces run by everyone show up in these functions.

Scripting Traces

There are five system stored procedures for creating and managing traces. They're listed in Table 17.2. The calling sequence and the codes for the parameters are listed in Books Online and won't be repeated here. The documentation on these stored procedures is important for understanding the fn_trace_* functions. The Books Online articles are the only places that the codes in the result set of the fn_trace_* functions are documented.

Table 17.2: Tracing system stored procedures

Procedure	Description
`sp_trace_create`	Creates the trace and returns the traceid used as a parameter to the other procedures and with the `fn_trace_*` functions
`sp_trace_setevent`	Adds or removes events and columns from the trace. Its documentation in Books Online is where you'll find the event codes and column codes.
`sp_trace_setfilter`	Adds and removes filters on traces. Its documentation in Books Online has the documentation for the `logical_operator` and `comparison_operator` columns returned by `fn_trace_getfilterinfo`.
`sp_trace_setstatus`	Starts, stops, and closes traces. SQL Profiler calls the stop status "Paused" and the closed status "Stopped."

A script that creates a trace usually follows this general order of calls:

1. The script is created with `sp_trace_create`.
2. `sp_trace_setevent` is called repeatedly to configure the events and columns to be monitored.
3. `sp_trace_setfilter` is called repeatedly to set up the filter on the trace.
4. `sp_trace_setstatus` is called with a status of 1 to start the trace.

To stop the trace, this sequence is usually used:

1. `sp_trace_setstatus` is called with a status of 0 to stop the trace.
2. `sp_trace_setstatus` is called with a status of 2 to close the trace.

The process of writing the script to perform a trace is tedious. Fortunately, SQL Profiler can do the job for you. Once you've used SQL Profiler to set up a trace, use the Profiler menu File ➤Script Trace ➤SQL Server 2000 option to create an almost equivalent script file. Listing 17.1 shows most of a script created for the SQLServerStandard.trc trace profile. The full script is in the chapter download in the file Chapter 17 Listing 1 SQL Trace.sql.

T-SQL scripts can't accept a rowset in the way that SQL Profiler does, so the script is created with the results sent to a file. The instructions in the beginning of the script tell you which lines of the script that you must modify to set the file name.

The script that SQL Profiler doesn't give you is the one that stops the trace. You need that one also. The script in Listing 17.1 returns the traceid, so you'll know which trace to stop. You can also get a list of traces that are defined in your system from the `fn_trace_getinfo` system UDF, which is the subject of the next section. I'll defer the code that stops a trace until near the end of that section.

Listing 17.1: Script for a SQL trace (abridged)

```
/****************************************************/
/* Created by: SQL Profiler                         */
/* Date: 10/30/2002  05:43:15 PM                    */
/****************************************************/

-- Create a Queue
declare @rc int
declare @TraceID int
declare @maxfilesize bigint
set @maxfilesize = 5

-- Please replace the text InsertFileNameHere, with an appropriate
-- filename prefixed by a path, e.g., c:\MyFolder\MyTrace. The .trc extension
-- will be appended to the filename automatically. If you are writing from
-- remote server to local drive, please use UNC path and make sure server has
-- write access to your network share

exec @rc = sp_trace_create @TraceID output, 0, N'InsertFileNameHere'
                                                , @maxfilesize, NULL
if (@rc != 0) goto error

-- Client side File and Table cannot be scripted

-- Set the events
declare @on bit
set @on = 1
exec sp_trace_setevent @TraceID, 10, 1, @on
exec sp_trace_setevent @TraceID, 10, 6, @on
...
exec sp_trace_setevent @TraceID, 17, 18, @on

-- Set the Filters
declare @intfilter int
declare @bigintfilter bigint

exec sp_trace_setfilter @TraceID, 10, 0, 7, N'SQL Profiler'

-- Set the trace status to start
exec sp_trace_setstatus @TraceID, 1

-- display trace id for future references
select TraceID=@TraceID
goto finish

error:
select ErrorCode=@rc

finish:
go
```

fn_trace_getinfo

Use this function to get information about the traces currently running on your server. The syntax of the call is:

```
::fn_trace_getinfo (@traceid)
```

@traceid, an `int`, is the only argument. It identifies the trace that the caller is requesting information about. If `@traceid` is `NULL` or `default`, then information for all traces is returned.

Each row of the returned rowset consists of the three columns shown in Table 17.3. A row only has information about a single property of the trace. To make the output of `fn_trace_getinfo` more readable, the results must be pivoted.

Table 17.3: Rowset returned by `fn_trace_getinfo`

Column	Data Type	Description
`Traceid`	`int`	Identifies the trace
`Property`	`int`	Identifies the property
`Value`	`sql_variant`	The value of the property. The data type depends on the property.

To illustrate the properties, I used SQL Profiler to start a trace. Figure 17.1 shows the Trace Properties screen as it is set up. SQL Profiler actually starts two traces as seen in the results of this query that was run just after the trace was started:

```
-- trace information for all traces
SELECT * from ::fn_trace_getinfo(default)
GO

(Results)

traceid     property    value
----------- ----------- -----------------------------------------------------
1           1           1
1           2           NULL
1           3           5
1           4           2002-09-20 00:36:02.123
1           5           1
2           1           2
2           2           C:\SampleTrace
2           3           5
2           4           2002-09-20 00:36:02.123
2           5           1
```

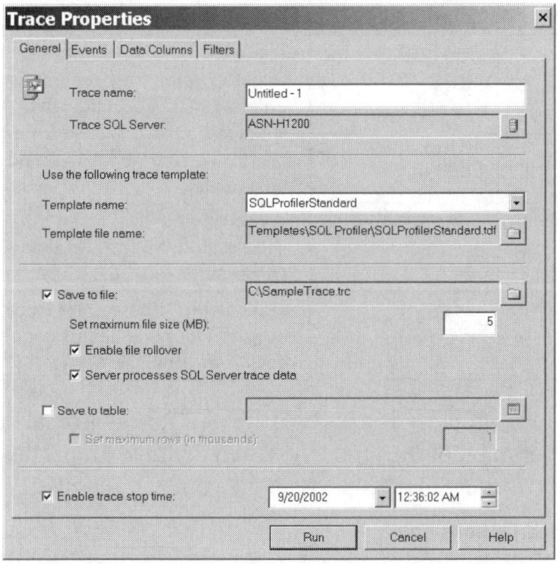

Figure 17.1: SQL Profiler Trace Properties screen starting a new trace

Two traces were started because "Server processes SQL Server trace data" was checked on the Trace Properties screen. Trace number 1 has the `TRACE_PRODUCE_ROWSET` status bit set and no output file. The rowset is sent to the Profiler to produce its GUI display. Trace number 2 is the server trace. It has the `TRACE_FILE_ROLLOVER` status bit set, and its output is written to the file C:\SampleTrace.trc. Both traces are set to stop at 36 minutes after midnight on 2002-09-20.

Server traces are written directly by the database engine and are not relayed to SQL Profiler or any other program. Only server traces are guaranteed not to lose any events. They're always written to disk files.

The next two tables contain the information that I used to interpret the table of output from `fn_trace_getinfo`. Table 17.4 has a description of each of the properties.

Table 17.4: Properties returned by `fn_trace_getinfo`

Number	Name	Data Type	Description
1	Trace Options	`int`	This is a bit field that holds four flags from the parameter to `sp_trace_create`. Table 17.5 describes each bit in the Trace Options property.
2	FileName	`nvarchar(254)`	Name of the file that the trace is being written to. It will be `NULL` if the trace is not being written to a file.

Number	Name	Data Type	Description
3	MaxSize	`bigint`	The maximum size of the file. Traces will stop when they reach this size unless `TRACE_FILE_ROLLOVER` has been specified, in which case a new file will be started after each file reaches 5 megabytes.
4	StopTime	`datetime`	The date and time when the trace should stop if it hasn't stopped for some other reason.
5	Status	`int`	The current status of the trace. Is it running or stopped? Status codes are shown in Table 17.6.

The `Trace Options` property is a bit field. Table 17.5 has a breakdown of the meaning of each bit of the property. When multiple properties are requested, the `Trace Options` property is the sum of the property values.

Table 17.5: Bits in the Trace Options field

Value	Trace Flag	Description
1	`TRACE_PRODUCE_ROWSET`	Results are sent to the trace client as rowsets. SQL Profiler and other GUI interfaces use a rowset to get events from the tracing facility. It is not used by a server trace.
2	`TRACE_FILE_ROLLOVER`	Files roll over when each reaches 5 megabytes.
4	`SHUTDOWN_ON_ERROR`	Specifies that if the file cannot be written for any reason, the SQL Server should shut down. This is available to ensure that the SQL Server is creating traces when required to satisfy the C2 security level.
8	`TRACE_PRODUCT_BLACKBOX`	Specifies that SQL Server will keep a record of the last 5 megabytes of trace information. This is used to produce the blackbox trace used by Microsoft product support. This flag must be set alone. When it is used, a trace file named blackbox.trc is created in the default \Data directory of your SQL Server.

The `Status` column is 0 or 1, as shown in Table 17.6. These are the same values used for the `@status` argument to `sp_trace_setstatus`. Of course, the third status, 2, meaning "close the trace," never shows up in `fn_trace_getinfo`. Closed traces are removed from memory, and SQL Server no longer has any knowledge of them. The last column in Table 17.6 is the name that the function `udf_Trc_InfoTAB` returns for each of the codes. That function is discussed in the next subsection of this chapter.

Table 17.6: Values for the Status property

Status	Description	Value from udf_Trc_InfoTAB
0	The trace is stopped.	Stopped
1	The trace is running.	Running

Interpreting the output of the fn_trace_getinfo function is a little painstaking, and two techniques make understanding the properties for each trace easier:

- Pivoting the properties so that each is a column in the output
- Breaking the Trace Options property into its constituent bits

The next function, udf_Trc_InfoTAB, does both jobs to produce a summary report for running traces.

udf_Trc_InfoTAB

For a quick summary of a single trace or all traces, try udf_Trc_InfoTAB. It's shown in Listing 17.2. Its sole argument is the traceid that the caller wants summarized. Like fn_trace_getinfo, if the traceid is NULL, a summary of all running traces is returned.

Listing 17.2: udf_Trc_InfoTAB

```
CREATE   FUNCTION dbo.udf_Trc_InfoTAB (

    @trace_id int = NULL -- which trace, NULL for all
)   RETURNS TABLE
    -- No SCHEMABINDING due to use of system UDF
/*
* Returns a table of information about a trace; these are the
* original arguments to sp_trace_create. The status field is
* broken down to four individual fields.
*
* Example:
SELECT * from udf_Trc_InfoTAB(default)
****************************************************************/
AS RETURN
SELECT TOP 100 PERCENT WITH TIES
       traceid
     , MAX(CAST(CASE WHEN property=5
                THEN CASE CAST(value as INT)
                          WHEN 1 THEN 'RUNNING'
                          ELSE 'STOPPED' END
                ELSE NULL END
              AS varchar(7))) AS [Status]
     , MAX(CAST(CASE WHEN property=1 and (CAST(value as int) & 1) = 1
                THEN 'YES' ELSE 'NO' END
            AS varchar(3))) AS PRODUCE_ROWSET
     , MAX(CAST(CASE WHEN property=1 and (CAST(value as int) & 2) = 2
                THEN 'YES' ELSE 'NO' END
            AS varchar(3))) AS FILE_ROLLOVER
```

```
    , MAX(CAST(CASE WHEN property=1 AND (CAST(value as int) & 4) = 4
                    THEN 'YES' ELSE 'NO' END
                AS varchar(3))) AS SHUTDOWN_ON_ERROR
    , MAX(CAST(CASE WHEN property=1 AND (CAST(value as int) & 8) = 8
                    THEN 'YES' ELSE 'NO' END
                 AS varchar(3))) AS TRACE_PRODUCE_BLACKBOX
    , MAX(CAST(CASE WHEN property=2
                    THEN value ELSE NULL end as nvarchar(254))) AS [FileName]
    , MAX(CAST(CASE WHEN property=3
                    THEN value ELSE 0 END AS int)) AS [MaxSize]
    , MAX(CAST(CASE WHEN property=4
                    THEN value ELSE NULL END AS datetime)) AS [StopTime]
   FROM ::fn_trace_getinfo(@trace_id)
   GROUP BY traceid
   ORDER BY traceid
```

Here's a query that uses `udf_Trc_InfoTAB` to show the properties for the currently running traces:

```
-- Show the properties as a readable table
SELECT TraceID as ID, Status, PRODUCE_ROWSET AS [RS], FILE_ROLLOVER [ROLL]
      , SHUTDOWN_ON_ERROR [SHUT], TRACE_PRODUCE_BLACKBOX AS [BB]
      , MaxSize [MS], StopTime [ST], FileName [FN]
    FROM dbo.udf_Trc_InfoTab(default)
GO
```

(Results - reformatted and truncated on the right)

```
ID Status  RS   ROLL SHUT BB   MS  ST                      FN
-- ------- ---- ---- ---- ---- --- ----------------------- --------------------
 1 RUNNING YES  NO   NO   NO     5 2002-09-20 00:36:02.123 NULL
 2 RUNNING NO   YES  NO   NO     5 2002-09-20 00:36:02.123 C:\Documents and Set
 3 STOPPED YES  NO   NO   NO     5 NULL                    NULL

Warning: Null value is eliminated by an aggregate or other SET operation.
```

The warning on the last line is produced because `ANSI_WARNINGS` is on and `NULL` was input to the `MAX` aggregation function on the `StopTime` and `FileName` columns.

Pivoting Data to Create the Columns

Data is often given to us as a series of rows similar to the output of `fn_trace_getinfo`. To turn it into a more user-friendly display, it helps to reorganize the data as a row with many columns. This is called pivoting the data. Many data analysis applications feature pivoting data as one of their primary functions. Pivoting is so useful that Excel and Access have pivot table functionality. T-SQL doesn't have explicit support for pivoting data. However, it does have the `CASE` expression; when cleverly applied, it can be used to pivot our data.

What we're after when we pivot the data from fn_trace_getinfo is one row for each trace with multiple columns instead of one row for each property. Each column in the pivoted output is one property of the trace. In order to produce the desired output, a GROUP BY clause must be employed. udf_Trc_InfoTAB groups the data by the traceid column, so there is one row of output for each traceid.

Next we want to create our columns. Here's the expression for the FileName column:

```
MAX(CAST(CASE WHEN property=2
              THEN value ELSE NULL END
         AS nvarchar(254))) AS [FileName]
```

Let's strip out the CAST since it doesn't have anything do to with the pivot operation, and we're left with:

```
MAX(CASE WHEN property=2
              THEN value ELSE NULL END
         ) AS [FileName]
```

The CASE expression is applied to every row of input, but it will return NULL for any row that doesn't have property=2. That is, it has a non-NULL value only when the input row is a file name. An aggregation function must be applied to the CASE expression because the SELECT has a GROUP BY clause that is not grouped by the CASE expression. If it were grouped by case when property=2 then value else NULL end and the other case expressions, there would be a separate row for each property, and that's the situation that's being pivoted in the first place.

The aggregation function chosen must aggregate the five rows in the input for every traceid. Four of the values, the ones where property!=2, are NULL. There's no aggregation function for: "Give me the one value that's not NULL." So I've used the MAX function. The only non-NULL value is MAX. If the value column is NULL in all rows, the result of the MAX function is NULL, as was the case for traceid=1 in the query above.

The cast(... as nvarchar(254)) expression that surrounds the case expression doesn't have anything to do with pivoting the data. It's used to convert the value column to nvarchar(254), even if the result of the aggregation is NULL. The user of udf_Trc_InfoTAB is going to want the data type to be something other than sql_variant, which can be difficult to work with.

Mining Bits from the Trace Options Field

The `Trace Options` property is an `int` that stores a bit field. Each of the four low-order bits is set to indicate a particular flag. The expression:

```
MAX(CAST(CASE WHEN property=1 AND (CAST(value as int) & 2) = 2
              THEN 'YES' ELSE 'NO' END
         AS varchar(3))) AS FILE_ROLLOVER
```

converts one bit in the `Status` property into a YES/NO character string that's easier to understand. The `case when property=1...` expression was explained above. The result of the `case` is going to be `'NO'` for rows that are not status columns. The test:

```
CAST(value AS int) & 2) = 2
```

tests the second bit in the `Status` column. Ampersand (&) is the bitwise AND operator. Because bitwise AND can't be applied to a `sql_variant`, `value` is first `CAST` to an `int`. The bitwise AND is applied, and the result is an `int`, which is 2 if the `TRACE_FILE_ROLLOVER` bit is set or 0 if it's not. The result dictates the choice between YES and NO. The `MAX` operator is used to choose between all the NOs and the one possible YES. The comparison is alphabetic, and the YES wins out, as the `MAX`, if it's present in the input.

If we're scripting traces, we need the T-SQL script to stop them. Now that we have `udf_Trc_InfoTAB`, the job will be pretty easy because it shows us the traceid and other characteristics of all running traces in your SQL Server instance.

Stopping Traces

In the section "Scripting Traces," you were shown the script to create a trace without SQL Profiler. Once a trace is started with a script, eventually it has to be stopped or it will run on and on until it fills the disk or you shut down SQL Server. This section shows the rather simple script required to stop a trace and then builds a useful stored procedure to stop either a specific trace or all traces.

All there is to stopping traces is a couple of calls to `sp_trace_setstatus`. It has to be called twice: first to stop the trace from running and the second time to close the trace and release it from memory. Assuming that there is a trace 1, the script at the top of the following page stops it and closes it.

Because you may not be the person running trace 1, the script is commented out when it appears in the Chapter 17 Listing 0 Short Queries.sql file. You don't want to do this to someone else on your server without a good reason.

```
-- Stop trace 1, assumes it's running
DECLARE @rc int
EXEC @rc = sp_trace_setstatus 1, 0 -- stop it from running
PRINT 'Return code from stop trace = ' + convert(varchar, @rc)
        + ' ' + dbo.udf_Trc_SetStatusMSG(@rc)
EXEC @rc = sp_trace_setstatus 1, 2 -- close it
PRINT 'Return code from close trace = ' + convert(varchar, @rc)
        + ' ' + dbo.udf_Trc_SetStatusMSG(@rc)
GO
```

(Results)

```
Return code from stop trace = 0 No Error.
Return code from close trace = 0 No Error.
```

udf_Trc_SetStatusMSG is a UDF that translates the return code from sp_trace_setstatus into a readable message. It's not listed, but you'll find it in the TSQLUDFS database.

If a trace is stopped—the equivalent of "Pause" in SQL Profiler—the first call gets a return code of 9, meaning illegal handle. But the second call will work, and the trace is closed and deallocated from memory.

Stopping someone else's trace and closing it without warning can be a bit disconcerting and won't win you any friends. But sometimes it has to be done. usp_Admin_TraceStop stops an individual trace or all traces. It's shown in Listing 17.3. To ease the impact on any unsuspecting SQL Profiler users, it only pauses traces that are being sent to the SQL Profiler window. It tells which traces are going to SQL Profiler by checking the PRODUCE_ROWSET column. If the trace is going to SQL Profiler, it's only stopped, not closed out.

System UDFs

Listing 17.3: usp_Admin_TraceStop, a stored procedure to stop a trace

```
CREATE      procedure usp_Admin_TraceStop
    @TraceID int = NULL -- Trace to stop or NULL for all traces
/*
* Stops a trace given by a TraceID (or NULL for all)
*
* Example:
exec usp_Admin_TraceStop NULL -- stop all traces
***********************************************************************/
AS
    -- Table built as the results are accumulated
    DECLARE @Traces TABLE (traceid int
                    , Status varchar(7)
                    , [FileName]  sysname NULL
                    , ActionDT datetime -- when was the trace stopped
                    , ActionDescription varchar(128)
                     )
    DECLARE @tr int -- trace ID of a trace
          , @Status varchar(7) -- Stopped or running status of the trace
          , @fn sysname -- filename the trace is going to
```

```
    , @Rowset varchar(3) -- Yes or NO to does it produce a rowset
    , @rc int -- return code
    , @Msg varchar(128)

SET NOCOUNT ON   -- SETs must be done before declaring the cursor
SET ANSI_WARNINGS OFF

DECLARE TraceCursor CURSOR FORWARD_ONLY TYPE_WARNING FOR
       SELECT traceid, status, [FileName], PRODUCE_ROWSET
          FROM udf_Trc_InfoTAB(@TraceID)

OPEN TraceCursor
FETCH TraceCursor INTO @tr, @status, @fn, @Rowset

WHILE @@Fetch_status = 0 BEGIN
   -- The trace gets stopped only if it's running
   IF UPPER(@Status) = 'RUNNING' BEGIN
      EXEC @rc = sp_trace_setstatus @tr, 0

      IF @RC = 0
         SELECT @MSG = 'Stopped'
              , @Status = 'Stopped'
      ELSE
         SET @MSG = 'Not Stopped (' + convert(varchar, @RC) + ') '
                    + dbo.udf_Trc_SetStatusMSG(@RC)
   END -- IF

   IF UPPER(@Rowset) = 'NO' BEGIN
      EXEC @rc = sp_trace_setstatus @tr, 2 -- Close it

      IF @RC = 0
         SELECT @Msg = @Msg + ' Closed'
              , @Status = 'Closed'
      ELSE
          SET @msg = @msg + ' Not Closed ('
                          + convert(varchar, @rc) + ') '
                          + dbo.udf_Trc_SetStatusMSG(@rc)
   END

   -- Clean up @Msg so it can be the ActionDescription
   SET @Msg = CASE WHEN @Msg IS NULL
                   THEN 'No Action'
                   ELSE LTRIM(@Msg)
                   END

   -- Store the result, whatever it was
   INSERT INTO @Traces (traceid, Status, [FileName]
                      , ActionDT, ActionDescription)
      VALUES (@tr, @Status, @fn, getdate(), @msg)

   FETCH TraceCursor INTO @tr, @Status, @fn, @Rowset
END -- of While LOOP

CLOSE TraceCursor -- Clean up the cursor
DEALLOCATE TraceCursor

SELECT TraceID , Status , [FileName] , ActionDT, ActionDescription
   FROM @Traces -- Return the result table
   ORDER BY Traceid
```

As you can see, usp_Admin_TraceStop first stops traces if they are running. Next, if no rowset is being created by the trace, which means SQL Profiler isn't showing it, the trace can be closed. This query shows the result of closing a few traces that were in different states when the SP was run:

```
-- Stop all traces
EXEC usp_Admin_TraceStop NULL -- all traces
GO

(Results - reformatted)

TraceID     Status  FileName              ActionDT   ActionDescription
----------- ------- --------------------- ---------- -------------------
          1 Stopped NULL                  2002-10-31 Stopped
          2 Stopped NULL                  2002-10-31 Stopped
          3 Closed  C:\temp\trace1.trc    2002-10-31 Stopped Closed
```

Since we're being such nice guys and not closing the traces started by everyone, how about being nicer and telling them what we're doing? They really ought to be told about what's going to happen before it happens, so I've separated the next stored procedure from usp_Admin_TraceStop.

Unfortunately, none of the fn_trace_* functions tell us which user started each trace. The best we can do is find out which users are running SQL Profiler. For all practical purposes, that strategy works pretty well. The information is in master..sysprocesses. Right now I'm the only one on the system, as shown by this query:

```
-- Who's running SQL Profiler
SELECT spid, hostname, hostprocess, nt_domain, nt_username
   FROM master..sysprocesses
   WHERE program_name = 'SQL Profiler'
   ORDER BY nt_username
GO

(Results - reformatted)

spid   hostname     hostprocess nt_domain
------ ------------ ----------- -----------------
    60 ASN-H1200    2148        ASN-H1200
```

I've turned the query, with a few additional columns, into an inline UDF, udf_Trc_ProfilerUsersTAB, which you'll find in the TSQLUDFS database.

udf_Trc_ProfilerUsersTAB and udf_Trc_InfoTAB show us information about traces that are running. The next system UDF, fn_trace_gettable, gives us access to the data in traces that are no longer running but have been saved to a disk file.

fn_trace_gettable

`fn_trace_gettable` converts a trace file stored on disk into a table format. The table can then be examined using whatever method you choose, such as:

- View it in SQL Profiler or some other tool.
- Analyze it with the Index Wizard or your own code.
- Save it to a SQL Server table for later use.
- Put it to another use that I haven't thought up.

The syntax of the function call is:

```
fn_trace_gettable( @filename
                 , @numfiles )
```

@filename is the path and name of the file. There is no default for this argument.

@numfiles is the number of files to load. If `default` is used for this argument, all the rollover files will be loaded.

There is a sample .trc file in the download directory for this chapter under the name ExampleTrace.trc. The next query loads ExampleTrace.trc using a sample call to `fn_trace_gettable`. The script assumes that you've copied that file to the root directory of your C drive. Please copy it before running this query:

```
-- sample call to fn_trace_gettable
SELECT CAST(replace(replace(Left(convert(varchar(30),TextData)
           , 30), char(10), ' '), char(13), ' ') as char(30)) as TextData
     , StartTime, EventClass
     , CPU, Reads, Writes
    FROM ::fn_trace_gettable('c:\ExampleTrace.trc', 1)
GO
```

(Results - reformatted and truncated)

```
TextData                       StartTime           EventClass CPU   Reads Writes
------------------------------ ------------------- ---------- ----- ----- ------
NULL                           2002-09-20 10:45:40 0          NULL  NULL  NULL
-- network protocol: LPC set q NULL                17         NULL  NULL  NULL
-- network protocol: LPC set q NULL                17         NULL  NULL  NULL
-- network protocol: LPC set q NULL                17         NULL  NULL  NULL
-- network protocol: LPC set q NULL                17         NULL  NULL  NULL
-- network protocol: LPC set q NULL                17         NULL  NULL  NULL
-- network protocol: LPC set q NULL                17         NULL  NULL  NULL
-- network protocol: LPC set q NULL                17         NULL  NULL  NULL
-- network protocol: LPC set q NULL                17         NULL  NULL  NULL
select * from dbo.udf_SQL_Trac 2002-09-20 10:46:06 12         10    125   0
SELECT *      FROM ::fn_helpco 2002-09-20 10:46:27 12         31    1155  16
SELECT *      FROM ::fn_liste 2002-09-20 10:46:36  12         91    983   0
```

```
select * from cust             2002-09-20 10:47:26 12      0     11    0
use pubs                       2002-09-20 10:48:04 12      0     14    0
select * from authors cross jo 2002-09-20 10:48:32 12      0     6     0
select * from authors cross jo 2002-09-20 10:48:41 12      0     6     0
select * from authors cross jo 2002-09-20 10:48:48 12      20    123   0
select * from authors cross jo 2002-09-20 10:48:58 12      70    954   0
select * from authors cross jo 2002-09-20 10:49:12 12      2664  9620  1
NULL                           NULL                5       NULL  NULL  NULL
```

As of SQL Server 2000 Service Pack 3, `fn_trace_gettable` returns 40-plus columns. Each column corresponds to a data column in a SQL Profiler definition. All the columns are returned, even if the data was not gathered in the trace. Columns that were not gathered are always returned as a `NULL` value.

The `EventClass` column is a numeric code, which is the same code that is used in the `sp_trace_setevent` procedure that creates the trace. The function `udf_Trc_EventName` translates `EventClass` into a more understandable name. The code is in Listing 17.4.

Listing 17.4: Partial text of `udf_Trc_EventName`

```
CREATE  FUNCTION dbo.udf_Trc_EventName (

    @EventClass int -- The ID from the trace file
)   RETURNS varchar(32) -- length of the longest description
/*
* Translates a SQL Trace EventClass into its descriptive name.
* Used when viewing trace tables or when converting a trace
* file with fn_trace_gettable.
*
* Example: -- assumes existence of the c:\ExampleTrace.trc file
select TextData, dbo.ufn_SQL_TraceEventName(EventClass)
     from ::fn_trace_gettable ('c:\ExampleTrace.trc', default)
****************************************************************/
AS BEGIN

     RETURN CASE @EventClass
                -- 0-9 Reserved
            WHEN 0 THEN 'TraceStart'
            WHEN 5 THEN 'TraceEnd'
            WHEN 10 THEN 'RPC:Completed'
            WHEN 11 THEN 'RPC:Starting'
            WHEN 12 THEN 'SQL:BatchCompleted'
            WHEN 13 THEN 'SQL:BatchStarting'
            WHEN 14 THEN 'Login'
...
            WHEN 117 THEN 'Audit Change Audit'
            WHEN 118 THEN 'Audit Object Derived Permission'
            ELSE
                CASE WHEN @EventClass BETWEEN 0 AND 118
                     THEN 'Reserved'
                     ELSE 'Unknown Event ' + CONVERT (varchar(20), @EventClass)
                     END
            END
END
```

A complete list of the codes with an explanation of what causes the events to occur is in Books Online in the documentation for `sp_trace_setevent`. A sample query shows what the translation looks like:

```
-- Query with translated event names
SELECT CAST(replace(replace(Left(convert(varchar(30),TextData)
          , 30), char(10), ' '), char(13), ' ') as char(30)) as TextData
     , dbo.udf_Trc_EventName(EventClass) as [Event Class]
     , CPU, Reads, Writes
   FROM ::fn_trace_gettable('c:\ExampleTrace.trc', 1)
GO
```

(Results - reformatted and abridged, columns truncated)

```
TextData                       Event Class          CPU   Reads   Writes
------------------------------ -------------------- ----- ------- -------
NULL                           Reserved             NULL  NULL    NULL
-- network protocol: LPC set q ExistingConnection   NULL  NULL    NULL
-- network protocol: LPC set q ExistingConnection   NULL  NULL    NULL
...
-- network protocol: LPC set q ExistingConnection   NULL  NULL    NULL
select * from dbo.udf_SQL_Trac SQL:BatchCompleted   10    125     0
...
select * from authors cross jo SQL:BatchCompleted   2664  9620    1
NULL                           Reserved             NULL  NULL    NULL
```

Analyzing trace data is beyond the scope of this book. There is additional information on using SQL Profiler to monitor UDFs in Chapter 3. That information also applies to traces that are stored in files and analyzed later using `fn_trace_gettable`.

Translating the numeric code for `EventClass` that `fn_trace_gettable` returns is only one of the translations that we need to make to create `udf_Trc_RPT`. When we retrieve event information and filter definitions using the next two system UDFs, we'll have to translate several more codes.

fn_trace_geteventinfo

Use `fn_trace_geteventinfo` to retrieve information about what events are being recorded by any particular trace. The syntax of the function call is:

::fn_trace_geteventinfo (*@traceid*)

@traceid is an `int` that identifies the trace. There is no default for `@traceid`; the number of a running trace must be specified to get any output.

A list of the traces that are running can be retrieved with the function `udf_Trc_InfoTAB`, which was shown earlier in Listing 17.2. `fn_trace_geteventinfo` returns the columns listed in Table 17.7.

Table 17.7: Result columns from fn_trace_geteventinfo

Column	Data Type	Description
EventID	int	ID of the traced event. This is the same as the EventClass returned by fn_trace_gettable in the previous section.
ColumnID	int	ID of the column collected by the event

To see how it works, I first started a SQL Profiler trace with minimal events and data columns. The first SELECT in this script gets a list of the traces. If a trace is found, the second SELECT uses the first traceid as the parameter to call fn_trace_geteventinfo.

```
-- Get the first running trace and request the event information
DECLARE @traceID int

SELECT TOP 1 @traceID = traceid
    FROM dbo.udf_Trc_InfoTAB(default)
    ORDER BY traceid

IF @traceID IS NOT NULL
    -- Get the event information from the first trace
    SELECT * FROM ::fn_trace_geteventinfo(@traceID )
ELSE
    PRINT 'No traces running'
GO
```

(Results - abridged)

```
eventid     columnid
----------- -----------
10          1
10          12
10          16
10          17
...
15          16
15          17
15          18
```

As you can see, the rows of this table have information for only one trace column each, and columnid is a numeric code. The output wasn't meant for you or me to understand.

Let's start by translating the columnid into something more understandable, like the column name. The complete list of column IDs is in the Books Online documentation for sp_trace_setevent. The function udf_Trc_ColumnName translates the columnid into a name. The code for the function is in Listing 17.5.

Listing 17.5: Partial script for udf_Trc_ColumnName

```
CREATE  FUNCTION dbo.udf_Trc_ColumnName (

    @ColumnID int -- The ColumnID from the trace file
)   RETURNS varchar(20) -- Descriptive name, <= 20 chars
    WITH SCHEMABINDING
/*
* Translates a SQL Trace ColumnID into its descriptive name.
* Used when viewing or retrieving event information from
* fn_trace_geteventinfo.
*
* Example: -- assumes existence of the c:\ExampleTrace.trc file
select EventID, dbo.udf_Trc_ColumnName(columnid)
        from ::fn_trace_geteventinfo (1)
***************************************************************/
AS BEGIN

     RETURN CASE @ColumnID
            WHEN 1 THEN 'TextData'
            WHEN 2 THEN 'BinaryData'
            WHEN 3 THEN 'DatabaseID'
...
            WHEN 43 THEN 'TargetLoginSID'
            WHEN 44 THEN 'ColumnPermissionsSet'
            ELSE 'Unknown:' + CAST(@columnid as varchar(20))
            END
END
```

There are a couple of reasonable ways to slice and dice the output from fn_trace_geteventinfo to make it more useful. A complete pivot of the table that listed the event name and then 44 columns, one for each possible columnid, is probably not very useful. When data is so sparse (let's say eight columns of data out of 44), it's often more useful to turn it into a single comma-separated list. Since the data columns are the same for every event, let's turn both the events and the columns into lists of names.

By the way, when the SQL Profiler starts the trace, it requests the same set of data columns on every event type. That's a lot of columns. When traces are created with the sp_trace_setevent stored procedure, a different set of columns can be requested for each event type, providing a level of control that isn't available in SQL Profiler.

Making a List of Events

In the TSQLUDFS database, but not listed, is udf_Trc_EventListCursorBased, which was my first crack at a function that makes the list of event names. It follows the pattern of other cursor-based list creation functions. As you might guess by the name, there's an alternative version that's not based on a cursor.

Since the cursor in udf_Trc_EventListCursorBased is used to concatenate strings, the string concatenation technique discussed in Chapter 8 and first shown with the function udf_Titles_AuthorList2 can be used to shorten and speed up the creation of the event list. I wouldn't show this technique again except that the circumstances of this function create a few interesting wrinkles. Listing 17.6 shows function udf_Trc_EventList that uses the cursor alternative technique. At first, I thought it wouldn't work.

Listing 17.6: udf_Trc_EventList

```
CREATE  FUNCTION dbo.udf_Trc_EventList (

    @trace_id int -- which trace. No valid default
  , @Separator nvarchar(128) = N', ' -- Separates enties in list
            -- usually this is a comma or NCHAR(9)
)   RETURNS nvarchar(4000) -- comma separated list of event names.
    -- NO SCHEMABINDING due to use of system UDF
/*
* Returns a separated list of events being monitored by a trace.
* Each event is given by its name. The separator supplied is
* placed between entries.  This could be N', ' or NCHAR(9)
* for TAB.
*
* Example:   assumes 1 is a valid trace id
select dbo.udf_Trc_EventList(1, N', ')
****************************************************************/
AS BEGIN

    DECLARE @EventList nvarchar(4000) -- working list

    SELECT @EventList = CASE WHEN @EventList IS NULL
                             THEN '' -- Empty String
                             ELSE @EventList + @Separator
                             END
                      + dbo.udf_Trc_EventName(EventID)
            FROM (SELECT DISTINCT TOP 100 PERCENT
                         EventID
                     FROM ::fn_trace_geteventinfo(@trace_id)
                     ORDER BY EventID
                 ) Events

    RETURN @EventList
END
```

I thought this technique wouldn't work at first because of the DISTINCT clause. DISTINCT is needed because an eventid can appear several times in the output of fn_trace_geteventinfo. My first attempt to write the SELECT was this:

```
    SELECT @EventList = @EventList
                      + @Separator
                      + dbo.udf_Trc_EventName(DISTINCT EventID)
            FROM ::fn_trace_geteventinfo(@trace_id)
            ORDER BY EventID
```

This isn't a legal place for the shaded DISTINCT keyword, and SQL Server won't create the function. I also tried putting the DISTINCT right after SELECT where I intuitively think it belongs. Here's what I tried:

```
    SELECT DISTINCT @EventList = @EventList
                  + @Separator
                  + dbo.udf_Trc_EventName(EventID)
          FROM ::fn_trace_geteventinfo(@trace_id)
          ORDER BY EventID
```

Although SQL Server accepts the function, it doesn't produce the desired result. That function, udf_Example_Trc_EventListBadAttempt, is in the TSQLUDFS database if you want to try it.

As you can see in Listing 17.6, the way to get the UDF to work is to move the SELECT on fn_trace_geteventinfo with its DISTINCT clause into a derived table. This isolates it from the looping SELECT, and we get the correct results. This query runs udf_Trc_EventList on trace number 1:

```
-- Run udf_SQLTraceEventList, assumes trace 1 is running
SELECT dbo.udf_Trc_EventList (1, N', ') as [Event List]
GO

(Results)

Event List
-------------------------------------------------------------------------------
RPC:Completed, SQL:BatchCompleted, Login, Logout, ExistingConnection
```

udf_Trc_EventList is one of the functions needed to translate the results of fn_trace_geteventinfo. The next section has a few more.

Additional UDFs Based on fn_trace_geteventinfo

There are several additional functions in TSQLUDFS that are based on fn_trace_geteventinfo. In the interest of space, these functions are not shown. If you want to see them, please retrieve them from the database. udf_Trc_ColumnList creates a list of columns using code similar to udf_Trc_EventList. The functions udf_Trc_EventCount and udf_Trc_ColumnCount return the number of events and columns in the lists. After discussing fn_trace_getfilterinfo in the next section, these functions will be used to create an enhanced version of udf_Trc_InfoTAB.

fn_trace_getfilterinfo

This function retrieves information about the active filters for a trace. The syntax of the call is:

```
::fn_trace_getfilterinfo( @traceid )
```

@traceid is an `int` that identifies the trace. There is no default for `@traceid`; the number of a running trace must be specified to get any output.

As we've done earlier in the chapter, we can retrieve the trace IDs of the current traces with the function `udf_Trc_InfoTAB`. These can be supplied to `fn_trace_getfilterinfo`.

The resultset returned by `fn_trace_getfilterinfo` is described in Table 17.8. It consists of codes that require more translation.

Table 17.8: Result columns from `fn_trace_getfilterinfo`

Column	Data Type	Description
`columnid`	`int`	ID of the column to which the filter is applied.
`comparison_operator`	`int`	Code for the logical operator that's used to combine the filters. 0 for AND and 1 for OR.
`logical_operator`	`int`	Code for the operator used to compare the column's value to the `value` column of this filter clause. The list of operators is in Table 17.9 in the next subsection.
`value`	`sql_variant`	The value compared to the trace's data column using the logical operator.

The process of making a human-readable filter expression starts by converting the `comparison_operator` and the `logical_operator` into something that you and I can read. The next sections create functions to take care of those tasks.

Converting Operator Codes to Readable Text

The list of `comparison_operator` codes is the same list that was used in `sp_trace_setfilter` when the filter was created. The function `udf_Trc_ComparisonOp` translates this code to its text equivalent.

Table 17.9: Comparison operator codes returned by `fn_trace_getfilterinfo`

Code Value	Operator	Operator Name
0	=	Equal
1	<> or !=	Not equal
2	>	Greater than
3	<	Less than

System UDFs

Code Value	Operator	Operator Name
4	>=	Greater than or equal to
5	<=	Less than or equal to
6	LIKE	Like
7	NOT LIKE	Not like

Also in the TSQLUDFS database is udf_Trc_LogicalOp, which translates from the logical_operator code to the text of the logical operator: 0 for AND and 1 for OR. OR operators can only be used between filters on the same columnid.

Sample Output from fn_trace_getfilterinfo

Let's take a look at the output from a simple call to fn_trace_getfilterinfo. I started a trace in SQL Profiler using the SQLProfilerStandard template. There were no other traces running on the system, so I assumed correctly that it was traceid 1. Here's the call:

```
-- Get filter info for trace 1. Assumes that there is a trace 1.
SELECT * from ::fn_trace_getfilterinfo(1)
GO

(Results)

columnid    logical_operator comparison_operator value
----------- ---------------- ------------------- ------------------------------
10          0                7                   SQL Profiler
```

This trace has one filter. If you look at the Filters tab of the profile definition, you'll see that it filters out events generated by SQL Profiler itself.

To translate this to more meaningful text, let's use the functions for translating comparison_operator and logical_operator that were created for the previous section:

```
-- Get filter info for trace 1 with translations. Assumes trace 1 is running.
SELECT dbo.udf_Trc_ColumnName(columnid) as [Column ID]
     , dbo.udf_Trc_LogicalOp(logical_operator) as [Logical Op]
     , dbo.udf_Trc_ComparisonOp(comparison_operator) as [Comp Op]
     , value
   FROM ::fn_trace_getfilterinfo(1)
GO

(Results)

Column ID            Logical Op Comp Op    value
-------------------- ---------- ---------- ------------------------------------
ApplicationName      AND        NOT LIKE   SQL Profiler
```

That's an improvement. The equivalent WHERE clause would be:

```
ApplicationName NOT LIKE 'SQL Profiler'
```

We're getting closer to text that's understandable for us SQL programmers. It would be easier for us to read if the filter expression used a syntax similar to a WHERE clause.

Converting the Filter into a WHERE Clause

The next step to a readable description in the filter is to combine the columnid, comparison_operator, and value into an equivalent logical clause in the style of the WHERE clause. The udf_Trc_FilterClause function does just that. It's shown in Listing 17.7. It relies on another function, udf_SQL_VariantToStringConstantLtd, which turns a sql_variant, such as the value column from fn_trace_getfilterinfo, into a character string constant. The intent is to translate the sql_variant to the string that represents it in a SQL statement. The Ltd on the end of the name implies that the version limits the length of the output.

Listing 17.7: udf_Trc_FilterClause

```
CREATE FUNCTION dbo.udf_Trc_FilterClause (

    @ColumnID int -- ColumnID from the trace filter definition
  , @Comparison_OperatorCode int -- Comparison op code =, >, etc.
  , @Value sql_variant -- value compared to the column
)   RETURNS nvarchar(64) -- Equivalent comparison expression
                          -- such as 'Database ID > 5'
    WITH SCHEMABINDING
/*
* Translates a SQL Profiler filter expression into text in a
* form similar to a WHERE clause. Used when retrieving event
* information from fn_trace_getfilterinfo.  The length of the
* output is limited to about 64 characters.
*
* Example: -- assumes existence of the c:\ExampleTrace.trc file
select dbo.udf_Trc_FilterClause(columnid, comparison_operator
               , value) from ::fn_trace_getfilterinfo (1)
****************************************************************/
AS BEGIN

    DECLARE @Comparison_OperatorText as nvarchar (8)

    SET @Comparison_OperatorText
          = dbo.udf_Trc_ComparisonOp(@Comparison_OperatorCode)

    -- Like and Not Like need spaces around them.
    -- Other operators do not.
     RETURN   dbo.udf_Trc_ColumnName(@ColumnID)
          + CASE WHEN @Comparison_OperatorText LIKE '%LIKE%'
                 THEN N' ' + @Comparison_OperatorText + N' '
                 ELSE @Comparison_OperatorText
                 END
          + dbo.udf_SQL_VariantToStringConstantLtd(@Value, 28)

END
```

System UDFs

To make our output interesting, I created a trace with several filter conditions. It started with the SQLProfilerStandard trace, which excludes output from the SQL Profiler itself. Then a few conditions were added to restrict the output of the trace to databases with IDs 5, 6, or 7. It also has "Exclude system IDs" checked. Figure 17.2 shows the Filters tab of the Trace Properties screen while the filter is being defined.

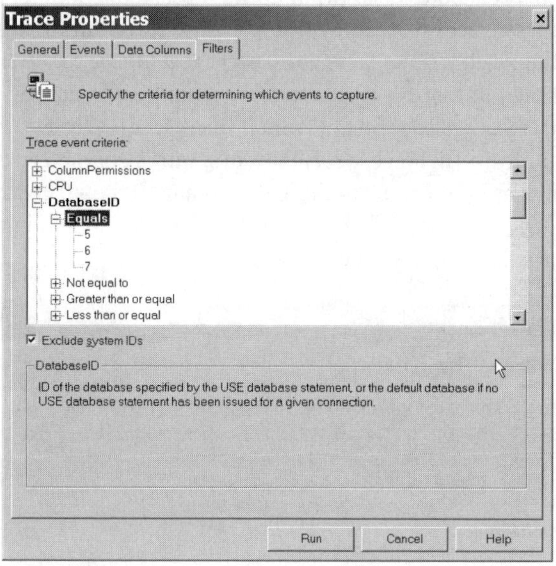

Figure 17.2: Defining a SQL Profiler filter

Here's a script that uses `udf_Trc_FilterClause` on the trace shown in Figure 17.2:

```
-- use udf_Trc_FilterClause on the trace 1 -- assumes it exists
SELECT dbo.udf_Trc_LogicalOp (logical_operator) as [Oper]
     , dbo.udf_Trc_FilterClause
            (columnid, comparison_operator, value) as [Expression]
    FROM ::fn_trace_getfilterinfo(1)
GO
```

(Results)

```
Oper Expression
---- -------------------------------------------------------------
AND  DatabaseID=5
OR   DatabaseID=6
OR   DatabaseID=7
AND  ObjectID>=100
AND  ApplicationName NOT LIKE N'SQL Profiler'
AND  ApplicationName NOT LIKE N'sqla%'
```

That's much better than the jumble of numbers returned by fn_trace_getfilterinfo. However, the logical_operator isn't just right. There's an extra AND in the first row, and the output is a rowset, not exactly a WHERE clause but not too far from the way that I write them. To construct the filter expression column of udf_Trc_InfoExTAB that's built later in this chapter, I want the filter expression as a single string or as a tab-separated list within a string.

udf_Trc_FilterExpression does what I really want: produce a single string that expresses the entire filter. You'll find it in Listing 17.8. It's similar to the udf_Trc_EventList function shown in Listing 17.6. This one uses a cursor to examine the results of fn_trace_getfilterinfo, translates each clause into text, and concatenates them together, returning the result. The parameters are the traceid, the separator character, and one bit compact option.

It's possible to convert this function from using a cursor to the alternate string concatenation technique used by udf_Trc_EventList. However, I looked at the complexity of the logic inside the loop and decided it wouldn't be that easy to convert. You have to weigh the effort that could be expended in improving the function against the frequency with which this function is run and the difficulty in maintaining it once it's changed. In this case, my decision is to leave the cursor in the function.

Listing 17.8: udf_Trc_FilterExpression

```
CREATE FUNCTION dbo.udf_Trc_FilterExpression (

    @trace_id int -- which trace. No valid default
  , @Separator nvarchar(128) = N', ' -- Separates entries
        -- usually this is something like ', ' or NCHAR(9)
  , @CompactBIT BIT = 0 -- Should the result be compacted.
)   RETURNS nvarchar(4000) -- separated list of filter expressions
               -- suitable for display or ready for word wrap.
/*
* Returns a separated list of filters being monitored by a trace.
* Each filter is given by its name. The separator supplied is placed
* between entries.  This could be ', ' or NCHAR(9) for TAB.
*
* Example:
select dbo.udf_Trc_FilterExpression(1, ' ', 1) -- assumes 1 is valid
*************************************************************************/
AS BEGIN

DECLARE @FilterExpression nvarchar(4000) -- working list
DECLARE @ColumnID int -- Single filter ID we're working on
      , @Logical_OperatorCode int -- logical operator code
      , @Comparison_OperatorCode int -- comparison operator code
      , @value sql_variant -- value being compared
      , @Logical_OperatorText nvarchar(8)
      , @Comparison_OperatorText nvarchar(10)
      , @LastColumnID int -- columnId of the previous entry in the list
      , @LastLogical_OperatorCode int -- Logical_Operator code of the previous entry
```

```
      , @LastComparison_OperatorCode int -- Comparison_Operator code
                                          -- of the previous entry
      , @FirstMemberBIT BIT -- keeps track of the need for separators

-- Create resultset of the filters handled by the trace.
DECLARE FilterCursor CURSOR  FAST_FORWARD FOR
    SELECT columnid
         , logical_operator
         , comparison_operator
         , value
        FROM ::fn_trace_getfilterinfo(@trace_id)

-- Open the cursor and fetch the first result
OPEN FilterCursor
FETCH FilterCursor INTO @ColumnID, @Logical_OperatorCode,
         @Comparison_OperatorCode, @Value

SET @FirstMemberBIT = 1 -- No separator needed after the first entry.
WHILE @@Fetch_status = 0  BEGIN
    -- add the name of the filter and separator, if needed.
    IF @FirstMemberBIT = 1 BEGIN
       SET @FilterExpression = dbo.udf_Trc_FilterClause(@ColumnID
                             , @Comparison_OperatorCode, @Value)
       SET @FirstMemberBIT = 0
       END -- IF Clause
    ELSE BEGIN
       SET @Logical_OperatorText =
                     dbo.udf_Trc_LogicalOp(@Logical_OperatorCode)

       IF @ColumnID = @LastColumnID and @CompactBIT = 1 BEGIN

           SET @Comparison_OperatorText =
                dbo.udf_Trc_ComparisonOp (@Comparison_OperatorCode)
           IF @Comparison_OperatorText LIKE '%LIKE%'
               SET @Comparison_OperatorText = @Comparison_OperatorText + N' '

           SELECT @FilterExpression = @FilterExpression
                        + N' ' -- instead of separator
                        + @Logical_OperatorText
                        + N' '
                        + @Comparison_OperatorText
                        + dbo.udf_SQL_VariantToStringConstantLtd(@Value, 28)

            END -- IFclause
       ELSE -- When not compact or when there is a new column
           SELECT @FilterExpression = @FilterExpression
                    + @Separator
                    + @Logical_OperatorText
                    + N' '
                    + dbo.udf_Trc_FilterClause(@ColumnID
                              , @Comparison_OperatorCode, @Value)
       -- END IF

    END -- Else clause

    -- Save the previous values so they can be used to compact the string
    SELECT @LastColumnID = @ColumnID
         , @LastLogical_OperatorCode = @Logical_OperatorCode
```

```
        , @LastComparison_OperatorCode = @Comparison_OperatorCode

    FETCH FilterCursor INTO  @ColumnID, @Logical_OperatorCode,
        @Comparison_OperatorCode, @Value -- retrieve next filter

END -- of the WHILE LOOP

-- Clean up the cursor
CLOSE FilterCursor
DEALLOCATE FilterCursor

RETURN @FilterExpression
END
```

With the compact option set to 0, a sample call shows the complete filter expression from trace 1. I've let the output wrap to a second line:

```
-- use udf_Trc_FilterExpression on trace 1 without Compact option
SELECT dbo.udf_Trc_FilterExpression (1, ' ', 0) as [Filter Expression]
GO

(Results - wrapped to a second line)

Filter Expression
-------------------------------------------------------------------------------
DatabaseID=5 OR DatabaseID=6 OR DatabaseID=7 AND ApplicationName NOT LIKE N'SQL
Profiler' AND ObjectID>=100
```

When the compact option is selected, the result is shorter and easier to fit onto a single line. It's shortened by not repeating the column name in successive comparisons to the same column. The output is a little smaller but still wraps based on the 80-character limit of the format of this book. As you can see in this query:

```
-- use udf_Trc_FilterExpression on trace 1 with Compact option
SELECT dbo.udf_Trc_FilterExpression (1, ' ', 1) as [Filter Expression]
GO

(Results - wrapped to a second line)

Filter Expression
--------------------------------------------------------------------------------
DatabaseID=5 OR =6 OR =7 AND ApplicationName NOT LIKE N'SQL Profiler' AND
ObjectID>=100
```

Whether your traces are created by scripts or by SQL Profiler, the `fn_trace_*` functions don't make it easy to understand what the traces are doing. Now that `udf_Trc_FilterExpression` is available to convert a filter to something that you and I understand, we've got all the functions needed to build a readable report of running traces. The next section does just that.

Reporting on All Running Traces

Previous subsections of this chapter have translated the raw information provided by the fn_trace_* functions into text that you and I can read. udf_Trc_InfoExTAB, which is not listed, extends udf_Trc_InfoTAB by including columns for the event list, column list, and filter expression. Its output is ideal for feeding into a report writer, which could take responsibility for placing fields on the page and word wrapping where necessary. But since I can't always count on having the same report writer available on every system that I work with, I've created another function, udf_Trc_RPT, to display all the information about running traces in a readable text format. It relies on udf_Trc_InfoTAB and the other UDFs created in this chapter. The UDF is shown in Listing 17.9.

Listing 17.9: udf_Trc_RPT

```
CREATE  FUNCTION udf_Trc_RPT (

    @trace_id int = NULL -- which trace, NULL for all
)  RETURNS @Rpt TABLE (rptline nVarChar(4000))
/*
* Returns a report of information about a trace. These are the original
* arguments to sp_trace_create and to the other sp_trace_* procedures.
* The status field for the trace is broken down to four individual fields.
* The list of events, list of columns, and the filter expression are each
* on their own line or wrapped to multiple lines.
*
* Example:
select rptline from udf_Trc_RPT(default)
*********************************************************************/
AS BEGIN

DECLARE @NewLine nvarchar(2)      , @Tab nvarchar(1)

SELECT @NewLine = nchar(13) + NCHAR(10)  + N' ' -- CR plus some spaces
     , @Tab = NCHAR(9) -- Tab character

INSERT INTO @Rpt
SELECT
        'Trace: ' + convert(varchar(10), traceid)
      + '  ' + Status
      + ' Rowset:' + PRODUCE_ROWSET
      + ' Rollover:' + FILE_ROLLOVER
      + ' ShutOnErr:' + SHUTDOWN_ON_ERROR
      + ' BlkBx:' + TRACE_PRODUCE_BLACKBOX
      + ' MaxSize:' + COALESCE(CONVERT(varchar(10), [MaxSize]), 'NULL')
      + @NewLine +' Stop At: ' + COALESCE(
                     CONVERT(varchar(32), [StopTime], 120), 'NULL')
      + '  Filename:' + COALESCE([FileName], 'NULL')
      + @NewLine + '  Events: ' + dbo.udf_TxtN_WrapDelimiters (
        dbo.udf_Trc_EventList(traceid, @Tab),78,@Tab,N', ',@NewLine,10,10)
      + @NewLine + ' Columns: ' + dbo.udf_TxtN_WrapDelimiters (
        dbo.udf_Trc_ColumnList(traceid, @Tab),78,@tab,N', ',@NewLine,10,10)
```

```
      + @NewLine + '  Filter: ' + dbo.udf_TxtN_WrapDelimiters (
         dbo.udf_Trc_FilterExpression(traceid, @Tab, 1)
                               , 78, @Tab, N' ', @NewLine, 10, 10)
      + @NewLine -- To provide space between lines of the report
     FROM udf_Trc_InfoTAB(@trace_id)

RETURN
END
```

To see how it works, start a few traces and choose various events, columns, and filter expressions. Set our output to text and be sure to set the Query Analyzer option “Maximum characters per column” to a big number like 4000. You'll find it on the Results pane of the Tools ➤ Options menu command. On the same tab, turn off “Print column headers (*)” or you'll get long lines of dashes when you try to send the output to a file. Then run this query:

```
-- Run udf_Trc_Rpt to see information about all running traces
--   be sure to start a few before testing it.
SELECT rptline from udf_Trc_RPT(default)
GO

(Results - abriged)

rptline
--------------------------------------------------------------------------------
Trace: 1   RUNNING Rowset:YES Rollover:NO ShutOnErr:NO BlackBox:NO MaxSize:5
  Stop At: NULL  Filename:NULL
   Events: RPC:Completed, SQL:BatchCompleted, Login, Logout, ExistingConnection
  Columns: TextData, NTUserName, ClientProcessID, ApplicationName,
           SQLSecurityLoginName, SPID, Duration, StartTime, Reads, Writes, CPU
   Filter: DatabaseID=5 OR =6 OR =7 AND ObjectID>=100
           AND ApplicationName NOT LIKE N'SQL Profiler'

Trace: 2   RUNNING Rowset:YES Rollover:NO ShutOnErr:NO BlackBox:NO MaxSize:5
  Stop At: 2002-09-25 11:14:20  Filename:NULL
   Events: RPC:Completed, RPC:Starting, SQL:BatchCompleted, SQL:BatchStarting,
           DTCTransaction, DOP Event, SP:CacheMiss, SP:CacheInsert,
           SP:CacheRemove, SP:Recompile, SP:CacheHit, SP:ExecContextHit,
           Exec Prepared SQL, Unprepare SQL, CursorExecute, CursorRecompile,
           CursorImplicitConversion, CursorUnprepare, CursorClose,
           Show Plan Text, Show Plan ALL, Show Plan Statistics
  Columns: TextData, BinaryData, DatabaseID, TransactionID, NTUserName,
           ClientHostName, ClientProcessID, ApplicationName,
           DatabaseUserName, TargetLoginName, TargetLoginSID,
           ColumnPermissionsSet
   Filter: DatabaseID=5 OR =6 OR =7 AND ObjectID>=100
           AND ApplicationName NOT LIKE N'SQL Profiler' AND NOT LIKE N'SQLAgent%'
...
```

I find this format readable and easy to print so the results can be e-mailed or shown to others when needed. The best way to get the results to print is to send the output to a file. There's a sample file, Output of udf_Trc_RPT.rpt, in the download directory for this chapter.

Now, you don't need the complete list of traces very often. But when you're trying to diagnose a performance problem and there are 15 traces running on the system, the traces are part of the problem. Even when you're trying to get realistic timing information, it's better not to be running any more traces than necessary and preferably only the one that is measuring the events that you're investigating.

Speaking of timing, if you have a bunch of traces running, you might notice that udf_Trc_RPT is surprisingly slow. How slow? I ran the two previous queries with just three traces running. The call to udf_Trc_InfoExTAB took 993 milliseconds. The call to udf_Trc_RPT took 2323 milliseconds. That's more than twice the amount of time. I'm pretty sure the difference is due to the large amount of procedural code used for text processing, particularly the calls to udf_TxtN_WrapDelimiters.

Summary

The trace is one of the most powerful tools in the SQL Server arsenal, as it is useful for debugging, monitoring, and analyzing performance. This chapter has produced a set of functions and stored procedures to aid in understanding and managing traces. Most of this information comes from a group of system UDFs whose name begins with fn_trace_.

The goal of most of the functions created in this chapter is to build a translation of the numeric codes used to create system traces into a readable description. The description is summarized by udf_Trc_RPT.

In addition, there was an introduction to creating traces with T-SQL script. While the SQL Profiler remains much easier to use, there are times when a script is better, such as when you just can't accept the loss of any events or when you want to have detailed control over which columns of data are gathered for each event.

In addition to creating traces with T-SQL script, you're also going to have to stop them. The stored procedure usp_Admin_TraceStop was created to make that easy. It's accompanied by udf_Trc_ProfilerUsersTAB, which can show you a list of users who are running SQL Profiler. Unfortunately, SQL Server doesn't provide the information needed to connect the trace to the user who is running that trace.

These last few chapters covered the documented system UDFs in depth and built useful UDFs based on their output. If you take a look at the list of functions in master, you'll see that there are many more than the ten documented UDFs. The next chapter explores some of the system UDFs that Microsoft left out of Books Online.

18

Undocumented System UDFs

The first four chapters of Part II of the book discussed the system UDFs that are documented in Books Online. Master is full of UDFs, few of which are documented. The undocumented UDFs in master fall into two groups:

- True system UDFs owned by `system_function_schema`
- Standard UDFs owned by **dbo**

The undocumented UDFs in master and owned by `system_function_schema` have the status of being system UDFs. That status confers on them two important characteristics:

- They can use T-SQL syntax that is reserved for system UDFs.
- They function as if they are running in the database from which they are called, instead of from the database in which they are defined.

That last point is subtle but can be very important. It only comes into play with a few of the undocumented system UDFs supplied by Microsoft, such as `fn_dblog`. Once we define our own UDFs in the next chapter, it's much more important.

There are also UDFs in master that are owned by **dbo**. While they're not actually system UDFs, you can use them to your advantage. A few of these are covered in this chapter. But there's nothing special about them; they're called like any UDF in any database and don't use the special syntax of system UDFs.

This chapter discusses these two groups of undocumented UDFs in master. It documents some of the more useful among them and shows examples of how they can be used.

Using any undocumented routine in any software product usually caries a risk that the vendor of the product (in this case Microsoft) will change the behavior of the routine in a future release. In the case of the undocumented system UDFs, this risk is mitigated by the presence of the source code that is used during the SQL Server installation process to create most of the system UDFs. The files that SQL Server uses when creating the system UDFs is left on your disk after the installation is complete. I'll give you a list of the files and their location so you can take a look for yourself.

When you want to retrieve the text of a function, you can either execute a query using `sp_helptext` or use one of the GUI tools, Enterprise Manager or Query Analyzer, to get the script. While these techniques work with the UDFs owned by **dbo** in master, it doesn't work on true system UDFs. As I just mentioned, you can get the text of many, but not all, system UDFs from the source code files. The rest are available from within SQL Server. We'll build a UDF, `udf_Func_UndocSystemUDFtext`, that can retrieve an undocumented function's source code. I'll also show why `sp_helptext` doesn't work on system UDFs. Understanding why reveals something of the status of system UDFs that sets them apart from other functions.

Once you have the text of a system UDF, you have options to insulate yourself from potential changes to the function in future releases. One option is to create an identical UDF using your own function name. That's a sensible approach for some of the undocumented system UDFs, such as `fn_chariswhitespace`, that use only standard T-SQL syntax and don't require the status of a system UDF to be effective. However, other system UDFs, such as `fn_dblog`, use syntax that is undocumented, is not part of standard T-SQL, and only works when executed in a system UDF.

The first step in using the undocumented UDFs is to get a list of them. This can be retrieved with a variety of tools. This chapter starts by showing how to get the list of system UDFs.

Listing All System UDFs

You can see the complete list of functions defined in master by querying the `INFORMATION_SYSTEM.ROUTINES` view in master and selecting the entries with `ROUTINE_TYPE = 'FUNCTION'`. This query was run on my development system, which is running SQL Server 2000 Service Pack 3:

```
-- get a list of all the system UDFs including the undocumented ones
USE master
GO

SELECT routine_schema
     , routine_name
     , data_type
    FROM information_schema.Routines
    WHERE ROUTINE_TYPE = 'FUNCTION'
    ORDER BY routine_schema, routine_name
GO
```

(Results)

```
routine_schema         routine_name                              data_type
------------------------------------------------------------------------------
dbo                    fn_isreplmergeagent                       bit
dbo                    fn_MSFullText                             TABLE
dbo                    fn_MSgensqescstr                          nvarchar
dbo                    fn_MSsharedversion                        nvarchar
dbo                    fn_sqlvarbasetostr                        nvarchar
dbo                    fn_varbintohexstr                         nvarchar
dbo                    fn_varbintohexsubstring                   nvarchar
system_function_schema fn_chariswhitespace                       bit
system_function_schema fn_dblog                                  TABLE
system_function_schema fn_generateparameterpattern               nvarchar
system_function_schema fn_getpersistedservernamecasevariation    nvarchar
system_function_schema fn_helpcollations                         TABLE
system_function_schema fn_listextendedproperty                   TABLE
system_function_schema fn_removeparameterwithargument            nvarchar
system_function_schema fn_repladjustcolumnmap                    varbinary
system_function_schema fn_replbitstringtoint                     int
system_function_schema fn_replcomposepublicationsnapshotfolder nvarchar
system_function_schema fn_replgenerateshorterfilenameprefix      nvarchar
system_function_schema fn_replgetagentcommandlinefromjobid       nvarchar
system_function_schema fn_replgetbinary8lodword                  int
system_function_schema fn_replinttobitstring                     char
system_function_schema fn_replmakestringliteral                  nvarchar
system_function_schema fn_replprepadbinary8                      binary
system_function_schema fn_replquotename                          nvarchar
system_function_schema fn_replrotr                               int
system_function_schema fn_repltrimleadingzerosinhexstr           nvarchar
system_function_schema fn_repluniquename                         nvarchar
system_function_schema fn_serverid                               int
system_function_schema fn_servershareddrives                     TABLE
system_function_schema fn_skipparameterargument                  nvarchar
system_function_schema fn_trace_geteventinfo                     TABLE
system_function_schema fn_trace_getfilterinfo                    TABLE
system_function_schema fn_trace_getinfo                          TABLE
system_function_schema fn_trace_gettable                         TABLE
system_function_schema fn_updateparameterwithargument            nvarchar
system_function_schema fn_virtualfilestats                       TABLE
system_function_schema fn_virtualservernodes                     TABLE
```

As you can see, the documented functions are on the list as well as many undocumented ones. The documented system UDFs have already been covered, so let's move on to those that Microsoft chose to leave out of Books Online.

Source Code for the Undocumented System UDFs

SQL Server uses a SQL script to create the undocumented system UDFs. You'll find the script files in the directory tree branch where you installed SQL Server in the subdirectory \MSSQL\INSTALL\. A search of that directory reveals that there are `CREATE FUNCTION` statements in these files:

instdist.sql
procsyst.sql
replsyst.sql
replcomm.sql
repltran.sql
sql_dmo.sql

The original definition of some of these functions was modified in the files:

sp1_repl.sql
sp2_repl.sql

It seems that in one of the service packs for SQL Server 2000, some additional protection has been added to hide the text of the system functions. If you try to get the text of a system UDF using `sp_helptext`, you just get an error. Try it:

```
-- Try to get the text of an undocumented system UDF
EXEC sp_helptext 'fn_serverid'
GO

(Results)

Server: Msg 15009, Level 16, State 1, Procedure sp_helptext, Line 53
The object 'fn_serverid' does not exist in database 'master'.
```

Variations on the name don't seem to work. The reason is that the `OBJECT_ID` metadata function returns `NULL` for the system UDFs, and `sp_helptext` depends on `OBJECT_ID`. This query shows it:

```
-- Get the Object_ID for fn_serverid
SELECT OBJECT_ID('fn_serverid') as [ID]
GO

(Results)

ID
-----------
NULL
```

Poking around reveals that most of the undocumented UDFs are still entries in `sysobjects` and `syscomments`, but the documented system UDFs have been removed as this query shows:

```
-- List the functions in sysobjects
SELECT * from sysobjects where (type = 'FN' or type = 'IF' or type = 'TR')
GO

(Results)

name
--------------------------------------------
fn_updateparameterwithargument
```

```
fn_repluniquename
fn_sqlvarbasetostr
...
fn_serverid
fn_isreplmergeagent
...
fn_replquotename
fn_chariswhitespace
fn_skipparameterargument
fn_removeparameterwithargument
```

Using these facts, it's possible to retrieve the text of the undocumented system UDFs using the function udf_Func_UndocSystemUDFtext, shown in Listing 18.1. I've included the CREATE FUNCTION script in the Listing 0 file so that you can easily create it in master. You should do this only in systems where you know it's okay. The script is commented out to prevent creating it unintentionally.

Listing 18.1: udf_Func_UndocSystemUDFtext

```
CREATE FUNCTION dbo.udf_Func_UndocSystemUDFtext (

    @FunctionName sysname -- name of the function
)  RETURNS @Script TABLE ( -- the text of the function
                [text] nvarchar(4000) -- a line of text
                )
    -- No SCHEMABINDING due to use of system tables
/*
* Returns the text of an undocumented system user-definded
* function. This function can only be used in the master
* database, where the text of the undocumented UDFs is stored.
* To work it must be created in master.
*
* Example:
select * from udf_Func_UndocSystemUDFtext('fn_serverid')
****************************************************************/
AS BEGIN

    DECLARE @ObjectID int -- the object id

    SELECT @ObjectID = id
        FROM sysobjects
        WHERE (type = N'FN' or type = 'IF' or type = 'TR')
          and name = @FunctionName

    INSERT INTO @Script
        SELECT [text]
            FROM syscomments
            WHERE id = @ObjectID

    RETURN

END
```

Running udf_Func_UndocSystemUDFtext on fn_serverid shows the script to create that function:

```
-- Get the text of select fn_serverid
SELECT [text]
    FROM udf_Func_UndocSystemUDFtext('fn_serverid')
GO

(Results)

text
-------------------------------------------------------------------------------CREATE
FUNCTION system_function_schema.fn_serverid(@servername sysname)
    RETURNS int
AS
BEGIN
    declare @srvid int
    select @srvid = srvid from master..sysservers where UPPER(srvname)
                    = UPPER(@servername) collate database_default
    RETURN (@srvid)
END
```

Since you've got the text to the function, you could pretty safely turn it into your own UDF in your own database or even a system UDF using the technique discussed in the next section. However, nothing guarantees that it will continue to work forever. A new version of SQL Server, or even a new service pack, could change the master..sysservers table that fn_serverid relies on. Proceed at your own risk.

Selected Undocumented System UDFs

This section documents some of the officially undocumented UDFs. I've tried to stick to the more general-purpose utility functions.

fn_chariswhitespace

This function is useful when trimming or word wrapping text. It accepts a string as input and responds with a result of 1 when the character is a whitespace character and 0 when the character is not whitespace.

The syntax of the call is:

```
fn_chariswhitespace (@char)
```

@char is an nchar(1) character.

The whitespace characters are listed in Table 18.1.

Table 18.1: ASCII values of whitespace characters

Name	Decimal Value	Hex Value
Tab	9	0x9
New Line	10	0xA
Carriage Return	13	0xD
Space	32	0x26

Notice that because it's a system UDF, the calling sequence for `fn_chariswhitespace` doesn't include the owner. Let's try a query in master, then move to pubs and try some more:

```
USE master
GO

-- check if various characters are whitespace characters
SELECT fn_chariswhitespace(CHAR(9)) as [Tab]
     , fn_chariswhitespace('A') as [A]
     , fn_chariswhitespace(' ') as [Space]
     , fn_chariswhitespace(N' ') as [Unicode Space]
     , fn_chariswhitespace(NCHAR(10)) [Unicode New Line]
     , fn_chariswhitespace(N'A') [Unicode A]
GO

(Results)

Tab  A    Space Unicode Space Unicode New Line Unicode A
---- ---- ----- ------------- ---------------- ---------
1    0    1     1             1                0

USE pubs
GO
SELECT fn_chariswhitespace(NCHAR(09)) as [Tab]
GO

(Results)

Tab
----
   1
```

Neither a two-part name nor a three-part name is required to invoke this scalar system UDF. The name alone is sufficient. This is a convenience of system UDFs.

You've seen the special double colon syntax that is used with the documented system UDFs. The undocumented system UDFs that return tables use the same syntax, as illustrated by `fn_dblog`.

fn_dblog

fn_dblog returns a table of records from the transaction log. The syntax of the call is:

```
::fn_dblog(@StartingLSN, @EndingLSN)
```

@StartingLSN and **@EndingLSN** are the start and end log sequence numbers, also known as LSNs. A NULL argument for the starting LSN requests log records from the beginning of the transaction log. A NULL value for the ending LSN requests information to the end of the transaction log.

To get an idea of what goes into the database log, I backed up my database to clear out the log. Actually, there were a few records left in, from open transactions I suppose. Then I ran this simple UPDATE statement that created records in the transaction log:

```
USE TSQLUDFS
GO

-- make a minor change to the database
UPDATE ExampleAddresses SET StreetNumber = StreetNumber + 1
GO
```

(Results omitted)

Next, I ran a query that uses fn_dblog. It's shown here with just two groups of the output columns. There are 85 or so columns of output. That's much too wide for display in this book, especially since most of the row values are NULL and I can explain only a few of them. Here's the query and output:

```
-- Get the entire database log from fn_dblog
SELECT * from ::fn_dblog(null, null)
GO
```

(Results - first group of columns)

```
Current LSN            Operation         Context        Transaction ID Tag Bits
---------------------- ----------------- -------------- -------------- --------
00000056:000000a0:0001 LOP_BEGIN_XACT    LCX_NULL       0000:00002adf  0x0000
00000056:000000a0:0002 LOP_SET_BITS      LCX_DIFF_MAP   0000:00000000  0x0000
00000056:000000a0:0003 LOP_MODIFY_ROW    LCX_CLUSTERED  0000:00002adf  0x0000
00000056:000000a0:0004 LOP_MODIFY_ROW    LCX_CLUSTERED  0000:00002adf  0x0000
00000056:000000a0:0005 LOP_MODIFY_ROW    LCX_CLUSTERED  0000:00002adf  0x0000
00000056:000000a0:0006 LOP_MODIFY_ROW    LCX_CLUSTERED  0000:00002adf  0x0000
00000056:000000a0:0007 LOP_MODIFY_ROW    LCX_CLUSTERED  0000:00002adf  0x0000
00000056:000000a0:0008 LOP_SET_BITS      LCX_DIFF_MAP   0000:00000000  0x0000
00000056:000000a0:0009 LOP_DELTA_SYSIND  LCX_CLUSTERED  0000:00002adf  0x0000
00000056:000000a0:000a LOP_COMMIT_XACT   LCX_NULL       0000:00002adf  0x0000
```

```
(Results - second group of columns)

Log Record Length Previous LSN           Flag Bits Object Name
----------------- ---------------------- --------- --------------------------
60                00000000:00000000:0000 0x0200    NULL
56                00000000:00000000:0000 0x0000    dbo.ALLOCATION (99)
76                00000056:000000a0:0001 0x0200    dbo.ExampleAddresses (98019
76                00000056:000000a0:0003 0x0200    dbo.ExampleAddresses (98019
76                00000056:000000a0:0004 0x0200    dbo.ExampleAddresses (98019
76                00000056:000000a0:0005 0x0200    dbo.ExampleAddresses (98019
76                00000056:000000a0:0006 0x0200    dbo.ExampleAddresses (98019
56                00000000:00000000:0000 0x0000    dbo.ALLOCATION (99)
80                00000056:000000a0:0007 0x0200    dbo.sysindexes (2)
52                00000056:000000a0:0001 0x0200    NULL
```

The entire output of the query is in the file Sample output of fn_dblog.txt in the chapter's download directory. It includes all columns and rows shown above as well as a few rows that remained in my log after I did the backup that preceded the update to `ExampleAddresses`.

There's no documentation of the format of a log record in Books Online, and I haven't been able to locate it anywhere else. However, there are a few obvious items of information in the log. `LOP_BEGIN_XACT` and `LOP_COMMIT_XACT` mark the beginning and ending of the implicit transaction that surrounds the statement. Each `LOP_MODIFY_ROW` operation on the object `dbo.ExampleAddresses` is an update to a single row. Beyond that, you're pretty much on your own.

Now that you know how to use `fn_dblog`, why would you? It could be used to analyze the patterns of updates or the frequency. Or you could use it to go back and check on all the updates that happened to a particular table.

There are products that produce database audit trails that use `fn_dblog` to ensure that they capture everything in the log. Microsoft has briefed these companies about the meaning of the output columns.

Before we move on, try `fn_dblog` in another database. Here's a script to try it in pubs:

```
-- Take a look at fn_dblog from pubs
USE pubs
GO

SELECT * from ::fn_dblog(NULL, NULL)
GO

(Results – omitted)
```

The results are different than when run in TSQLUDFS. System UDFs get their data from the database in which they are run, rather than the database in which they are defined. That lets them be defined just once and used in any script, assuming that the tables that they refer to exist in the database being queried. In the case of fn_dblog, it's querying information that is internal to SQL Server. It's not in base tables.

Most of the issues that I envision resolving with fn_dblog can also be resolved with the SQL Profiler. The difference is that fn_dblog can look back into the log, whereas the SQL Profiler can only capture data while it's running.

fn_mssharedversion

This function returns a part of the server version that's used to create a directory in the path used to set up the current instance of SQL Server. This is used by the SQL Server installation. It's how the directory named 80 ends up just below the Microsoft SQL Server directory in Program Files.

If you need information about the version of SQL Server, you're better off using the SERVERPROPERTY function, as in this query:

```
-- Get the product version
SELECT SERVERPROPERTY ('ProductVersion') as ProductVersion
GO

(Results)

ProductVersion
------------------------------
8.00.760
```

SERVERPROPERTY takes many other arguments. It serves as the source of data for some of the library functions such as udf_Instance_InfoTAB and udf_Instance_EditionName. Both of these UDFs are better sources of information than fn_mssharedversion.

fn_replinttobitstring

This function converts an integer to a 32-character string of ones and zeros that represent the bit pattern of the integer. It's the complement to fn_replbitstringtoint, which is documented next in this chapter. The syntax of the call is:

fn_replinttobitstring (@INT)

@INT is any int or number that can be converted to an int. It is typically used to hold a bit field.

The return value of fn_replinttobitstring is a char(32) string of ones and zeros. Each character position represents one bit of the int. Here are two examples:

```
-- Sample queries for fn_replinttobitstring
SELECT fn_replinttobitstring (26) as [26 in binary]
     , fn_replinttobitstring (-1) as [-1]
GO

(Results)

26 in binary                     -1
-------------------------------- --------------------------------
00000000000000000000000000011010 11111111111111111111111111111111

SELECT fn_replinttobitstring (0x8FFFFFFF) as [Most positive number]
     , fn_replinttobitstring (0x80000000) as [Most negative number]
GO

(Results)

Most positive number             Most negative number
-------------------------------- --------------------------------
01111111111111111111111111111111 10000000000000000000000000000000
```

The numbers in the last query that start with 0x are T-SQL's "binary" constants. I've put the word binary in quotes because T-SQL's binary constants are actually hexadecimal constants.

The TSQLUDFS database has three functions that are very similar to fn_replinttobitstring but work in slightly different ways: udf_BitS_FromInt, udf_BitS_FromSmallint, and udf_BitS_FromTinyint. In addition to taking a numeric argument, they each take a BIT argument that requests that leading zeros be eliminated.

udf_BitS_FromInt is shown in Listing 18.2. It's based on fn_replinttobitstring but handles the elimination of leading zeros to produce a more readable and compact result. Many bit fields use only the first few low-order bits.

Listing 18.2: udf_BitS_FromInt

```
CREATE  FUNCTION dbo.udf_BitS_FromInt (

    @INT int -- the input value
  , @TrimLeadingZerosBIT bit = 0 --  1 to trim leading 0s.
)   RETURNS varchar(32) -- String of 1s and 0s representing @INT
    -- No schemabinding due to use of system UDF.
/*
* Translates an int into a corresponding 32-character string
* of 1s and 0s. It will optionally trim leading zeros.
*
* Related Functions: fn_replinttobitstring used in this UDF.
* Common Usage:
select dbo.udf_BitS_FromInt(26, 0) as [With leading 0s]
     , dbo.udf_BitS_FromInt(26, 1) as [Sans leading 0s]
* Test:
PRINT 'Test 1    ' + CASE WHEN '11010' =
  dbo.udf_BitS_FromInt (26, 1) THEN 'Worked' ELSE 'ERROR' END
***************************************************************/
```

System UDFs

```
AS BEGIN

    DECLARE @WorkingVariable varchar(32)
          , @PosOfFirst1 int

    SELECT @WorkingVariable = fn_replinttobitstring (@INT)

    IF @TrimLeadingZerosBIT=1 BEGIN

       SET @PosOfFirst1 = CHARINDEX( '1', @WorkingVariable, 1)

       SET @WorkingVariable =
            CASE @PosOfFirst1
                 WHEN 1 THEN @WorkingVariable -- Negative Number
                 WHEN 0 THEN '0' -- return at least 1 of the 0s
                 ELSE SUBSTRING (@WorkingVariable
                               , @PosOfFirst1
                               , 32 - @PosOfFirst1 + 1)
                 END
    END -- IF

    RETURN @WorkingVariable
END
```

Here's a query that shows the difference between fn_replintotbitstring and udf_BitS_FromInt.

```
-- Show difference between fn_replinttobitstring and udf_BitS_FromInt
SELECT fn_replinttobitstring (37) as [37 from fn_replinttobitstring]
     , dbo.udf_BitS_FromInt (37, 1) [37 from udf_BitS_FromInt]
GO

(Results)

37 from fn_replinttobitstring    37 from udf_BitS_FromInt
-------------------------------- --------------------------------
00000000000000000000000000100101 100101
```

udf_BitS_FromSmallint and udf_BitS_FromTinyint are not listed here. You'll find them in the TSQLUDFS database. They're very similar to udf_BitS_FromInt, as these queries illustrate:

```
-- udf_BitS_FromSmallint and udf_BitS_FromTinyint
SELECT dbo.udf_BitS_FromSmallint (255, 0) as [Small 255 cum 0s]
     , dbo.udf_BitS_FromSmallint (255, 1) as [Small 255 no 0s]
     , dbo.udf_BitS_FromSmallint (-3, 0) as [Small -3 no 0s]
     , dbo.udf_BitS_FromSmallint (255, 1) as [Small 255 no 0s]
GO

(Results)

Small 255 cum 0s Small 255 no 0s  Small -3 no 0s   Small 255 no 0s
---------------- ---------------- ---------------- ----------------
0000000011111111 11111111         1111111111111101 11111111


SELECT dbo.udf_BitS_FromTinyInt (26, 0) as [Tiny 26]
     , dbo.udf_BitS_FromTinyInt (255, 0) as [Tiny 255]
     , dbo.udf_BitS_FromTinyInt (127, 0) as [Tiny 127]
```

```
     , dbo.udf_BitS_FromTinyInt (127, 1) as [Tiny 127 no 0s]
GO

(Results)

Tiny 26  Tiny 255 Tiny 127 Tiny 127 no 0s
-------- -------- -------- --------------
00011010 11111111 01111111 1111111
```

Back in the days of $25,000 disk drives, we used to pack bits as tight as sardines. Functions like `udf_Bits_FromInt` and `fn_replinttobitstring` would have come in handy for examining the data. These days, I prefer to spread my data out rather than use bit fields. If you must use them, you might also want to take a look at the function `udf_Bit_Int_NthBit`, which plucks individual bits from an `int` that's being used as a bit field.

Once the bit field is converted to a string, there are times when it has to be converted back to an integer type. The next UDF takes care of that.

fn_replbitstringtoint

In the previous section we've seen how the bit fields used by many system functions can be turned into more human-readable strings using `fn_replinttobitstring` or the alternative UDFs. `fn_replbitstringtoint` is the complement of `fn_replinttobitstring`, as it converts a string that holds a 32-bit bit pattern back into the corresponding `int`. It's a scalar system UDF with the syntax:

`fn_replbitstringtoint (@Bitstring)`

@Bitstring is a 32-character string of ones and zeros that represent the bits of an integer.

For example, `'00000000000000000000000000000010'` represents 2.

Some examples of using `fn_replbitstringtoint` are:

```
-- examples of fn_replbitstringtoint
SELECT fn_replbitstringtoint ('00000000000000000000000000000010') as [2]
     , fn_replbitstringtoint ('11111111111111111111111111111111') as [-1]
     , fn_replbitstringtoint ('10000000000000000000000000000000')
                                              as [Most negative number]
     , fn_replbitstringtoint ('01111111111111111111111111111111')
                                              as [Most positive number]
GO

(Results)

2           -1          Most negative number Most positive number
----------- ----------- -------------------- --------------------
2           -1          -2147483648          2147483647
```

This function doesn't handle missing leading zeros well. In fact, it assumes that they're missing trailing zeros. That's not a very useful interpretation, as shown in this query:

```
-- what happens when there are missing leading zeros
SELECT fn_replbitstringtoint ('00000000000000000000000000001100') as [12]
     , fn_replbitstringtoint ('1100') as [12 without leading zeros]
GO

(Results)

12          12 without leading zeros
----------- ------------------------
12          -1073741824
```

The functions udf_BitS_ToINT, udf_BitS_ToSmallint, and udf_BitS_To-Tinyint work better than fn_replbitstringtoint. They each assume missing leading zeros and return their respective data types. Since this type of bit string is usually used as a way to represent bit fields as opposed to numbers, leading ones are not propagated to the left to form negative numbers. Each of these three functions has a slightly different implementation.

udf_BitS_ToINT, which is not listed in this book, pads the input on the left with zeros and then passes the result to fn_replbitstringtoint to complete the conversion. This query shows how it handles leading zeros in a way different from fn_replbitstringtoint:

```
-- try out udf_BitS_ToINT and compare with fn_replbitstringtoint
SELECT dbo.udf_BitS_ToINT ('00000000000000000000000000011010') as [26]
     , dbo.udf_BitS_ToINT ('11111111111111111111111111111111') as [-1]
     , dbo.udf_BitS_ToINT ('01111111111111111111111111111111')
                                           as [Most positive number]
     , dbo.udf_BitS_ToINT ('11010') as [26 without leading 0s]
     ,    fn_replbitstringtoint ('11010') as [fn_replbitstringtoint]
GO

(Results)

26      -1      Most positive number 26 without leading 0s fn_replbitstringtoint
------- ------- -------------------- --------------------- ---------------------
     26      -1           2147483647                    26            -805306368
```

udf_BitS_ToSmallint is shown in Listing 18.3. It uses a technique that's similar to the one used in fn_replbitstringtoint. However, the bitwise operators | and & work on 32-bit values. To propagate the negative sign to 32 bits, it's translated into 0XFFFF8000.

Listing 18.3: udf_BitS_ToSmallint

```
CREATE  FUNCTION dbo.udf_BitS_ToSmallint (

    @BitString varchar(16) -- Bit pattern for the input
)   RETURNS smallint -- Equivalent smallint
/*
* Converts a bit string of up to 16 one and zero characters into
* the corresponding smallint. The string is padded on the left to
* fill in any missing zeros.
*
* Related Functions: the undocumented built-in function
*     fn_replbitstringtoint is similar but it works on an int and
* does not handle missing leading zeros the same way.
*
* Example:
SELECT dbo.udf_BitS_ToSmallint('1101') -- should return 13
*
* Test:
PRINT 'Test 1   13        ' + CASE WHEN 13=
dbo.udf_BitS_ToSmallint ('1101') THEN 'Worked' ELSE 'ERROR' END
PRINT 'Test 2   -1        ' + CASE WHEN -1=dbo.udf_BitS_ToSmallint
             ('1111111111111111') THEN 'Worked' ELSE 'ERROR' END
PRINT 'Test 3 bigest smallint ' + CASE WHEN 32767=
                 dbo.udf_BitS_ToSmall  ('0111111111111111')
                                 THEN 'Worked' ELSE 'ERROR' END
***************************************************************/
AS BEGIN
DECLARE @Number int -- We have to work with an INT
      , @sWorking varchar(16)


SELECT @number = 0
      ,@sWorking = RIGHT ('0000000000000000' + @BitString, 16)

IF (SUBSTRING(@sWorking, 1,1) = '1') SELECT @number = @number | 0xFFFF8000
IF (SUBSTRING(@sWorking, 2,1) = '1') SELECT @number = @number | 0x00004000
IF (SUBSTRING(@sWorking, 3,1) = '1') SELECT @number = @number | 0x00002000
IF (SUBSTRING(@sWorking, 4,1) = '1') SELECT @number = @number | 0x00001000
IF (SUBSTRING(@sWorking, 5,1) = '1') SELECT @number = @number | 0x00000800
IF (SUBSTRING(@sWorking, 6,1) = '1') SELECT @number = @number | 0x00000400
IF (SUBSTRING(@sWorking, 7,1) = '1') SELECT @number = @number | 0x00000200
IF (SUBSTRING(@sWorking, 8,1) = '1') SELECT @number = @number | 0x00000100
IF (SUBSTRING(@sWorking, 9,1) = '1') SELECT @number = @number | 0x00000080
IF (SUBSTRING(@sWorking,10,1) = '1') SELECT @number = @number | 0x00000040
IF (SUBSTRING(@sWorking,11,1) = '1') SELECT @number = @number | 0x00000020
IF (SUBSTRING(@sWorking,12,1) = '1') SELECT @number = @number | 0x00000010
IF (SUBSTRING(@sWorking,13,1) = '1') SELECT @number = @number | 0x00000008
IF (SUBSTRING(@sWorking,14,1) = '1') SELECT @number = @number | 0x00000004
IF (SUBSTRING(@sWorking,15,1) = '1') SELECT @number = @number | 0x00000002
IF (SUBSTRING(@sWorking,16,1) = '1') SELECT @number = @number | 0x00000001

RETURN CAST (@number as smallint)
END
```

Here's a query that illustrates how it works in comparison to `fn_replbitstringtoint`:

```
-- try out udf_BitS_ToSmallint and compare with fn_replbitstringtoint
SELECT dbo.udf_BitS_ToSmallint ('0000000000011010') as [26]
     , dbo.udf_BitS_ToSmallint ('11010') as [26 sans leading 0s]
     , dbo.udf_BitS_ToSmallint ('1111111111111111') as [-1]
     , dbo.udf_BitS_ToSmallint ('0111111111111111')
                                              as [Most positive number]
     , dbo.udf_BitS_ToSmallint ('1000000000000000')
                                              as [Most negative number]
GO

(Results)

26     26 sans Leading 0s -1     Most positive number Most negative number
------ ------------------ ------ -------------------- --------------------
26     26                 -1     32767                -32768
```

`udf_BitS_ToTinyint` is shown in Listing 18.4. `tinyint` doesn't have negative values, so there's no issue of propagating the negative sign. To make the function slightly more efficient, the strategy for handling each bit is changed. Instead of having an `IF` statement for each character in the input, each `IF` statement is turned into a `CASE` expression, and they're bitwise `OR`'ed together. That turns what would have been 16 statements (one `IF` and one `SELECT` for each input character) into one statement.

Listing 18.4: `udf_BitS_ToTinyint`

```
CREATE FUNCTION dbo.udf_BitS_ToTinyint (

    @BitString varchar(16) -- Bit pattern for the input
)   RETURNS TINYINT
    WITH SCHEMABINDING
/*
* Converts a bit string of up to 8 one and zero characters into
* the corresponding tinyint. The string is padded on the left to
* fill in any missing zeros.  The result is a value from 0 to
* 255.  There are no negative tinyint values.
*
* Related Functions: the undocumented built-in function
* fn_replbitstringtoint is similar but it works on an int and
* does not handle missing leading zeros the same way.
*
* Example:
select dbo.udf_Bits_ToTinyint('0101') -- should return 5
*
* Test:
PRINT 'Test 1   5       ' + CASE WHEN 5=
dbo.udf_Bits_ToTinyint ('0101') THEN 'Worked' ELSE 'ERROR' END
PRINT 'Test 2 bigest TINYINT ' + CASE WHEN 255=
                      dbo.udf_BitS_ToTinyint ('11111111')
                      THEN 'Worked' ELSE 'ERROR' END
***************************************************************/
AS BEGIN
```

```
DECLARE @Number int -- We have to work with an INT
      , @sWorking varchar(16)


SELECT @number = 0
      ,@sWorking = RIGHT ('00000000' + @BitString, 8)

SELECT @Number =
           CASE WHEN substring(@sWorking, 1,1) = '1' THEN 0x80 ELSE 0 END
         | CASE WHEN substring(@sWorking, 2,1) = '1' THEN 0x40 ELSE 0 END
         | CASE WHEN substring(@sWorking, 3,1) = '1' THEN 0x20 ELSE 0 END
         | CASE WHEN substring(@sWorking, 4,1) = '1' THEN 0x10 ELSE 0 END
         | CASE WHEN substring(@sWorking, 5,1) = '1' THEN 0x08 ELSE 0 END
         | CASE WHEN substring(@sWorking, 6,1) = '1' THEN 0x04 ELSE 0 END
         | CASE WHEN substring(@sWorking, 7,1) = '1' THEN 0x02 ELSE 0 END
         | CASE WHEN substring(@sWorking, 8,1) = '1' THEN 0x01 ELSE 0 END

RETURN CAST (@number as TINYINT)
END
```

This query illustrates `udf_BitS_ToTinyint` at work:

```
-- try out udf_BitS_ToTinyint and compare with fn_replbitstringtoint
SELECT dbo.udf_BitS_ToTinyint ('00011010') as [26]
     , dbo.udf_BitS_ToTinyint ('11010') as [26 sans leading 0s]
     , dbo.udf_BitS_ToTinyint ('11111111') as [255]
     , dbo.udf_BitS_ToTinyint ('01111111') AS [127]
     , dbo.udf_BitS_ToTinyint ('10000000')
                                          as [No negative numbers]
GO
```

(Results)

```
26   26 sans leading 0s 255  127  No negative numbers
---- ------------------ ---- ---- -------------------
26   26                 255  127  128
```

The three UDFs created in this section all work better than `fn_replbitstringtoint`, and I use them in preference to it. Along with the functions that convert numbers to bit strings, these functions make it pretty easy to use bit fields.

fn_replmakestringliteral

`fn_replmakestringliteral` accepts a string as input and turns its value into a Unicode string literal that is suitable for use in a SQL statement. The syntax of the call is:

`fn_replmakestringliteral (@string)`

@string is an `nvarchar(4000)` containing the name to be quoted.

System UDFs

The return value is also an nvarchar(4000), which contains @String surrounded by quotes and the leading N that indicates a Unicode string literal.

This query illustrates how fn_replmakestringliteral works:

```
-- Turn some characters into string literals
SELECT fn_replmakestringliteral (43) as [43]
     , fn_replmakestringliteral ('abcd') as [abcd]
     , fn_replmakestringliteral (N'ABCD') as [Unicode ABCD]
GO

(Results)

43          abcd         Unicode ABCD
---------- ----------- ---------------
N'43'       N'abcd'      N'ABCD'
```

This might be useful when writing code that writes SQL statements, but Listing 18.5 shows a function that I've found to be more useful. udf_SQL_VariantToStringConstant converts a sql_variant to a string that is the constant value for the sql_variant in SQL script. Be warned, however: It only works on a subset of the possible data types.

Listing 18.5: udf_SQL_VariantToStringConstant

```
CREATE FUNCTION udf_SQL_VariantToStringConstant (

    @InVal sql_variant -- input variant
) RETURNS nvarchar(4000) -- String constant
/*
* Converts a value with the type sql_variant to a string constant
* that is the same as the constant would appear in a SQL
* statement.
*
* Example:
select dbo.udf_SQL_VariantToStringConstant
                (CONVERT(datetime, '1918-11-11 11:11:11', 120))
* Test:
PRINT 'Test 1 date    ' + case when '''1918-11-11 11:11:00.000'''
                = dbo.udf_SQL_VariantToStringConstant
                    (CONVERT(datetime, '1918-11-11 11:11', 120))
                          THEN 'Worked' else 'Error' end
PRINT 'Test 2 Nstring ' + CASE WHEN 'N''ABCD''' =
                  dbo.udf_SQL_VariantToStringConstant (N'ABCD')
                          THEN 'Worked' else 'Error' end
****************************************************************/
AS BEGIN

DECLARE @Result as nvarchar(4000)
      , @BaseType sysname
      , @Precision int    -- # digits of the numeric base type
      , @Scale int -- # of digits to the right of the decimal of
                -- numeric base btypes
      , @TotalBytes int -- Storage consumed
      , @Collation sysname -- the collation name of the variant
```

```
    , @MaxLength int -- Maximum data type length

-- Get the properties of the variant that we'll need.
SELECT @BaseType  = CAST(SQL_VARIANT_PROPERTY
                            (@InVal, 'BaseType') as sysname)
     , @Precision = CAST(SQL_VARIANT_PROPERTY (@InVal, 'Precision') as int)
     , @Scale     = CAST(SQL_VARIANT_PROPERTY (@InVal, 'Scale') as int)
     , @MaxLength = CAST(SQL_VARIANT_PROPERTY (@InVal, 'MaxLength') as int)

IF @InVal IS NULL RETURN 'NULL'

IF @BaseType in ('char', 'varchar') BEGIN
     SET @Result = N'''' + CAST(@InVal as nvarchar(3998)) + N''''
     END
ELSE IF @BaseType in ('nchar',  'nvarchar') BEGIN
     SET @Result = N'N''' + CAST(@InVal as nvarchar(3998)) + N''''
     END
ELSE IF @BaseType in ('smallint', 'int') BEGIN
     SET @Result = CAST(@InVal as nvarchar(128))
     END
ELSE IF @BaseType in ('smallmoney', 'money', 'numeric', 'decimal'
                    , 'real', 'float') BEGIN
     SET @Result = CAST(@InVal as nvarchar(128))
     -- If there is no decimal point, add one with a 0 after it
     IF charindex(N'.', @Result) =0
         SET @Result = @Result + N'.0'
     END
ELSE IF @BaseType in ('datetime', 'smalldatetime') BEGIN
     SET @Result = '''' + CONVERT(nvarchar(128), @InVal, 121) + ''''
     END
ELSE
     SET @Result = CAST (@InVal as nvarchar(3990)) + N' (' + @BaseType + N')'

RETURN @Result
END
```

This query illustrates udf_SQL_VariantToStringConstant at work:

```
-- Show various constants from udf_SQL_VariantToStringConstant
SELECT dbo.udf_SQL_VariantToStringConstant (getdate()) as [Current Date/Time]
     , dbo.udf_SQL_VariantToStringConstant ('ASDF;LKJ') as [Char]
     , dbo.udf_SQL_VariantToStringConstant (N'ASDF;LKJ') as [NChar]
     , dbo.udf_SQL_VariantToStringConstant (16) as [int]
     , dbo.udf_SQL_VariantToStringConstant (CAST (37 as numeric (18,5)))
             as [Numeric (18,5)]
GO
```

(Results)

```
Current Date/Time           Char         NChar        int   Numeric (18,5)
-------------------------- ------------ ------------ ----- --------------
'2002-10-03 09:56:32.403'  'ASDF;LKJ'   N'ASDF;LKJ'  16    37.00000
```

In the past I've used this function to create SQL statements. For example, this query creates INSERT statements for the ExampleDataTypes table that was created with one record to demonstrate this function:

```
-- Demonstrate udf_SQL_VariantToStringConstant (c_) + ', '
SELECT 'INSERT INTO ExampleDataTypes VALUES('
     + dbo.udf_SQL_VariantToStringConstant (c_int) + ', '
     + dbo.udf_SQL_VariantToStringConstant (c_datetime) + ', '
     + dbo.udf_SQL_VariantToStringConstant (c_char3) + ', '
     + dbo.udf_SQL_VariantToStringConstant (c_varchar) + ', '
     + dbo.udf_SQL_VariantToStringConstant (c_nvarchar) + ', '
     + dbo.udf_SQL_VariantToStringConstant (c_money) + ', '
     + dbo.udf_SQL_VariantToStringConstant (c_numeric_18_5)
     + ') ' as [Insert Script]
    FROM ExampleDataTypes
GO
```

(Results - Word wrapped)

```
Insert Script
-------------------------------------------------------------------------------
INSERT INTO ExampleDataTypes VALUES(1, '1911-11-11 11:11:11.000', 'abc',
                                'acbdef', N'ABCDEF', 3.17, 1234.56789)
```

This comes in handy from time to time. Be careful though: It's not a complete solution to writing INSERT scripts for a table. That requires handling situations such as computed columns, timestamps, identity columns, text, ntext, images, and other special columns.

fn_replquotename

This function turns its string argument into a name surrounded by brackets, which is suitable for use as a name in a SQL statement. The syntax of the call is:

```
fn_replquotename (@string)
```

@String is an nvarchar(1998). It's the name to be quoted.

The return value for the function is an nvarchar(4000) string that includes the name surrounded by brackets. In the process, any right brackets (]) in the name are doubled up so they will remain part of the name.

Here's a sample:

```
-- sample quoted name
SELECT fn_replquotename('My column name with embedded spaces') as [Quoted Name]
GO
```

(Results)

```
Quoted Name
-------------------------------------------------------------------------------
[My column name with embedded spaces]
```

Although it's impossible to execute dynamic SQL in a user-defined function, you can use UDFs to construct all or part of a dynamic SQL statement that will be used elsewhere. fn_replquotename can help.

That help is used in the function udf_View_ColumnList, shown in Listing 18.6. It produces the select list for all the columns in a view. Each column name is bracketed in case it's a keyword, starts with a number, contains embedded spaces, or contains special characters.

Listing 18.6: udf_View_ColumnList

```
CREATE  FUNCTION dbo.udf_View_ColumnList (

    @ViewName sysname -- Name of the view
  , @Prefix sysname = NULL -- Prefix to prepend to each column
      -- NULL indicates no prefix. Brackets can be used around
      -- prefix. Don't include the period that separates the
      -- prefix from the column name. Often used for an alias.
  , @Owner sysname = NULL -- owner name, NULL for none
     )
RETURNS nvarchar(4000) -- Column names quoted.
/*
* Creates a quoted list of the columns in a view, suitable for
* creation of a dynamic SQL statement.
* Depends on INFORMATION_SCHEMA.VIEW_COLUMN_USAGE. This prevents
* use with views with only one column.
*
* Example:
select dbo.udf_View_ColumnList(
'ExampleViewWithKeywordColumnNames', null, null)
****************************************************************/
AS BEGIN

DECLARE @Result nvarchar(4000) -- the result
      , @view_catalog sysname -- a database name
      , @view_schema sysname -- owner
      , @column_name sysname -- column
      , @FirstColumnBIT BIT -- has the first column been added.

DECLARE ColumnCursor CURSOR FAST_FORWARD FOR
    SELECT VIEW_CATALOG, VIEW_SCHEMA, COLUMN_NAME
    FROM INFORMATION_SCHEMA.VIEW_COLUMN_USAGE
    WHERE VIEW_NAME = @Viewname
       and (@Owner IS NULL
           or @Owner = VIEW_SCHEMA)

SELECT @Result = ''
     , @FirstColumnBIT = 1 -- No separator after the 1st entry.

OPEN ColumnCursor -- Open the cursor and fetch the first result
FETCH ColumnCursor INTO @view_catalog, @view_schema, @column_name

WHILE @@Fetch_status = 0 BEGIN
    -- add the name of the Column and separator, if needed.
    IF @FirstColumnBIT = 1 BEGIN
        SET @Result =
          + CASE WHEN @Prefix is NOT NULL and LEN(@Prefix) > 0
                 THEN @Prefix + '.'
                 ELSE ''
                 END
          + fn_replquotename (@column_name)
        SET @FirstColumnBIT = 0
```

```
        END
    ELSE
       SELECT @Result = @Result + ', '
           + CASE WHEN @Prefix is NOT NULL and LEN(@Prefix) > 0
                  THEN @Prefix + '.'
                  ELSE ''
                  END
           + fn_replquotename (@column_name)

    FETCH ColumnCursor INTO @view_catalog
                          , @view_schema, @column_name
END -- of the WHILE LOOP

-- Clean up the cursor
CLOSE ColumnCursor
DEALLOCATE ColumnCursor

RETURN @Result
END
```

Here's an example that uses the output from `udf_View_ColumnList` to create a `SELECT` statement on the view and then dynamically execute the statement:

```
-- Construct a dynamic SQL statement to get all the columns from a view
DECLARE @view sysname, @SQLStatement nvarchar(4000)-- our temporary view
SET @view = 'ExampleViewWithKeywordColumnNames'
SET @SQLStatement = 'SELECT ' + dbo.udf_View_ColumnList(@view, null, null)
                    + ' FROM ' + @view
SELECT @SqlStatement as [SQL Statement]
EXECUTE (@SqlStatement)
GO

(Results)

SQL Statement
------------------------------------------------------------------------------
SELECT [END], [VALUES], [CROSS] FROM ExampleViewWithKeywordColumnNames

END        VALUES     CROSS
---------- ---------- ----------
```

There are two resultsets returned from the batch. The first one is the SQL statement. The second one is produced by executing the SQL statement dynamically. Since `ExampleViewWithKeywordColumnNames` is a view on `ExampleTableWithKeywordColumnNames`, which contains no rows, the second resultset is empty.

The importance of quoting the column names is easy to illustrate. Trying to execute the `SELECT` created in the previous query without quoting the column names gives an error. Try it:

```
-- Select with keywords as column names.
SELECT END, VALUES, CROSS FROM ExampleViewWithKeywordColumnNames
GO

(Results)

Server: Msg 156, Level 15, State 1, Line 2
Incorrect syntax near the keyword 'END'.
```

fn_replquotestring is a system UDF. As I mentioned, there are a few UDFs in master that are owned by **dbo**. The next one fits that bill.

fn_varbintohexstr

This function can be used to convert almost any data to a hex representation. The syntax for the function is:

```
master.dbo.fn_varbintohexstr (@Input VarBinary(8000))
```

@input is a varbinary(8000). There is no automatic conversion to that type. That implies that unless the input starts out as varbinary, you'll have to CAST it to varbinary(8000). Of course, that's not really difficult; the CAST or CONVERT functions do the conversion for you.

fn_varbintohexstr is not a real system UDF. It's owned by **dbo** in the master database, not by system_function_schema. That makes it an ordinary UDF that is created in master. Thus, the qualifiers master.dbo are required when using it outside of the master database. In master, dbo.fn_varbintohexstr is sufficient.

The length of @Input is misleading. The function returns a nvarchar(4000) string that represents the input as hex. Each byte of the input is going to be turned into two hex characters of Unicode output. Effectively, the input is limited to 2,000 bytes.

A pretty simple example is:

```
-- Simple use of fn_varbintohexstr
SELECT master.dbo.fn_varbintohexstr(CAST('ABCD' as varbinary)) as Hex
GO

(Results)

Hex
-------------------------------------------------------------------------------
0x41424344
```

It's time to drag out your ASCII charts and check to be sure it's correct. (Don't worry—I checked, and it's correct.) Here are some more data types:

System UDFs

```
-- Show a variety of data types being converted to varbinary
     SELECT N'   ASCII Characters  ABCD ->'
       + master.dbo.fn_varbintohexstr(CAST('ABCD' as varbinary)) + '<-' as Demo
UNION SELECT N' Unicode Characters  ABCD ->'
          + master.dbo.fn_varbintohexstr(CAST(N'ABCD' as varbinary)) + '<-'
UNION SELECT N'            Integer 100 ->'
          + master.dbo.fn_varbintohexstr(CAST(100 as varbinary)) + '<-'
UNION SELECT N'                  BIT 1 ->'
      + master.dbo.fn_varbintohexstr(CAST(CAST (1 as BIT) as varbinary)) + '<-'
UNION SELECT N'      Numeric (18,3) 100 ->'
          + master.dbo.fn_varbintohexstr
                 (CAST(CAST (100 as numeric(18,3)) as varbinary)) + '<-'
UNION SELECT N'              float 100 ->'
          + master.dbo.fn_varbintohexstr
                  (CAST(CAST (100 as float) as varbinary)) + '<-'
GO

(Results)

Demo
------------------------------------------------------------------------------
                   BIT 1 ->0x01<-
               float 100 ->0x4059000000000000<-
             Integer 100 ->0x00000064<-
      Numeric (18,3) 100 ->0x12030001a0860100<-
  ASCII Characters  ABCD ->0x41424344<-
 Unicode Characters  ABCD ->0x4100420043004400<-
```

One of the useful things that can be done with `fn_varbintohexstring` is produce a readable hex dump of a string. It can help you find embedded carriage returns or accented characters that may not be displayed correctly elsewhere.

There are more undocumented UDFs. In this section, we've seen a few, but I have neither the time nor the space to write about them. Every once in a while I discuss one in the Transact-SQL User-Defined Function of the Week newsletter. You'll find it, along with the newsletter archives, on my web site at http://www.NovickSoftware.com.

Summary

There are many useful undocumented UDFs. However, you may or may not decide to use any of them due to their undocumented status. After all, they could be changed by Microsoft in any service pack.

Mitigating any risk is the fact that the text for the functions is available. This chapter has shown you two places to find the `CREATE FUNCTION` script for any of the undocumented UDFs:

- In `master.dbo.syscomments` by using the `udf_Func_UndocSystemUDFtext` function
- In SQL files that are used during SQL Server installation

If you really want to use one of these functions, you might want to copy the script, give it your own name, and make a normal UDF out of it. What's more, you'll be able to create it using the `WITH SCHEMABINDING` clause if there's any reason to use it in a schemabound object.

What you lose by turning a system UDF into a normal UDF is the special status that system UDFs enjoy. That status can be important enough for you to want to create your own system UDFs. For example, when referencing scalar UDFs, such as `fn_chariswhitespace`, there was no need to use the owner name prefix when referencing the UDF. That's one small advantage. The method for creating a system UDF is the subject of the next and final chapter.

19

Creating a System UDF

The system user-defined functions can be used from any database and invoked without referring to their database or owner. Those are powerful advantages in simplifying the function's distribution. The chapters in Part II have discussed the system UDFs distributed with SQL Server, both documented and undocumented. You can make your own system UDFs using the procedure outlined in this chapter.

Be aware that the procedure outlined here is not supported by Microsoft and might cease working in some future release or service pack of SQL Server. That might cause any SQL that uses the function to stop working until all references to the UDF can be changed.

Note:

If this technique stops working, there is a quick fix: Create the function in every database in which it is used and change all references to any scalar functions to include the owner name.

As mentioned earlier, system UDFs have common characteristics that we'll mimic as we create our own system UDFs:

- The name always begins with `fn_`.
- The name consists only of lowercase letters.
- The owner is `system_function_schema`.
- They're in the master database.

For a function to be available in all databases, it must have all of these characteristics. Any deviations either prevent the function from being created or leave you with an ordinary UDF.

Previous chapters showed how the special status of system UDFs grant them additional capabilities not shared by ordinary UDFs. Chapter 14 showed the special syntax that some system UDFs use. This is pretty much off limits to you and me and shouldn't be touched. Other chapters, including Chapter 18, showed how system UDFs are referenced differently than normal UDFs. The double colon syntax for system UDFs that return tables is unique to system UDFs. Also, scalar system UDFs aren't required to include the owner name every time they are used.

This chapter highlights a third difference: Table references in system UDFs are made to tables in the database in which the function is run, not the database in which the function is created, which is always master. The difference is necessary in order to make any general-purpose functions that have table references.

Of course, any table references must be to tables that exist in the database where the UDF is run. The most likely candidates are the set of system tables that SQL Server puts into every database that it creates.

Before we take a look at how a system UDF behaves, let's start by examining how an ordinary UDF that has table references works when it is run from different databases. It's the contrast between the two types of UDFs that really shows the differences between them.

Where Do UDFs Get Their Data?

For an example, let's start with the function `udf_Tbl_COUNT`, which was created in the TSQLUDFS database and is shown in Listing 19.1. It accesses the `sysobjects` system table to produce a count of the number of user tables in the database. The advantage of using a system table rather than a user table for a system UDF is that there is a group of system tables that exist in every database. `sysobjects` is one of those tables.

Listing 19.1: `udf_Tbl_COUNT`

```
CREATE   FUNCTION dbo.udf_Tbl_COUNT (

    @table_name_pattern sysname = NULL -- NULL for all
          -- or a pattern that works with the LIKE operator
)   RETURNS int -- number of user tables fitting the pattern
/*
* Returns the number of user tables in the database that match
* @table_name_pattern
*
* Example:
select dbo.udf_Tbl_COUNT(NULL) -- count all user tables
select dbo.udf_Tbl_COUNT('Currency%') -- tbls in currency group.
****************************************************************/
AS BEGIN

    DECLARE @Result int -- count

    SELECT @Result=COUNT(*)
        FROM sysobjects
        WHERE TYPE='U'
             and (@table_name_pattern is NULL
                   or [name] LIKE @table_name_pattern)
```

```
    RETURN @Result

END
```

Let's test this function. The first test should be performed in the TSQLUDFS database where the function was created:

```
-- Move to TSQLUDFS and try udf_Tbl_COUNT
USE TSQLUDFS
GO

SELECT dbo.udf_Tbl_COUNT(default) as [All Tables]
     , dbo.udf_Tbl_COUNT('Currency%') [Currency Tables]
GO

(Results)

All Tables  Currency Tables
----------- ---------------
         21               4
```

Those look like reasonable numbers. The answer you see when you run the query might be slightly different if tables have been added or dropped from the database since the book was published.

Now, move into the pubs database and use the function as it is defined in TSQLUDFS:

```
-- Move to pubs and try udf_Tbl_COUNT
USE pubs
GO

SELECT TSQLUDFS.dbo.udf_Tbl_COUNT(default) as [All Tables]
     , TSQLUDFS.dbo.udf_Tbl_COUNT('Currency%') [Currency Tables]
GO

(Results)

All Tables  Currency Tables
----------- ---------------
         21               4
```

The answer is the same! How can that be? Does pubs have 21 user tables, four of which begin with the string "Currency"? I don't think so. Let's check by running an equivalent query without using `udf_Tbl_COUNT`:

```
-- Get the tables in pubs without using udf_Tbl_COUNT
SELECT COUNT(*) as [All pubs Tables]
     , SUM (CASE WHEN name like 'Currency%' THEN 1 ELSE 0 END)
               as [Currency Tables in pubs]
    FROM sysobjects
    WHERE TYPE = 'U'
GO
```

(Results)

```
All pubs Tables Currency Tables in pubs
--------------- -----------------------
             11                       0
```

That looks better. You can verify it for yourself.

So what happened when we tried to use `udf_Tbl_COUNT` to count the tables in pubs? The answer is that a normal UDF refers to tables in the database in which it is created, not in the database in which it is invoked. `TSQLUDFS.dbo.udf_Tbl_COUNT` counts the rows in the `TSQLUDFS.dbo.sysobjects` table, not in `pubs.dbo.sysobjects` even when it's run in pubs. Had we recreated `udf_Tbl_COUNT` in pubs and removed the references to TSQLUDFS, we would have received the count that we expected.

Having to recreate a function in every database in which it is used makes code control difficult. What happens when the UDF is updated? It has to be updated in every database where it's defined. What if objects are schemabound to the UDF? The `WITH SCHEMABINDING` clause has to be removed before the UDF can be altered.

These types of code control issues must have been a factor that led Microsoft to create the special category of system UDFs in the first place. Creating your own system UDFs lets you avoid them also.

Creating the System UDF

All of the rules listed in the chapter introduction must be obeyed to create a system UDF. In addition, a simple protocol is needed to allow updates in master so that the function can be created. This section performs all the steps necessary to turn `udf_Tbl_COUNT` into `fn_tbl_count`, a system UDF that can be used from any database. The name `fn_tbl_count` obeys all the rules for system UDFs.

To create an object owned by `system_function_schema`, you must enable updates in the master database. This script gets the process started:

```
-- Reconfigure master to allow updates
USE master
GO

EXEC sp_configure 'allow updates', 1
GO

reconfigure with override
GO
```

Once updates are allowed in master, it's possible to run a CREATE FUNCTION script. The script to create fn_tbl_count is in the Chapter 19 Listing 0 Short Queries.sql file and shown in Listing 19.2. It's deliberately omitted from TSQLUDFS.

Listing 19.2: fn_tbl_count

```
SET QUOTED_IDENTIFIER ON
GO
SET ANSI_NULLS ON
GO

CREATE FUNCTION system_function_schema.fn_tbl_count (

    @table_name_pattern sysname = NULL -- NULL for all
          -- or a pattern that works with the LIKE operator
)   RETURNS int -- number of user tables fitting the pattern
/*
* Returns the number of user tables in the database that match
* @table_name_pattern
*
* Example:
select dbo.fn_tbl_count(NULL) -- count all user tables
select dbo.fn_tbl_count('Currency%') -- tbls in currency group.
****************************************************************/
AS BEGIN

    DECLARE @Result int -- count

    SELECT @Result=COUNT(*)
        FROM sysobjects
        WHERE TYPE='U'
             and (@table_name_pattern is NULL
                   or [name] LIKE @table_name_pattern)

    RETURN @Result

END
GO

GRANT EXEC on system_function_schema.fn_tbl_count to PUBLIC
GO
```

This script includes the SET statements for connection options that should be run before all UDFs are created and the GRANT permission is given to PUBLIC. These were omitted from most listings in the book since Chapter 2 because the functions are already created. In this listing, the function doesn't exist, and you must run the script to be able to execute any of the queries in the rest of the chapter.

Leaving master in a state where updates are allowed would be inviting trouble. After you create the UDF, you should turn off updates in master with this script:

```
-- Now turn updates back off
exec sp_configure 'allow updates', 0
go

RECONFIGURE WITH OVERRIDE
GO
```

Now that fn_tbl_count has been created as a system function, let's run it in master, TSQLUDFS, and pubs to see what answer it gives to the query we tried with udf_Tbl_COUNT. Start in master:

```
-- Use the new system UDF
SELECT fn_tbl_count (null) [All Tables]
     , fn_tbl_count ('Currency%') [Currency Tables]
GO

(Results)

All Tables  Currency Tables
----------- ---------------
         10               0
```

So master has a few user tables. You can use Enterprise Manager to check the answer on your system.

Next, move to TSQLUDFS and see if we get the same answer that was given by udf_Tbl_COUNT:

```
-- Try fn_tbl_count in TSQLUDFS
USE TSQLUDFS
GO

SELECT fn_tbl_count (null) [All Tables]
     , fn_tbl_count ('Currency%') [Currency Tables]
GO

(Results)

All Tables  Currency Tables
----------- ---------------
         21               4
```

fn_tbl_count gives us the same answer as TSQLUDFS.dbo.udf_Tbl_COUNT when run from inside TSQLUDFS.

The pièce de résistance is to run it in pubs and get the correct answer. Let's see:

```
-- Try fn_tbl_count in pubs
USE pubs
GO

SELECT fn_tbl_count (null) [All Tables]
     , fn_tbl_count ('Currency%') [Currency Tables]
GO
```

```
(Results)

All Tables  Currency Tables
----------- ---------------
         11               0
```

That's right! `fn_tbl_count` is a system UDF, and as such it uses the tables in the database in which it's invoked (in this case `pubs.dbo.sysobjects`) instead of the database in which it is created, master. If you don't want to copy the function definition into every database, that difference in behavior can make all the difference in the world.

Summary

This chapter and the other chapters in Part II showed the differences that the special status accorded to system UDFs provides. The most important difference illustrated here is the ability to reference tables in the database where the function is running. That, plus the simpler syntax for referencing them, makes system UDFs special.

The third major difference, the ability to run reserved SQL syntax, was discussed in Chapter 14. It should really be left to Microsoft. Using it in your own UDFs is asking for trouble.

If you find yourself creating your own system UDFs, please remember that the technique shown in this chapter is an unsupported feature of SQL Server and it might not always be around. Fortunately, there are workarounds if something were to change, but you might find yourself scrambling to fix your code.

This also concludes Part II, "System User-Defined Functions." The system UDFs are a useful feature introduced in SQL Server 2000. I expect that we'll see more of them in future versions of SQL Server.

This chapter is also the last in this book. I hope that you've found it interesting and useful in your work as a SQL Server developer or DBA. The accompanying library of functions is yours to use in your own projects. I hope you'll find a few functions that you can use and you have learned the techniques that you need to create your own.

Appendix A

Deterministic and Nondeterministic Functions

Although Books Online has information about which built-in functions are deterministic and which are nondeterministic, the information is a bit scattered. This appendix lists all of the built-in functions in SQL Server 2000 as of Service Pack 3. The Status column displays D for a built-in function that's always deterministic, N for built-in functions that are never deterministic, and C for built-in functions that are conditionally deterministic. The Comment column describes what factors make the difference when using the conditionally deterministic functions.

Table A.1: Built-in functions and their status as deterministic

Status	Function Name	Comment
D	ABS	
D	ACOS	
N	APP_NAME	
D	ASCII	
D	ASIN	
D	ATAN	
D	ATN2	
D	AVG	
D	BINARY_CHECKSUM	
C	CAST	Deterministic unless used with datetime, `smalldatetime`, or `sql_variant`. Use `CONVERT` with `datetime` and `smalldatetime` for a deterministic result.
D	CEILING	
D	CHAR	
N	CHARINDEX	

Status	Function Name	Comment
C	CHECKSUM	Deterministic, unless CHECKSUM(*)
D	CHECKSUM_AGG	
D	COALESCE	
N	COL_LENGTH	
N	COL_NAME	
N	COLUMNPROPERTY	
N	@@CONNECTIONS	
C	CONVERT	Always nondeterministic when used with `sql_variant`. Always deterministic when used with other types except `datetime` and `smalldatetime`. For the time formats, using a style format other than 0, 100, 9, or 109 makes the result deterministic. You can use the style when converting to a `datetime` or `smalldatetime`. See `udf_DT_NthDayInMon` for an example.
D	COS	
D	COT	
D	COUNT	
D	COUNT_BIG	
N	@@CPU_BUSY	
N	CURRENT_TIMESTAMP	
N	CURRENT_USER	
N	@@CURSOR_ROWS	
N	CURSOR_STATUS	
N	DATABASEPROPERTY	
N	DATABASEPROPERTYEX	
D	DATALENGTH	
D	DATEADD	
D	DATEDIFF	
N	@@DATEFIRST	
N	DATENAME	
D	DAY	
N	DB_ID	
N	DB_NAME	
N	@@DBTS	
D	DEGREES	
D	DIFFERENCE	
N	@@ERROR	
D	EXP	
N	@@FETCH_STATUS	

Status	Function Name	Comment
N	FILE_ID	
N	FILE_NAME	
N	FILEGROUP_ID	
N	FILEGROUP_NAME	
N	FILEGROUPPROPERTY	
N	FILEPROPERTY	
D	FLOOR	
N	fn_getsql	
N	fn_helpcollations	
N	fn_listextendedproperty	
N	fn_servershareddrives	
N	fn_trace_geteventinfo	
N	fn_trace_getfilterinfo	
N	fn_trace_getinfo	
N	fn_trace_gettable	
N	fn_virtualfilestats	
N	fn_virtualservernodes	
N	FORMATMESSAGE	
N	FULLTEXTCATALOGPROPERTY	
N	FULLTEXTSERVICEPROPERTY	
N	GETANSINULL	
N	GETDATE	
N	GETUTCDATE	
D	GROUPING	
N	HAS_DBACCESS	
N	HOST_ID	
N	HOST_NAME	
N	IDENT_INCR TEXTPTR	
N	IDENT_SEED	
N	IDENTITY	
N	@@IDENTITY	
N	@@IDLE	
N	INDEX_COL	
N	INDEXKEY_PROPERTY	
N	INDEXPROPERTY	
N	@@IO_BUSY	
N	IS_MEMBER	
N	IS_SRVROLEMEMBER	

Status	Function Name	Comment
C	ISDATE	Only deterministic if used with a `CONVERT` function call that specifies a style other than 0, 100, 9, or 109.
D	ISNULL	
D	ISNUMERIC	
N	@@LANGID	
N	@@LANGUAGE	
D	LEFT	
D	LEN	
N	@@LOCK_TIMEOUT	
D	LOG	
D	LOG10	
D	LOWER	
D	LTRIM	
D	MAX	
N	@@MAX_CONNECTIONS	
N	@@MAX_PRECISION	
D	MIN	
D	MONTH	
D	NCHAR	
N	@@NESTLEVEL	
N	NEWID	
D	NULLIF	
N	OBJECT_ID	
N	OBJECT_NAME	
N	OBJECTPROPERTY	
N	@@OPTIONS	
N	@@PACK_RECEIVED	
N	@@PACK_SENT	
N	@@PACKET_ERRORS	
D	PARSENAME	
N	PATINDEX	
N	PERMISSIONS	
D	POWER	
N	@@PROCID	
D	QUOTENAME	
D	RADIANS	
C	RAND	Only deterministic when a seed parameter is supplied.
N	@@REMSERVER	

Status	Function Name	Comment
D	REPLACE	
D	REPLICATE	
D	REVERSE	
D	RIGHT	
D	ROUND	
N	@@ROWCOUNT	
D	RTRIM	
N	@@SERVERNAME	
N	@@SERVICENAME	
N	SESSION_USER	
D	SIGN	
D	SIN	
D	SOUNDEX	
D	SPACE	
N	@@SPID	
N	SQL_VARIANT_PROPERTY	
D	SQRT	
D	SQUARE	
N	STATS_DATE	
D	STDEV	
D	STDEVP	
D	STR	
D	STUFF	
D	SUBSTRING	
D	SUM	
N	SUSER_SID	
N	SUSER_SNAME	
N	SYSTEM_USER	
D	TAN	
N	@@TEXTSIZE	
N	TEXTVALID	
N	@@TIMETICKS	
N	@@TOTAL_ERRORS	
N	@@TOTAL_READ	
N	@@TOTAL_WRITE	
N	@@TRANCOUNT	
N	TYPEPROPERTY	
D	UNICODE	
D	UPPER	
N	USER	

Status	Function Name	Comment
N	USER_ID	
N	USER_NAME	
D	VAR	
D	VARP	
N	@@VERSION	
D	YEAR	

Appendix B

Keyboard Shortcuts for Query Analyzer Debugging

Table B.1 shows the icons and the function key equivalents for the T-SQL debugger windows. Books Online shows the icons, but I try to use function keys instead.

Table B.1: Debugging icons and keyboard shortcuts

Icon	Keyboard Shortcut	Function
	F5 or Ctrl+E	GO
	F9	Toggle Breakpoint
	Ctrl+Shift+F9	Remove All Breakpoints
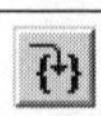	F11	Step Into
	F10	Step Over
	Shift+F11	Step Out
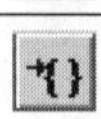	Shift+F10	Run to Cursor
	Ctrl+Shift+F5	Restart Debugging
	Shift+F5	Stop Debugging
		Auto Rollback
	F1	Help

Appendix C

Implementation Problems in SQL Server 2000 Involving UDFs

During the course of writing this book, I've encountered various problems in the implementation of SQL Server 2000. Some of these, particularly the first one, might be considered bugs. The status of the others is less clear. These problems were verified as of SQL Server 2000 Service Pack 3:

- sp_rename doesn't work correctly on a UDF. Although the function runs and the name is changed in sysobjects, the name isn't changed in syscomments. Thus, when the UDF is scripted, it's incorrect. This problem may also occur with other object types.
- If you have a check constraint on the return TABLE variable of a multistatement UDF, you can't alter the UDF. See udf_Example_Runtime_Error_Multistatement in the TSQLUDFS database.
- @@ERROR is not available to T-SQL code after an error is generated inside a UDF. See Chapter 5 for more details.
- COLUMNPROPERTY IsDeterministic doesn't work for computed columns in functions. It's NULL. See Chapter 9.
- COLUMNPROPERTY IsPrimaryKey doesn't work for columns returned by multistatement UDFs. See Chapter 9.
- OBJECTPROPERTY IsPrimaryKey and IsQuotedIdentOn return NULL for UDFs. See Chapter 9.
- SQL Server won't allow the use of sp_trace_generateevent in a UDF, even though it's an extended stored procedure.

- Running `sp_recompile` on a UDF doesn't force the recompile to happen. I realize that there are no statistics on UDFs, but there might be a reason to force a recompile. It doesn't look like the UDF is forced out of the cache.

User-Defined Functions

The following table lists all the UDFs included in the TSQLUDFS database, which is available in the download file. The page number, if any, is where the CREATE FUNCTION script for the UDF can be found in the book.

Function	Type	Page	Description
fn_tbl_count	SCALAR	417	User-created system UDF to return the number of user tables in the database in which it is run.
getcommaname	SCALAR	113	Example UDF to show really bad formatting.
udf_BBTeam_AllPlayers	TABLE	168	Returns a list of all players on all BBTeams.
udf_BBTeams_LeagueTAB	INLINE	142	Returns the ID, name, and manager of all teams in a league.
udf_Bit_Int_NthBIT	SCALAR		Returns the Nth bit in a int. Bits are numbered with zero beginning with the least-significant bit up to 31, which is the sign bit of the int. If @Nth is > 31, it returns NULL.
udf_BitS_FromInt	SCALAR	397	Translates an int into a corresponding 32-character string of 1s and 0s. It will optionally trim leading zeros.
udf_BitS_FromSmallint	SCALAR		Translates a smallint into a corresponding 16-character string of 1s and 0s. It will optionally trim leading zeros.
udf_BitS_FromTinyint	SCALAR		Translates a tinyint into a corresponding 8-character string of 1s and 0s. It will optionally trim leading zeros.
udf_BitS_ToInt	SCALAR		Converts a bit string of up to 32 characters into the corresponding int. The string is padded on the left with any missing zeros.
udf_BitS_ToSmallint	SCALAR	401	Converts a bit string of up to 16 one and zero characters into the corresponding smallint. The string is padded on the left to fill in any missing zeros.
udf_BitS_ToTinyint	SCALAR	402	Converts a bit string of up to eight one and zero characters into the corresponding tinyint. The string is padded on the left to fill in any missing zeros. The result is a value from 0 to 255. There are no negative tinyint values.
udf_Category_BigCategoryProductsTAB	TABLE	159	Returns a table of product information for all products in all categories with at least @MinProducts products.
udf_Category_ProductCountTAB	INLINE	138	Categories and their count of products.
udf_Category_ProductsTAB	INLINE		Returns a table of product information for all products in the named category.

Function	Type	Page	Description
udf_Currency_DateStatus	SCALAR	288	Used together with udf_Currency_XchangeNearDate to understand the status of the exchange rate.
udf_Currency_RateOnDate	SCALAR		Converts from one currency to another on a specific date. The date must be in the database or the result is NULL.
udf_Currency_StatusName	SCALAR		Returns a meaningful name for the return code from udf_Currency_DateStatus.
udf_Currency_XlateNearDate	SCALAR	286	Converts from one currency to another using a rate that's on or near the specified date. If the date is not found in the table, an approximate result is returned.
udf_Currency_XlateOnDate	SCALAR	284	Converts from one currency to another on a specific date. The date must be in the database or the result is NULL.
udf_DT_2Julian	SCALAR		Returns the Julian date — the number of days since 1990-01-01.
udf_DT_Age	SCALAR		Returns the age of a person, in years, for a given date of birth, as of a given date. If no @AsOfDate is supplied, then today is used.
udf_DT_CurrTime	SCALAR	87	Returns the time as a CHAR(8) in the form HH:MM:SS. This function bypasses SQL Server's usual restriction against using getdate by selecting it from a view.
udf_DT_DaysTAB	TABLE		Returns one row for each day that falls in a date range. Each date is the SOD.
udf_DT_dynamicDATEPART	SCALAR		Does the same job as DATEPART but takes a character string as the datepart instead of having the datepart in the script.
udf_DT_FileNameFmt	SCALAR		Formats a date/time so that it can be used in a file name. It changes any colons and periods to dashes and includes only the parts the user requests. Time and milliseconds are optional.
udf_DT_FromYMD	SCALAR		Returns a smalldatetime giving the Year, Month, and Day of the month.

Function	Type	Page	Description
udf_DT_MonthsTAB	TABLE	12	Returns a table of months that are between two dates including both end points. Each row has several ways to represent the month. The result table is intended to be used in reports that are reporting on activity in all months in a range.
udf_DT_NthDayInMon	SCALAR		Returns a datetime for the Nth occurrence of a day in the month, such as the third Tuesday. Returns NULL if the date doesn't exist, such as the fifth Monday in June, 2002. Sensitive to setting of DATEFIRST. Assumes default value of 7.
udf_DT_SecSince	SCALAR		Seconds since a time.
udf_DT_SOD	SCALAR		Returns a smalldatetime with just the date portion of a datetime.
udf_DT_WeekdayNext	SCALAR		Returns the next weekday after @Date. Always returns a start-of-day (00:00:00 for the time). Takes into account @@DATEFIRST and works with any setting, but it is always based on Saturday and Sunday not being weekdays.
udf_DT_WeekdaysBtwn	SCALAR		Computes the number of weekdays between two dates. Does not account for holidays. They're counted if they're M-F. It counts only one of the end days. So if the dates are the same, the result is zero. Order does not matter. Will swap dates if @dtEnd < @dtStart. This function is sensitive to the setting of @@DATEFIRST. Any value other than 7 (the default) would make the results incorrect, so a test for this condition causes the function to return NULL when @@DATEFIRST is not 7.
udf_EP_AllTableLevel2EPsTAB	TABLE	329	Returns a table of extended properties for a property (or NULL for all), for an owner (or NULL for all), for a table (or NULL for all) in the database. The Level 2 object name must be specified (NULL means on the table itself). The Level 2 object name may be given to get info-specific Level 2 object or use NULL for all Level 2 objects.
udf_EP_AllUsersEPsTAB	TABLE	326	Returns the extended property value for a property (or NULL for all properties) on all USERS in the database. The Level 1 object type must be specified. Useful for finding a property for all tables, views, etc. The cursor is needed because it does not assume that every object is owned by dbo.

Function	Type	Page	Description
udf_Example_Inline_WithComputedColumn	INLINE		Inline UDF that returns a table with a computed column. It turns out that the column isn't marked as computed even though it's the result of an expression. Run sp_help to see that PRODUCT isn't considered computed by SQL Server.
udf_Example_Multistatement_With ComputedColumn	TABLE		Example UDF that returns a table with a computed column. Use sp_help to see that SQL Server considers PRODUCT a computed column.
udf_Example_OAhello	SCALAR	225	Example UDF to exercise the TSQLUDFVB.cTSQLUDFVBDemo OLE automation object.
udf_Example_Palindrome	SCALAR	30	A palindrome is the same from front to back as it is from back to front. This function doesn't ignore punctuation as a human might.
udf_Example_Runtime_Error	SCALAR	102	Example UDF to demonstrate what happens when an error is raised by a SQL statement.
udf_Example_Runtime_Error_Inline	INLINE	104	Example UDF to demonstrate what happens when an error is raised by a SQL statement. This is an inline UDF.
udf_Example_Runtime_Error_MultiStatement	TABLE		Example UDF to demonstrate what happens when an error is raised by a SQL statement. It returns a table of results.
udf_Example_TABLEmanipulation	SCALAR	35	An example UDF to demonstrate the use of INSERT, UPDATE, DELETE, and SELECT on table variables. Uses data from the Northwind Employees table.
udf_Example_Trc_EventListBadAttempt	SCALAR		This is an incorrect attempt to write the equivalent of udf_Trc_EventList. See the text for a further explanation.
udf_Example_User_Event_Attempt	SCALAR	79	Example UDF that attempts to call the extended stored procedure sp_trace_generateevent. This demonstrates that the call fails with server message 557 in spite of sp_trace_generateevent being an extended and not a regular stored procedure.
udf_Exchange_MembersList	INLINE	130	Returns a table with a list of all brokers who are members of the exchange @ExchangeCD.

Function	Type	Page	Description
udf_Func_BadUserOptionsTAB	INLINE		Returns a table of functions that have been created without the proper QUOTED_IDENTIFIER and ANSI_NULLS settings. Both of these should be ON. These UDFs may cause problems in the future, particularly with INDEXES on computed columns.
udf_Func_ColumnsTAB	INLINE	190	Returns a table of information about the columns returned by a function. Works on both inline and multistatement UDFs.
udf_Func_COUNT	SCALAR		Returns the number of functions in the database that match @function_name_pattern.
udf_Func_InfoTAB	INLINE	189	Returns a table of information about all functions in the database. Based on INFORMATION_SCHEMA.ROUTINES and OBJECTPROPERTIES.
udf_Func_ParmsTAB	INLINE	192	Returns a table of information about the parameters used to call any type of UDF. This includes the return type that is in Position=0.
udf_Func_TableCols	INLINE		Returns a single column table. Each row is the declaration of a column in the output of a UDF. It works for both inline and multistatement UDFs but is most useful as an aid to converting an inline UDF to a multistatement UDF.
udf_Func_Type	SCALAR		Returns a character description of the function type SCALAR, INLINE, or TABLE.
udf_Func_UndocSystemUDFtext	TABLE	391	Produces a listing of an undocumented system UDF in master. Gets the text from syscomments.
udf_Instance_EditionName	SCALAR		Returns the edition name of the SQL Server. Obtained from the SERVERPROPERTY function.
udf_Instance_InfoTAB	INLINE		Returns a single row table of information about the system the SQL Server is running on. Interprets information from SERVERPROPERTY.
udf_Instance_UptimeSEC	SCALAR	345	Returns the number of seconds since the instance started.
udf_Lst_Stooges	TABLE		Returns a table of the Stooges. This function illustrates what happens when you try to write a book. After a while, you've got to do anything but really work on the book. Serious research into the Stooges is an alternative.

Function	Type	Page	Description
udf_Name_Full	SCALAR	5	Concatenates the parts of a person's name with the proper amount of spaces.
udf_Name_FullWithComma	SCALAR	114	Creates a concatenated name in the form @sLastname, @sFirstName @sMiddleName @SuffixName. In the process it is careful not to add double spaces. Prefix names such as Mr. are not common in this type of name and are not supported in this function.
udf_Name_SuffixCheckBIT	SCALAR	126	Returns 1 when the name is one of the common suffix names such as Jr., Sr., II, III, IV, MD, etc. Trailing periods are ignored.
udf_Num_FactorialTAB	TABLE	158	Returns a table with the series of numbers and factorials.
udf_Num_FpEqual	SCALAR		Checks for equality of two floating-point numbers within a specific number of digits to the right of the decimal place. Returns 1 if equal, otherwise 0.
udf_Num_IsPrime	SCALAR	33	Returns 1 if @Num is prime. Uses a loop to check every odd number up to the square root of the number.
udf_Num_LOGN	SCALAR	106	The logarithm to the base @Base of @n. Returns NULL for any invalid input instead of raising an error.
udf_Num_RandInt	SCALAR		Returns a random integer between @MinNum and @MaxNum inclusive. Note that while the query SELECT RAND(), RAND() always returns the same two values, select dbo.udf_NumRandIntFromRange (1, 100) , dbo.udf_NumRandIntFromRange (1, 100) returns two different values. That's because the view is executed separately for each function invocation.
udf_OA_ErrorInfo	SCALAR	217	Consolidates information about an error from the sp_OA* routines into a single error message.
udf_OA_LogError	SCALAR	220	Creates an error message about an OA error and logs it to the SQL log and NT event log.
udf_Object_SearchTAB	INLINE	194	Searches the text of SQL objects for the string @SearchFor. Returns the object type and name as a table.

Function	Type	Page	Description
udf_Object_Size	SCALAR		Returns the bytes taken by the object definition in syscomments. The definition may be split over multiple rows. These objects types have definitions in syscomments: CHECK constraints, DEFAULT constraints, user-defined functions, stored procedures, triggers, and views.
udf_Order_Amount	SCALAR	53	Returns the amount of an order by summing the order detail.
udf_Order_RandomRow	INLINE		Returns a random row from the Northwind Orders table.
udf_Paging_ProductByUnits_Forward	SCALAR	149	Forward paging UDF for ASP page ProductsByUnit.
udf_Paging_ProductByUnits_REVERSE	INLINE	152	Reverse paging UDF for ASP page ProductsByUnit.
udf_Perf_FS_ByDbTAB	INLINE	349	Returns a table of total statistics for one database or a group of databases where the name matches a pattern. NULL for all. Done by grouping by database.
udf_Perf_FS_ByDriveTAB	INLINE	352	Returns a table of statistics by drive letters for all drives with database files in this instance. They must match @Driveletter (or NULL for all). Returns one row for each drive. Information about physical files is taken from master..sysaltfiles, which has the physical file name needed. Warning: Drive letters do not always correspond to physical disk drives.
udf_Perf_FS_ByPhysicalFileTAB	INLINE	350	Returns a table of statistics for all files in all databases in the server that match the @File_Name_Pattern. NULL for all. The results are one row for each file including both data files and log files. Information about physical files is taken from master..sysaltfiles, which has the physical file name needed.
udf_Perf_FS_DBTotalsTAB	TABLE	348	Returns a table of total statistics for one particular database by summing the statistics for all of its files.
udf_Perf_FS_InstanceTAB	INLINE		Returns a table of statistics for all databases in the instance. There is only one row for each database, aggregating all files in all databases.
udf_Proc_WithRecompile	INLINE		Returns a table of names of procedures that have been created with the WITH RECOMPILE option. These procedures are never cached and require a new plan for every execution. This can be a performance problem.

Function	Type	Page	Description
udf_Session_OptionsTAB	TABLE	95	Returns a table that describes the current execution environment inside this UDF. This UDF is based on the @@OPTIONS system function and a few other @@ functions. Use DBCC USEROPTIONS to see some current options from outside the UDF environment. See the BOL section titled "User Options Option" in the section "Setting Configuration Options" for a description of each option. Note that QUOTED_IDENTIFER and ANSI_NULLS are parse time options and the code to report them has been commented out. See also MS KB article 306230.
udf_SQL_DataTypeString	SCALAR		Returns a data type with full length and precision information based on fields originally queried from INFORMATION_SCHEMA.ROUTINES or from SQL_VARIANT_PROPERTIES. This function is intended to help when reporting on functions and about data.
udf_SQL_DefaultsTAB	INLINE		Returns a table of all defaults that exist on all user tables in the database.
udf_SQL_LogMsgBIT	SCALAR	203	Adds a message to the SQL Server log and the NT application event log. Uses xp_logevent. xp_logevent can be used in place of this function. One potential use of this UDF is to cause the logging of a message in a place where xp_logevent cannot be executed, such as in the definition of a view.
udf_SQL_StartDT	SCALAR	344	Returns the date/time that the SQL Server instance was started.
udf_SQL_UserMessagesTAB	INLINE		Returns a table of user messages in the SQL Server.
udf_SQL_VariantToDatatypeName	SCALAR		Returns the data type name of a sql_variant.
udf_SQL_VariantToStringConstant	SCALAR	404	Converts a value with the type sql_variant to a string constant that is the same as the constant would appear in a SQL statement.
udf_SQL_VariantToStringConstantLtd	SCALAR		Converts a value with the type sql_variant to a string constant that is the same as the constant would appear in a SQL statement. The length of the constant is limited for display purposes to a specified length. Ellipsis is used when truncation is performed to let the caller know that it has happened. This may make the constant unsuitable for use as SQL script text.

Function	Type	Page	Description
udf_SYS_DriveExistsBIT	SCALAR	221	Uses OLE automation to check if a drive exists.
udf_Tax_TaxabilityCD	TABLE	173	Code table for taxability of the entity.
udf_Tbl_ColDescriptionsTAB	INLINE	328	Returns the description extended property for all columns of user tables in the database. A specific owner or table can be named. If @TableOwner is NULL, extended properties for all owners is returned. If @TableName is NULL, columns for all tables are returned.
udf_Tbl_ColumnIndexableTAB	INLINE		Returns a table of the columns in tables whose name matches the patterns in @tbl_name_pattern and @col_name_pattern. Includes the status of the columns as indexable, deterministic, and precise.
udf_Tbl_COUNT	SCALAR	414	Returns the number of user tables in the database that match @table_name_pattern.
udf_Tbl_DescriptionsTAB	INLINE	325	Returns the description extended property for all user tables in the database.
udf_Tbl_InfoTAB	INLINE		Returns a table of information about a table. Information is from sysobjects, sysowner, sysindexes, extended properties, and OBJECTPROPERITES. Intended as input to a report writer.
udf_Tbl_MissingDescrTAB	INLINE	332	Returns the schema name and table name for all tables that do not have the MS_Description extended property.
udf_Tbl_NotOwnedByDBOTAB	INLINE		Returns a table of tables not owned by DBO.
udf_Tbl_RowCOUNT	SCALAR		Returns the row count for a table by examining sysindexes. This function must be run in the same database as the table.
udf_Tbl_RptW	INLINE	333	Returns a report of information about a table. Information is from sysobjects, sysowner, extended properties, and OBJECTPROPERITES. Intended to output from Query Analyzer. It can be sent to a file and then printed from the file with landscape layout.
udf_Test_ConditionalDivideBy0	SCALAR	108	Creates a divide-by-zero error conditionally based on the @bCauseError parameter.

Function	Type	Page	Description
udf_Test_Quoted_Identifier_Off	SCALAR	93	Test UDF to show that it's the state of the quoted_identifier setting when the UDF is created that matters, not the state at run time. This UDF was created when quoted_identifier was OFF.
udf_Test_Quoted_Identifier_On	SCALAR	93	Test UDF to show that it's the state of the quoted_identifier setting when the UDF is created that matters, not the state at run time. This UDF was created when quoted_identifier was ON.
udf_Test_RenamedToNewName	SCALAR		Example UDF to show that sp_rename doesn't work correctly for user-defined functions.
udf_Title_AuthorsTAB	INLINE		Returns a table of information about all authors of the title.
udf_Titles_AuthorList	SCALAR	170	Returns a comma separated list of the last name of all authors for a title.
udf_Titles_AuthorList2	SCALAR	171	Returns a comma separated list of the last name of all authors for a title. Illustrates a technique for an aggregate concatenation.
udf_Trc_ColumnCount	SCALAR		Returns the number of columns being reported by a trace.
udf_Trc_ColumnList	SCALAR		Returns a comma separated list of columns being monitored by a trace. Each column is given by its name.
udf_Trc_ColumnName	SCALAR	374	Translates a SQL Trace ColumnID into its descriptive name. Used when retrieving event information from fn_trace_geteventinfo.
udf_Trc_ComparisonOp	SCALAR		Translates a SQL Trace comparison operator code into its text equivalent. Used when retrieving event information from fn_trace_getfilterinfo. The code numbers are originally used when creating the filter with sp_trace_setfilter.
udf_Trc_EventCount	SCALAR		Returns the number of events being reported by a trace.
udf_Trc_EventList	SCALAR	375	Returns a separated list of events being monitored by a trace. Each event is given by its name. The separator supplied is placed between entries. This could be N', ' or NCHAR(9) for TAB.

Function	Type	Page	Description
udf_Trc_EventListCursorBased	SCALAR		Returns a separated list of events being monitored by a trace. Each event is given by its name. The separator supplied is placed between entries. This could be ', ' or NCHAR(9) for TAB.
udf_Trc_EventName	SCALAR	371	Translates a SQL Trace EventClass into its descriptive name. Used when viewing trace tables or when converting a trace file with fn_trace_gettable.
udf_Trc_FilterClause	SCALAR	379	Translates a SQL Profiler filter expression into text in a form similar to a WHERE clause. Used when retrieving event information from fn_trace_getfilterinfo. The length of the output is limited to about 64 characters.
udf_Trc_FilterExpression	SCALAR	381	Returns a separated list of Filters being monitored by a trace. Each Filter is given by its name. The separator supplied is placed between entries. This could be ', ' or NCHAR(9) for TAB.
udf_Trc_InfoExTAB	INLINE		Returns a table of information about a trace. These are the original arguments to sp_trace_create and to the other sp_trace_* procedures. The status field for the trace is broken down to four individual fields. The list of events, list of columns, and the filter expression are each string columns. There are two arguments available to provide the separator character one for the two lists and the other for the filter expression. When displaying the results, the defaults work well. When passing the lists to a wrapping function, such as udf_Text_WrapList, a tab (NCHAR(9)) is cleaner.
udf_Trc_InfoTAB	INLINE	363	Returns a table of information about a trace. These are the original arguments to sp_trace_create. The status field is broken down to four individual fields.
udf_Trc_LogicalOp	SCALAR		Translates a SQL Trace Logical operator code into its text equivalent. Used when retrieving event information from fn_trace_getfilterinfo. The code was originally used when creating the filter with sp_trace_setfilter. Result is 0 for AND or 1 for OR.
udf_Trc_ProfilerUsersTAB	INLINE		Table listing user information for processes running SQL Profiler.

Function	Type	Page	Description
udf_Trc_RPT	TABLE	384	Returns a report of information about a trace. These are the original arguments to sp_trace_create and to the other sp_trace_* procedures. The status field for the trace is broken down to four individual fields. The list of events, list of columns, and the filter expression are each on their own line or wrapped to multiple lines.
udf_Trc_SetStatusMSG	SCALAR		Returns the textual equivalent of a return code from sp_trace_setstatus.
udf_Trig_TANH	SCALAR		Returns the hyperbolic tangent of a number. It's equal to sinh(x)/cosh(x) or the expression found below. See http://mathworld.wolfram.com/HyperbolicTangent.html.
udf_Txt_CharIndexRev	SCALAR	18	Searches for a string in another string working from the back. It reports the position (relative to the front) of the first such expression that it finds. If the expression is not found, it returns zero.
udf_Txt_FixLen	SCALAR		Returns the input string in a character string of a specified length.
udf_Txt_FixLenR	SCALAR		Right justifies @sSource String in a field of @nTargetLength. Padding is done with @sPadCharacters.
udf_Txt_FmtInt	SCALAR		Formats an integer with no decimal and right justification to the specified number of characters, padding with @sPadChar.
udf_Txt_FullLen	SCALAR		Returns the length of a character string including trailing blanks. The built-in LEN function excludes trailing blanks when it calculates the length. This function uses a sql_variant so that both Unicode and ANSI strings can be @input.
udf_Txt_IsPalindrome	SCALAR		A palindrome is the same from front to back as it is from back to front. This function removes spaces, periods, question marks, quotes, and double quotes and then checks to see if the string is the same in both directions.
udf_Txt_RemoveChars	SCALAR		Removes characters from a string.

Function	Type	Page	Description
udf_Txt_SplitTAB	TABLE	165	Returns a table of strings that have been split by a delimiter. Similar to the Visual Basic (or VBA) SPLIT function. The strings are trimmed before being returned. NULL items are not returned, so if there are multiple separators between items, only the non-NULL items are returned. Space is not a valid delimiter.
udf_Txt_Sprintf	SCALAR	208	Uses xp_sprintf to format a string with up to three insertion arguments.
udf_TxtN_SpreadChars	SCALAR		Spreads the input string out by placing characters between each character of the input.
udf_TxtN_WrapDelimiters	SCALAR		Wraps text that is separated by a set of delimiters. The wrap allows the first line and subsequent lines to be padded for alignment with other text.
udf_Unit_CONVERT_Distance	SCALAR	260	Converts a distance measurement from any unit to any other unit.
udf_Unit_EqualFpBIT	SCALAR	269	Checks for equality of two floating-point numbers within a specific number of digits. Returns 1 if equal, otherwise 0.
udf_Unit_EqualNumBIT	SCALAR	271	Checks for equality of two floating-point numbers within a specific number of digits by converting to numeric and comparing those digits.
udf_Unit_Km2Distance	SCALAR	258	Returns a distance measure whose input is a kilometer measurement. The parameter @UnitSystemOfOutput requests that the output be left as kilometers "M" or converted to the U.S. standard system unit miles signified by a "U."
udf_Unit_Km2mi	SCALAR	263	Converts kilometers to miles.
udf_Unit_KmFromDistance	SCALAR		Returns a kilometer measure whose input is a distance measurement in the unit system given by the parameter @UnitSystemOfOutput.
udf_Unit_lb2kg	SCALAR	267	Converts pounds (advp) to kilograms (kg).
udf_Unit_mi2Km	SCALAR		Converts miles to kilometers.
udf_Unit_mi2m	SCALAR	256	Converts miles to meters.

Function	Type	Page	Description
udf_Unit_Rounding4Factor	SCALAR	254	Returns the number of digits of precision that a units conversion is performed on a measurement with @nDigits2RtofDecimal of precision and a conversion factor of @fConversionFactor. The result is intended to be used as input into the ROUND function as the length parameter.
udf_Unit_RoundingPrecision	SCALAR		Returns the number of digits of precision in a result after a units conversion is performed on a measurement with @nDigits2RtOfDecimal of precision and a conversion factor of @fConversionFactor. The result is intended to be used as input into the ROUND function as the length parameter.
udf_View_ColumnList	SCALAR	407	Creates a quoted list of the columns in a view, suitable for creation of a dynamic SQL statement. Depends on INFORMATION_SCHEMA.VIEW_COLUMN_USAGE. This prevents use with views with only one column.

Index

Index

T-SQL UDF of the Week Newsletter

If you've read this far, you're probably interested in the topic of user-defined functions. The T-SQL User-Defined Function of the Week Newsletter is a free service of Novick Software. Each issue has a new UDF with a short article describing how it's used. Subscribing to the UDF of the Week Newsletter is a great way to keep in touch with the wide range of possibilities for UDFs.

Sign up for the newsletter at:

http://www.NovickSoftware.com/UDFofWeek/UDFofWeekSignup.htm

The newsletter archives with all the past issues is available at:

http://www.NovickSoftware.com/UDFofWeek/UDFofWeekArchive.htm

About the Author

Andrew Novick develops applications as consultant, project manager, trainer, and Principal of Novick Software. His firm specializes in implementing solutions to business operations problems using the Microsoft tool set: SQL Server, ASP, ASP.NET, Visual Basic, and VB .NET. 2003 marks his thirty-second year of computer programming, starting in high school with a PDP-8 and moving on to a degree in computer science and an MBA, and then programming mainframes, minicomputers, and for the last 17 years, PCs.

When not programming, Andy enjoys coaching Little League baseball, woodworking, mowing the lawn, and seeing the occasional movie with his wife. He can be found on the web at www.NovickSoftware.com or by e-mail at anovick@NovickSoftware.com. Check out the web site for articles, tips, code samples, and instructional videos about programming SQL Server, VB, C#, ASP.NET, and other environments.